Unconventional Wisdom

UNCONVENTIONAL
Wisdom

ESSAYS ON ECONOMICS
IN HONOR OF
John Kenneth Galbraith

EDITED BY
Samuel Bowles, Richard Edwards,
AND *William G. Shepherd*

HOUGHTON MIFFLIN COMPANY · BOSTON 1989

For information about permission to reproduce selections from
this book, write to Permissions, Houghton Mifflin Company,
2 Park Street, Boston, Massachusetts 02108.

Library of Congress Cataloging-in-Publication Data

Unconventional wisdom : essays on economics in honor of John
Kenneth Galbraith / edited by Samuel Bowles, Richard Edwards,
and William G. Shepherd.
p.   cm.
"Books by John Kenneth Galbraith": p.
Includes bibliographical references.
ISBN 0-395-49179-7
1. Galbraith, John Kenneth, date — Contributions in economics.
I. Galbraith, John Kenneth, date.   II. Bowles, Samuel.
III. Edwards, Richard, date.   IV. Shepherd, William G.
HB119.G33U53   1989   89-11244
330.1 — dc20   CIP

Printed in the United States of America

V   10 9 8 7 6 5 4 3 2   1

Contents

III/GLOBAL PERSPECTIVES

IV/PERSONAL PERSPECTIVES

Preface

Galbraith and Economics

It is our great pleasure to introduce this volume of essays in honor of John Kenneth Galbraith. Given his own penchant for the unconventional, it will perhaps not seem unacceptably novel that we will not here review his career and note his many contributions, as is often done on such occasions. These are both too well known to need repetition and too varied to be adequately chronicled by any except a Galbraith specialist. Rather we will reflect on Galbraith's contributions to economics and on the difficulty which the economics profession has had in coming to terms with Galbraith.

The generous assessments of Galbraith's work that appear in the essays which follow and the distinguished cast of economists who have chosen here to honor him attest to the admiration, respect, and affection which so many feel for the man. He is rightly considered to be one of the preeminent economists of our age. According to the *Social Science Citation Index* he is more frequently referred to than any but a handful of economists. His election as President of the American Economic Association in 1972 confirms his elevated stature in the profession. Those who are not economists often seem to believe that Galbraith *is* economics. The following observation by C. Richard Hatch, a professor of architecture, may bemuse economists, but is not atypical: "Mainstream economics has until recently been dominated by the Galbraithian concept of the giant firm . . ."[1]

---

1. "Italy's Industrial Renaissance: Are American Cities Ready to Learn?" *Urban Land* (January 1985): 20.

It is curious, then, that so few economists *teach* Galbraith to their students. This is particularly the case in graduate programs; in economic theory courses for doctoral students at major U.S. universities, his works are not frequently assigned or mentioned.

The reason why economists can neither dismiss nor teach Galbraith, we think, is that Galbraith is one of those misfits whose transgressions point to a basic flaw in the now dominant approach to economics, a flaw at once too obvious to ignore, but too major to repair without extensive and embarrassing ramifications. At issue is the manner in which economics banishes the question of power to the far-flung periphery of the discipline and even beyond into the seldom traveled territory of political science. Galbraith's Presidential Address to the American Economic Association (presented in Toronto, not far from his boyhood Ontario home) makes the point with characteristic incisiveness:

> The most commonplace features of neo-classical and neo-Keynesian economics are the assumptions by which power, and therewith political content, is removed from the subject. The business firm is subordinate to the instruction of the market and, thereby, to the individual or household. The state is subordinate to the instruction of the citizen.

The result, he continues, is not only that economists are often wrong, but that (here one notes his acute sense of what will persuade) they are increasingly irrelevant:

> The decisive weakness in neoclassical and neo-Keynesian economics is not the error in the assumptions by which it elides the problem of power. The capacity for erroneous belief is very great, especially where it coincides with convenience. Rather, in eliding power — in making economics a nonpolitical subject — neoclassical theory by the same process destroys its relation with the real world. . . . In consequence neoclassical and neo-Keynesian economics is relegating its players to the social sidelines where they either call no plays or urge the wrong ones.

Galbraith's concern with power puts him out of step with the *way* economists think no less than with what they think *about*. If one were really interested in the economic consequences and sources of power, one would quickly find that the demanding but rewarding pursuit of general models of great abstraction — the flowering of general equilibrium economics which coincided in time with

Galbraith's early works comes to mind — is simply the wrong way to go. The way in which power is exercised in consumer goods markets differs in fundamental ways from the manner in which employers boss workers and again from the manner in which the ownership of wealth confers power in money markets or in the electoral process. There is no general theory of economic power, and Galbraith places very little value on attempting to create a common underlying model that would explain the workings of, say, the planning system and the market system of the U. S. economy.

The methodological signpost raised by Galbraith's work pointed toward a differentiated and multidisciplinary theory of the economy, not a general and purely economic one. It was a signpost well worth ignoring for a generation of graduate students who implicitly understood that tenure went most readily to those who knew how to reduce anything worth saying to the canonical form: maximize u(·) subject to f(·).

The mélange of attraction and discomfort occasioned by Galbraith and his work can hardly be separated from his engagement in the world. Sometimes masked by irony and wit, and often tempered by understatement, his passion for a more just and civilized human existence and his lifelong commitment to act politically toward those ends challenged a profession espousing an improbable and vacuous neutrality on questions of public morality. No one ever doubted which side Galbraith was on:[2]

> This is what economics now does. It tells the young and susceptible and the old and vulnerable that economic life has no content of power and politics . . . Such an economics is not neutral. It is the influential and invaluable ally of those whose exercise of power depends on an acquiescent public. If the state is the executive committee of the great corporation and the planning system, it is partly because neoclassical economics is its instrument for neutralizing the suspicion that this is so. I have spoken of the emancipation of the state from economic interest. For the economist there can be no doubt as to where this task begins. It is with the emancipation of economic belief.

This exemplary intellect has been the conscience of the econom-

---

2. This quote and those above are from "Power and the Useful Economist," *American Economic Review* LXIII, no. 1 (March 1973): 1–11.

ics profession (and sometimes its unhappy conscience) for more than a generation. It is the deep appreciation of Galbraith's insight, his intelligence, and his dogged and not wholly unsuccessful effort to engage economics in the task of making a better life for all that unites the authors of this book in his honor. We present you these essays with fondness and gratitude.

Samuel Bowles
Richard Edwards
William G. Shepherd
University of Massachusetts
Amherst, Massachusetts
April 1989

The enemy of the conventional wisdom
is not ideas but the march of events.

JOHN KENNETH GALBRAITH,
The Affluent Society

I

ECONOMICS AND
PERSUASION

Kenneth E. Boulding

The Pathologies
of Persuasion

Persuasion as a Critical but Neglected Element in Social Systems

Persuasion is a human relationship of great universality and significance. It is surprising, therefore, that it has been so much neglected, both by social scientists and by moral philosophers. Nowhere in the social sciences do we find anything that looks like a general theory of persuasion as a social relationship. In the study of rhetoric and in the underworld of what used to be called speech departments, we find a certain classical literature, going back at least to Aristotle, on the art of persuasion, the various techniques which may be used, and so on. We find something of this also in modern psychology, especially in applied psychology. What we do not find is much discussion of the role of persuasion in the total social system, or even its role in the total decision-making process, either in the organization or in the person.

Yet it is clear that persuasion plays a crucial role in all social systems, that without it society probably could not exist. It forms the matrix, indeed, within which other social organizers, such as the threat system and the exchange system, are able to come into being. Unless we can persuade someone that a threat is credible, or that an offer to exchange is genuine, neither threats nor exchange can serve to organize social relations and role structures.

At the level of the integrative system, also, it is clear that persuasion plays an absolutely crucial role in the awakening of love, in the development of community, honor, sacrifice, legitimacy, and in the whole development of the human identity. People become lovers, spouses, citizens, church members, party members, employees or employers, mainly because they are persuaded to do so by their own minds, by other people, or perhaps by circumstances.

To be persuaded, indeed, is a wider concept than to persuade. We are persuaded that there is a force of gravity the first time we take a fall. All sorts of information input, both verbal and nonverbal, take part in the persuasion process. To persuade, however, as a human activity, is to add messages, which again may be either verbal or nonverbal, to the vast input of another person in the hope of "changing the mind." Persuasion is a part of the human learning process, and the human learning process is the essence of the social dynamics of society. In the light of its crucial importance, it is all the more astonishing that this phenomenon should have been so long neglected.

Persuasion Ignored by Economics and the Other Social Sciences

Economics knows little of persuasion, which has seldom emerged from the practically oriented, earthy underworld of marketing into the empyrean ether of economic theory. Economic man never has to be persuaded to do anything, just as he never has to learn anything because he knows everything already. He makes his maximizing choices in the light of a given value system, a known set of choices, and a known set of consequences. How he learned all this the economist never inquires. What I have elsewhere called the doctrine of the "immaculate conception of the indifference curve" is so firmly established in economics that it is a very rare economist indeed who questions it. There are hints indeed in Adam Smith's *Wealth of Nations* that people learn to be what they are and that the differences between the philosopher and the porter, in preferences no doubt as well as in abilities, depend on their life experiences, that is, on their total input of information rather than on their genetic heritage.[1]

Of the twentieth-century economists, I can think of only three who have ever raised the question as to how people are persuaded to have the preferences they do: Thorstein Veblen, especially in *The Theory of the Leisure Class*,[2] recognized very clearly that preferences are learned from the subculture in which they operate; John Kenneth Galbraith suggests that businesses themselves help to create the preferences which enable them to survive in the market;[3] and I should modestly add myself to this distinguished but not very persuasive company.[4]

The general assumption of economic theory, therefore, than there is an equilibrium set of prices which can be derived from the existing preferences of individuals and the production functions of commodities seems to be true only in short periods, for as we consider the total dynamics of society the impact of the price structure on preferences may be just as important as the impact of preferences on the price structure. However, Veblen also remained in the underworld of institutional economics, and the mainstream of economic theory flowed on cheerfully into a vast slough called "welfare economics," which is based solidly on the principle that nobody is ever persuaded of anything and nobody ever learns anything. The very concept of the Paretian optimum, that *summum bonum* of welfare economics, implies that all preferences are given and all utilities are independent, so that everybody is selfish and exhibits neither malevolence nor benevolence, envy or pride, or indeed any of the seven deadly sins, nor of course do they exhibit any of the corresponding virtues.[5] The only place for economic man indeed is limbo. He is too virtuous for hell and not virtuous enough for heaven.

---

1. Adam Smith, *The Wealth of Nations* (New York: Random House/Modern Library, 1937).

2. Thorstein Veblen, *The Theory of the Leisure Class* (New York: Random House/Modern Library, 1937).

3. John Kenneth Galbraith, *The New Industrial State* (Boston: Houghton Mifflin, 1967).

4. Kenneth E. Boulding, "Economics as a Moral Science," *American Economic Review* 59, no. 1 (March 1969): 1–12.

5. Kenneth E. Boulding, "The Economics of Pride and Shame," *Atlantic Economic Journal* 15, no. 1 (March 1987): 10–19.

Of the other social sciences, psychology has probably made the largest contribution to the study of persuasion, especially through the theory of the subconscious. We are all familiar with the doctrine that the prune is a witch. All this, however, is rather superficial, simply because our ignorance of the human learning process is so enormous. One should not scold psychologists; they are like the rest of us, doing their little best, but they are faced with a system of almost inconceivable complexity. The human nervous system has about 10 billion neurons, so that its capacity is of the order of 2 to the 10 billionth power. A system of such enormous complexity cannot be reduced to explicit formulations and it is not surprising, therefore, that psychology retreats into animal behavior.

Sociology, which should perhaps have had a theory of persuasion at its very core, has neglected the problem even more single-mindedly than the economists. There is, of course, a literature on socialization and on child development and on the learning of roles, but the part played by persuasion in all this is very rarely recognized. The moral philosophers have neglected the problem in any systematic sense, again with remarkable unanimity. I know of no systematic treatise on this subject. And while this may only reflect my own ignorance, if any such cases exist they have certainly not made very much impact.

Persuasion in the Learning Process

The concept of persuasion, like all other important concepts, has fuzzy edges. We are faced with a spectrum of phenomena rather than with a clear-cut boundary which divides what is persuasion from what is not. At its widest definition, we could include in persuasion almost the whole of the human learning process and a good deal of animal learning as well. The learning process consists of the modification of what might be called the internal universe, or the image of the world which is possessed by the knower. This modification takes place in a number of different ways. It takes place partly through the internal generation of messages and images in the imagination. The knowledge structure is changing all the time because of the enormous internal activity of the nervous system within which it is embodied.

The earlier concept of the mind as a kind of *tabula rasa,* on which the messages coming in from the outside world through the senses were simply imprinted, is now seen to be hopelessly inadequate. Even in modern perception theory, the mind is now seen as an enormously active organization constantly producing vast numbers of images, even at the unconscious level. The senses, and the information coming in from them, act much more as critics than as authors. This is not to deny, of course, that we do receive imprints from the senses, but for perception, and still more for an increase in knowledge to take place, the inputs from the senses must be processed through a huge active system, the nature of which at the moment we are only just beginning to understand. It is not a mere quirk of language, therefore, to say that I am "persuaded" that I am now sitting on the porch at my cabin, looking at a blue sky flecked with clouds, at rocks and pine trees, at rough furniture, and at the Dictaphone which I am using. I am persuaded of all this because I have an input through my eyes and from other sense preceptors which persuade me, that is, change my knowledge structure in the direction of accepting the image of the real world around me. When the senses no longer persuade, the person is in real trouble. I can imagine a pink elephant sitting in front of me. As I have a good imagination, I can imagine it in considerable detail, but my senses inform me that it is not there. If I were drunk, or still more, schizophrenic, my senses would lose their power of persuasion and I would be at the mercy of my imagination, and I might see the pink elephant.

Knowledge consists partly in the memories and the internal records of perception, but it involves much more than a simple roster of memories. It involves, for instance, the perception of regularities in the perceived world. This is true even at the level of what I have called "folk knowledge," the kind of knowledge we acquire in the ordinary business of life. I am able to get out of bed in the morning because I have learned the regularities in the law of gravity, which have been somehow coded into my nervous system, into my muscles, and the rest of me. Without the knowledge of such regularities, that is, of laws, action would be impossible. I have suggested elsewhere that if the gravitational constant was in fact not constant, we would find it extremely difficult to learn how to get out of bed in the morning or how to do any of the commonest activities of daily life.

At the more sophisticated level of scientific knowledge, of course, these laws and regularities become explicit. They are embodied in mathematical formulae, from which precise images of the future are derived that can then be tested. The testing process, however, is crucial to the development of knowledge of all kinds. It involves having some sort of image of the regularities of the world; it involves making an inference from these images, that is, a prediction about the future; it involves observing the future as the present passes over and it becomes the past; and it involves comparing the image of the future as we had it in the past with the image of the same thing after it has become the past. If there is a mismatch between the image of the future as we hold it in the past and the image of the same thing as we remember it after it has occurred, then there has to be some sort of reorganization. These reorganizations can be of many kinds, some of which produce more knowledge than others. Without mismatch, however, there can be no learning, though what we learn and whether what we learn is true is not determined by the mismatch alone, but by our reactions to it.

Ethics as Persuasion about Valuations

Ethics begins to come into the picture when we consider that some part of our knowledge structure is a set of values or preferences. Some such assumption as this is absolutely necessary to the theory of choice, for choice involves contemplating at least two alternative futures over which we have some control and selecting one of them. The moment we make a selection we have in effect made a value ordering. We have decided that the future that we chose is "better" than the future that we did not. I have sometimes accused decision theory of being merely a set of mathematical variations on the theme that "everybody does what he thinks best at the time," but even so, the concept of "best" involves a scalar ordering of the world on some kind of scale of better or worse. Usually this need only be an ordinal scale, that is, we have to order possible alternatives — first, second, third — but we do not have to measure the value of each alternative in a cardinal number, although there are situations in which cardinality of value measurement may be necessary.

Ordering the world on a scale of better or worse is something that we do all the time, and it is something that we have to *learn* how to do. In some cases, values are "learned" genetically, that is, are built into the structure of the nervous system by the genes as they organize the phenotype. This seems particularly true of the insects, who learn very little, if anything, in their lifetimes. The behavior of the ant is governed by quite a complex value system. It "chooses" some objects rather than others, some directions rather than others, even though its activity also seems to have a large random component. These choices, however, are not learned, but are presumably built into the nervous system of the ant by its genetic code. Birds, likewise, have preferences that are mainly genetic. Orioles prefer other orioles and oriole nests to robins and robins' nests, but this preference does not seem to be learned much from their life experience.

There are some kinds of learning even in the birds, for instance, in bird song, some of which has to be learned, some of which is genetically controlled. As we move into the mammals, especially as we move toward humans, the learning component in the development of value orderings increases until in humans it becomes completely dominant. The human being starts out with certain primitive genetic values determined by the structure and composition of the baby's nervous system as it is created by the genetic code, but this genetic value system is extremely elementary and almost the whole preference structure of the adult has been learned. Even many things that we previously thought of as instinct, such as sex, are in fact very largely learned, even though the genetically created physical structure of the nervous system introduces certain predispositions into the learning process.

It is clear, therefore, that just as we are persuaded that the world around us is what we think it is, so we are persuaded of our values. An American is persuaded to be an American by his upbringing and by the innumerable information inputs which he has perceived. In much the same way, the average Russian is persuaded to be a Russian. The whole process of socialization, as the sociologists call it, indeed, is nothing more than an elaborate piece of persuasion, simply because it is a learning process.

The Persuader-Persuadee Relation
as Part of Human Learning

This may, however, be carrying the concept of persuasion too far. As noted earlier, to be persuaded is not the same thing at all as to persuade. Persuasion, in the active sense of persuading, is by no means coextensive with the learning process. It is indeed only a part of it, and perhaps quite a small part of it at that. It is with this part, however, that we are most concerned in this paper. Here we are concerned with the persuader rather than with the persuaded, with those who seek to influence rather than those who are influenced. Even when we narrow the concept down to this point, however, we still find that it includes a very large area of human relationships in social life. We can think indeed of at least five areas of social life where the relationship between an active persuader and a more passive persuadee is an essential element in the system.

We start first of all with the family. Each spouse is constantly trying to persuade the other to do something or to believe something which he or she prefers. In a successful marriage presumably some kind of an equilibrium is reached fairly soon between the spouses, after which relatively little persuasion takes place, because the tastes of the parties are similar enough so that they are not a severe source of discord. In the relations of parents with children, however, persuasion goes on constantly and intensely. The value structure of the child, particularly, is open to parental persuasion, simply because of the basic relationship of dependency. Persuasion is frequently at a rather unconscious level, as, for instance, in the learning of language. However, a child growing up in an English-speaking home is easily persuaded to learn English, and one who grows up in a French-speaking home similarly is persuaded to learn French.

In the institutions of formal education, it is clear that persuasion is a major enterprise. In the classroom the teacher takes an active role in trying to transmit certain knowledge structures from his own nervous system to the nervous systems of the students. All the arts of persuasive rhetoric indeed are part of the stock in trade of the good teacher, whose success may be judged by the amount of persuasion that he manages to perform. Here persuasion becomes a good deal more conscious than it is in the family, where the child often grows up persuaded more by what the parents are than by what they consciously do.

As we move from education into religion, the role of persuasion becomes even more prominent. The sermon is almost the ideal type of the persuasive rhetorical exercise. The architecture of the church, the stained-glass windows, the symbolism of the ritual are all means of persuasion, designed to change the mind of the visitor or the participant in directions which the church quite self-consciously desires. It is not surprising, therefore, that children growing up in a Christian community easily become Christian; those growing up in a Buddhist community become Buddhists.

An interesting question is that of the extent to which art from different cultures should be regarded as persuasive in its essential character. A great deal of art clearly is persuasive. The Ravenna mosaics, medieval stained glass, the Gothic cathedral, the Palladian temple, the state capital, the triumphal arch, Collegiate Gothic, fashionable paintings, and fine clothes . . . all carry persuasive messages. In the last century a certain feeling has grown up in the artistic community that to use art for persuasive purposes, especially for the persuasive purposes of other people, is in some sense prostitution. This is the movement of "art for art's sake." Even here, however, unless the artist is performing a purely individual act, which hardly deserves the name of art, he is presumably seeking to persuade the viewer of the art at least to enjoy it and appreciate it.

Politics is another area of life where persuasion is of enormous importance. This is true even in the most dictatorial regime. Indeed, frequently the more dictatorial the regime, the more effort has to be put into propaganda and persuasion. The cynical arts of Madison Avenue pale almost into bland virtue beside the persuasive activities of Goebbels or the persuasive appeal of Mao's "Little Red Book," both of which ended up in the garbage can. In democratic societies, of course, the rhetoric of politics is almost wholly the rhetoric of persuasion. The major activity of all candidates for office consists largely of attempts to change the value preferences of the voters in their favor. It is a nice question as to whether Billy Graham or Ronald Reagan is more skilled at persuasive rhetoric, but from this point of view they are clearly birds of a feather.

Finally, we come to the uses of persuasion in business and economic life. This constitutes a major part of industrial relations on the one hand and marketing on the other. The economist's ideal type, the seller in perfect competition, facing a market which will take any quantity of what he has to sell at a price that he cannot himself determine, is described unflatteringly in the marketing literature as an "order taker." The wheat farmer and the gold miner may indeed conform to this ideal type. Over the whole range of manufacturing and service industries, however, imperfect competition is the rule and imperfect competition almost always implies marketing, that is, positive activity devoted specifically to increasing the demand for the product. All of this falls under the head of persuasion, that is, activity devoted to changing the image of the world and especially the values or preference orderings in the minds of somebody else — Galbraith's "revised sequence."[6]

Industrial relations can be thought of as marketing in the labor market and involves a great deal of persuasion on both sides. Bargaining of any kind, and collective bargaining in particular, has to be visualized as an exercise in mutual persuasion, to the point where both parties are persuaded to accept the bargain on the same terms. Within organizations, also, a great deal of persuasion has to go on in order to get people to accept the roles to which they are assigned in the hierarchy. Indeed, I suspect that the further up the hierarchy one goes, the more time is spent on persuasion, even in hierarchies which appear at first sight to be highly authoritarian and dictatorial. Even the Pope must persuade the cardinals; the cardinals, the archbishops; the archbishops, the bishops and the priests; and the priests, the laity. In military organizations as well, an enormous amount of persuasion goes on. Otherwise there would not be so many meetings. The committee indeed is the altar at which the rites of persuasion are mainly performed. Show me an organization without committees and you will show me one without persuasion. The persuasive activities of more powerful people may be more mixed with threat, and those of less powerful people more dependent on rhetoric, but naked threat is rarely effective, and even threat has to be clothed in the language of persuasion.

---

6. Galbraith, *The New Industrial State.*

The "Production Function" of Persuasion

Let us now look briefly at what might be called the "production function" of the persuasion enterprise, that is, what inputs into it produce what outputs, particularly from the point of view of the persuader. It is clear that the immediate product of the persuader is information of some kind, whether this is an advertisement, a speech, a sermon, a poem, a piece of architecture, or a punch to the jaw. The persuader's special production function is that which involves the inputs of resources which are necessary to produce a given output of information. Information, however, is only an intermediate product; the final product is the change in the knowledge structure or the value structure in the nervous system of the persuadee. This is much more difficult to estimate.

We might postulate certain very rough aggregate parameters of this system: first, the ratio of information output of the persuader to the value of the resources used; second, the ratio of the change in the knowledge structure of the persuadee per unit of information received; and third, the value of this perceived change in the mind of the persuader. The decision as to whether it is worthwhile to try to persuade somebody clearly depends on the ratio between the value in the mind of the persuader of the change that he believes will take place in the mind of the persuadee, to the value of the inputs which the persuader has to employ in producing the information, or whatever it is that will produce this change. This, of course, is a statement of the obvious, as cost-benefit analysis usually is. It does point up the fact, however, that in this calculation there are enormous uncertainties. Persuasion indeed is one of the most uncertain of all the operations of the human mind. The persuader may have a pretty fair idea what his output is costing him. He usually has very little idea as to the impact of this output of information on the mind of the persuadee. Under these circumstances, we would not be surprised to find that the persuasion industry, if we may call it that, is subject to all sorts of nonrational phenomena, such as rules of thumb (a given percentage of sales spent for advertising), habits (preachers go on preaching sermons long after they have had any effect), and waves of fashion as we find them in advertising, in education, and elsewhere.

Any theory of persuasion obviously has to revolve around the study of these highly uncertain production functions. Thus, the theory of operant conditioning assumes that persuasion is accomplished by the association of some kind of reward with the change which the persuader is going to bring about. This, in effect, supposes that persuasion is closely related to the phenomenon of exchange. The persuader achieves an objective by rewarding the persuadee for the changes which he is trying to bring about. Operant conditioning tends to assume that the rewards have to be almost immediate and have to be clearly related in the mind of the persuadee with the change which is taking place in him.

No one could doubt, of course, that these processes do take place, and that the rewards play an important part in the learning process. Nevertheless, the weakness of this kind of theory (also, I suspect, of the practice based on it) is that it assumes that the human mind, and especially the human value structure, is almost indefinitely malleable. Its malleability, however, has sharp limits. There are limitations imposed, for instance, by the genetic composition of an individual's nervous system. We are not going to be able to persuade a person who is genetically tone deaf to respond to any kind of music, simply because he cannot differentiate one note from another, no matter what the reward structure. It is no use rewarding him for Beethoven and penalizing him for rock if he cannot tell one from the other. This is merely an extreme case of a general problem of the ability to discriminate. In obvious physiological cases such as tone deafness and color blindness, the non-malleability of the system is fairly clear. There may, however, be much more subtle failures of discrimination of which we are now barely aware. Discrimination in the bad sense of the word, for instance, such as stereotyping and racial and religious discrimination, is often the result of a failure to discriminate in the good sense, in the sense, for instance, that we say that people have discriminating tastes. This in turn is a basic failure in the learning process. Why this happens and how it happens, however, I think we do not really understand.

We might perhaps postulate a concept of a "persuadability gradient," or perhaps since elasticity is such a good word in economics, we might almost call it the "elasticity of persuadability." Some people are very firm in their opinions and values and are very hard to persuade; other people are indeed malleable and are easy to persuade. Again, I think we really do not know what makes the difference. It certainly has something to do, in the mathematical sense, with the "strength" of the orderings of a person's value system. A person who has strong orderings, who always knows whether he prefers A to B, is apt to be less persuadable than somebody who has weak orderings and does not really care whether he has A or B. This is a personality trait which seems to have been studied very little by psychologists. Just how it is learned, or whether indeed it has any genetic base, is, again, something that we do not know.

The problem is enormously complicated by the fact that we are not dealing here with easily quantifiable inputs and outputs, but rather with complex multidimensional structures in which the structure and composition, or inputs or outputs, may have much more significance than any simple measure of quantity. The psychology of persuasion has, of course, some wisdom about these matters. We are all familiar, for instance, with the principle of association, the logic of which is highly dubious, the psychology of which may have some truth in it. Thus, the syllogism "Sex is agreeable, I see an advertisement with a pretty girl smoking a cigarette, therefore cigarettes must be agreeable" must be an example of one of a large class of false syllogisms. In the psychology of persuasion, however, this kind of false logic seems to be very successful, and it is perhaps the first major principle of the rhetoric of persuasion. Jones has a kind face, kind faces are good, therefore Jones would make a good mayor, is the sort of logic which all too often guides the voters.

The Pathologies of Persuasion in the Creation of Error

Finally, we come to the title of this paper: What about "the pathologies of persuasion"? The greatest pathology of persuasion is that it may produce error, that is, images in the minds of the persuaded that do not correspond to something in the real world. If I am persuaded by a charismatic preacher that I can jump off the Empire State Building and fly, and I try it, my disillusionment will end very rapidly. Unfortunately, many erroneous images are not so easily tested. Rain dances are sometimes followed by rain, development policies are sometimes followed by development; revolutions occasionally, though very rarely, improve a society; a criminal justice system may even reduce crime. Nevertheless, as we move into complex systems, the problems of testing become acute. It becomes easy to persuade people of things that are not so, often to their severe detriment. The things that the human race has believed that are not so would fill a very large encyclopedia.

We see this persistence of error as a result of persuasive skills even in scholarly knowledge. Alchemy lasted for a very long time, and even now persists in a few underworlds, in spite of the fact that the elements are not earth, air, fire, and water. Even chemists at one time believed in phlogiston. A pattern of believing plausible but hard-to-test images of the world, what Kuhn has called "normal science,"[7] has been quite common, even in the history of the physical sciences, still more so in the case of the social sciences. Marxism has persisted for well over a hundred years now on a large scale, in spite of the fact that "classes" are heterogenous aggregates, about as useful in understanding the real complexities of social interaction as the alchemist's elements were for chemistry.

Mainline economics, as defined, say, by most of the Nobel Prize winners, is not in much better shape. The younger generation has gotten trapped in a set of mathematical and statistical variations on models which are not really adequate to describe the complexity of social life, especially in the modern world. The pathology of persuasion here is the persuasiveness of the Ph.D. committee, which is pretty powerful in persuading younger people to develop eloquent elaborations on the mistakes of their elders. As Lester C. Thurow, one of the few younger economists who has not lost interest in the real world, says of John Kenneth Galbraith in his delightful article in *The New Palgrave*, "His books have been written always in the form of verbally persuasive economic tracts, without a hint of mathematics."[8] Why, then, have these verbally persuasive tracts failed to persuade? The economics profession has gone deeper and deeper into its mathematical and statistical morass, with its

---

7. Thomas S. Kuhn, *The Structure of Scientific Revolutions* (Chicago: University of Chicago Press, 1962).
8. Lester Thurow, "John Kenneth Galbraith," in *The New Palgrave: A Dictionary of Economics*, vol. 2; ed. John Eatwell (New York: Stockton Press, 1987), p. 455.

eighteenth-century mathematics and nineteenth-century statistics, quite inappropriate to investigating a system, which like most systems in the real world, is fundamentally topological and structural rather than numerical and algebraic. Even though it is true that all knowledge is gained by the orderly loss of information, most statistical analysis throws away the essential information, especially information about extreme positions of systems, which is necessary to fulfill an understanding of complexity. Mainline economics for the last fifty years now has been in a condition of "normal science," becoming increasingly remote from the realities of the world, with evidence accumulating against the existing models. It seems to be time for a scientific revolution. Perhaps this can only be done, however, by a topological mathematician using a mathematics which still remains to be written in the twenty-first century.

Economics, of course, is not the only victim of pathological persuasive systems. International and strategic studies have built a huge fairy tale on models of deterrence and threat power, which are wholly inappropriate to the nuclear age. Psychology is only now beginning to recover from behaviorism, with its absurd denial of the capacity of humans to have knowledge about their own consciousness. Even in the physical sciences, geology, which resisted the enormous evidence in favor of plate tectonics and continental drift for a generation or more, finally succumbed in the face of some overwhelming evidence on the mid-Atlantic rift. Now what used to be heresy has become orthodoxy.

Pathologies of Persuasion in Marketing

We are fairly familiar with the pathologies of persuasion in advertising and marketing. Cigarette advertising is a classic case, where people are being persuaded to shorten their own lives. Persuasions that lead to addictions are perhaps the most pathological, addictions being the satisfaction of certain desires in which the satisfaction increases the future desire. Tobacco, alcohol, and drugs are obvious examples. Some forms of radicalism, conservatism, fundamentalism, and the desire for power may be even more dangerous, as they are addictive mental states.

Even though there is no addiction, there may be dishonesty in persuasion both at the marketing level and at the political, religious, and even academic levels. But there are certain offsetting factors here. The fact that liars can be found out does give an important modicum of truth to the old saying that honesty is the best policy. Even if it is only the reputation for honesty, that it is the best policy, still, such a reputation can be destroyed by a single instance of being found out. This is as true of politicians and preachers as it is of business people.

One pathology of the persuasive system which is perhaps harder to deal with, perhaps because it is hard to identify, is what might be called "vulgarization." When the persuasive powers of the artist and architect are directed toward bishops and princes, the very smallness of the subculture may result in beauty. However, when the powers of persuasion are democratized, they may degenerate into kitsch or mere functionalism, like modern architecture. I am not sure that this is a serious problem, but it cannot be wholly brushed aside.

We are reminded constantly nowadays that we are moving into an information age. I suspect this really started with DNA. Nevertheless, the information industry is increasing very rapidly as a percentage of the total economy. This may mean that persuasion becomes a larger and larger part of social activity and the pathologies of persuasion become more and more important. In simpler societies, where a large part of human activity consisted of growing things and making things, persuasion was not so important, though it certainly began to increase with the rise of civilization, empires, and organized religions. In the world of the future, persuasion may become increasingly important and the pathologies of persuasion all the more dangerous.

Remedies for the Pathologies
of Persuasion

The question of the remedies for the pathologies of persuasion, therefore, becomes increasingly important as time goes on, and the situation is not at all clear. Here again, one of Galbraith's great concepts, "countervailing power," is at least a wedge to enter into a rather impenetrable problem. There are undoubtedly countervailing powers to pathologies of persuasion. We see this, for instance, in the tremendous development of citizen initiatives, the development of the environmental movement, the consumer movement, innumerable private organizations to check on the sins both of corporate business and of government. The computer age seems to be generating an enormous spread of person-to-person communication, as evidenced, for instance, by the "minitel" system in France, the development of worldwide computer networks such as BITNET, the enormous rise of private citizen diplomacy and local government diplomacy undermining the almost inherently pathological persuasion system of the national state. The increase of diversity within such organizations as the Catholic Church, and now the Soviet Union and China, and even the large corporations is a straw in the wind which suggests that the pathologies of persuasion are not wholly incurable and that the very technology of information itself provides a countervailing power.

Just what countervailing power countervails against, however, is not always clear. The power of trade unions may countervail against unorganized labor and household purchases rather than against the employer. Protests against apartheid may actually strengthen it. Protest in many fields has often backfired. Even the Prohibition movement was a countervailing power against the liquor industry, but created a still greater countervailing power for the moderate drinkers and probably did less to solve the alcoholism problem than Alcoholics Anonymous does. There is a large field of study opening up here, also one which is by no means devoid of hope. Galbraith's persuasive economic tracts and other voices in the wilderness may still turn out to be really persuasive, and in that there is much hope for the future.

Albert O. Hirschman

How the Keynesian Revolution Was Exported from America[1]

KEN GALBRAITH WROTE his famous article "How Keynes Came to America" in the midsixties. In the introduction to *Economics, Peace, and Laughter* (Boston: Houghton Mifflin, 1971), the collection where it was republished, he notes that "for whatever reason [it is] by far the most extensively reprinted piece I have ever written." Actually the reason is not far to seek: the article is highly informative (even a bit gossipy), as well as characteristically acute and witty, and it does deal with a fascinating topic: the transmission and diffusion of economic ideas that become politically powerful.

The purpose of this note is not to go over the ground already so well covered by Ken. Rather, I am principally interested in a complementary aspect of the story in which I was involved while working on the Marshall Plan in Washington from 1946 to 1952: the *reexport* of Keynesian ideas and doctrines *from* the United States during that postwar period. In addition, I am writing more than twenty years after Ken: his article dates from the time when the influence of Keynesian ideas was at its zenith, whereas my observations cannot help but be affected by the considerable change in the intellectual climate that has occurred since.

As a result of this change, one is tempted to paraphrase a famous pronouncement of the sixties and to proclaim, "We are all *post*-Keynesians now." From that vantage point, a number of new observations come into view. For example, a remarkable parallel can now be drawn between the fate of the Free Trade Doctrine in the nineteenth century and the rise and decline of Keynesianism in the twentieth, and this topic can serve to introduce my story.

In 1846, Free Trade won its major domestic victory in Great Britain, then the dominant world power, with the abolition of the Corn Laws. The doctrine soon acquired a considerable degree of international hegemony, which was manifested and further propelled by the Cobden-Chevalier Treaty of 1860. But it suffered reverses with the coming of the "Great Depression" in the 1870s and was superseded by neo-mercantilist and imperialist policies that were adopted not only by the major Continental powers and the United States, but eventually also won politically powerful converts in the original protagonist, the United Kingdom.

Keynesianism, the economic doctrine fashioned by Keynes in *The General Theory of Employment, Interest and Money* (1936), gained its first major success in acquiring influence over the economic policy of a great power in the United States, in the course and as a result of the 1938 recession.[2] This influence was substantially strengthened during World War II. Through the war's outcome, the United States was then propelled to superpower status, and it proceeded to promote Keynesian-type policies not only because of its new position in the world, but also because it acquired, through its postwar aid programs, considerable direct influence on the economic policies of other major countries. In spite of many resistances, Keynesianism curiously acquired a good measure of intellectual hegemony for just about as long as the Free Trade Doctrine, and during the identical decades of "its" century — thirty years, from the forties to the seventies. It went into decline with the oil shocks of the seventies and the concomitant unsettling experience of "stagflation." Increasingly, the theoretical predominance Keynesianism had long exercised was contested by neo-monetarist and "supply-side" doctrines which largely originated in the very country — the United States — that had originally been spreading the Keynesian message.

The purpose of sketching this historical parallel is not to insinuate that influential economic doctrines come and go at regular intervals, like schools of painting such as Impressionism or Abstract Expressionism, nor to ponder the curiosum that they both achieved hegemony during the middle decades of succeeding centuries. Rather it is to bring out how the two episodes have three characteristic elements in common:

First, a newly arisen economic doctrine came to acquire dominant influence *within* a very special country: one that is outstandingly endowed both with military power and with the prestige that comes from being a principal beacon of economic progress.

Second, this country then became eager to export the doctrine to others and initially achieved a measure of international hegemony for it.

Third, in spite of the seemingly invincible combination of a persuasive body of thought with its sponsorship by the most "modern" country which is also a leading world power, the doctrines soon met with numerous resistances and their reigns turned out to be unexpectedly short-lived. Moreover, they came to be contested within the very countries which had originally spread them.

The comparative look at the spread of Free Trade and of Keynesianism also calls attention to an important difference between the two stories. The Free Trade Doctrine arose in England, became that country's official policy, and was "exported" from it, along with its prized manufactures, to the rest of the world; Keynesianism also arose in England, but won its most significant battle for influence over domestic policy making in the United States during the thirties and the Second World War, and then was spread primarily from that country after the war's end. It is perhaps not of overwhelming interest that the originating and the missionary country were identical in the Free Trade story, whereas in the case of Keynesianism two different countries assumed successively the function of "invention" and that of worldwide diffusion. The arresting features lie rather in some specific aspects of "How Keynes Came to and was Spread from America," to expand on the title of the Galbraith article.

Galbraith told us how Keynesian ideas came to a key university (Harvard) and to some key Washington agencies (Federal Reserve Board, Treasury, Bureau of the Budget) in the wake of the protracted depression of the 1930s, particularly the steep and troubling 1938 recession.[3] Seldom in history were some basic propositions of an economic theory so strikingly confirmed by events as during the 1938–1945 period in the United States: the new and heterodox Keynesian concept of underemployment equilibrium illuminated the continuing difficulties of the late thirties that were particularly evident in the United States; shortly thereafter, the ability of government spending to energize the economy and to drive it to full employment (with wartime controls restraining the inflationary impulses) was taken as another, more positive demonstration of the correctness of Keynesian analysis. These experimental verifications of the theory — so uncharacteristic for social science propositions — might have been sufficient to cause many economists to take Keynes's ideas seriously, but, as has often been remarked, the rhetoric of the *General Theory* also contributed to forming a band of sectlike initiates and devotees on the one hand, as well as a group of out-and-out opponents on the other.

It is useful to dwell briefly on the latter point. As Salant points out, Keynes showed how, in an underemployment situation, numerous common-sense intuitions about economic relationships are by no means fallacious, as had long been believed and taught by the economics profession: contrary to Say's Law, general overproduction *can* exist, deficit spending by the government *can* activate the economy, and, horror of horrors, the "mercantilist" imposition of import duties and export subsidies *can* improve the trade balance and domestic employment. In propounding these popular and populist heresies, Keynes threatened traditional economists, not just in their beliefs but in their hard-won *status* as high priests of an arcane science that owed its prestige in good part to its claim that much of common-sense understanding of economic relationships was pitifully wrong. Here is one reason for the undying hostility of some important members of the profession to the Keynesian system.

But while rehabilitating common sense, Keynes hardly presented his own theory in common-sensical terms. Rather, his message was delivered in a text of "fascinating obscurity," as Galbraith put it. Moreover, Keynes frequently presented his propositions as counterintuitive rather than as confirming common sense: for example, instead of telling his readers that converging individual decisions to cut consumption can set off an economic decline (common sense), he dwelt on the equivalent but counterintuitive proposition that a spurt of individual decisions to save more will fail to increase aggregate savings. In this manner, he managed to present common sense in paradox's clothing and in fact made his theory doubly attractive: it satisfied at the same time the intellec-

tuals' craving for populism and their taste for difficulty and paradox.

The Keynesian system thus attracted a group of extraordinarily
devoted followers. It gave them the exhilarating feeling of pos-
sessing the key to truth while being beleaguered by a coalition of
ignoramuses and sinister interests. Moreover, the thirties were a
highly ideological or "creedal" period and Keynesianism, with its
reevaluation of the proper roles of the state, the world of business,
and the intellectuals (the economists in particular) supplied an attractive "third way" that could compete with the various Fascist
and Marxist creeds of the time.

It was in the United States that these various factors converged
most effectively to create an energetic and influential group of
Keynesians during the years just prior to and during World War
II. Then comes the peculiar "exogenous" twist of the story: the
outcome of the war. With the United States suddenly propelled to
military and political world leadership, its group of devoted and
inspired Keynesians could now fan out to the far corners of the
U.S.-controlled portion of the globe to preach their gospel to a
variety of as yet unconverted natives. And this is what they did,
backed up by U.S. power and prestige, first by occupying positions
with the military governments established in Germany and Japan
and then by providing much of the qualified manpower needed
for the administration of Marshall Plan aid, both in Washington
and in the missions accredited to the countries receiving that aid.

By flocking to the newly opening and highly attractive opportunities to spread the message and exert power overseas, the U.S.
Keynesians, who were after all still a rather small group, left the
domestic front dangerously unprotected. The retreats that were
imposed on the Keynesian cause in the United States in the immediate postwar period (with the emasculation of the Full Employment Bill, for example) may in part be explained by this factor. On the other hand, the difficulties of maintaining their grasp
on domestic policy in the more contentious and conservative climate of the Truman era may have convinced many prominent and
gifted U.S. Keynesians that they would have a far easier and more
profitable time applying their skills in the newly opened overseas
theaters of operation. Such are the dialectics of Empire, especially
when it is of the instant variety.

In sum, what spread of Keynesianism occurred after World War

II was due to an extraordinary constellation of circumstances: first the formation of a core group of Keynesians in the United States, in function of *domestic* economic problems, then the military victory of that country, and then the attempt at "colonization" of the rest of the "free world" with Keynesian ideas. The peculiar shape of the story is perhaps better understood by invoking a seemingly odd historical parallel. In the fifteenth century, the Catholic kings of Spain completed, after centuries of fighting, the reconquest of that country from the Muslims. In the course of this epochal event, the ruling circles of the kingdom became imbued with an extraordinary spirit of fervor, missionary zeal, and power. With the discovery of the New World in America (the exogenous event in this story), that ardent spirit then found a ready-made outlet and inspired both the soon-to-be-staged military conquest of the new continent and the intensive subsequent proselytizing efforts by the Spanish State and Church. One significant difference between the two stories is that, unlike the United States, Spain did not switch to spreading a wholly different faith after some thirty years.

But this exotic parallel only serves to underline the nonreplicable character of the story I have chosen to tell. It certainly does not yield anything like a usable "model" of the process through which economic ideas gain political influence. Or, if it does, it is in the nature of the old advice "Get yourself a rich grandfather" to a young man who wishes to know the secret of how to become rich. It would seem that, to achieve worldwide influence, an economic idea must first win over the elite in a single country, that this country must exert or subsequently chance to acquire a measure of world leadership, and that the country's elite must be motivated and find an opportunity to spread the new economic message.

I have evidently been stressing the unique features of the spread of Keynesianism. My account does not lend itself, therefore, to deriving any stable set of "preconditions" for the diffusion of ideas. The story may, nevertheless, have another kind of utility: it intimates and puts us on guard that next time around we may have to look for a very different combination of circumstances to explain (or promote) the acquisition of political influence by an economic idea.

Something remains to be said, from the perspective here adopted, about the highly different degrees of influence wielded by Keynesianism in the various countries that, immediately after World War II, were all exposed to considerable American influence and, along with that, to Keynesian ideas. The specific historical factors that are peculiar to each country, and explain some of the variance, are well known: the revulsion in Italy and Germany, after the Fascist and Nazi experiences, against state interference in the economy, as opposed to the openness to economic policy innovation in France which had stagnated lamentably in the thirties, largely under the dictates of "orthodox" economic management (resistance to devaluation and insistence on deflation). There remains nevertheless a puzzle: if American influence meant exposure to Keynesian ideas as a result of the fanning out of U.S. Keynesians, why was it that in Germany and Japan, which were under U.S. military occupation and government and where U.S. power was therefore strongest, the influence of Keynesian ideas on policy making was far weaker than in France and Italy, countries that were merely subject to U.S. advice as recipients of substantial U.S. aid? To help explain this paradox, I wish to propose a hypothesis which needs to be confirmed by archival research, but which, as an active participant in those events, I sense to be correct.

At the end of World War II, the U.S. Keynesians formed a cohesive, combative, and influential yet, as already noted, a multiply beleaguered group. It was based in various government agencies in Washington and in a still quite small number of the major universities. In government, these Keynesian economists had mostly influential advisory, rather than outright managerial, positions, in line with the Washington quip that economists should be "on tap, but not on top." When the U.S. government was suddenly called upon to improvise an apparatus of military government in Germany and Japan, the top positions were given to military officers and to experienced businessmen, bankers, lawyers, and other managerial types. These groups had by no means been converted to Keynesianism and tended in fact to be hostile to it to the extent they had an opinion on the matter. (In the militarily occupied countries, in Germany in particular, there was often conflict between the top administrators and the Keynesian advisers within the U.S. military government.) To the contrary, in the other countries the top jobs available to Americans were those of economic advisers to Allied governments, and they largely went to the U.S.

Keynesians, who therefore had virtually the last word on the economic policy that was being urged on the local government by the United States. Hence the U.S. Keynesians were *more* influential in those countries where the United States had *less* power and exercised it indirectly via advisers rather than directly, via outright administrators.

NOTES

1. This paper draws on the author's contribution to *The Political Power of Economic Ideas: Keynesianism across Nations,* ed. Peter A. Hall (Princeton, N.J.: Princeton University Press, 1989).
2. The importance of the 1938 recession in making Keynesian ideas persuasive in the United States is stressed by Walter Salant in "The Spread of Keynesian Doctrines and Practices in the United States," also in *The Political Power of Economic Ideas.*
3. A number of other accounts with somewhat different emphases are now also available. See Salant's article cited above and the literature there noted.

Barbara R. Bergmann

Why Do Most Economists Know So Little about the Economy?

THIS PAPER EXPOUNDS the thesis that most academic economists lack interest in the actual economy and know very little about it. In this respect, John Kenneth Galbraith is way out of the mainstream of the economics profession. Galbraith is one of the few economists (Alan Greenspan is another) who has brought to his work a warm and abiding interest in the real economy run by the flesh-and-blood folks. The mainstream members of our profession "study" instead those shadowy folks who always resort to perfectly competitive markets to transact their business, whose tastes are never influenced by advertising, and who have no political aims. There is in our profession a willful and crucial failure to make contact with reality, and a resultant inability to advance our knowledge of the realities of economic functioning.

When mainstream economists get together, they tend to congratulate themselves on their many "discoveries." They award one another Nobel Prizes. But there is, I think, an unacknowledged worry that perhaps our "science" is based on a faulty investigative technique. One indication of the existence of this worry is that economists are remarkably reticent in telling the world (including their students) how the "wisdom" they purvey, conventional or otherwise, was found out.

Most books designed to introduce a science to beginning students describe not only what the scientists know but also how they have come to know it. They let the students look in on the scientists as they go about advancing knowledge by observing the phenomena that form their subject matter. The biologists' books tell about cells, but also about looking through microscopes. The physicists tell about the gravitational formula, but also about throwing balls off the Leaning Tower of Pisa. In the social and behavioral sciences, the anthropologists talk about their field trips to the Trobriand Islands and the rat psychologists tell about their mazes.

By contrast, when we teach economics we tell the students nothing about economists' methods of finding things out. It is no accident that the authors of college texts fail to portray in a plain way the process of finding things out in economics. The authors would have to reveal to the students (and to themselves) that our profession's method of finding things out are very different from those of any other branch of knowledge calling itself a science.

The Methodology of Economic Discovery

Why are explicit descriptions of economists' methods of extending their knowledge absent from teaching materials for high school and college students? Why in this respect are our textbooks so unlike those of the other sciences?

Some might answer that economists find things out about the world by running regressions on economic data collected by the government, which would be difficult to explain to beginners. But running regressions is not at all the main way economists find things out or, more properly, decide what they believe. What we "know" about the way the economy works owes very little to regression running, as the inconclusive controversy over Keynesian and monetarist models showed. Most of what each economist believes to be true was arrived at by methods of research that predate econometrics.

Most of what we represent ourselves as knowing we have learned from "theory" — which in economics takes the form of musing at length on the implications of the few facts we know about the economy. Regressions on government-collected data have been used mainly to bolster one theoretical argument over another. But the bolstering they provide is weak, inconclusive, and easily countered by someone else's regressions. This leaves theorizing as our major method of finding out about the world and explaining it to ourselves — just sitting in our offices and thinking.

There are some crumbs of factual content in our theorizing. These crumbs don't come from regressions on government data, but have been gathered casually in the course of our everyday lives. They include tidbits like the fact that more income is generally preferred to less, all else being equal, and that businesses use labor and space and equipment to produce output, that unemployment rises and falls. The impoverished factual content of our thought doesn't embarrass us economists; we are used to it. But it is somewhat embarrassing to explain explicitly to noneconomists that we find things out by sitting and thinking and mulling over a few factual crumbs, and that the systematic, firsthand observation of economic functioning has no place whatever in economic science.

I first became aware that our methods of discovery had best be kept under wraps a number of years ago when I was retained as an expert witness in a lawsuit. One of my functions in the case was to give testimony that would help the judge to understand how a well-working unbiased competitive labor market was supposed to work. The day before I was to testify, the attorney who had engaged me asked me to go through what I planned to say. I started with great confidence and self-possession, giving my little lecture about how human capital costs and requirements affect the supply and demand for various kinds of labor.

In the middle of my spiel, the attorney interrupted me and asked how I knew all that. I was quite taken aback. I bumbled around and finally blurted out that it was agreed-upon theory, and that all economists subscribed to it. This didn't please the attorney. After a pause, she finally said, "Well, you had better say that you know those things as a result of the studies you have made. You've made a lot of studies, haven't you?" I hurriedly agreed that, indeed, I had made many, many studies.

What the attorney meant was that, if I were asked, I had better represent to the judge that the methodology of my science and the basis of my expertise were on a par with those of the other experts who customarily make appearances in court. The medical expert has done studies on actual, individual hearts or livers; the psychologist has seen a lot of patients; the textile expert has done studies of what fibers look like under the microscope; the handwriting expert has done studies of writing samples.

We may label the "science" of those other experts as primitive and certainly may disparage their objectivity as witnesses, but it must at least be admitted that they have a hands-on knowledge of their subjects that economists lack utterly, except for what they can pick up in their daily lives. Economists do not get the material for presentations about the labor market by "doing studies" like those of experts in other disciplines. I did not "know" that stuff I was spouting about the labor market because I or any other economist was in the habit of studying the behavior of unemployed people or had made direct studies of the practices of people who are in charge of hiring or wage setting. Nor did any of it come from regressions, mine or anyone else's.

My encounter with the lawyer made me realize that everything I am supposed to "know" about the labor market comes from no-where but the private musings of economists. In fact, economists' main method of contributing to their field is the same as mathematicians'. This partly explains the mystery of why there is nothing about discovery methods in the economics textbooks. Mathematicians' textbooks don't have anything about their method of discovery either. In the case of mathematics, it is obvious that mathematicians just sit around wherever they are comfortable and introspect in a special way. No one would feel there was something lacking or that they should feel embarrassment because they don't use microscopes or go to the Trobriand Islands.

But if virtually all the "knowledge" in economics books is the product of introspection, so what? After all, mathematics is a high-prestige field, practiced by people acknowledged by the world to be very clever. Ditto for economics. So what?

Unfortunately, only a very limited idea of the way the actual economy works is deducible by logic from first principles. When the day comes that we leave off musing and regression running on secondhand data, I predict we will be amazed at the doctrines that fall. The cross-point on the supply-demand diagram may even have to go. When Edward Chamberlin (1948) tried running a market experimentally, he found that few trades occurred at the price that would equate amount supplied and amount demanded, and that the average price was systematically lower.

Economics concerns the behavior of cantankerous humans, their habits and rules and institutions, and the results of the interactions conditioned by all that. If we are talking about the real world (as opposed to the fictional worlds that Gary Becker and Robert Lucas and Paul Samuelson conjure up when they write their articles), the subject matter of economics is a lot closer to anthropology than to mathematics. That fact should inform our methodological practice.

Finding Out and Measuring

The sad state of finding things out in economics is well illustrated by the controversies on unemployment. A good example is the much-cited paper of Lucas and Rapping (LR) (1969), and the regression running inspired by the paper, which goes on to this very day. I have chosen that paper to illustrate the products we get when we take musings as a way of finding things out, and then run regressions to try to support or falsify the musings. I happen not to believe that the Lucas and Rapping musings, as they stand, represent an addition to our store of knowledge. Nor do the hundreds or thousands of regressions they have inspired. But I do think those musings are highly suggestive of factual issues that ought to be explored in ways that are different from those we ordinarily use.

The story Lucas and Rapping tell seems simple, despite the equations with which it is tricked out. They tell us (1) that a person who has been laid off and is currently out of work could, between the layoff and the present, have taken a job at a lower wage, probably by getting a job in a different occupation or location, (2) that those who remain unemployed have chosen not to take that lower-wage job in the light of current wage rates, expected wage rates, interest rates, and so on, because that seems best for them. LR then say that (3) when you see a person in a state of unemployment you see a person who has chosen leisure over work.

Statement 1 asserts a fact about opportunities of individuals. We can easily accept, as a microeconomic truth, that at any time at least some currently out-of-work individuals could have previously left unemployment if they had chosen to fill vacancies that offered a wage lower than the wage they had in their last job. This is the crumb of real information from everyday life on which the LR musings are based.

However, LR want also to assert a macroeconomic fact by Statement 1 — that total employment would be sure to rise if all or many unemployed people decided to find and accept vacant jobs at lower wages. That goes way beyond the crumb of knowledge of everyday life that LR have available to them. They assure themselves that it is so by writing down an equation in which the aggregate demand for labor has the wage rate as one of its determinants. But I have no knowledge of the world that gives warrant for that equation, and neither do they. We don't have even crumbs of knowledge about how individual businesses manage their employment policy and wage-rate setting. We have some musings about it, which I would guess are dead wrong. Nor do LR have a good way of taking any microknowledge that comes their way and showing with any realism how it all hangs together. I will come back to both of these points later.

Statement 2 says that the unemployed did not take advantage of their opportunities. It offers no new assertion of fact, just a reassertion of the proposition that opportunities for lower-paying jobs were there for an unspecified number of unemployed people.

Statement 3 also offers no new assertions of fact. Although formally it is just a restatement of 1 in other words, it uses words that are loaded emotionally. LR admit that there might be some "social cost" to measured unemployment. But we are conditioned not to feel sorry for people characterized as choosing leisure over work. LR, by redefining unemployment this way, are telling us not to get upset when the unemployment rate rises. They do not quite say that a severe recession triggers a lot of simultaneous decisions to go on vacation, or maybe vice versa. But the psychological tendency for the incautious reader — most of us — to feel that way is there.

Lucas and Rapping's paper do bring up factual issues it would be valuable to have some real-world knowledge on. What are the options that laid-off people think they face? What are their attitudes and behaviors when faced with such options? One might imagine someone seriously interested in the purely factual issues trying to explore these microeconomic issues of fact in a direct manner. Such a person might try to interview a few dozen or a few hundred laid-off workers. The workers could be asked about how they explore their options, what they think their options are, and what their attitudes toward those options are.

What want ads does the unemployed worker answer, and why? What does the laid-off male worker say about why he hasn't (or hasn't yet) gone down and applied to be a cashier at McDonald's? Why hasn't he knocked on the door of my suburban home and offered to do the yard work I have so much trouble hiring someone to do, as Willy Fellner used to tell me he ought? Why has the unemployed female worker neglected to apply to me for a job as a maid? What would her friends and family think if she did? How would it affect her chances for reemployment in her old occupation?

Someone interested in the factual issues raised by Lucas and Rapping might also interview the manager of the worker's old establishment, and ask a series of questions artfully designed to elicit why he doesn't offer more work at lower wages. One might interview the manager at McDonald's and ask what reception the worker laid off from a higher-wage job would get if he were to show up there and ask to be taken on. Perhaps we might assign a participant-observer to a business establishment, with instructions to try to discern the do's and don'ts of hiring and wage setting. After that kind of research, one might be in a better position to decide whether the laid-off workers deserved our sympathy and policy help (if we know any that will do them any good), or whether we should simply wish them a happy vacation.

There are influential voices in our profession who say that the kind of direct research I have just described would lead to systematically misleading results. That might well happen at the beginning, but after a while we would get better at it. In addition to learning how to explore the microreality in a systematic, direct way, we would have to learn to incorporate the behavior we found out about into a framework in which the dynamic interactions of the unemployed, the employed, the plant managers, the money managers, the bank managers, and so on, were portrayed. See Bennett and Bergmann, 1986, for one such framework, using Orcutt-type computer simulation.

Lucas and Rapping did not, of course, proceed to investigate the factual issues they had raised in the direct way I have suggested would be appropriate. Instead, they proceeded in what I think deserves to be characterized as an insanely indirect way. They got some macroeconomic time series data on employment, the money wage rate, the GNP deflator, real GNP, and so on. Hiding under a clutch of equations the vagueness of the connection of these macrodata to the microbehaviors posited, Lucas and Rapping threw the data into the computer and ran some regressions. It is hard to understand how anyone could believe that such an exercise could be expected to throw any light on the factual matter of workers' and managers' options and attitudes. But out of the computer came a printout. Having read the printout, Lucas and Rapping reported that the printout gave only modest support to their ideas, but was not inconsistent with them. (The entrails of the next chicken they ate were probably also not inconsistent with the Lucas-Rapping ideas, but they refrained from reporting that.)

Someone not in our profession, hearing about such an article, might well have predicted that the "unemployment is leisure" factual-conjecture-cum-redefinition followed by wildly inappropriate regressions would have been rejected by all refereed journals and died. The same person might further predict that the reputation of those who had offered it would suffer grave damage. But such, of course, has not been the result.

The "unemployment is leisure" idea itself did not die in its cradle, as it richly deserved to do. It became an industry that is flourishing to this day and will soon enter its third decade of lusty lfe.

Methodological Reform

David Ricardo was capable of advancing economic knowledge by just sitting in his office and thinking. He probably made a high proportion of the discoveries that are findable by such a methodology. But today's economists don't have Ricardo's opportunities, talent, or practical knowledge. For one thing, Ricardo had a lot of firsthand knowledge of business. After Ricardo, there should have been a turn, at least on the part of some members of the profession, to a more observational style.

Today there are some signs that such a style is increasingly respectable. One such sign is the increasing interest in experimental economics. Another is the work that is being done in survey research. Still another is the search for business firms that will allow their records to be analyzed. Computer simulation offers a methodology to model interactions of the economic actors, based on realistic observations of their operating procedures.

Economics will eventually become a science like all the others — based on firsthand observation of reality rather than solely on cloistered musings on made-up simple models. When the economists of the future look back to our era, they will find a few who bucked the tide, who were realists rather than fabulists, to whom common sense and observation were important. Ken Galbraith will then surely be honored as one in advance of his time.

REFERENCES

Bennett, Robert L., and Barbara R. Bergmann. *A Microsimulated Transactions Model of the United States Economy.* Baltimore: The Johns Hopkins University Press, 1986.

Chamberlin, Edward H. "An Experimental Imperfect Market." *Journal of Political Economy* 56 (April 1948): 95–108.

Lucas, R. E., Jr., and L. A. Rapping. "Real Wages, Employment, and Inflation." *Journal of Political Economy* 77 (September 1969): 721–54.

Samuel Bowles and Richard Edwards

Varieties of Dissent: Galbraith and Radical Political Economy

THE MODERN STREAM of radical political economy, roughly that of the past two decades, is distinctive in its treatment of what may be termed the three dimensions of the economy: the horizontal dimension of competition, the vertical dimension of command, and the time dimension of change.[1] The radical model departs from the neoclassical model not only in the greater emphasis on the command and change dimensions of economic life — often referred to as class and history — but in the theoretical representations of each of the three dimensions. The result is a theoretical approach which supports normative conclusions quite at odds with neoclassical economics and an econometric and historical research agenda which has propelled radical economists into novel areas of investigation.

The radical political economy model has developed along lines seemingly quite independent of John Kenneth Galbraith's work.[2] Galbraith's books have not been a prominent departure point in the radical political economy literature. Nor have key Galbraithian concepts, such as countervailing power, the technostructure, the revised sequence, and the planning system, been critically examined or frequently taken up. Nor can it be said that Galbraith's method has been widely emulated. Yet radical political economy and Galbraith's work share some common intellectual commitments and features, and these commonalities may now be coming into clearer view after some two decades or so of the former's development.

One feature that characterizes both bodies of work is their orientation to neoclassical economics. Radical political economy, like Galbraith's own project, has attempted to challenge the dominance of the neoclassical orthodoxy, but neoclassicism's predominance has perhaps marked each challenger more than either realizes. In effect, each has intruded upon a landscape already defined by neoclassicals, and in arguing against orthodox views, each has been forced to concede much of this territory in order to contest the terrain elsewhere. For example, despite Galbraith's scathing rejection of neoclassicism's conventional wisdom on consumer sovereignty, he does not appear bothered by accepting its view of the labor process. And despite radical political economy's refusal to adopt the orthodoxy's presumption that all economic relations may be understood as if they are voluntary exchanges, it has not developed an analysis of the modern corporation that successfully distinguishes it from neoclassicism's anonymous, timeless, and omniscient competitive firm. This feature of arguing against neoclassical economics on neoclassicism's own grounds simply highlights the difficulty of displacing a prevailing paradigm.

A second common feature in Galbraith's work and that of radical political economists is a concern for understanding the exercise of power in everyday economic life. In the neoclassical world, power exists only as anomaly, market failure, or a manifestation of government; elsewhere, voluntary exchange prevails. For both Galbraith and radical political economy, however, power is a central constituent element in economic relations and as necessary a construct in analyzing capitalism (or socialism) as are competition and markets. For Galbraith, the language of power (such as "the shift in power from ownership and the entrepreneur to the technostructure," "control," and "planning" as "the comprehensive exercise of power") peppers virtually every page and emphasizes that for him the understanding of how power is exercised is of the first importance in economic analysis. For radical political economy, the concerns of class, hierarchy, control, and dominance, concerns that have in particular motivated the development of radical microeconomics, demonstrate the centrality of power issues within radical analysis.

Other shared features could be mentioned: endogenous preferences, the state as an intrinsic player in capitalist economies, the importance of historically contingent development and hence of history, and the commitment to a democratic vision of society.

Yet despite these many commonalities, radical political economy has developed in a direction quite different from that of Galbraith's work. In what follows, we review that development, the results now of some two decades' effort. At the end we speculate on how this development (as well as parallel developments within neoclassical theory) has taken a roundabout and perhaps ironic path leading to a better understanding of the enduring contributions in Galbraith's work.

Command: The Microeconomics of Class Conflict

> One aspect of the relationships between the factors of production has, however, been less examined. That is why power is associated with some factors and not with others.
>
> — *The New Industrial State*

The most obvious beginning point for a discussion of radical political economy is the importance given to relationships of domination, power, subordination, and hierarchy — in short, what may be called "command." Two concerns motivate this focus: a democratic commitment to the elimination of arbitrary and unaccountable forms of authority and a theoretical commitment to the proposition that capitalist society is simply unintelligible to those who abstract from the question of power. Early contributions to radical political economy focused almost entirely on command relationships in markets and in firms and gave rise to a rich literature on what might be called the political structure of the capitalist firm, the relationship between technology and hierarchy, and the racial and gender segmentation of labor markets.

Within this framework, class played a major conceptual role, and one quite different from that played by the distribution of property rights in the neoclassical model. A class relationship is generally defined as a relationship of domination based on ownership and control of capital goods used in production.[3] The dominant class is dominant in the sense that it exercises command (in a capitalist economy through ownership) over the surplus product.[4]

Terminological differences aside, the concept of the surplus product differs little from the analogous concepts used in linear growth models, Sraffa-based systems, and input-output accounting frameworks. Further, the economic importance of the claims exercised on the surplus product by owners of productive assets is recognized in virtually all schools of economic thought. But the treatment of class in radical political economic models distances these approaches considerably from neoclassical or Cambridge (England) economics. The fundamental difference is that the radical political economic conception of class is not restricted to a distribution of property claims, the effects of which are exercised exclusively through its impact on income distribution (and hence its influence on macroeconomic aggregates). Rather, the radical model of class encompasses the effects of the structure of ownership and control of capital goods on the production process itself, on the choice of technology, and on the structure and nature of equilibrium in labor markets. Thus the power of capital is not reducible to purchasing power but includes power over production and even — through the actual or threatened withholding of investment — power over public policy.

Class may thus be considered a microeconomic as well as a macroeconomic concept; but unlike classical Marxism, which rooted its analysis in the labor theory of value, radical political economy bases the microeconomics of class on a particular model of the production process no less Marxian in spirit but owing nothing to his labor theory of value.[5] This model conceives of the production process as composed of two conceptually distinct but in fact always intertwined aspects: the translation of inputs into outputs (which may be described by a production function) and the control of workers by employers in the interest of regulating the pace and intensity of work (which Marx termed the extraction of labor from labor power). Understanding this second aspect of the production process requires a model of the conflict of interest between worker and owner, of the strategies adopted by each, and of the institutional and other environments affecting the ability of workers to pursue collective as opposed to individual strategies.

A number of models of the production process embodying both a production function and a labor extraction function have been developed.[6] In all of them the threat of job loss is a major employer weapon in controlling the work process.[7] Because the magnitude of the threat of job loss depends on the level of the wage, novel results immediately ensue. For example, the cost of an effort unit of work may actually fall with a rise in the wage, for a higher wage will increase the threat of job loss to the worker and may thus evince a greater amount of work effort or allow the employer to economize on supervisory inputs. Further, it will generally be in the interest of the employer to offer workers a wage in excess of the workers' next best alternative, implying that involuntary unemployment will persist even in a competitive labor market equilibrium.

The radical view of class and the resulting nonclearing nature of labor markets thus provides a microeconomic basis for the functioning of unemployment — Marx's reserve army of the unemployed — in regulating the bargaining strength between capital and labor, and hence in supporting a positive profit rate. When these models are applied to the problem of technical change, they demonstrate that profit-maximizing technical choice will not generally be efficient, thus inviting an analysis of the institutional determinants of technical change of the type suggested by Marx and pioneered in recent years by Stephen Marglin's work on the role of hierarchy in production.[8]

Competition:
Beyond Walrasian Exchange

> . . . prices are no longer of unique importance in telling how resources are distributed. What counts is the whole deployment of power — over prices, costs, consumers, suppliers, the government.
>
> — *Economics and the Public Purpose*

The radical economists' focus on command relationships entailed a new view of how markets work. Of particular analytical and political interest, of course, was the question of unemployment and the segmented nature of labor markets. Relationships between core and peripheral firms — a theme stressed by Galbraith — also received attention. In recent years, radical economists have taken up the question of credit markets, seeking to understand why it is that wealth confers power in a highly competitive economy and why it is that workers (and most others) are often credit rationed. In this framework markets (even highly competitive ones) are not seen as antithetical to command relations but rather as complementary.[9]

Because in this new theory of exchange, quantity constraints are ubiquitous rather than exceptional, both rents and bargaining relationships assume an important role in the theory of exchange. The result is a theory of markets which permits a more coherent and less ad hoc treatment of such elements as oligopoly, collusion among agents, market segmentation, price rigidities, managerial deviations from profit maximization, and the absence of competition.[10] Moreover, while neoclassical economics is quintessentially a theory of markets and marketlike interactions, radical economists have focused much theoretical attention on social relationships in which market-type interactions assume a relatively minor importance. Thus, for example, in developing a feminist model of household labor and demography, radical economists have eschewed the marriage-market metaphor of the new family economics and developed an analysis of conflict and accommodation within a general framework of gender-based domination.[11] Similarly, conflict theories of inflation stress the integral importance of nonmarket (e.g., political) forces.[12] This same radical understanding of markets also informs the conflict theory of discrimination and racial inequality.[13]

The distinct treatment of markets in radical models, however, neither requires ad hoc assumptions about collusion or rigidities nor presumes the unimportance of market institutions relative to nonmarket structures. Rather, the introduction of class or command challenges the coherence of the conventional textbook model more or less on its own grounds. The radical analysis thus moves us towards a Galbraithian rather than Walrasian conception of markets.

The most general difference is that radical economists consider as endogenous a range of phenomena generally considered to be exogenous in neoclassical models. The above radical model of the production process, for example, is distinct from the usual neo-classical model in that it treats the problem of labor-contract enforcement as endogenous to the firm. Equally important, the firm is represented as a price maker and wage maker rather than regarding these market phenomena as parametric. Firms are thus active rather than passive, interacting in ways better captured by analogy to military strategy than to the hydraulic metaphor which appears to inform so much of neoclassical price theory.

Moreover, the endogenization of what are in the neoclassical model exogenous elements, including, in particular, the preferences and interests of the actors, implies that the concept of market equilibrium as it is usually defined is of marginal significance. Even when markets do clear, they do not reach an "equilibrium" (meaning stasis in the absence of an exogenous change).[14] Although not always recognized even in radical models, this redefinition of the market process allows for the true introduction, within the model, of the third dimension in the economic process, "change" or history. Such models therefore use such terms as "accumulation" and "development" rather than "profit-maximization" and "equilibrium."

Even in those radical models where the "equilibrium" concept continues to play an important part, equilibria are generally not regarded as unique and pressures for the attainment of equilibria are often counterposed by what may be considered disequilibrating tendencies.[15] In radical models of dynamic competition these disequilibrating pressures are often summarized as the tendency toward "uneven development," the bases of which are structurally determined inequalities in access to credit, information, and political power, giving rise to the disproportionate ability of some groups to profit from market disequilibria.

This, in radical political economy, markets appear more as battlegrounds for contending economic actors than as the slate upon which are registered the prices and quantities uniquely determined through the interaction of pregiven tastes, technologies, and endowments. This perspective has immediate application to product markets and the analysis of corporations, and corporate-government interactions.[16]

Corporate strategies for competing in markets and the consequences of such strategies are not in general confined to a national economy. The model therefore pushes analysts to consider the workings of an open economy with generalized worldwide competition. The results of this perspective are apparent not only in those subject areas which have traditionally forced economists to consider an open economy — areas such as monetary movements and regional specialization — but also in novel areas with sometimes novel results. International capital flows and domestic power relations are seen as conditioned by differential opportunities between corporations and bankers for reaping offshore profits. Employers' attention to opening production facilities abroad, rather than simply reflecting lower production costs, is understood in part as a strategy for extracting labor from domestic employees. Domestic investment and savings behavior is analyzed in a regime in which domestic savings does not equal domestic investment.[17]

Change: Learning, History, and Irreversible Time

> A curiosity of modern economic life is the role of change. It is imagined to be very great; to list its forms or emphasize its extent is to show a reassuring grasp of the commonplace. Yet not much is supposed to change. The economic system of the United States is praised on all occasions of public ceremony as a largely perfect structure. This is so elsewhere also. It is not easy to perfect what has been perfected. This is massive change but, except as the output of goods increases, all remains as before.
>
> — *The New Industrial State*

Radical economists, like Galbraith, have focused on the analysis of a particular set of institutions — those of modern capitalism — and the evolution of these institutions through time. The institutional peculiarities of an epoch are regarded as essential characteristics of the historical evolution of the age, not as superficial variations on an unchanging underlying model. This perspective has given rise to the concept of a social structure of accumulation — the rules of the game which regulate the profit-making and investment process, ranging from labor relations and the international monetary order to tax policy and the structure of educational institutions. Three characteristics of this approach to the evolution of institutions may be noted: time is treated historically, people are endogenous, and institutions matter.

Historical time is simply a conception of time and change in which history matters. What came before makes a difference because, in the radical economic model, time is irreversible, more or less as we think of it in everyday discourse, but not as it is treated in most economic models.

The paradigmatic model of change in neoclassical economic theory is the exogenous displacement of an equilibrium of agents with exogenously given preferences and capacities, as, for example, when the equilibrium price and quantity are altered through some shift in a supply or demand function. Neither the mathematics of Cramer's Rule nor the substantive theory of comparative static analysis gives us any reason to doubt that should the exogenous shock be withdrawn, the system would return to its *status quo ante*.

The radical economic model of change is historical rather than comparative static: time goes on, it does not go back and forth; it is not differentiable in either direction. The irreversibility of time is founded on one of the most basic axioms of contemporary radical political economy: people are endogenous to the economic system. Our tastes, capacities, identifications, and other aspects of what we are like as people depend in important measure on our experiences in the economy, including the process by which we are brought up and schooled for entry into adult economic life. When the "givens" of an economic situation change, we change with them, and should they change back again, we continue changing, but only by accident would we return to where we started.

Historical time is part of a view of economic change which displaces the favored dichotomy of comparative static analysis — exogenous/endogenous — with an alternative model of change based on the interaction of action and system or, in the more traditional language, practice and structure. By system or structure is meant any relevant set of rules of the game imparting regularity to actions and their effects. By action or practice is meant any intentional project — either individual or collective — structured by these rules of the game. According to this view, change in economic systems takes place through the effects of structures in limiting actions and forming actors and the reciprocal effect of actors in transforming and consolidating systems.

The familiar example of profit maximization may illustrate the point. Within neoclassical economics profit maximization is represented primarily as the choice of an input structure and level of output which yields the highest profit for a given set of technologies and market prices. This process may have dynamic effects, as new technologies become available, or as tastes or endowments change, resulting in the perturbation of the firms first-order conditions in the manner which the displacement of equilibrium was described above. In radical political economy, firms maximize profits, but they do so primarily through attempting to alter precisely those parameters taken as exogenously determined in the neoclassical model: tastes, state policy, technologies, the structure of competition. Rent-seeking behavior along the lines described by Schumpeter (entrepreneurial profits) and Marx (superprofits) thus becomes central to the theory, as does the exercise of power over variables considered parametric in the textbook neoclassical model stressed by Galbraith.

To take a rather different illustration, work on the critical role of credit and debt in the macroeconomy follows Keynes in emphasizing institutional features and such aspects as expectations and speculation.[18] These are areas in which the analysis must incorporate real historical events rather than presumptions of an unchanging structure for understanding how, for example, the global credit expansion of the past decade has occurred.

Just as the actors seek to transform the structures, the process results in a transformation of the actors. In this case the process of competition endogenously generates changes in its own structure: a competitive process of small firms may be transformed into a dual economy of giant corporations and small firms and then perhaps to a system of competition among the few or a highly competitive global system.

As is clear, social institutions — public policy, contract enforcement, international relations, labor organization, ideology — are treated as endogenous.[19] Investigation of the manner in which social institutions regulate the accumulation process and are at the same time transformed by it has barely begun, but the social structure of accumulation framework appears to have provided a fruitful starting point for this research. Among its many attractive features, the social structure of accumulation model allows a complex theoretical demarcation of epochs of capitalist history at once supplementing the otherwise overly abstract concept of the capitalist mode of production (capitalism in general) and the overly simple earlier formulations such as the distinction between monopoly capitalism and competitive capitalism.[20]

Do (Analytical) Systems Converge?
Galbraith and the Future of Economic Analysis

The time has come for a concluding word on economics. Lord Keynes, in a famous forecast, thought the subject would eventually become unimportant — in social significance it would rank about with dentistry. . . . But, though in a sense Keynes was right that the subject is in decline, in a larger sense he was wrong. . . . the future of economics could be rather bright. It could be in touch with the gravest problems of our time. Whether this is so — whether economics is important — is up to economists. They can, if they are determined, be unimportant; they can, if they prefer a comfortable home life and regular hours, continue to make a living out of the infinitely interesting gadgetry of disguise.

Or economists can enlarge their system. They can have it embrace, in all its diverse manifestations, the power they now disguise.

— *Economics and the Public Purpose*

Neoclassical microeconomics, Galbraith's analysis of the corporation, and radical political economy's three-dimensional analysis represent three approaches to understanding the firm. Many of the microeconomic concerns of radical economics — nonclearing markets, endogenous claim enforcement, and bargaining problems, for example — are echoed in recent developments throughout the economics profession. While nobody ever accused Galbraith of an excessive concern with formal microeconomic theory, the implications of much of the new research in microeconomic theory point unambiguously — if ironically — to the enduring importance of Galbraith's institutionalism. This is so because the new microeconomics — radical and otherwise — has left the Walrasian world with its simple problems and unique answers far behind. If one were to draw a single conclusion from the last couple of decades of research on game theory, incomplete contracts, property rights, nonclearing markets, and the like, it would have to be that the results of theoretical investigations must be far more open-ended than the determinate and unique solutions that the textbook Walrasian model suggested. The nonuniqueness of equilibria (where they exist) and the general indeterminateness of results in small numbers exchange problems might well foster a healthy if unaccustomed modesty among theorists.

The growing dissatisfaction with the physics-based economics models and the awareness of the sheer complexity of modeling interactions among real people in society rather than *Homo economicus* in abstract markets may promote a return to the theoretically informed but concrete study of institutions as they are, motivated by the quest not for the highest level of generality but for historically contingent answers to questions concerning what might be done to design an economy more conducive to fairness, wellbeing, and freedom. If economists do take up this more relevant, more useful, and hardly modest task, they will find Galbraith's work an exemplary guide.

NOTES

1. The starting point for this approach may be taken as Richard Edwards, Arthur MacEwan, et al., "A Radical Approach to Economics: Basis for a New Curriculum," Proceedings of the American Economic Association, May 1970, and Richard Edwards, Michael Reich, and Thomas Weisskopf, *The Capitalist System* 3rd. ed. (Englewood Cliffs, N.J.: Prentice-Hall, 1986). Other comprehensive approaches are presented in Stephen Marglin, *Growth, Distribution, and Prices* (Cambridge: Harvard University Press, 1984), and Donald Harris, *Capital Accumulation and Income Distribution* (Stanford, Calif.: Stanford University Press, 1978). No recent work matches the compass of Paul Sweezy's now somewhat dated *Theory of Capitalist Development* (London: Denis Dobson, 1942). Introductory critiques of neoclassical economics are presented in a number of important textbooks, e.g., E. K. Hunt and Howard J. Sherman, *Economics: An Introduction to Traditional and Radical Views* (New York: Harper & Row, 1978), and Tom Riddell, Jean Shackleford, and Steve Stamos, *Economics: A Tool for Understanding Society* (Reading, Mass.: Addison Wesley, 1982). A general model along these lines is presented in Samuel Bowles and Richard Edwards, *Understanding Capitalism: Competition, Command, and Change in the U.S. Economy* (New York: Harper & Row, 1985).

2. For this discussion, Galbraith's most important works are *The Affluent Society, The New Industrial State,* and *Economics and the Public Purpose.*

3. The theory of class relationships, which derives from the original theoretical work of the classical economists and Marx, has been developed considerably in recent years. Major works indicative of the diversity of these contributions include John Roemer, *A General Theory of Exploitation and Class* (Cambridge: Harvard University Press, 1982); *Free to Lose* (Cambridge: Harvard University Press, 1988); Erik Olin Wright, *Class, Crisis and the State* (London: New Left Books, 1978); and Stephen Resnick and Richard Wolff, "The Concept of Class in Marxian Theory," *Review of Radical Political Economics* 13, no. 4 (1981).

4. The surplus product is gross output minus both intermediate goods inputs (including those used to repair wear and tear on capital goods) and the outputs which make up the wage bundle. The surplus product may be measured as a vector of heterogeneous goods, in the hours of labor time directly and indirectly required to produce these goods, in money terms as total property income derived from the ownership of the capital goods used in production, and in other ways.

5. Contributions to this literature include Herbert Gintis, "The Nature of the Labor Exchange and the Theory of Capitalist Production," *Review of Radical Political Economics* 8, no. 2 (Summer 1976); Stephen Marglin, "What Do Bosses Do? The Origins and Function of Hierarchy in Capitalist Production," *Review of Radical Political Economics* 6, no. 2 (Spring 1974); Richard Edwards, *Contested Terrain: The Transformation of the Workplace in the Twentieth Century* (New York: Basic Books, 1979); and David Gordon, Richard Edwards, and Michael Reich, *Segmented Work, Divided Workers: The Historical Transformation of Labor in the United States* (Cambridge, England: Cambridge University Press, 1982).

6. See Herbert Gintis and Tsuneo Ishikawa, "Wages, Work Discipline, and Unemployment," *Journal of Japanese and International Economics* 1 (1987): 195–228, and Samuel Bowles, "The Production Process in a Competitive Economy: Walrasian, Neo-Hobbesian, and Marxian Models," *American Economic Review* 75, no. 1 (March 1985): 16–36. Others working outside the radical tradition have developed similar models. See Janet Yellen, "Efficiency Wage Models of Unemployment," *American Economic Review* 74, no. 2 (May 1984): 200–205; Robert Solow, "On Theories of Unemployment," *American Economic Review* (March 1980); and Carl Shapiro and Joseph Stiglitz, "Equilibrium Unemployment as a Worker Discipline Device," *American Economic Review* (June 1984). A post-Keynesian variant is presented in Eileen Appelbaum, "The Labor Market in Post Keynesian Theory," *Challenge* (January–February 1979): 39–47.

7. Juliet Schor and Samuel Bowles, "Employment Rents and the Incidence of Strikes," *Review of Economics and Statistics* 64, no. 4 (November 1987): 584–92.

8. This result is central to the radical critique of capitalist technology. It follows trivially when the labor extraction function is not formally separable from the production function — due to the effects of alternative production technologies on the ease with which labor is controlled.

9. Herbert Gintis, "Financial Markets and the Political Nature of the Enterprise," *Journal of Economic Behavior and Organization* (forthcoming). For a sketch of what the authors term the theory of contested exchange, see Samuel Bowles and Herbert Gintis, "Contested Exchange: Political Economy and Modern Economic Theory," *American Economic Review* 78, no. 2 (May 1988): 145–50.

10. The radical reconsideration of the workings of markets owes much to the stimulus of recent works in the theory of imperialism and international economic relations, many of which have suggested the inadequacy of both the neoclassical treatment of markets and the classical Marxian preoccupation with the production process (often to the exclusion of any sustained analysis of markets) as the key to understanding exploitation. Not surprisingly three of the influential works in this area are authored by noneconomists: Immanuel Wallerstein, *The Modern World System: Capitalist Agriculture and the Origins of the European World-Economy in the Sixteenth Century* (New York: Academic Press, 1974); Eric R. Wolf, *Europe and the People without History* (Berkeley: University of California Press, 1982); and Fred Block, *The Origins of International Economic Disorder* (Berkeley: University of California Press, 1977).

11. Nancy Folbre, "Of Patriarchy Born: The Political Economy of Fertility Decisions," *Feminist Studies* 9, no. 2 (Summer 1983): 261–84; and "Exploitation Comes Home:

A Critique of the Marxian Theory of Family Labor," *Cambridge Journal of Economics* 6, no. 4 (December 1982): 317–29; Heidi Hartmann, "The Family as the Locus of Gender, Class and Political Struggle: The Example of Housework," *Signs: Journal of Women in Culture and Society* 6, no. 3 (Spring 1981): 366–94; and Elaine McCrate, "Gender Inequality and Marital Choice: The New Home Economics and an Alternative," mimeo, University of Massachusetts, Amherst, 1984.

12. See Leonard Rapping, "The Domestic and International Aspects of Structural Inflation," in James Gapinski and Charles Rockwood, eds., *Essays in Post-Keynesian Inflation* (Cambridge, Mass.: Ballinger, 1979).

13. See Michael Reich, *Racial Inequality* (Princeton, N.J.: Princeton University Press, 1981).

14. For an important discussion on this point from a post-Keynesian perspective, see Douglas Vickers, "On Relational Structures and Non-Equilibrium in Economic Theory," *Eastern Economic Journal* 11, no. 4 (Summer 1985).

15. Few general equilibrium theorists of any stripe would claim that equilibria are unique except under quite stringent conditions. But the absence of any general theoretical reasoning as to why an economy might "locate" at one or another of a number of possible equilibria suggests that at least in textbook practice most neoclassical economists are content to act as if equilibria were unique.

16. See David Kotz, *Bank Control of Large Corporations in the U.S.* (Berkeley: University of California Press, 1978), and Joseph Bowring, *Accumulation in the Dual Economy* (Princeton, N.J.: Princeton University Press, 1985).

17. Arthur MacEwan, "Slackers, Bankers, Marketers: Multinational Firms and the Pattern of U.S. Foreign Direct Investment," mimeo, University of Massachusetts, Boston, 1982; Barry Bluestone and Bennett Harrison, *The De-Industrialization of America* (New York: Basic Books, 1983); and Bowles and Edwards, *Understanding Capitalism,* especially part IV.

18. See Hyman Minsky, *John Meynard Keynes* (New York: Columbia University Press, 1975); Leonard Rapping, "The Interest Rate and Third World Debt," in *The Donald S. MacNaughton Symposium, Proceedings 1983* (Syracuse: Syracuse University, 1983); and James Crotty, "The Centrality of Money, Credit, and Financial Intermediation in Marx's Crisis Theory: An Interpretation of Marx's Methodology," in Stephen Resnick and Richard Wolff, eds., *Rethinking Marxism* (New York: Autonomedia, 1985).

19. The most developed work on the endogeneity of social institutions focuses on the manner in which state policy — and particularly macroeconomic policy — responds to the interests of dominant groups within the capitalist class. While this literature dates back at least to Kalecki's writings in the 1940s, it has received important recent impetus in James O'Connor, *The Fiscal Crisis of the State* (New York: St. Martin's, 1973); Raford Boddy and James Crotty, "Class Conflict and Macro Policy: The Political Business Cycle," *Review of Radical Political Economics* 8 (1975); and Andrew Glyn and Robert Sutcliffe, *British Capitalism, Workers, and the Profit Squeeze* (London: Penguin, 1972).

20. The social structure of accumulation concept was introduced in David Gordon, "Stages of Accumulation and Long Economic Cycles," in *Processes of the World-System,* T. Hopkins and I. Wallerstein, eds. (Beverly Hills, Cal.: Sage, 1980), and developed more extensively in Gordon, Edwards, and Reich, *Segmented Work, Divided Workers.* Econometric estimates of the post–World War II U.S. social structure of accumulation appear in Samuel Bowles, David Gordon, and Thomas Weisskopf, "Business Ascendancy and Economic Impasse: A Structural Retrospective on Conservative Economics, 1979–1986," *Journal of Economic Perspectives,* 3, no. 1 (Winter 1989): 107–34.

Robert Lekachman

The Power of Words

THE FIRST TIME I saw Ken Galbraith plain was at 2:30 P.M., December 28, 1953, at the Sixty-Sixth Annual Meeting of the American Economic Association in Washington, D.C. The session, chaired by Edward H. Chamberlin, inventor of the theory of monopolistic competition, was devoted entirely to discussion of a single book. The item at issue was not a mathematical treatise. It contained no equations and no technical jargon. The style was direct and frequently ironic. Elegant prose, a pleasure wherever encountered, never startles more than when an economist perpetrates it. Galbraith did not intend to charm economists. He had attempted to convert if not charm the professionals in a closely argued case for price and wage controls in an earlier book, *A Theory of Price Control.* Its small sales and lack of resonance in the journals convinced him that the path to attention was neither journal articles nor reputable monographs. If the economists were recalcitrant, the public just might be more receptive. The cost-benefit computations of the guild assign small value to charm, a quality perilously close to frivolity and profoundly subversive of sober maximization. His intended audience was that mysterious group who prefer accessible discussion of public issues to Harold Robbins, Judith Krantz, Sidney Sheldon, Stephen King, Jackie Collins, and other titans of trash.

No need to prolong suspense. Galbraith had published his first major popular success the preceding year, *American Capitalism: The Concept of Countervailing Power.* Delighted, like any other proud literary parent, to praise his achievement, Galbraith began in the style with which his admiring readers have become familiar over the last three and a half decades: "One is greatly favored in being allowed to speak about a book which he himself has written. He can fairly claim to be an authority on what the author said or meant to say. He is not expected to conform to especially high standards of scientific detachment. On the contrary, a certain partiality and even admiration for the work under discussion is permissible — in fact commonplace." Quickly, Galbraith segued into a lucid précis of his argument and an elegant rebuttal of most of the criticisms levied up to that time against it. His two concluding sentences were exhortatory: "Unrestrained economic power is still an enemy of the good society. I only urge that we have a full view of the processes by which it is restrained."

Up stood George J. Stigler, a slender pillar then but a massive column now in the temple of Chicago free-market economics. His remarks, entitled "The Economist Plays with Blocs," raked countervailing power fore and aft and back again. Good clean fun, and the better for the audience that between them Galbraith and Stigler exceeded thirteen feet in height. In his infinite wisdom, the Lord had matched a tall conservative against a tall liberal — heavenly affirmative action.

Rereading the disputants, I'd call the exchange a draw. Those like me who venerate bright ideas couched in attractive prose even, or perhaps especially, when the ideas are not smothered in presumably supporting data, thought Galbraith had the better of the argument. Bright ideas are so rare that each one merits tender nurture. Stigler's strategy was conventional. Much was wrong with Galbraith's analytical framework. Worse still, the man had done none of the required investigation of how well in the real world of commerce and manufacturing countervailing power fared. He had not set a platoon of graduate students to work on suitably unreadable dissertations devoted to the breakfast cereal, chain store, pharmaceutical, auto, and other industries where countervailing power might or might not lurk.

At a guess, a majority of the large audience awarded Stigler the palm of victory. Like other specialists, most economists won their advanced degrees, progressed to tenure, and aged into retirement by working within safe, conventional paradigms. Socialized into respectability in graduate school, they tend to view novelty as a devaluation of their arduously acquired and professionally indispensable intellectual capital. It takes a Keynes aided by a calamitous depression to drag his colleagues, kicking and screaming, into a new world of mysterious concepts, strange terminology, and dangerous public policy novelties. Better to be respectably wrong than prematurely right. And even Keynes needed World War II as a practical demonstration of the efficacy of public spending in generating full employment.

I do not recall this episode in order to revive an elderly controversy. My point is quite different, a comment on contrasting careers. George Stigler has won the Nobel Prize. He is a sharp and witty controversialist. His work in industrial organization is appropriately respected even by those who differ from its thrust and conclusions. Many of his essays in the history of economic thought and others concerned with the education of economists, the profession's appropriate role in the formulation of public policy, and similar themes are written in clear, seemly English. As a former student during the man's brief exile at Columbia, I can testify to his exciting, contentious classroom style, admirably calculated to challenge belligerent radicals and timid liberals. His many students have preached the Chicago gospel in universities at home and abroad. Some of its acolytes have advised the Chilean government. In Chile they are known, derisively or respectfully according to taste, as the Chicago boys. Undeterred by evidence as good economists should be, they continue to believe that free markets must in the end culminate in political democracy.

Pause to contrast Stigler's and Galbraith's public reputation or mere name recognition. I hazard the conjecture that for every literate soul who can identify Stigler there are millions here and abroad who if queried will readily recognize Galbraith. A sizable cohort, particularly of the mature, have read *The Affluent Society, The Great Crash, The New Industrial State,* or perhaps that charming memoir of Canadian childhood and adolescence, *The Scotch,* one of my favorites in the canon. In case one wanted to refresh one's recollection of Galbraith, during a week in June 1988, he was visible on the morning network TV programs and numerous radio stations, in the company of Stanislav Menshikov, an authentic Russian Communist intellectual. The duo had jointly written *Capitalism and Coexistence,* based upon lengthy, recorded conversations about such matters as *glasnost* and *perestroika.* To their mutual benefit, Galbraith and William Buckley have sparred on the latter's long-running "Firing Line," the commercial networks, and other public forums.

Galbraith is a prime example of a shrinking breed — the public intellectual, the woman or man who commands often grudging respect from peers in spite of a deplorable habit of writing readable, even enjoyable books directed at the literate public and a positively despicable tendency to wax positively wealthy on the royalties. A short list of the quick and the dead would feature such names as Hannah Arendt, Rachel Carson, Simone de Beauvoir, Daniel Bell, Irving Howe, Michael Harrington, Milton Friedman (alas!), Lionel Trilling, Edmund Wilson, and Alfred Kazin. What unites them is their successful preference for large audiences and the corollary desire to influence public policy in counterpoint to the cloistered scholars who read each other in technical journals safe from the comprehension of the great, unwashed public. As reviewers they are as likely to appear in the *New York Review of Books* as the *New York Times Book Review.* Galbraith and Friedman have presided over a multipart public television series.

As Russell Jacoby persuasively argues in his 1987 *The Last Intellectuals,* younger replacements for this valuable group are difficult to locate. At least one cause, Jacoby plausibly emphasizes, is the malignant influence of university tenure criteria. Rachel Carson and Edmund Wilson flourished outside the university. Before the success of *The Other America,* Michael Harrington shared the poverty he so effectively described and deplored. His two years with Dorothy Day's *Catholic Worker* were an exercise in voluntary mortification of the flesh. But the shrinking number of serious magazines and other sources of free-lance income almost compels young writers to seek steady income from academe. And increasingly what is demanded of the young scholar is command of narrow technique. Harvard denied tenure to Paul Starr, author of the popular (damning word!), prize-winning *The Social Transformation of American Medicine.* Alan Brinkley, winner of awards in history, was a second Harvard casualty. There's a lesson for young scholars cursed by literary talent. Publish for the general public and you will surely perish. Write long enough in specialized jargon and your literary flair will extinguish itself — one of the unstated objectives of the tenure process.

What unites public intellectuals is their common desire to advance ideas directed at large political objectives or notions that challenge what Galbraith has memorably termed the "conventional wisdom." Rachel Carson's *Silent Spring* sparked the environmental movement which has survived even eight years of Reagan sabotage. Michael Harrington's *The Other America* recalled poverty to an inattentive public, caught the attention of John Kennedy, and spurred Lyndon Johnson's "unconditional" war against poverty. Daniel Bell's *The End of Ideology* became a much-cited argument during the placid Eisenhower years that Marxism primarily but also other coherent general theories of society had lost their appeal. As the upheaval of the next decade demonstrated, prophecy is risky.

There is no set of literary devices common to public intellectuals. The prose of *The Other America* was simple, direct, and passionate. Daniel Bell's and Hannah Arendt's most influential works were intricately argued and dotted with scholarly allusions. Allan Bloom's best-selling *The Closing of The American Mind* is a furious, frequently incoherent polemic against rock music, popular culture, and above all the cowardice of academics who have, according to Bloom, defaulted on their central mission — the education of the elite in the great classics of western culture, according to Plato's prescription in *The Republic*. Education Secretary William Bennett embraced Bloom warmly, apparently heedless or ignorant of the fact that *The Republic* is a profoundly antidemocratic screed and that the Platonic dialogues positively celebrate homosexuality. Has the vociferous secretary recently reread *The Symposium* in moments spared from bashing Harvard, Duke, and Stanford? Bloom touched a nerve, public apprehension that something was seriously amiss at all levels of our untidy educational nonsystem. Descending rapidly into the lower levels of intellectual discourse, one can cite George Gilder's hysterical claim in *Wealth and Poverty* that God is a capitalist and investors are motivated by altruism. Ronald Reagan held up the book, title foremost, on TV, and the tract won instant celebrity as a vindication of supply-side economics.

As my two final examples demonstrate, the public intellectual's message may be nonsense bathed in gibberish. Nevertheless, if the time is right, if the evil attacked worries the public, and if the agenda chimes with dominant political forces, rest assured that the Book-of-the-Month Club, the book chains, the TV talk shows, and other mighty engines of marketing promotion will place the book on the coffee tables of middle-class America. It is all but irrelevant how many of the purchasers actually read their acquisition. Fully to disentangle Bloom, a reader should be acquainted with Plato, Aristotle, Machiavelli, Dante, Rousseau, Locke, Hobbes, and many other eminences of the last two and a half millennia.

This is only to state the obvious. Public intellectuals, good, bad, or indifferent, are fiercely individualistic, in appealing contrast to specialists whose prose is homogenized to the requirements of their guild. Nor do they aspire to the ideological neutrality, the apparently value-free analysis of economists and the social scientists who imitate them. They are advocates. More power to them.

Let me turn to the agreeable task of comment on Ken Galbraith's literary strategy. I shall use *The Affluent Society* as my major text but stray from time to time to other works. A preliminary warning. One can enjoyably identify some of the devices used by a gifted writer to attract and sustain attention and, object of the public intellectual's efforts, nudge readers to accept novel notions and unfamiliar proposals. But no such guide will improve the prose style of those whose ear is not responsive to the music of seemly word patterns. Long ago I worked for a year with an intelligent student ambitious to write better. At year's end, I commented that it was too bad time had run out. His prose now was for the most part grammatically correct. He was capable of coherent sentences and even entire paragraphs. The next stage, I mused, was progress from grammatical accuracy toward grace of expression. He looked at me with utter astonishment that words on a printed page could be so arranged as to convey pleasure. Sadly, he represents a large public, so heedless of language as to make best-sellers of semiliterate Ludlum thrillers and ponderous Michener tomes composed for the prose-deaf by one of their own.

Not the least of Galbraith's services to his adopted country has been the creation of a public of his own better attuned to literary virtuosity. How does the man his wonders to perform?

Alliance with Readers

It helps to make clear at the start what you intend to do. On page three of *The Affluent Society,* its author states his agenda.

> The first task is to see the way our economic attitudes are rooted in the poverty, inequality, and economic peril of the past. Then the partial and implicit accommodation to affluence is examined. The next task is to consider the devices and arguments, some elaborate, some meretricious, some in a degree dangerous, by which, in vital matters, we have managed to maintain an association with the older ideas which stemmed from a world where nearly all were poor. For no one should suppose that there is anything convenient or agreeable about the assumption of affluence. On the contrary, it threatens the prestige and position of many important people. And it exposes many of us to the even greater horror of new thought. We face here the greatest of vested interests, those of the mind.

In less than half a page, Galbraith lays out the plan of his book and promises those who stay with him a risky exploration of new intellectual terrain. He reinforces his challenge to readers two pages later.

> These are the days when men of all social disciplines and all political faiths seek the comfortable and the accepted; when the man of controversy is looked upon as a disturbing influence; when originality is taken to be a mark of instability; and when, in minor modification of the scriptural parable, the bland lead the bland. Those who esteem this world will not enjoy this essay. Perhaps they should return it to the shelf unread. For there are negative thoughts here, and they cannot but strike an uncouth note in the world of positive thinking.

Are you a woman or man of vision unafraid of challenges to orthodoxy, avid for originality, a devotee of negative thought, a passionate debater, or are you meekly willing to consume the bland fare dished up by respectable pundits and place iconoclasm behind you as a temptation of the devil? Galbraith has cunningly loaded the dice. If the choice is between him and Norman Vincent Peale, then any individual who fancies herself a free spirit can only opt for the devil.

The devil rewards his retinue. There are memorable phrases, like "the conventional wisdom" and "social balance." There are several chapters which sketch in acid terms nineteenth- and twentieth-century economics and invite readers to participate in the formulation of a more enlightened vision of getting and spending, buying and selling. Nor — and here I approach a second literary device — does Galbraith neglect appropriate illustrative anecdotes and revelations of folly from the mouths of the foolish.

Stories

The following is a pointed example of association in the past, if different in the present, of power and wealth, a sermon in a story:

> The power that was once joined with wealth has been impaired in a more intimate way. In 1194, the crusading knight, Henry of Champagne, paid a visit to the headquarters of the Assassins at the castle at al-Kahf on a rugged peak in the Nosairi Mountains. The Assassins, though a fanatical Moslem sect, had, in general, been on good terms with the Christians, to whom they often rendered, by arrangement, the useful service of resolving disputes by eliminating one of the disputants. Henry was sumptuously received. In one of the more impressive entertainments, a succession of the loyal members of the cult, at a word from Sheik, expertly immolated themselves. Before and ever since, the willing obedience of household coteries has been a source of similar satisfaction to those able to command it. Wealth has been the most prominent device by which it has been obtained. As may indeed have been the case at al-Kahf, it has not always endeared the master to the men who rendered it.

As the ancient corporate wheeze goes, when the boss says jump, the appropriate response is, how high? Fortunately our tedious statutes against homicide inhibit the bosses from directing disfavored subordinates to jump out of windows on high floors.

An admirably ironic telling of a rather grisly tale. Galbraith spares us the technique of self-immolation no doubt out of deference to the feelings of the tender-hearted.

Or consider the self-mockery (still another way of enlisting readers on one's side) in the following recollection of passionate youth from *The Scotch:*

> At some time during adolescence, I encountered a novel by Anatole France which made unlicensed sexual transactions, especially if blessed by deep affection and profound mutual understanding, seem much more defensible than I had previously been allowed to suppose. It was summer and I was deeply in love. One day the object of my love, a compact golden-haired girl who lived on Willey's

Sideroad, a half mile away, came over to visit my sisters. They were away and we walked together through the orchard and climbed onto a rail fence which overlooked a small field between our place and Bert McCallum's. Our cows were pasturing on the second-growth clover in front of us. The hot summer afternoon lay quiet all around.

With the cows was a white bull named O. A. C. Pride, for the Ontario Agricultural College where my father had bid him in at an auction. As we perched there the bull served his purpose by serving a heifer which was in season.

Noting that my companion was watching with evident interest, and with some sense of my own courage, I said "I think it would be fun to do that."

She replied: "Well, it's your cow."

Can you think of a better-told story — the pastoral setting, the intrusion of animal nature, its application to a human couple, and the concluding zinger?

When he can, Galbraith extracts a lesson from his instructive youth. A second anecdote from *The Scotch* exemplifies his technique:

My own introduction to politics occurred in these days. My father was a prodigious orator and from the age of six or eight, I began accompanying him to meetings. It was of some educational value, and I learned, among other things, the uses of humor. Once at an auction sale, my father mounted a large manure pile to speak to the assembled crowd. He apologized with ill-concealed sincerity for speaking from the Tory platform. The effect on this agrarian audience was electric. Afterward, I congratulated him on the brilliance of the sally by which I too had been deeply impressed. He said, "It was good but it didn't change any votes."

Ruefully, Galbraith recalled his father's conclusion when he participated in Adlai Stevenson's stylish but unsuccessful campaigns against the unstylish Dwight Eisenhower in 1952 and again in 1956. Eisenhower was a national hero. Stevenson, worse luck, was a mere politician:

In 1952 and 1956, the speeches of Adlai Stevenson were spiced by similar if somewhat more elevated sallies. The best he wrote himself. Quite a number were by Arthur Schlesinger. Some were mine. Often, with appropriate circumspection, other members of the campaign party would congratulate me on some particularly pointed thrust, including ones with which I had nothing to do. I always found myself recalling the earlier warning. Humor is richly rewarded to the person who employs it. It has some value in gaining and holding attention. But it has no persuasive value at all.

Galbraith has always rejoiced in the idiocies and misadventures of the rich and powerful. Indeed his elegant, succinct account of the 1929 misadventure, *The Great Crash,* was dotted with virtuoso passages like this one:

> In the autumn of 1929 the mightiest of Americans were, for a brief time, revealed as human beings. Like most humans, most of the time, they did some very foolish things. On the whole, the greater the earlier reputation for omniscience, the more serene the previous idiocy, the greater the foolishness now exposed. Things that in other times were concealed by a heavy façade of dignity now stood exposed, for the panic suddenly, almost obscenely, snatched this façade away. We are seldom vouchsafed a glance behind this barrier; in our society the counterpart of the Kremlin walls is the thickly stuffed shirt. The social historian must always be alert to his opportunities, and there have been few like 1929.

Sometimes the stuffed shirts indict themselves. Galbraith cites a 1930 exchange between Senator James Couzens and Walter E. Sachs of Goldman, Sachs:

> SENATOR COUZENS: Did Goldman, Sachs and company organize the Goldman Sachs Trading Corporation?
> MR. SACHS: Yes, sir.
> SENATOR COUZENS: And it sold its stock to the public?
> MR. SACHS: A portion of it. The firm invested originally in 10 percent of the entire issue for the sum of $10,000,000.
> SENATOR COUZENS: And the other 90 percent was sold to the public?
> MR. SACHS: Yes, sir.
> SENATOR COUZENS: At what price?
> MR. SACHS: At 104. That is the old stock . . . the stock was split two for one.
> SENATOR COUZENS: And what is the price of the stock now?
> MR. SACHS: Approximately 1¾.

The Uses of Eloquence

Galbraith transparently enjoys entertaining himself and his readers, but the entertainment, it should not be forgotten, is in the pursuit of a serious idea. Two examples, again from *The Affluent Society,* underline the man's objectives. In the first, he makes the point to which much of the book's preceding pages have been leading, an assault upon the standard assumption of conventional price theory that consumer demand is an autonomous phenomenon. Individuals "reveal" their wants by the pattern of their market purchases. It is none of the business of economists to inquire into the ways these urges are generated. Here is Galbraith to the contrary:

> As a society becomes increasingly affluent, wants are increasingly created by the process by which they are satisfied. This may operate passively. Increases in consumption, the counterpart of increases in production, act by suggestion or emulation to create wants. Or producers may proceed actively to create wants through advertising and salesmanship. Wants thus come to depend on output. In technical terms it can no longer be assumed that welfare is greater at an all-round higher level of production than at a lower one. It may be the same. The higher level of production has, merely, a higher level of want satisfaction. There will be frequent occasion to refer to the way wants depend on the process by which they are satisfied. It will be convenient to call it the Dependence Effect.

For respectable economists, few notions can be more subversive than the proposition that it is the wielders of market power and its manifestations in marketing and advertising manipulations who shape consumer markets, not each isolated consumer furiously maximizing her utility.

Remember, in this second passage, that Galbraith was deploring the poverty of the public sector late in the 1950s. Matters, of course, are far worse after two doses of Ronald Reagan.

> The contrast was and remains evident not alone to those who read. The family which takes its mauve and ccrisc, air-conditioned, power-steered, and power-braked automobile out for a tour passes through cities that are badly paved, made hideous by litter, blighted buildings, billboards, and posts for wires that should long since have been put underground. They pass on into a countryside that has been rendered largely invisible by commercial art. (The goods which the latter advertise have an absolute priority in our value system. Such aesthetic considerations as a view of the countryside accordingly come second. On such matters we are consistent.) They picnic on exquisitely packaged food from a portable icebox by a polluted stream and go on to spend the night at a park which is a menace to public health and morals. Just before dozing off on an air mattress, beneath a nylon tent, amid the stench of decaying refuse, they may reflect vaguely on the curious unevenness of their blessing.
> Is this, indeed, the American genius?

Such is Galbraith's way of imprinting on his readers' memories the concept of social balance between private and public needs and

America's outrageous deviations from a balance more likely to promote public welfare than our nation's infatuation with private goods and derogation of public goods. Plus ça change, plus c'est la même chose. Déjà vu all over again.

In concentrating with the admiration and envy of a fellow practitioner upon Galbraith's linguistic virtuosity, I have said little about the power of his ideas and the prescience of his vision. Other contributors to this volume, I assume, will comment authoritatively on the new industrial state, Galbraith's support of price and wage controls, his advocacy of sales taxes (to the horror of liberal friends), and the variety of proposals he has floated and positions he has taken.

Yet I cannot conclude without uttering a few words of wonder at the combination of prescience and enlightenment that has distinguished his career as a public intellectual. Examples are legion. One of the final chapters of *The Affluent Society,* "The New Position of Poverty," anticipates by half a decade Michael Harrington's classic *The Other America.* He makes a key distinction between case poverty and insular poverty that early on anticipates the endless arguments over the extent of individual and community responsibility for the persistence of poverty in a rich society.

Years ago Galbraith advocated nationalization of large military contractors on grounds quite similar to those that the current wave of weapons-procurement scams have made familiar. Why support two symbiotic bureaucracies — one corporate, one military, when one will suffice? And when the players shuffle back and forth between public employment and private ventures as consultants or high officials of the corporations with which only recently they dealt as generals and admirals the predictable companion of inefficiency is corruption.

The Affluent Society can be and has been read, particularly in Great Britain, as an environmental tract fit to stand in the company of Rachel Carson's *Silent Spring.* Galbraith has been ahead of his time on women's issues, détente, income distribution, and much else. That he shows no sign of slowing down as he enters the ninth decade of life should reassure us all about the sturdy qualities of this Scotch Canadian as well as his unquenched taste for the never-ending battle of ideas to which he has contributed so much.

Herbert Gintis

The Power to Switch:
On the Political Economy
of Consumer Sovereignty

Introduction

In the three decades following the Second World War, the distance between traditional economic theory and institutional economics, of which John Kenneth Galbraith is doubtless the most illustrious living exponent, was probably greater than any other epoch in the history of economic thought. Following the formidable contributions of Paul Samuelson (1947), Kenneth Arrow (1951), and Gerard Debreu (1959), economic theory entered a sustained phase of neoclassical orthodoxy in which institutional structure was ignored in favor of a minute analysis of Walrasian equilibrium and the logic of constrained maximization.

By the mid-1970s, however, many economists, including those located within the neoclassical tradition, came to realize that key aspects of the functioning of market economies remain anomalous within traditional microeconomic theory. Macroeconomic fluctuations (Okun, 1981), variations in labor productivity (Aoki, 1984), the pattern of control in the modern corporation (Williamson, 1978; Jensen and Meckling, 1979), and the locus of residual claimancy in the enterprise (Alchian and Demsctz, 1972; Grossman and Hart, 1983) have all been cited as requiring new principles of analysis.

The "new institutional economics" emerging from this realization has nevertheless remained true to traditional neoclassical principles in at least two ways: (a) its commitment to explaining institutions in terms of the rational maximizing behavior of individuals, and (b) its methodological avoidance of issues concerning "power" or "political structure" in explaining economic institutions.

In our recent work on the foundations of political economy, Samuel Bowles and I have accepted (at least in many areas) the assumption of rational maximizing behavior while arguing that the capitalist economy has a political structure which cannot be ignored in an adequate model of general economic equilibrium (Bowles and Gintis, 1986, 1988). In this paper I shall outline the general approach, which we refer to as the "theory of contested exchange," and then apply this approach to the political economy of consumer sovereignty.

Of all the areas of economic life, neoclassical theory is arguably the strongest in dealing with the issue of consumer sovereignty. Barring external diseconomies and increasing returns to scale, and given the distribution of wealth and income, says this theory, the free market is the optimal instrument for allocating consumer goods to maximize consumer welfare. At least by contrast to its rather less compelling treatment of such recalcitrant areas as labor and capital markets, money, and historical change, the neoclassical treatment of consumption appears apt and unexceptionable.[1]

Yet several major characteristics of consumer product markets are ignored in the traditional model. Most visible is the prevalence of large established firms which are *quantity-constrained* and engage in *nonprice competition* through advertising, establishing extensive marketing networks, and promoting brand-name recognition in competition with other firms in the industry (Galbraith, 1955, 1967).

Equally evident is the fact that firm size and the pattern of market shares are determined by the relative capacity of firms to attract and retain customers rather than by the shape of their cost curves. The notion that optimum firm size is determined by the minimization of long-run average costs is therefore inaccurate. The same industry (e.g., automobile, soft drink, fast food, insurance, retail food) may include firms facing virtually the same cost curves, yet whose sizes are orders of magnitude apart.

Finally, from a political perspective consumers do not favor competitive product markets simply as a Pareto superior form of resource allocation any more than they approve of democratic government simply as a more efficient form of state administration. Rather, consumers experience their sovereignty as a form of personal power: *the power to switch*. Receiving shoddy merchandise, poor service, or insulating personal treatment by sellers is viewed by consumers not simply as a reduction in well-being, but as an attack on their dignity and integrity as citizens. The power to punish the offending supplier by switching is, accordingly, viewed as a contribution not to net wealth, but rather to freedom.

In this paper, I will argue that consumer sovereignty, which involves the power of consumers over the enterprises that satisfy their needs, can be explained by the same model that accounts for the power of employers over workers and the power of banks and the wealthy over production and investment and growth.

Contested Exchange

In neoclassical economics, market exchange is modeled as a transfer of property titles among economic agents. This model makes the exogenous enforcement assumption that contractual exchanges can be costlessly enforced by an independent third party — the judicial system. In the absence of exogenous enforcement, however, the axioms of neoclassical theory are violated. While the market exchange typically depicted in elementary textbooks (e.g., buying lemonade at a roadside stand) approximates this assumption, some of the most basic areas in a capitalist economy involve *endogenous enforcement:* in these areas the transacting parties cannot depend upon the state and are thus themselves responsible for contract enforcement.

One such area is the *labor market:* an employer offers a wage in exchange for which the employee offers not some fully specifiable *quid pro quo,* but rather at best an unenforceable promise to perform with sufficient intensity, care, and initiative (Gintis, 1976). The employer rarely sues an employee in a court of law for an inadequate level of performance. Rather, the employer develops a monitoring system (the system of authority in the firm) to determine whether this level has been achieved, and it must have means to discipline an employee whose performance is deemed unsatisfactory.

Another major instance of endogenous enforcement involves *fi-*

nancial markets: an investor makes funds available to an enterprise, receiving *ex ante* neither a determinate return nor even a specific probability distribution of returns, but rather a vague and contractually unenforceable promise of future returns. For instance, a stockholder may receive, in exchange for money, the right to a specified share of a random variable (profits) whose mean and variance are both contractually unspecifiable and unobservable. Similarly, a bank may receive a fixed return on its loans, but cannot fix the probability of repayment: the conditions of borrower insolvency remain outside contractual specification and enforcement. The lender's interests in this case are protected only by the lender providing financial incentives and penalties sufficient to inducing borrowers to remain solvent.

Labor and finance capital are instances of a general category of goods that are subject to what we term "contested exchange." An exchange is contested when some aspect of the good exchanged possesses an attribute which is valuable to the buyer, is costly to provide, is contractually unspecifiable, and hence requires endogenous enforcement. Power matters in competitive exchange because *who has power determines how exchanges are enforced and in whose interest.*

How are exchanges endogenously enforced? Since individuals are generally enjoined, according to both civil and criminal law, from visiting harm upon others, the best an unsatisfied partner to exchange normally can do is simply to refuse to enter into further contracts with the offending party. In neoclassical theory, it is never assumed that the same parties engage in multiple exchange. By contrast, in the contested exchange approach endogenous enforcement is predicated upon *contingent renewal:* agents enforce their claims by forming economic transactions consisting of an indefinite series of exchanges through time, terminated at will by a disgruntled party.[2]

In labor markets, contingent renewal takes the form of worker dismissal when the employer is dissatisfied.[3] In financial markets, contingent renewal is also operative: firms and individuals who default on their loans become uncreditworthy and are refused further financial support, and managers who jeopardize the financial integrity of their firms lose their jobs.[4]

Contingent renewal necessarily entails nonclearing markets, for nonrenewal of a customary contractual exchange is a threat only if the buyer offers terms better than the seller's next best alternative. The buyer must thus offer the seller an *enforcement rent* as a premium added to the price paid. For instance, an employer in a competitive labor market normally pays a higher wage than the expected value of the worker's next best alternative, thus generating a positive cost of job loss and rendering the threat of dismissal effective. Similarly, credit must be rationed in a financial market, agents with access to credit enjoying rents in the form of low interest rates, in order that the threat of nonrenewal of credit be credible.

This enforcement rent, it should be clear, persists in competitive equilibrium, since it embodies the optimal strategies of buyers and sellers alike. Those on the short side of the market (e.g., employers) have the power to change the terms of the exchange (e.g., raise the wage) but have no incentive to do so. Quantity-constrained agents on the long side of the market (e.g., unemployed workers) thus cannot compete away the rent by offering to work for lower wages than the currently employed.

Where contingent renewal is operative, and hence where there are positive enforcement rents, markets do not clear. Indeed, the principle of *short-side power* holds: under competitive conditions, power in a capitalist economy accrues to agents on the short side of the market, i.e., those whose trading partners are in a chronic state of excess supply. To identify these short-siders, we offer the principle of *the power of the purse:* a buyer offering money (or, more generally, a liquid financial asset) in exchange for a contested good or service is on the short side of the market. That is because money tends to be the commodity least subject to imperfect measurement and contractual unspecifiability.

In sum, neoclassical theory ignores power by assuming that contract enforcement is costlessly ensured by exogenous forces. In a market economy, economic power exists and has substantive allocative and distributive effects, because contracts must be endogenously enforced. Power lies with agents whose option of nonrenewal of contract is a credible threat. These agents are short-siders, such as employers and lenders, who offer liquid financial assets under conditions of excess supply of contested commodities.[5]

Consumer Sovereignty as Contested Exchange

Consumers, like employers and lenders, pay for services which are not completely contractually specifiable. Like employers and lenders, consumers rarely seek redress through the judicial system when dissatisfied. Instead, they simply switch to a different supplier. In the case of consumer goods, the noncontractual aspect of the good is its "quality." Excess supply consists of (potential) units of the commodity that firms would be happy to produce and sell at prevailing (or even lower) prices, but for which they cannot attract buyers. Suppliers are induced to provide an adequate level of quality through the threat of brand change on the part of buyers. The price is not bid down to clear the market, because informed buyers possess enough knowledge concerning the production costs that they are assured that in equilibrium, the margin of price over cost of production is precisely the premium ensuring that an adequate level of quality will be forthcoming.

Consumers are thus short-siders. Consumer sovereignty in the contested exchange model involves consumer power in that sellers are driven by the chronic excess supply of their product to pander to consumers' tastes. Whereas in neoclassical theory the term "sovereignty" is used purely figuratively, the concept in contested exchange is considerably closer to its usage in political theory. Consumer power is exercised through the direct ability to punish an offending supplier, much as voters in a democracy have the power to reward and punish persuants of office.

The contested exchange model of consumer sovereignty has comparative static properties in many respects similar to those of a neoclassical market. For instance, as in traditional demand and supply analysis, an increase either in demand or in the price of a factor price induces an increase in price. However, novel comparative static behavior can occur as well. For example, it can be shown that "market tightening" (i.e., a decline in equilibrium excess supply) entails higher firm rents and lower product quality.

Contested exchange in consumer products differs in two important ways from the more familiar cases of capital and labor markets. First, the relationship between employer and worker, or between lender and borrower, involves bilateral exchange. In this setting, the idea that the short-sider's strategic decisions can affect the behavior of the other party is reasonable. In consumer goods markets, however, there are many buyers facing each seller. Hence, an individual consumer cannot affect the behavior of producers. Thus while "brand change" has the same role in commodity markets as "dismissal" in labor markets and "loss of credit" in financial markets — that of inducing sellers to supply a high level of the noncontractual quality (work intensity, probability of default, product quality), the consumer cannot in general change brands in order to affect the behavior of the firm with which it deals. Hence the usual model of buyer behavior in contested exchange, involving nonrenewal as a threat to ensure an adequate level of quality, is not applicable to consumer markets. Consumers change brands because they believe they can do better elsewhere.[6]

Profit Maximization and Excess Supply Equilibrium

Consider a firm supplying a set of consumers with homogeneous preferences. We will investigate the equilibrium price, quantity, and quality of goods supplied, assuming quality cannot be directly measured and contractually specified.

Suppose a consumer purchases one unit per period at price P and sets a certain acceptable level of quality which either is or is not attained when the purchased item is consumed. We assume the consumer knows the cost curves of firms in the industry and knows (or believes) that the true quality of the product is, in fact, unchanged from period to period. The consumer then continues to purchase from the same firm until dissatisfaction induces a switch of brands.

We may consider the consumer as taking repeated samples from a population of unknown mean quality, continuing until the estimated quality falls below the acceptable level. Since the sample mean is a sufficient statistic in this case, it is reasonable to assume that the consumer will continue buying the product as long as the number of satisfactory experiences ("successes") exceeds that of unsatisfactory ("failures"). Let $\phi_t(p)$ be the probability that the customer stays with the firm precisely t periods before switching, assuming the probability the product will fail in any single period is p. If $\phi(s)$ is a generating function for $[\phi_t \mid t \geq 0]$, it can be shown that [7]

$$\phi(s) = [1 - (1 - 4p(1-p)s^2)^{1/2}] / 2(1-p)s. \qquad (1)$$

Now suppose for the firm, profit per unit sold is π and the discount rate is $\rho > 0$. We assume that when a consumer leaves the firm, the firm has a fallback position with present value $\eta \geq 0$. Here η represents the expected present value of the use of the resources released by the loss of a customer.[8] We may think of the firm as having, for each new customer, an infinite income stream with value π while the customer remains with the firm, and value $\rho\eta$ thereafter. Hence $(\pi - \rho\eta)$ represents the "cost of customer loss" as an income flow.

It is easy to see that expected profit for an n-period customer is thus given by $\pi\delta\phi_n(1-\delta^n)/(1-\delta) + \phi_n\eta\delta^n$, where $\delta = 1/(1+\rho)$. Summing over n, expected profit π^e for a new customer satisfies

$$\pi^e = [\pi\phi(1) - (\pi - \rho\eta)\phi(\delta)] / \rho. \qquad (2)$$

Since quality cannot be measured prior to purchase, the firm's choice of quality affects only the *length of time* each remains with the brand.[9] The firm then maximizes profit using objective function (2).

Competition forces the firm to accept the going price P, but the firm remains free to vary product quality. Measuring the quality of the product by the probability p that it will prove unacceptable to a consumer on any given occasion, we posit a concave cost $c(p)$ per unit of output.[10] We then have $c'(p) < 0$, reflecting the increasing cost of quality, and $c''(p) > 0$ reflecting diminishing returns in the production of quality. For simplicity we shall also assume that $c(0) = \infty$, and $c'(1) = 0$, so that the marginal cost of providing positive quality is zero, while providing "perfect" quality is infinitely expensive.[11] Then assuming the firm operates in a range over which constant returns to scale holds,[12] profit per sale is given by $\pi = P - c(p)$.

Clearly if $\pi < \rho\eta$, the firm will not produce. We shall call a product price P feasible if $\pi > \rho\eta$ for $p = 1$. Since P must be feasible in order that there be any production of goods with positive quality. We then have

Theorem 1: For every feasible price P there is a unique profit maximizing quality. This quality corresponds to a failure rate p^* (P) at which $\pi > \rho\eta$. In particular, equilibrium price exceeds marginal cost, and the firm earns a positive rent per unit in competitive equilibrium.

It follows from Theorem 1 that market equilibrium involves excess supply. Some traditional comparative static conditions nevertheless continue to hold. For instance, we have

Theorem 2: Quality is an increasing function of price and a decreasing function of the firm's fallback position η.

Consumer Demand and the Determination of Price

We have assumed that consumers are sophisticated to the extent of knowing the cost curves of producers. We now add the assumption that consumers know the firm's fallback position η. Such a consumer can, in effect, set a quality-optimizing price, refusing to accept a lower price,[13] while depending upon free entry and market competition to drive the price down to this level.

For any desired quality q, the consumer must choose a critical quality level q_{min} (q) such that a failure is registered when observed quality q^o falls below q_{min}. The consumer's optimal critical quality is that which minimizes the price $P(q)$ of ensuring that the firm supplies a product with quality q. We call the corresponding price P_{min} the consumer's optimal price. Suppose for the sake of exposition that the error in observed quality, $q^o - q$, is normally distributed with mean 0 and positive standard deviation σ.[14] We then have

Theorem 3: For any desired quality q there is an optimal price p_{min} which offers the firm a positive rent per unit equal to $(\pi - \rho\eta)$. This price corresponds to an optimal critical quality $q_{min} > q$. The level of rent increases with the variance in quality measurement error and with the discount rate. As measurement error and the discount rate tend to zero, enforcement rents also tend to zero, and the allocation approaches the neoclassical equilibrium.

Theorem 3 clarifies the nature of competition in contested exchange. A consumer knowing the firm's cost function can offer a price p_{min} at which production is profitable to the firm, but which cannot be undercut by competitors. Thus the whole competitive structure of the industry is captured by the fallback position η, and the fact that competitive pressures may be central to the revelation of the firm's cost function. Price competition is, at least at this level of generality, not operative.

Market Equilibrium

A theory of market equilibrium must explain firm size, market shares, and the conditions of firm entry to and exit from the industry. The contested exchange approach suggests that firm size is not determined by price structure or the shape of cost functions. In addition to relative unit product costs, factors critical to the size distribution of firms include the level of quality measurement costs, initial conditions (i.e., historically given patterns), and the cost of attracting new customers.

To stress the nonprice aspect of market equilibrium, let us take the array of fallback positions $[\eta_j]$, and hence the equilibrium price P, as given for a product of quality q. Suppose the market consists of n firms serving M customers, where firm j has m_j^t customers in period t. We may normalize $M = 1$, so m_j^t is the market share of firm j in period t.

Let $f_j \in (0,1)$ for $j = 1, \ldots , n$. We call $f = (f_j)$ the *leaving vector* for the industry if in each period firm j loses the constant proportion f_j of its customers. Suppose also $0 < \alpha_j$ for $j = 1, \ldots , n$ and $\Sigma_j \alpha_j = 1$. We call $\alpha = (\alpha_j)$ an *arriving vector* if firm j relative power α_j to attract new customers in the following sense: of k customers leaving firm i, firm j will attract $\alpha_j k / (1 - a_i)$ for each $j \neq i$. We say the industry is in equilibrium if the market share of each firm is constant over time. We have

Theorem 4: For every pair (f, α) of leaving and arriving vectors, there is a unique industry equilibrium. This equilibrium is asymptotically stable and is approached from any initial distribution of market shares. Conversely, any pattern of market shares is an equilibrium for some leaving vector f and some some arriving vector α.

Theorem 4 shows that it is reasonable to posit a competitive market structure leading to a determinate equilibrium, yet in which price exceeds marginal cost, while firm size and market shares are set by interactions among firms not mediated by factor costs or product prices. In particular, the (f_j) are dependent not only upon cost functions, but upon the fallback positions $[\eta_j]$, which reflect the cost of attracting new customers by means other than lowering the price of the good (e.g., by advertising or by raising quality temporarily above its equilibrium value). Similarly, the $\{\alpha_j\}$ represent the relative power of firms to attract customers by means other than lowering price (e.g., via reputation of another form of "market presence").

The limitations of Theorem 4 must be clearly recognized. First, it may be reasonable to assume that the dynamics of price and market share determination can be analytically separated, but that requires derivation from more fundamental principles. The notion that the leaving and arriving vectors are independent from the pattern of market shares is not reasonable. Second, in general the arrival vector α may depend upon the past history of the system. In this case, the system may have steady state equilibria dependent upon the initial distribution of market shares, or the behavior of the system may consist of steady state orbits. Third, if there are significant returns to scale over a portion of firms' cost curves, then we must add the contingency of bankruptcy when market share is sufficiently small. Finally, we must add a mechanism allowing for the entry of new firms. In general, we would expect entry costs to include setup costs and fixed costs, plus the costs involved in establishing an arrival weight α_j, plus losses sustained while the firm builds up to its equilibrium market share.

Conclusion

The power of the contested exchange model lies in its ability to capture the institutional and political dynamics ignored in traditional microeconomic theory, while generalizing the neoclassical model in the sense that the latter is a limiting case of contested exchange as enforcement costs tend to zero. The model, moreover, employs consistent microeconomic logic, thus undermining the notion that political economy and institutional economics are methodologically incompatible.[15]

This paper demonstrates that consumer goods markets can be insightfully treated as instances of contested exchange. Just as in such contested exchange markets as labor and credit, consumer goods markets are characterized by repeated transactions (note that buyers in such markets are *"customers")*, and the assurance of quality is based on the threat of nonrenewal of contractual relations. Moreover, as the transactions rate becomes large, and as quality measurement costs become small, contested exchange equilibrium approaches neoclassical equilibrium.

The basic elements of contested exchange theory of consumer goods are easily summarized. Given a product price, each quality level entails a certain probability distribution of the number of periods a customer will remain with the firm. The firm chooses a quality level which equates the marginal cost of quality with the marginal revenue resulting from increased sales. The consumer estimates production costs and considers price offers only if they are compatible with the firm's supplying adequate quality at the given cost. The consumer also chooses an optimum threshold quality which serves to indicate when switching suppliers is justified. In equilibrium there is excess supply in the sense that each supplier would be willing to lower price in order to expand output, but buyers will not accept lower prices. Firm size is determinate, as are market shares, by virtue of a dynamic process of consumers switching suppliers at given rates, while entry and exit are determined by minimum feasible firm size and the costs of setting up production and attracting a clientele.

NOTES

1. I argued exactly this position in Gintis (1972).
2. A second important endogenous enforcement mechanism is *collateralization:* agents ensure that their trading partners have too great a stake in a satisfactory outcome of a transaction to fail to live up to its explicit or implied conditions (Stiglitz and Weiss, 1983; Gintis, 1988*a*). This mechanism does not carry over to consumer goods markets and will be ignored in this paper.
3. For theoretical and empirical analysis of contingent renewal in labor markets, see Shapiro and Stiglitz (1984), Bowles (1985), Gintis and Ishikawa (1987), Schor (1983), Schor and Bowles (1987).
4. See Fama (1980), Stiglitz and Weiss (1983), Williamson (1983), Gintis (forthcoming).
5. It may appear that the short-side, long-side taxonomy is simply a recasting of the traditional class division of economic agents into owners and nonowners. The con-

tested exchange taxonomy, in fact, draws somewhat finer distinctions, since individual agents may be on the long side of some markets and on the short side of others. For instance, the manager of a firm may have power over workers, while owners may have power over the manager, both instances of power stemming from the threat of job loss. Similarly, an individual may be on the long side of the market as a worker, but on the short side as a consumer — a possibility discussed below.

6. This instrumental treatment of brand switching, while sufficient to validate the claims of the contested exchange model, may be too narrow. Disgruntled consumers, like voters, may reject a utilitarian free-rider logic and switch brands simply out of a sense of social obligation; they may also switch out of vindictiveness, even though they do not expect to do better elsewhere.

7. Proofs and derivations of material in the remainder of this paper, when not supplied, are given in Gintis (1988b).

8. Alternatively, we may treat η as the present value of having a new customer π^e, minus the cost of actively acquiring a new customer, or as π^e discounted by the expected number of periods before a replacement customer arrives. The exact formulation will be immaterial for our argument, except that we will assume $\eta = 0$ when $\pi^e = 0$.

9. The dynamics of markets in which reputation and quality are assessed by word of mouth obey quite different dynamics from the types of consumer markets investigated in this paper. For our purposes, reputation is limited to identifying which quality level a firm competes in. See Satterthwaite (1979) for a model with endogenous reputation.

10. The continuity of $c(q)$ and the assumption that $c'(0) = 0$ imply that the firm will have no incentive to promise high quality and deliver low. The possibility of this behavior, which has been analyzed by Klein and Leffler (1981), would not substantively alter the contested exchange model.

11. These assumptions are made for the most part to simplify the exposition of the central argument. Convexity of the cost function $c(p)$ implies (though not trivially) that any local extremum of profits is a global maximum, thus permitting comparative static analysis with continuous supply curves.

12. Allen (1984) develops a variable returns to scale model to explore a rather different set of issues. Variable returns to scale could be applied to the current model with little substantive change in our conclusion if we make the "franchise assumption" that increasing costs apply to "plants" rather than firms, and multiplant firms suffer no costs of integration. This assumption has the attractive property that cost considerations do not determine optimal firm size.

13. In neoclassical theory, competitive markets ensure the equality of supply and demand. In contested exchange equilibrium, by contrast, competition serves to reveal to consumers the shape of supplier cost functions and to limit rents to the minimum required to elicit appropriate product quality.

14. In fact, all we need is that the density of the error have a unique maximum at 0, be differentiable there, and that this maximum become infinite as σ approaches zero.

15. Indeed, the relationship between quality and price has been previously investigated in the microeconomic literature, with important contributions by Smallwood and Conlisk (1979), Kotowitz and Mathewson (1979), Shapiro (1982, 1983), Satterthwaite (1979), Klein and Leffler (1981), Shapiro (1983), Rogerson (1983), and Allen (1984).

REFERENCES

Alchian, Armen, and Harold Demsetz. "Production, Information Costs, and Economic Organization." *American Economic Review* 62 (December 1972): 777–95.

Allen, Franklin. "Reputation and Product Quality." *Rand Journal of Economics* 15, 3 (Autumn 1984: 311–27.

Aoki, Masahiko. *The Co-operative Game Theory of the Firm* (London: Clarendon, 1984).

Arrow, Kenneth J. "An Extension of the Basic Theorems of Classical Welfare Economics," in J. Neyman, ed., *Proceedings of the Second Berkeley Symposium on Mathematical Statistics and Probability* (Berkeley: University of California Press, 1951) pp. 507–32.

Bowles, Samuel. "The Production Process in a Competitive Economy: Walrasian, Neo-Hobbesian, and Marxian Models." *American Economic Review* 75, 1 (March 1985): 16–36.

Bowles, Samuel, and Herbert Gintis. *Democracy and Capitalism: Property, Community, and the Contradictions of Modern Social Thought* (New York: Basic Books, 1986).

———. "Contested Exchange: Political Economy and Modern Economic Theory." *American Economic Review* 78, 2 (May 1988): 145–50.

Debreu, Gerard. *Theory of Value* (New York: Wiley, 1959).

Fama, Eugene F. "Agency Problems and the Theory of the Firm." *Journal of Political Economy* 88, 2 (1980): 288–307.

Galbraith, John Kenneth. *The Affluent Society* (Boston: Houghton Mifflin, 1955).

———. *The New Industrial State* (Boston: Houghton Mifflin, 1967).

Gintis, Herbert. "Consumer Behavior and the Concept of Sovereignty." *American Economic Review* 42, 2 (May 1972): 267–78.

———. "The Nature of the Labor Exchange and the Theory of Capitalist Production." *Review of Radical Political Economics* 8 (1976): 36–54.

———. "The Principle of External Accountability in Financial Markets." Working Paper, Department of Economics, University of Massachusetts, February 1987.

———. "Savings, Investment, and the Interest Rate: Credit Rationing in Competitive Equilibrium." Working Paper, Department of Economics, University of Massachusetts, February 1988a.

———. "A Contested Exchange Theory of Consumer Sovereignty." Department of Economics, University of Massachusetts, 1988b.

———. "Financial Markets and the Political Structure of the Enterprise." *Journal of Economic Behavior and Organization* (forthcoming).

Gintis, Herbert, and Tsuneo Ishikawa. "Wages, Work Discipline, and Unemployment." *Journal of Japanese and International Economies* 1 (1987): 195–228.

Grossman, Sanford, and Oliver Hart. "An Analysis of the Principal-Agent Problem." *Econometrica* 51 (1983): 7–45.

Jensen, Michael C., and William H. Meckling. "Rights and Production Functions: An Application to Labor-Managed Firms and Codetermination." *Journal of Business* 52 (1979): 469–506.

Klein, B., and K. Leffler. "The Role of Market Forces in Assuring Contractual Performance." *Journal of Political Economy* 89 (August 1981): 615–41.

Kotowitz, Yehuda, and Frank Mathewson. "Advertising, Consumer Information, and Product Quality." *Bell Journal of Economics* 10, 2 (Autumn 1979): 566–88.

Okun, Arthur. *Prices and Quantities: A Macroeconomic Analysis* (Washington, D.C.: The Brookings Institution, 1981).

Rogerson, William P. "Reputation and Product Quality." *Bell Journal of Economics* 14, 2 (Autumn 1983): 508–16.

Samuelson, Paul. *The Foundations of Economic Analysis* (New York: Atheneum, 1947).

Satterthwaite, Mark A. "Consumer Information, Equilibrium Industry Price, and the Number of Sellers." *Bell Journal of Economics* 10, 2 (Autumn 1979): 483–502.

Schor, Juliet B. "Social Wages and the Business Cycle: Measuring the Cost of Job Loss," in M. Jarsulec, ed., *Money and Macro Policy* (Boston: Kluwer-Nijhoff, 1983).

Schor, Juliet B., and Samuel Bowles. "Employment Rents and the Incidence of Strikes." *Review of Economics and Statistics* 64, 4 (November 1987): 584–91.

Shapiro, Carl. "Consumer Information, Product Quality, and Seller Reputation." *Bell Journal of Economics* 13, 1 (Spring 1982): 20–35.

———. "Premiums for High Quality Products as Returns to Reputations." *Quarterly Journal of Economics* 98 (November 1983): 659–79.

Shapiro, Carl, and Joseph E. Stiglitz. "Unemployment as a Worker Discipline Device." *American Economic Review* 74, 3 (June 1984): 433–44.

Smallwood, Dennis E., and John Conlisk. "Product Quality in Markets Where Consumers Are Imperfectly Informed." *Quarterly Journal of Economics* 93, 1 (February 1979): 1–23.

Stiglitz, Joseph, and Andrew Weiss. "Incentive Effects of Terminations: Applications to the Credit and Labor Markets." *American Economic Review* 73, 5 (December 1983): 912–27.

Williamson, Oliver E. *Markets and Hierarchies* (New York: The Free Press, 1978).

———. "Credible Commitments: Using Hostages to Support Exchange." *American Economic Review* 73, 4 (September 1983): 519–40.

Mancur Olson

Esthetics, Economics, and Wit

WE KNOW ALMOST NOTHING about the future, and even very little about how the writers of the future will assess the ideas and writers of our own time. I am especially hesitant to make forecasts and sometimes look down on those colleagues who do not know that they do not know what is going to happen. Yet for all this hesitancy I cannot repress a confident conviction about the way in which the writings of John Kenneth Galbraith will be regarded in the intellectual histories of the future. I believe the honoree of this volume will be celebrated not primarily as a theorist of how our economy or political system works, but rather as a supremely witty critic of our manners, mores, and patterns of consumption. My hunch is that his contemporary criticisms of the tail-fins on the pointlessly large American automobiles of the 1950s, for example, will impress the detached and discriminating historians of the future more than his criticisms of the economic thought of his time.

To be sure, on the matter of John Kenneth Galbraith's severe commentary on the economic thought of his contemporaries, I cannot claim detachment. As a hardened professional economist who, in spite of occasional intellectual eccentricities, argues that the modern economist stands on the shoulders of giants, I have a vested interest in the matter. At least some of our honoree's attacks presumably apply as much to my articles in the economics journals as to the others. Thus it could be that, in spite of my conviction to the contrary, I am just being defensive.

With respect to John Kenneth Galbraith's criticisms of what Thorstein Veblen called "conspicuous consumption," on the other hand, I have no professional stake, and may have no greater bias than any other American of my vintage. I shall accordingly in this essay need to support my objections to some of his economic arguments more fully than I shall need to document my awe at his wit, prose style, esthetic discernment, and social criticism. Since serious criticism is itself a tribute, I hope that even those parts of my essay that express disagreement will be taken as a sign of my respect. This essay is intended partly as a token of my appreciation for the favors John Kenneth Galbraith did for me in my graduate student days.

1

There are three themes that seem to me the most important in Galbraith's writings. One is that the growth of large-scale business makes the economist's conception of the benefits of competition increasingly irrelevant to modern conditions. A second is that the large-scale organizations of the modern age, with their professional "technostructures" or skilled staffs, are the main source of efficiency and technical innovation. A third is that the pretension and display inherent in much modern consumption are unworthy of civilized men and women.

The first theme seems to me to have some merits but to have been greatly overstated. My objection is mainly to the often implicit tendency to identify small-size enterprises with competition and large-scale firms with the absence of competition. The basis for my objection is evident when we consider some of the causes of the growth in the size of the average firm over time. Galbraith tells us that in the early nineteenth century and before, the typical unit for organizing production in the United States was the family-sized farm, the family-owned store, or the shop of the village craftsman. I agree. Galbraith further tells us that a large proportion of the goods we consume are manufactured by giant corporations with thousands of employees and are often also marketed by retail chains of impressive scale. Again, I do not see how anyone can disagree.

One of the most important sources of the large enterprise of the modern day is the improvement of transportation and communication. Some surviving records reveal that in the Middle Ages the cost of transporting a staple item of consumption such as wheat for fifty miles could double its price. By and large, only items of extraordinary value in relation to their size and weight, such as spices, were transported very far on land. Staple items could often be profitably transported over longer distances by water, but only to that tiny fraction of the land that was near navigable waterways. The hazards of navigation, weather, and piracy often made even water-borne commerce costly. In the seventeenth century, as Fernand Braudel tells us, the main device for maritime navigation on the Mediterranean was to stay within sight of land.

With the slow and costly transportation and communication systems of earlier times, no enterprise producing typical and important items of consumption could expect to market them to a vast population spread across continents. An enterprise might on occasion sell produce across the sea, but not over land areas the size of the large countries of today, much less to the several continents of consumers that are reached by some firms in our time. Even if a firm in premodern times could economically reach the whole populations of relatively large countries, these populations were then so very much smaller than they are today that the number of millions of people could usually be counted on the fingers of the hands. The inputs needed for productive enterprises would similarly have to be acquired over large areas, and this would also limit the size of enterprises. The high costs of transportation of both outputs and inputs gave an enormous advantage to small-scale firms that served a small area.

Obviously the steamship, the railway, the truck, and the jet airplane have changed all this. We regularly see household appliances made, say, in the nations of the Pacific rim, and manufactured out of materials mined in Australia or Brazil, in the department stores of the Middle West. The cost of transportation even over such vast distances is relatively small for many products in relation to their value.

Modern communication systems, in conjunction with the computer and other advances, have also made it possible to coordinate large enterprises operating in several locations. The worldwide chains of hotels, car-rental agencies, and even fast-food restaurants, though their production is often localized, owe their existence and their (sometimes depressing) uniformity to the modern media of transportation and communication.

2

A visit to surviving medieval towns, such as Bruges or Ghent, or even to a theater showing a movie on the Wild West of the nineteenth-century United States, tells us something about the number of competitors our consumer ancestors in the ages of small enterprise had to choose from. In the typical rural village there might well have been only a single miller to grind the flour needed for daily bread and only a single blacksmith as a source of metal manufactures. The farmer on the American frontier might have been limited to a single general store. Even the customer in the larger medieval cities was typically restricted to suppliers who were members of a single cartelistic guild.

Surely, all would agree that the typical modern consumer has access to a number of different supermarkets and department stores, as well as to many smaller vendors. And these establishments, in any country without high levels of protection, happily supply the wares of many different manufacturers from diverse countries. Even some products, such as automobiles, that are most economically produced in relatively large scale are characteristically manufactured by giant multinational firms that face more than a dozen competitors.

3

There are other factors besides transportation and communication costs that influence the size of surviving firms. Some advantageous new technologies are only advantageous at a scale that is greatly different from that which was optimal for the old technology. For example, the invention of the steam-powered railway transportation system called for larger firms than those that were appropriate for carts drawn by oxen or horses. The indivisibilities inherent in railway lines also left patrons, especially in rural areas, at the mercy of a single supplier of long-distance transportation, even as new technology gave the local rural store the competition of the mail-order houses and brought much of the populace to large cities that contained many competing vendors.

The development of the truck, the bus, the automobile, and the modern highway system, by contrast, increased the number of competitors even in transportation itself. It did this not only by increasing the competition among different modes of transportation, but also because the indivisibilities for these newer modes of transportation are normally less than for the railroad. If lobbying by associations of trucking companies does not prevent entry of smaller firms, there will characteristically be many more competitors for freight-hauling among trucking companies than railroads. In general, the degree of indivisibility of new technologies, and the economically most advantageous size of the productive establishment, changes over time, sometimes in the direction of bigger enterprises and sometimes in the direction of smaller ones. Though some technologies, such as the computer, are clearly evolving in ways more favorable to smaller establishments, I would guess that the net effect of the change in indivisibilities has been one that has worked in the direction of increasing concentration and reducing competition, but I am by no means certain about this and know of no compelling study of the matter.

4

Whatever may be the direction of effect of the degree of indivisibility inherent in successive new technologies, they are surely overwhelmed by the awesome improvements in transportation and communication. These improvements not only create a "global village," they make what is (in the absence of tariff and quota protection) a global shopping mall. The stores in this shopping mall are incomparably bigger than the shops of earlier ages, and the firms that control them are bigger still. But the numbers of firms in competition with each other in the global shopping center are surely much larger than those in competition with each other in prior periods of history. The same advances of transportation and communication that have brought us larger firms have literally given us a world of choice and thus more competition in most industries than ever before.

Since the managers of many of these firms are (excessively, to my mind) anxious to command even larger conglomerate firms, there is a crucially important potential competition in each line of industry and trade from existing giant firms in other lines of industry; if the firms in one industry enjoy exceptional monopoly profits, they will (in those many markets that are relatively "contestable") invite entry by aggressive managements of firms in other industries, as well as by new firms.

A *Festschrift* for John Kenneth Galbraith is not, perhaps, the most natural place to cite econometric evidence in favor of the hypothesis that the degree of competition has not decreased over the historical periods over which the scale of enterprise has increased. But such evidence, while not comprehensive or compelling, is by no means lacking.

5

I shall soon be dealing elsewhere with the efficiency of what Galbraith calls the "technostructure" of large organizations,[1] so I shall turn now to the criticism of sumptuary styles that I believe will be his most enduring achievement. The advances in transportation, communication, and other technologies, as well as capital accumulation and other factors, have indeed created what is, by historical standards, an "affluent society" in all the developed nations. There is still the urgent problem that this affluence does not extend to all residents of these countries, and especially not to most of the peoples of the less-developed areas.

There is also the problem that our industrial culture naturally could not adjust immediately and ideally to the vast array of additional products, firms, and quantities that the affluent society made available. Some of the new consumer choices, I believe, were unreflective, ill-considered choices. The gigantic gas-guzzling automobiles of the United States in the 1950s and 1960s, and other products like them, were utterly beyond the reach of previous societies. Accordingly, our cultures, even though they go back for millennia, had not accumulated the type of wisdom needed to deal in a fully civilized fashion with these choices.

---

1. In a book tentatively entitled *Beyond the Measuring Rod of Money*.

There was a case for less ostentation and more civility in sumptuary choices, and John Kenneth Galbraith presented that case compellingly. What Veblen called "pecuniary decency" was not the kind of decency we needed most, and Galbraith pointed this out more eloquently than anyone else. The need for cultural adaptation to the new choices — the need for guides to civilized behavior in the global shopping center — is with us still, and Galbraith's discussions of the matter are still much the wittiest. Just as there is a need for criticism of literature, theater, and art, so there is a need for criticism of everyday consumption and display. John Kenneth Galbraith has met the need far better than anyone else. He is the Thorstein Veblen of our time.

Thus it is not as a creator or critic of economic theory, but as a contributor to the debate on how our consuming culture should adapt to new conditions, that John Kenneth Galbraith made his largest contribution. It is a contribution of ultimate importance.

Lloyd G. Reynolds

Dissent a Century Ago:
The Veblen Era

I ENCOUNTERED Thorstein Veblen in 1927, as a sophomore. He was, of course, too heterodox to be assigned in economics courses, but he had an active circulation under the counter. We read him for his sparkling prose style and biting social criticism. Many of us were college radicals, and the fact that Veblen disliked the financial manipulators whom we also disliked was enough to commend him to us.

The invitation to contribute to this symposium seemed to provide an excuse for revisiting Veblen and considering how his work appears sixty years later. I thought that Galbraith would be comfortable in the company of another notable dissenter.

To associate Galbraith and Veblen is not mere whimsy. Both came from rural areas far from the seats of economic power. Both were obliged briefly to teach courses on the economics of agriculture, though both wisely abandoned that subject. There is the same independence of mind, irreverence toward the rich and well-born, distrust of accepted economic doctrine. They share a knack for coining phrases which have passed into the language, an ability to communicate with the public that arouses deep suspicion among colleagues confined to an academic audience. Substantively, both were concerned with the shift from small-scale competitive capitalism to an economy dominated by big business.

Indeed, both were considered for appointment at Harvard. F. W. Taussig admired Veblen and tried to bring him to Harvard, but was rebuffed by the conservative economics department of that day. Decades later, when a more enlightened department recommended the appointment of Galbraith, there was opposition from conservative members of the board of overseers, but President James B. Conant overrode this opposition, to Harvard's great benefit.

But we should not press similarity too far. Veblen was in many ways a quite different individual, and his academic failure, which contrasts so strongly with Galbraith's academic success, is rooted in his personal characteristics.

Veblen the Man

Background

Veblen's father migrated from Norway in 1847, settling with other Norwegian immigrants in a community near Manitowoc, Wisconsin. (This community, Valders, derives its name from a valley in Norway). There Veblen was born in 1857. In 1864 the family moved to a larger farm near Northfield, Minnesota, again in an area heavily populated by Norwegian and Swedish families. There Veblen grew up speaking Norwegian in the home, in a distinctive Norwegian culture of which he was always proud, and which included a strong devotion to Lutheran tradition and church attendance.

Veblen's later excellence in English may be due partly to the fact that for him, as for Joseph Conrad, it was a second language which he labored to perfect. He had a flair for languages and linguistics and eventually was fluent in a dozen tongues. In one of his essays Veblen comments on the critical and skeptical tone of many Jewish writers, attributing this to their freedom from the preconceptions which beset the Christian tradition, their grounding in B.C. rather than A.D., which enables them to view contemporary situations in a different light. One suspects that in this comment Veblen is speaking partly about himself, about his grounding in rural, Norwegian culture which was deeply suspicious of the Yankee town-dwellers.

Veblen's early years were shaped also by the context of western agrarian discontent and populist rhetoric. Farmers complained of the millers who controlled the grain elevators and who, it was alleged, short-weighted and downgraded their wheat. They complained about the exorbitant freight rates charged by the railroad monopolists. They complained about the middleman who inserted a large and growing wedge between the price of wheat and the price of bread. The long economic downswing of 1873–1896 naturally intensified their complaints.

Other features of the period are familiar to readers of economic and political history. There was continuing labor unrest — the rise and decline of the Knights of Labor, the formation of the American Federation of Labor, the Pullman strike, and the Haymarket affair. Henry George's *Progress and Poverty* was published, as was Bellamy's *Looking Backward.* There was Eugene V. Debs and the rise of a socialist party, stronger in the 1900s than ever before or since. There was the trust movement of the 1890s, followed by the muckraking literature of the early 1900s. So it is not surprising that Veblen grew up with no belief in the natural beneficence of capitalism. To the extent that the economic writings of 1890–1910 served as an apologia for capitalism, they aroused in Veblen an intuitive repugnance.

Education

The normal thing for a bright young Norwegian would have been to attend a Lutheran college, perhaps to train for the ministry. But Veblen chose instead to follow an older brother to the newly established Carleton College in Northfield. Founded under Congregational auspices in 1867, Carleton had a strongly Christian and evangelical tone. Most of the faculty were clergymen, and many students were preparing for the ministry. The curriculum was dominated by classics, theology, and philosophy. There was no U.S. history, only one quarter of English literature, little science. John Bates Clark, however, was there as a young faculty member, serving as librarian and teaching everything from English composition to moral philosophy. His lectures on political economy were considered a branch of this latter subject. Veblen was a philosophy major, and he did his "senior oration" on an aspect of John Stuart Mill's philosophy.

Veblen appeared to fellow students as supercilious and cynical but good-natured and witty. In the weekly "declamation exercises," he regaled his peers with such topics as "A Plea For Cannibalism," "An Apology for a Toper," and "The Science of Laughter." The faculty distrusted his brilliance but could not deny his ability. He graduated with top honors in 1880.

Johns Hopkins was being advertised at this time as the first real graduate school in America, so Veblen went there to prepare for a teaching career in some place like Carleton. Among other things he took a course by Richard T. Ely, who was only three years older than himself, in the history of political economy, which focused heavily on the German historical school. He wrote an essay on John Stuart Mill's theory of the taxation of land. But he failed to obtain a fellowship at Hopkins and, having virtually no money, was forced to leave after less than a year. He ended up at Yale, which did provide a stipend sufficient for subsistence.

At Yale he became a protégé of the philosopher Noah Porter, who was president of Yale in an era when the president had enough leisure to take long walks with Veblen to discuss philosophical problems. Veblen worked mainly on Kant and wrote a thesis in moral philosophy under Porter which earned him a Ph.D. in 1884, after two and a half years of study. Economics at this time had not yet penetrated the Yale curriculum. Veblen may have had some contact with William Graham Sumner, a divinity school graduate who later turned against theology and began to teach sociology at Yale, with emphasis on Herbert Spencer's doctrine of social evolution. This doctrine, under which the rich exemplify survival of the fittest and the natural order of private property plus competition is invariably beneficial, was not likely to arouse Veblen's enthusiasm.

Despite strong recommendations from Noah Porter, J. B. Clark, and others, Veblen failed to obtain a teaching appointment. At this time, professors of philosophy were still drawn mainly from divinity schools (most of his Yale classmates were divinity students), and this qualification Veblen conspicuously lacked. So he returned to his father's farm as an unemployed Ph.D. and remained so for seven years. Meanwhile, in 1888, he married his college classmate Ellen Rolfe, a highly intelligent woman with tastes very similar to Veblen's and with the further advantage of an independent income. They lived for several years in a cabin on land owned by her father in Iowa — reading and discussing endlessly, making botanical forays into the woods, and being as happy as an unemployed intellectual can be.

Veblen's spotty formal training was only a small part of his education. In the main, he was self-educated through reading. He was an omnivorous reader, and nothing relating to human affairs was beyond his ken. He read philosophy, history, archeology, linguistics, anthropology, psychology, and sociology as well as politics and economics and paid scant attention to the supposed boundaries between these disciplines. And he had the faculty of putting all this into a mental storage bank. He claimed never to have forgotten anything he had read. Students remarked that he seemed to know everything in the world.

His formal training in economics was negligible. But at some point — perhaps during the nineties when he was teaching economics at Chicago and editing the *Journal of Political Economy* — he read his way through the literature: the Physiocrats, the classical writers (including Marx), the German historical school, and the then moderns such as Marshall, Clark, and Fisher. It is clear from his writings that he understood what he had read — in his fashion. Everything was viewed through the prism of philosophy, and his rather long-winded critiques are preoccupied with methodology. He was generous in conceding intellectual skill to the mainstream economists and in recognizing positive contributions. But in the main, he thought that they were on the wrong track and that it was up to him to turn the subject in a new direction.

Career

After seven years in the forest, Veblen and his wife decided that he really should get a job. He failed to get an appointment in philosophy at Iowa because he lacked a degree in divinity. Sensing that the intellectual drift was away from philosophy, he departed in 1891 for Cornell, which was offering four graduate fellowships in social science. There he came into contact with a rising young economist, J. Laurence Laughlin, who was impressed with his abilities. In 1893, when Laughlin was invited to head the department of economics at the newly founded University of Chicago, he took Veblen along as a junior colleague. Thus when Veblen began his teaching career he was already thirty-six, the same age as the president of the university, William Rainey Harper.

The fifteen years at Chicago were Veblen's most productive period. He published two major books, *The Theory of the Leisure Class*

(1899) and *The Theory of Business Enterprise* (1904), along with a flood of articles and book reviews, many published in the *Journal of Political Economy,* which he edited for most of the period. He attained a substantial national reputation. But at Chicago he climbed only slowly up the long academic ladder which President Harper had established: from fellow to reader, to tutor, to docent, to instructor, and finally to assistant professor. Harper didn't like Veblen and made it clear that he would be quite happy to see him go elsewhere. Laughlin continued to get him reappointed, with some difficulty. But in 1905 he was finally forced to leave, apropos of an entanglement with a woman admirer.

Fortunately, President David Starr Jordan of Stanford was at that time trying to build the scholarly reputation of that still largely undergraduate institution by buying up "big names." Allyn Young, then department chairman at Stanford (and later a noted figure at Harvard), arranged an appointment for Veblen as associate professor. The Stanford career (1906–1909) was a small replica of the Chicago career: much reading and writing, a reputation in the faculty as a brilliant eccentric, failure to make much contact with the undergraduates who dominated campus life, continued domestic difficulties. In 1909, when a woman admirer from Chicago moved in on him, he was forced to leave. He landed this time at the University of Missouri, where the chairman of the department, H. D. Davenport, admired him and offered a position as lecturer on annual appointment. He taught at Missouri until 1917, always as a lecturer, and never getting back to his Stanford salary of $3,000.

In 1918 Veblen served for six months in the wartime Food Administration, an appointment arranged by an admiring former student, Isador Lubin (later commissioner of labor statistics in the New Deal era). From there he went to New York, as one of several editors of *The Dial* magazine. In 1919 he joined a distinguished faculty at the New School for Social Research, but this ended when the school's finances collapsed in 1922. Soon afterward he returned to his cabin in Palo Alto, where he died in low spirits and near poverty in 1929.

By the usual standards, then, Veblen would have to be considered a failure. His academic career shows downward mobility — in quality of institutions and of students, in academic rank, in real income. How can one account for this combination of great intellectual ability and marked lack of success? The answer is partly that Veblen was a loner, a reclusive scholar with no talent for self-promotion. He would have scorned to curry academic favor even if he had known how. He was considered a poor teacher, in an era when teaching was valued, relative to scholarship, even more highly than it is today. He had a stormy domestic life. After the happy early years, there were quarrels and long periods of living apart, leading eventually to divorce in 1912. Veblen was attractive to women and always had a bevy of admirers. While he does not seem to have been the pursuer in these relationships, neither did he make much effort to fend them off. As he complained at one point to a friend at Stanford, "What is one to do if the woman moves in on you?"[1] While friends might sympathize, presidents did not.

Curiously enough, Veblen seems never to have been persecuted for his opinions. It was women, not ideas, that did him in.

Teaching and Scholarship

Veblen exemplifies the scholarship that we all exalt in the abstract, but may not appreciate when we see it in the flesh. He was a solitary, almost a recluse — the opposite of the genial clubman. He avoided social life, usually refusing even to turn up when his wife gave a party. He was not easy to know, and it was hard to get from him a definite opinion on anything. Acquaintances commented that he seemed always to be wearing a mask. He sat silently through college courses and later through faculty meetings and other gatherings. To observers he gave an impression of passivity, amounting almost to indolence.

But along with this external passivity went an extremely active inner life, which consisted in reading, thinking out problems, writing out conclusions. He was a "night person," usually sitting down to work about 8 P.M. and going on until 2 A.M. (Galbraith, on the other hand, is a "morning person," who writes every day from 9 A.M. until 1 P.M., as I do myself.)

Veblen was objective and dispassionate to an extraordinary degree. He could discuss the most controversial issues without giving a clue to his own opinions and even enjoyed teasing students in this respect. Dorfman reports that "of Veblen's opinions no one was quite certain. Students suspected that he was an agnostic . . . but they were not sure . . . A student in the course on trusts would ask what could be done about the situation he described. Veblen's eyes would sparkle, the lines of his face would be drawn into a quizzical smile, and he would answer, in effect . . . We are interested in what is, not what ought to be . . . Sometimes in his course on socialism his remarks would start excited arguments among members of the class . . . but he did not give much clue to his own judgment."[2] One day after class H. D. Davenport said in exasperation, "You are outside class now, and can say what you think of socialism." But Veblen never gave him a direct answer.

Veblen was not an advocate of political causes. He was applauded by socialists and other social critics who found his ideas congenial. But they joined *him*. He did not join *them*. As Galbraith comments, "Veblen . . . was not a reformer. His heart did not beat for the proletariat or otherwise for the downtrodden and poor. He was a man of animus but not of revolution."[3]

Veblen's great course was called Economic Factors in Civilization, an unorthodox course in economic history, which began with the savage tribes and came gradually down to 1900. He usually taught a course on socialism, again with a heavy historical flavor and a review of all the major socialist writings. At various times he taught courses on agriculture, on industrial organization, and on the history of political economy.

Most undergraduates considered Veblen a poor teacher, and this view is understandable. He had no patience with the ordinary academic routines. He never recruited students, trying if anything to discourage them. He placed no stock in class attendance even when, as at Missouri, this was compulsory. Examination requirements he treated with amusement, and everyone in the class received a C grade. He refused to hold office hours, though he was always available for a stroll and a talk. His lectures were disorganized, filled with a great jumble of everything from ancient times to the present, with many detours along the way. As Veblen slouched in his chair, he talked away in a low mumble which was difficult to hear, let alone to understand. He discouraged note taking, averring that what he was saying wasn't very important anyway.

Veblen believed that most undergraduates were not much interested in education, and he was not about to force it upon them. But he responded quickly to anyone with the spark of an original idea and was kind and patient in helping such students to develop their ideas. There was always a limited band of superior students, primarily graduate students, who found Veblen both intelligible and exciting. Some of these disciples, such as Wesley Mitchell, later became prominent figures in economics, and all retained an affection and respect for their master. So, if Veblen failed as a teacher, he was perhaps the kind of failure that more of us should try to become.

Veblen's Economics

The Critique of Mainstream Economics[4]

The economics of 1890, with which Veblen grew up, was not an attractive system of thought. Nor did it undergo major changes during his lifetime. He could not have foreseen the revolutions in both macro and micro theory in the 1930s. It is interesting to speculate on whether they would have softened his critical stance. Probably not.

Veblen's own bent was inductive. Any science must be grounded in reality, must start from an observation of facts. It seemed to him that contemporary economics proceeded by a clever avoidance of facts. Institutions are disposed of by assuming a hypothetical, competitive economy. Human nature is disposed of by resorting to utilitarian psychology, which Veblen rejected as long since superseded by modern psychology.

"The hedonistic interpretation of man is that of a lightning calculator of pleasures and pains, who oscillates like a homogeneous globule of desire of happiness under the impulses of stimuli that shift him about the area, but leave him intact . . . He has neither antecedent nor consequent. He is an isolated, definitive human datum, in stable equilibrium except for the buffets of the impinging forces that displace him in one direction or another. Self-imposed in elemental space, he spins symmetrically about his own spiritual axis."[5] In this view, human nature is indeed constant. In fact, there is no human nature. He proceeds to contrast this with the view of "modern psychology" that man is essentially an *actor* and that the activities through which he tries to realize his goals evolve as the result of past experience and changes in the cultural and technological environment.

Human nature and economic organization having been eliminated, economics reduces to a set of algebraic relations among
quantities. These results of deduction are characterized by such
terms as "normal," "underlying tendencies," "basic principles." The
deductive results, to be sure, are sometimes checked against observed behavior. But "features of the process that do not lend
themselves to interpretation in terms of the formula are abnormal
cases and are due to disturbing causes. In all this the agencies or
forces causally at work in the economic life process are neatly
avoided. The outcome of the method, at its best, is a body of logically consistent propositions concerning the normal relation of
things — a system of economic taxonomy. At its worst, it is a body
of maxims for the conduct of business and a polemical discussion
of disputed points of policy."[6]

This theoretical system is also entirely static. Though economists
often talk about "dynamics," this turns out to be only pseudodynamics. They do not advance a coherent theory of economic change.
A proper economics, Veblen thought, should focus on processes
of change. This would give it the evolutionary character found in
all other modern sciences — except mathematics, which alone resembles economics in its taxonomic structure.

Nor did Veblen think that economic history could usefully be
separated from social history in general: "The economic interest
does not act in isolation, for it is but one of several vaguely isolable
interests on which the complex of technological activity carried out
by the individual proceeds . . . an evolutionary economics must
be the theory of a process of cultural growth as determined by the
economic interest, a theory of a cumulative sequence of economic
institutions."[7] Change induced by cumulative causation, not a perpetually recurring equilibrium, was the proper object of study.

While Veblen's critique of conventional economics was based on
methodology, he was also repelled by its tendency to slip over from
analytical results to moralistic approval of those results. The results of private ownership and free competition are not only "normal" but beneficent. The distribution of income measures contribution to production. In the words of Arthur Twining Hadley's
Economics, ". . . to the medieval economist the businessman was a
licensed robber, to the modern economist he is a public benefactor
. . . So confident are we of the substantial identity of interest be-

tween the businessman and the community as a whole, that we give
our capitalists the freest choice to direct the productive resources
of the community."[8] Veblen thought that there were still many
robbers around and that much business income arose from predatory rather than productive activity.

Among the economists whom Veblen studied and taught was
Karl Marx. One might have expected him to be sympathetic to
Marx, who did advance a theory of historical change. But in fact
he was critical of Marx, not on points of detail (such as the labor
theory of value) but on general methodological grounds.[9] Marx's
system is based partly on an inversion of the Hegelian dialectic but
is also heavily overlaid with British utilitarianism, from which Veblen dissented. He did not think workers would necessarily realize
that enlightened self-interest dictated an overthrow of the capitalist class. They might instead decide to share the spoils of capitalism
through union organization. Or they might accept the culture of
capitalism and end up submissive and subservient. Nor did Veblen
like the Marxian doctrine that history comes to an end "after the
revolution." In Darwinian evolution, which Veblen favored, there
is no end of the road, but simply a continuing adaptation of the
human species to changing material circumstances.

Veblen notes also that some of Marx's economic predictions, such
as the immiserization hypothesis, have not been validated by history, that lack of a theory of population is a serious defect, and
that the Marxian system, rooted in industrial processes, is not applicable to peasant agriculture. He did not think that peasants could
ever be converted to socialism.

The Veblenian System

Veblen's economic writings[10] are somewhat wordy and repeti-
tive. He liked language and was not economical in its use. Reading
him is like listening to a fugue. One encounters a statement which
turns out to be a major theme. Then this theme is embroidered
and repeated at many other points. He convinces partly by repeated assertion rather than by systematic proof.

There is also a certain myopia in Veblen. His focus is on manufacturing, which he regarded as the core of the modern economy.
And within this sector he focuses on the company promoters, financiers, "captains of industry." He shows little interest in the rou-

tine management of production, in what Schumpeter called "the circular flow of economic life." Within this realm he would probably have accepted the conventional conclusion that rewards are in proportion to productivity. But he sets this aside as being so well known as to be uninteresting. He is concerned rather with the top corporate managers and their allies, the investment bankers. These people are concerned, not with furthering production, but with restricting production in the interest of profit. They profit, not from smooth operation of the circular flow, but from spontaneous or contrived disturbances in the flow. Their gains are predatory gains, bearing no necessary relation to productivity or service to the community. While these people are a small percentage of the gainfully active population, they occupy a dominant position and are able to appropriate a large amount of income.

Basic to his thinking is a distinction between *the industrial system* and *the business system.* The industrial system is a physical reality. It comprises the apparatus of machinery and plants involved in producing and transporting goods. This apparatus becomes ever more complex, specialized, and interrelated because of the progress of machine industry, which is the driving force in Veblen's view of history. The industrial system employs the bulk of the labor force, including foremen, production managers, and engineers. These are the "good guys" in Veblen's world. They display the instinct of workmanship, which he regarded as a basic human characteristic, and labor to turn out serviceable goods for community use.

The business system, on the other hand, is a pecuniary reality, concerned with prices, profit, credit, and capital values. It comprises the people who manage the pecuniary linkages among component parts of the industrial system. This excludes production managers and engineers. The "businessmen" in Veblen's system are concerned with advertising and marketing, pricing, finance, and overall corporate strategy, including mergers and acquisitions. These "bad guys" control the activities of the "good guys," who are allowed to produce goods only in such quantities and qualities as will yield profit.

The sole aim of the business system is profit. Production, serviceability, and industrial efficiency are all subordinate to that end. He thought that businessmen were not very good at promoting efficiency. As the productive system grows more complex and as corporate organizations grow larger, the managers at the top increasingly lose touch with the engineers and production people at the bottom. They no longer know how to enforce efficiency even if they wanted to do so. He notes that, when things get so bad that efficiency engineers have to be called in, "they have no hesitation in speaking of preventable wastes amounting to ten, twenty, fifty, or even ninety percent, in the common run of American industries."[11] This long before Leibenstein and "X-efficiency."

Businessmen are concerned, not with the *serviceability* of goods, but with their *vendibility* — not what is most useful, but what will sell. Product quality will be deteriorated if that will increase profit. Price is set at "whatever the traffic will bear," and then output is restricted by as much as necessary to sustain this price. These controls of quantity and quality Veblen terms "capitalist sabotage" or "conscientious withdrawal of efficiency."

Strictly speaking, charging what the traffic will bear applies only to monopoly. But Veblen thought that there was an element of monopoly in almost every business. "But it is very doubtful if there are any successful business ventures within the range of modern industries from which the monopoly element is wholly absent . . . the endeavor of all such enterprises . . . is to establish as much of a monopoly as may be. Such a monopoly position may be a legally established one, or it may be a monopoly of a less definite character resting on custom or prestige (good-will) . . . The end sought by the systematic advertising of all the larger business concerns is such a monopoly of custom and prestige. This form of monopoly is sometimes of great value, and is frequently sold under the name of good-will, trade-mark, brands, etc."[12] This thirty years before Chamberlin and Robinson.

He goes on to note that the object of advertising is to shift demand among competitors. This may be profitable, even essential, for the firms involved. But the resources used are largely wasted from a social standpoint. He was skeptical of new consumer goods, asserting that they often complicated life without enhancing it. Still "Invention is the mother of necessity."[13] Once a new good has appeared, it will work its way into consumption patterns. Here, as in the discussion of marketing strategy, there is an overtone of Galbraithian "producer sovereignty."

The modern economy has emerged from a long process of technological, cultural, and institutional change. At various points in his writings, Veblen traces this process all the way from savage times through the classical civilizations to the Middle Ages and beyond. (He believed, correctly, that he knew much more about these earlier periods than did most modern economists. The pictures which they sometimes draw for illustrative purposes are simply fables, what Veblen called "conjectural history.")

In modern times he distinguishes three phases: (1) the handicraft period, in which the instinct of workmanship operates with full force, (2) machine industry, operated by small owner-managers under essentially competitive conditions. Here business principles of price and profit have already made their appearance, but the instinct of workmanship is still powerful because the small business owner is still close to production management. This period began in the third quarter of the eighteenth century and reached full flower around 1850. Since that time the economy has been moving gradually into phase (3), marked by consolidation of business into large, quasi-monopolistic corporations, dominated by "captains of industry" and financiers. Essentially, he argues that the economics of his day is still stuck in the past, giving an idealized version of phase 2. His concern is with the physiology and pathology of phase 3.

When Veblen was writing, people like Carnegie, Judge Gary, Rockefeller, Morgan, Vanderbilt, and others had recently burst on the economic scene with apparently irresistible force, and so it was natural for him to put them in the center of the stage. These "captains of industry" he regarded as buccaneers, who aimed through mergers and takeovers to conquer a larger economic territory. Their depredations are financed on credit from the investment bankers. In the complex process of recapitalizing the merged enterprises the promoters come out with large equity holdings. But the size of their loot bears no relation to services performed. In "the financing operations of the great captains of industry . . . the amount of the businessman's gains from any given transaction . . . bear nor traceable relation to any benefit which the community may derive from the transaction."[14]

On the efficiency impact of consolidations he is ambivalent. If the merger promoters are operating with a view to continuing ownership, this may conduce to an interest in efficiency. Very often, however, they are interested only in manipulation and resale for gain, in which case their interest in industrial operations is purely transient. Where costs are reduced this will come mainly through eliminating those formerly engaged in managing rival businesses, including marketing and advertising people, i.e., reducing the number of unproductive "businessmen." Veblen was certainly not against large industrial units per se. But he would have liked to see them controlled by the people he trusted, the engineers, rather than by the investment bankers.

His concern with financial manipulation led Veblen to define "capital" in monetary rather than physical terms. The amount which has been spent on plant and equipment is irrelevant. The value of a going concern depends on capitalization of its future earning power. This reflects not only whatever productivity may be imputed to the physical plant, but also "good-will," monopoly power, and other intangibles. The typical outcome of an industrial consolidation, he thought, was that the new enterprise comes out with debt somewhat equivalent to the value of its plant and equipment. The equity issues, appropriated mainly by the promoters, derive their value largely from intangibles.

The capital of an enterprise, then, is the value of its securities, and this value fluctuates from day to day in the market. The "capital market," Veblen thought, has now superseded the "goods market" as the central feature of the economy. The capital market, incidentally, provides an opportunity for insiders to profit from superior knowledge of company affairs. The market value of a stock depends on outsider estimates of future earning power. But a manager may know that these estimates are inaccurate, that the market valuation is accordingly too high or too low, and so can profit from trading in company securities. Moreover, management can manipulate outsider estimates by adroit action. A clever manager "will aim to manage the affairs of the concern with a view to an advantageous purchase and sale of its capital rather than with a view to the future prosperity of the concern . . . the interest of the managers of a modern corporation need not coincide with the permanent interest of the corporation as a going concern."[15] There is, in fact, a three-way split between:

1. The public interest, which consists in lowest-cost production
2. The corporate interest, which consists in profitability

3. The management interest, which consists in "a discrepancy, favorable for purchase or sale as the case may be, between the actual and the putative earning capacity of the corporation's capital."

The interest of the management is thus removed by one degree from that of the corporation and by two degrees from that of the public. "In so far as invested property is managed by the methods of modern corporation finance, it is evident that the management is separated from the ownership of property, more and more widely as the scope of corporation finance widens."[16] Again, this is thirty years before Berle and Means.

Economics at this time was almost entirely microeconomics. So it is not surprising that there is virtually no macroeconomics in Veblen. He seems to have believed that technical progress was creating an ever-wider gap between potential output and what the market can absorb. But this is asserted rather than proved, except by casual reference to the depressed conditions of the eighties and nineties. There is an embryonic monetary theory of the business cycle. The upswing is marked by excessive credit creation, rising prices, speculation. This is followed by a "liquidation," with falling prices and a redistribution of ownership in favor of creditors.

Where is the system going over the long run? Most economists of the day regarded it as stable, even near-perfect. Veblen was convinced that it was unstable and would continue to evolve toward some new form of economic organization. But this future era is never clearly outlined. There is a suggestion that at some point the gap between the financiers and the engineers will become so wide that the former will lose their ability to control production and that the engineers may then be called on to take over. In the early twenties, when the aging Veblen had become part propagandist, he made some effort to alert the engineers to their responsibility for keeping the system running and even suggested formation of a "guild of engineers." The technocrats of the thirties looked to Veblen for inspiration. There are also suggestions that ownership of very large enterprises might pass peaceably from private to public hands, an anticipation of Schumpeter's "march into socialism." But Veblen was essentially a scientist. He was not much interested in predicting the future, and even less in influencing its course.

The Lighter Side

There is a lot of fun in Veblen, and we should not leave him without a word about *The Theory of the Leisure Class* and *The Higher Learning in America*. These books do not really fit into his analysis of the economy. While Veblen meant them as serious studies, they were widely received as social satire, and many passages have a distinct tongue-in-cheek air.

Why do people strive to accumulate goods? We usually say "because of their utility in consumption." Veblen conceded that this may be true for "those classes who are habitually employed at manual labor, whose subsistence is precarious, and who own little." But it is not true of the owning class, "the superior pecuniary class." Their desire for wealth stems from the motive of invidious distinction, or emulation, which he regarded as one of the strongest human motives. This desire is competitive, involving a ranking of oneself relative to others and, in the nature of the case, can never be satiated. "The invidious comparison can never become so favorable to the individual making it that he would not gladly rate himself still higher relative to his competitors in the struggle for pecuniary reputability. . . . In the nature of the case, the desire for wealth can scarcely be satiated in any individual instance, and evidently a satiation of the average or general desire for wealth is out of the question."[17]

It is not enough to be wealthy. One must be seen to be wealthy. "In order to gain and hold the esteem of men it is not sufficient merely to possess wealth or power. The wealth or power must be put in evidence, for esteem is awarded only on evidence . . . a life of leisure is the readiest and most conclusive evidence of pecuniary strength . . . the characteristic feature of leisure-class life is a conspicuous exemption from all useful employment."[18]

Conspicuous leisure does not require idleness. It is all right to engage in government, war, sports, and devout observances — none of these is "productive." It is all right to spend time studying dead languages, appreciating art and music, mastering the niceties of gentlemanly behavior, leading an elaborate social life. But one must not *produce* anything.

The other way of displaying wealth is through consumption of a wide variety and superior quality of goods. "Conspicuous consumption of valuable goods is a means of reputability to the gentleman of leisure."[19] And since it is difficult to consume enough one-self, it is necessary to rely partly on conspicuous consumption by others — giving presents to friends, mounting elaborate feasts and entertainments, keeping many retainers, decking out women of the family with clothes and jewelry. All these people are "vicarious consumers."

Conspicuous consumption and conspicuous leisure are commensurable: "From the foregoing survey of the growth of conspicuous leisure and consumption, it appears that the usefulness of both alike for the purposes of reputability lies in the element of waste that is common to both. In the one case it is a waste of time and effort, in the other it is a waste of goods. Both are methods of demonstrating the possession of wealth, and the two are conventionally accepted as equivalents. The choice between them is a question of advertising expediency simply."[20] The trade-off terms will vary with the stage of development. In modern urban society, dominated by numerous and transient contacts, it may be easier to make an instant impression by conspicuous consumption.

He is at pains to point out that "invidious" and "waste" are not used in a deprecatory sense. To the individual, any expenditure is an expression of preference and yields utility. "Waste is a technical term, denoting expenditures which are purely emulative or competitive, which "do not serve human life and human well-being on the whole." Clearly, an article may be *both* useful and wasteful, in varying degree. He is making an analytical distinction, not a classification of objects.

Standards of living are habitual, and habits are hard to break. So it is difficult to bring about any reductions in standards of living. But they are very flexible upward: "This suggests that the standard of expenditure which commonly guides our efforts is not the average, ordinary expenditure already achieved; it is an ideal of consumption that lies just beyond our reach, or to reach which requires some strain. The motive is emulation — the stimulus of an invidious comparison which prompts us to outdo those with whom we are in the habit of classing ourselves. Substantially the same proposition is expressed by the commonplace remark that each class envies and emulates the class next above it in the social scale . . . in this way all standards of consumption are traced back by insensible gradations to the usages . . . of the highest social and pecuniary class, the wealthy leisure class."[21] The Duesenberry consumption function is thoroughly in the spirit of Veblen.

There is an amusing discussion of "the classes given over to scholarly pursuits. Because of a presumed superiority and scarcity of the gifts and attainments that characterize their life, these classes are by convention subsumed under a higher social grade than their pecuniary grade should warrant. The scale of decent expenditure in their case is pitched correspondingly high, and it consequently leaves an exceptionally narrow margin disposable for the other ends of life."[22] This is clearly written with feeling by an impecunious faculty member.

In *The Higher Learning in America*, Veblen hits back at the academic apparatus into which he fitted so badly. The modern university, he thought, was essentially a business organization operated on business principles. Boards of trustees are drawn increasingly from the business class. He does not accuse these people of encroaching on academic freedom. Indeed, he thought that they did very little, except to appoint a president in their own image and to require that the institution be managed with an eye to the bottom line.

The university president typically falls short of the average faculty member in academic attainments. ". . . a plausible speaker with a large gift of assurance, a businesslike educator, or clergyman, some urbane pillar of society, some astute veteran of the scientific *demi-monde*, will meet all reasonable requirements. Scholarship is not barred, of course, though it is commonly the quasi-scholarship of the popular *raconteur*."[23]

The university itself is "conceived as a business house dealing in merchantable knowledge, placed under the governing hand of a captain of erudition, whose office is to turn the means in hand to account for the largest feasible output."[24] It is, in fact, rather like a department store. The field of knowledge is sliced up into "subjects" (this process sometimes involving fierce interdepartmental struggles), each of which is sliced up in turn into standardized units (credit hours), to be dispensed to the customers. Like a department store, too, each university competes for custom with other universities, and much of the energy of university administrators goes into this competitive activity. This whole apparatus of administration, curriculum requirements, undergraduate forced feeding, and interuniversity competition has little to do with — is in fact antithetical to — the pursuit of knowledge which Veblen regarded as the proper purpose of a university. Pursuit of knowledge is a cooperative, not a competitive, activity.

Veblen thought that vocational training, even for the "learned professions," had no proper place in a university and should be left to other institutions. He is particularly severe on business schools, which were then beginning to appear around the country: These do not have even the justification which attaches to law, medicine, or engineering. They do not draw on any body of established scientific knowledge, nor is their output useful to the community. "No gain comes to the community at large from increasing the business proficiency of any number of its young men. There are already much too many of these businessmen, much too astute and proficient in their calling, for the common good. A higher average business efficiency simply raises activity and avidity in business to a higher average pitch of skill and fervor, with very little material result than a redistribution of ownership; since business is occupied with the competitive acquisition of wealth, not with its production."

The ideal university of Veblen's dreams would look rather like the Institute of Advanced Studies at Princeton. One would begin by abolishing the board of trustees and the central university administration. Then each group of scholars, freed from the "coordination" they do not need, could set about their proper work of advancing knowledge. Students would be admitted only in the status of apprentices and would learn by observing and working with senior scholars. Veblen thought that most undergraduates were not interested in learning but wanted rather to accumulate "credits" with minimum effort and otherwise to spend their time on sports and social life. If their needs must be served, this could be done in separate institutions which would not draw scholars away from their proper work.

Coda

I have tried to let Veblen speak for himself, without implying agreement or disagreement. It is easy to show that his portrait of the economy is distorted, highlighting the warts on the system while taking its accomplishments for granted. It is easy to show that the black-and-white distinctions which Veblen loved — the industrial system and the business system, productive activity and predatory activity, competition and monopoly, necessary consumption and conspicuous consumption — have at most some analytical significance and that the real world consists of varying shades of gray. The reader may find satisfaction in carrying out such a critique. But I have neither space nor inclination to play that game here. I like the old curmudgeon.

Why does one find Veblen attractive? His mind was powerful, wide-ranging, and highly original. He had no mentor, nor did he seek disciples. In the nature of things he could not have created a "Veblen school." He was *sui generis*. Then there is his freshness of view, his honesty, his freedom from cant. At a time when politicians, educators, and economists were voicing unstinted praise of the businessman, he ventured to assert that the emperor had no clothes. At a time when most economists were portraying stable equilibrium within a fixed institutional framework, Veblen maintained that the economy was continually changing its skin and that this evolution would continue indefinitely into the future. His vision was akin to that of Marx and Schumpeter: "this too will pass away."

On rereading Veblen after sixty years one is surprised, too, at the way in which he anticipated ideas which have now become commonplace: the element of monopoly in most markets, the economics of advertising activity, the element of rivalry in consumers' budget decisions, the divorce of management from ownership, the technique of corporate mergers (as relevant in the era of Icahn and Perot as in that of Morgan and Gary). Others were to make more of these ideas later on. But to have suggested them as early as 1900 showed strong creative power.

Veblen's ambition was to derail conventional economics and set it on a new track. In this, as we now know, he failed. When he wrote, it might have seemed that the subject had reached a dead end — an ever more refined microeconomics, going nowhere. Veblen could not have anticipated the transformation of the subject by the upsurge of macroeconomics in the twenties and thirties, by innovations in micro theory which began in the thirties and achieved full force in the sixties and seventies, and by the increased quantification of economic research. Today's econometrician does not worry, as Veblen did, about shaky metaphysical foundations, provided that the R^2 is satisfactory. So the ship of economics did not sink but sailed on, leaving Veblen behind.

Foundation officials, university administrators, and other outsiders often urge that we should not live too narrowly within the bounds of one discipline but should seek instead to become broad, multidisciplinary scholars. Veblen's works illustrates both the seductiveness and the shortcomings of this approach. No one could have been more multidisciplinary than he was. He ranged beyond the social sciences into philosophy and the methods of natural science. He wanted to create a unified theory of the evolution of human civilizations, with economic motives and institutions in the forefront but embedded in their cultural matrix. He did not succeed. The task was too large, perhaps even ill advised. But what a fine way to fail.

NOTES

1. Joseph Dorfman, *Thorstein Veblen and His America* (New York: Viking, 1934), p. 295.
2. Dorfman, *Thorstein Veblen*, pp. 246–47.
3. "Who Was Thorstein Veblen?," written originally as an introduction to a new edition of Veblen's *The Theory of the Leisure Class* (Boston: Houghton Mifflin, 1973). Reprinted in J. K. Galbraith, *Annals of an Abiding Liberal* (Boston: Houghton Mifflin, 1979), p. 141.
4. Veblen's views on the economics of his day appear primarily in "Why Is Economics Not an Evolutionary Science?" *Quarterly Journal of Economics* (July 1898), 373–97; in three articles titled "The Preconceptions of Economic Science," *Quarterly Journal of Economics* (January 1899), 121–50; (July 1899), 396–426; (January 1900), 240–69; and "The Limitations of Marginal Utility," *Journal of Political Economy* 16 (November 1909).
5. "Why Is Economics Not an Evolutionary Science?," as reprinted in *The Place of Science in Modern Civilization*.
6. Ibid., p. 67.
7. Ibid., p. 77.
8. Quoted in Dorfman, *Thorstein Veblen*, p. 129.
9. See "The Socialist Economics of Karl Marx and His Followers," *Quarterly Journal of Economics* (August 1906 and February 1907).
10. The most important of these is *The Theory of Business Enterprise*. Other relevant material can be found in *The Instinct of Workmanship* and *The Engineers and the Price System*.
11. *Instinct of Workmanship*, p. 223.

12. *Theory of Business Enterprise*, pp. 54–55.
13. *Instinct of Workmanship*, p. 314.
14. *Theory of Business Enterprise*, p. 61.
15. *Theory of Business Enterprise*, p. 157.
16. *Theory of Business Enterprise*, pp. 175–76.
17. *The Theory of the Leisure Class*, pp. 31–32.
18. *Theory of the Leisure Class*, pp. 36, 38.
19. *Theory of the Leisure Class*, p. 75.
20. *Theory of the Leisure Class*, p. 81.
21. *Theory of the Leisure Class*, pp. 103–4.
22. *The Higher Learning in America*, p. 83.
23. *Higher Learning*, p. 85.
24. *Higher Learning*, p. 208.

SELECTED WORKS BY THORSTEIN VEBLEN

The Theory of the Leisure Class (New York: Macmillan, 1899). References herein are to the Modern Library edition (New York: Random House, 1931).

The Theory of Business Enterprise (New York: Charles Scribner's Sons, 1904). References herein are to the Reprints of Economic Classics edition (New York: Augustus M. Kelley, 1965).

The Instinct of Workmanship (New York: Macmillan, 1914). References herein are to the Reprints of Economic Classics edition (New York: Augustus M. Kelley, 1965).

The Place of Science in Modern Civilization (New York: B. W. Huebsch, 1919). References herein are to a later edition (New York: Russell and Russell, 1961).

The Higher Learning in America (New York: B. W. Huebsch, 1918). References herein are to the Academic Reprints edition (Stanford, Cal.; Stanford University, 1954).

The Engineers and the Price System (New York: B. W. Huebsch, 1921). References herein are to the Reprints of Economic Classics edition (New York: Augustus M. Kelley, 1965).

Eric Roll

What Is Economics?
What Is an Economist?
The Case of J. K. Galbraith

THIS TITLE MAY WELL be puzzling, especially as it heads a contribution to a *Festschrift* honoring on his birthday one of the world's best-known writers on economic topics. Moreover, among the contributors are many distinguished economists, including no less than three Nobel Prize winners. In terms of worldly success and fame, Ken Galbraith has achieved as much as is humanly possible. He is widely read, and the sale of his books puts him firmly in the best-seller class. A poll among reasonable educated people in most countries of the world would certainly find his name better known than that of any other contemporary writer in the same field — often perhaps the only one to be known at all by name. He has been honored by a number of countries and remains today, as ever, a much-sought-after speaker in all parts of the world. Even his professional colleagues who for a long time hesitated, despite his tenure of a coveted Harvard chair, to count him as fully one of their own, did elect him to the presidency of the American Economic Association: a distinction that could be regarded as the ultimate accolade of professional recognition.

Nevertheless, some traces of the old doubt linger here and there. He is included in a recent *Who's Who* type of register of the one hundred *Great Economists since Keynes* by Mark Blaug (many of the inclusions may, incidentally, not command universal support), but the article on him ends with the statement that "he remains a renegade in the eyes of his fellow economists," and it speaks of his racy style "full of undocumented assertions" and of "his contempt for rigorous analysis." Even if one discounts this judgment in the light of its author's evident ideological preferences (no such criticism is offered in the article on a recent Nobel Prize winner renowned for his "public choice theory"), the description of Galbraith's standing among professional economists is not, alas, entirely without foundation.

Lester Thurow in his appreciative entry in *The New Palgrave* calls Galbraith "an economist out of the mainstream of economic thought," though he rightly acknowledges that he is "in the mainstream of economic events." A young English economist, David Reisman, who has written, on the whole, an admiring book on Galbraith, while acknowledging that he is "witty, provocative, stimulating, intelligent, etc.," also says that he is "vague, repetitious, arrogant, mercenary, journalistic, dogmatic, etc."

One may well feel that the best thing to do with these opinions is to ignore them, and, no doubt, Galbraith himself is highly unlikely to be much troubled by them. Even the fact that he has not yet been awarded the Nobel Prize — an omission which he shares with a number of other eminent twentieth-century economists (some now dead) who would certainly fall in the class of those who practiced "rigorous analysis" — need not be surprising, since one is unlikely to find many people who would support all the choices so far made. (In this regard, economics, the newcomer among Nobel Prize disciplines, has been no more successful than some of the old established ones such as literature or peace. Nor, in the nature of things, is this ever likely to be the case.)

It is thus, in my view, not for the sake of any in itself wholly unnecessary advocacy of Galbraith's merits as such that the question deserves a little analysis, but rather for the sake of at least attempting to bring some clarity into the question of how the scope and method of economics is nowadays understood by many of its practitioners as well as by the consuming public. The man whom we are honoring in this volume will, I am sure, tolerate to have his work used, at least in part, as a touchstone for this purpose, particularly since in his writings there are many explicit, and even more implicit, references to his views on the scope and method of economic enquiry. In his latest book, *Economics in Perspective,* he has included at the end some reflections on the future of the discipline which echo earlier views but also have some novel and even surprising features.

The first point is to examine what precise aspect of Galbraith's work has led some fellow economists to doubt his membership in good standing of the club. And here the first question is whether it is his method of argument or the conclusion to which it leads that is at issue. A phrase, clearly used slightingly, in the *Great Economists since Keynes* to which I have already referred is possibly a guide, namely "his [Galbraith's] fond belief in planning and more state control." On a very rough inspection, it seems to be the case that criticism of Galbraith has come mainly from those who object to his skepticism of the beneficent omnipotence of the free market; its ability always to produce the economically and socially optimal results. In consequence, he is generally found to be on the side of those who advocate specific forms of state intervention to correct what might otherwise be undersirable results. Galbraith's writings tend to place him within the broad spectrum of Keynesian economists and thus to make him inevitably a target for the followers of the anti-Keynesian, monetarist, *laisser-faire* counterrevolution. Whether the Galbraithian views which provoke criticism are rightly lumped together as a "fond belief in planning and more state control" is, however, doubtful. By temperament as well as by practical experience it is highly unlikely that Galbraith can really be guilty of such a naive view as is ascribed to him; though, of course, if any kind of state intervention (presumably outside the ambit of the "nightwatchman-state") is to be condemned, then the fact that there are limits of his own, or anyone else's, acceptance of some degree of intervention becomes irrelevant.

I have myself found only one piece of evidence of weight in Galbraith's work of a belief in the virtue of economic planning in general, and that is in *Economics and the Public Purpose*, where the need for a national plan is produced as a reply to criticism (e.g., by Meade) of Galbraith's belief in a sort of spontaneous overall plan emerging from the planning proclivities of the large corporations. Surprisingly, he reached this view not in the days when the concept of general planning was much more fashionable than it is today. I am inclined to discount this particular example and to place more emphasis on the fact that where he has advocated intervention it has been specific and in response to what he considered observed flaws in the uncontrolled operation of individually directed economic forces. Indeed, much of his theoretical work is a critical analysis of the degree of private (i.e., not state-engendered) economic planning by powerful groups which he regards as characteristic of modern developed economies.

That the "Keynesian" approach to economic analysis — and, more important, the consequential economic policy — which held sway, roughly speaking, from the Great Depression through the controlled economy of wartime and through the period of postwar reconstruction with its undoubted successes, led to a certain "ideological" presumption, and here and there a certain "hubris," is easily explicable (though this is not the place for such an explanation). That it was followed by a counterrevolution, a well-attested fact of recent intellectual history, is not surprising. What is unfortunate is that the intensity of the counterrevolution has not only not abated but has continued to have, and even increasingly, an almost religious fervor. (The extraordinarily intemperate, indeed strident, criticism which *The New Palgrave* has evoked in certain quarters is an interesting example reminiscent of the attitude of the more extreme followers of some religious sect.)

The politicization of so many issues of current economic policy and the evident inability of the more reasonable mainstream economic analysts — even the most eminent — to provide satisfactory and, above all, practicable answers that politicians can make use of, has perhaps led to a tendency for some economists to take refuge in ideological fortresses. This has led them to identify one view with virtue, the other with vice, a tendency which, it must be said, seems to be particularly marked on the "right" of the economic spectrum.

It may be possible to resign oneself to this situation in the (perhaps vain) hope that calmer, more reasonable attitudes would eventually prevail. On the other hand, one may also hope that the progress of mainstream analysis, for example, in the areas of fiscal and monetary policy and their international repercussions, would produce more practical guidance for those in authority in respect of policies for economic growth and for the avoidance of violent fluctuations in the most important economic categories. However, the present state of affairs does demand some early reconsideration since it has begun to affect the view of what is and what is not properly within the definition of economics and so has created an uncertainty which has even affected, admittedly in a few cases only, opinion as to the legitimacy of Galbraith's work as a part of economics.

Since too many highly respected economic analysts (including happily still a majority of Nobel Prize winners!) have from time to time been known to advocate, or at least not to avert their gaze, from specific intervention, this stance cannot in the end be a very effective target for the attack on Galbraith, or indeed on anyone else with similar views. It becomes tempting, therefore, to rest criticism not so much on the policy conclusions as on the method by which they are arrived at, in the hope, perhaps, of thus questioning the legitimacy of attaching the label "economic" to the underlying analysis.

Here, however, the critics who talk about broad generalizations, vague assertions, or absence of rigorous analysis (whatever that means, unless it is meant to be a plea for greater, or even exclusive use of mathematics — hardly acceptable as a general proposition) are not on very solid ground.

Throughout its history, economic thought has had distinguished and important practitioners of many kinds, including some of the most seminal ones, who have built substantial systems on a very few broad hypotheses, not only within the narrow limits of economic analysis but in the wider field of social speculation as it affects the actual economic process at any one time or economic development over time.

Beginning with old Adam Smith himself, it can hardly be denied that *The Wealth of Nations* is full of very broad generalizations (not surprising in the author of *The Theory of Moral Sentiments*) of human conduct in society: the "invisible hand" itself is simply an extension into the social field, the validity of which could quite reasonably be considered to be much more limited than it is nowadays fashionable in some circles to claim. Beyond that, apart from the theory of value, or such more specific analytical aspects as the principles of taxation, much of the material, historical or descriptive, belongs very much in the category of structural or organizational theorizing.

It is interesting in this connection to recall that in a popular short history of economics of the interwar period, Ricardo's analytical method, described as the result of a certain "inherited Jewish subtlety," is compared to its disadvantage with Smith's much broader approach. (Alfred Marshall, incidentally, had something very similar to say in his Inaugural Lecture.) It is arguable that the impact of Smith's views on practical policy was due much more to the appeal of his "broad theorizing" than to the more specific analytical parts of his work, even though some of these were to become building blocks for the work of later economists.

In more recent times, Schumpeter is another economist whose work could usefully be juxtaposed and compared with that of Galbraith. Schumpeter's position in the ranks of the foremost economists of this century has rightly never been questioned. Yet if the criteria that are sometimes used (and apparently occasionally applied to Galbraith), i.e., whether his work includes contributions to the corpus of strict, rigorous analysis such as, shall we say, Samuelson's *Foundations of Economic Analysis* or (chosen at random) the work of Patinkin, Arrow, and Domar, were to be applied to Schumpeter, probably only his *Business Cycles* would qualify as suitable for a test. This work, however, would by quite wide consent be judged his least successful: certainly not one that has had any seminal influence on subsequent work in the same field. To this day, Schumpeter's achievement in economics (not, I fear, repeated in either public policy — as finance minister — or in private enterprise — as a banker) rests on his earliest major work, *The Theory of Economic Development* and, to some extent, on a later even more "speculative" work, *Capitalism, Socialism and Democracy*. The author is described in an earlier *Who's Who* by Mark Blaug, *Great Economists before Keynes,* in almost lyrical terms: "Schumpeter is one of the giants of twentieth-century economics whose majestic vision of the economic process can rank with that of Adam Smith or Karl Marx." Yet, leaving aside one's view about the respective validity of the theory of innovation and the role of the entrepreneur in Schumpeter and, say, the role of the large corporation and the concept of the technostructure in Galbraith — on which one may legitimately have strong and strongly opposing views — the surprising thing is that the method and approach should be questioned in one case and not in the other.

Much of the work of a more recent economist (and Nobel Prize winner), James Buchanan, which is clearly on the margins of Economics and Political Theory, could also be grouped within the "broad speculative" realm. The theory of public choice developed by him with Gordon Tullock rests on a very simple foundation, namely, on the proposition that politicians and those who vote them into power are rational beings motivated by the desire to maximize the fulfillment of their self-interest. This proposition puts the whole of their subsequent edifice of, for example, the theory of democracy, the role of the bureaucracy and many other aspects of government, firmly on the same foundation as some modern versions of neoclassical economic theory; though in this, its simplest form, it is tempting to say with Horatio, "There needs no ghost come from the grave to tell us this," a remark which can be made about many of the broad speculative hypotheses on which much more refined work is subsequently built. The point, however, is to recognize that starting out from such hypotheses is a well-practiced method of both the great and not so great in the history of economic thought and cannot in itself provide proof or disproof of qualification as an economist.

A very large and important area of economics, modern and ancient, including some of Galbraith's work, concerns the problem of economic development, as in Schumpeter, or growth as it is more commonly known nowadays. This field exhibits, *par excellence,* the great variety of treatment, each in principle legitimate, which different writers have accorded to it. To mention only some in addition to Schumpeter, it is hard to imagine greater differences of approach and method applied to this subject than for example those of Bob Solow (related to the work of Harrod and Domar) and that of Walt Rostow — with Ed Dennison somewhere in between and Galbraith's *New Industrial State* also of considerable relevance in the same context.

Clearly, we are free to assign our own values to each of these treatments. Some may find Galbraith's views, as in *The Affluent Society* or *The New Industrial State* (arguably his two most important books), as little convincing as some would consider Veblen's *Absentee Ownership* or his *Theory of Business Enterprise* (with which Galbraith's books have a clear family resemblance). His basic concepts may well be superseded by other equally daring propositions or by changes in the economic structure which may make the concepts themselves irrelevant. Walt Rostow's *Stages of Economic Growth* seems to have suffered that kind of fate. On the other side, the theory of public choice may in future prove itself more pregnant with valuable insights that enlarge our understanding of human society and, perhaps, be even more productive of practical policy guidance than seems likely at the moment. The history of ideas shows some surprising belated revelations of truth or resuscitations of discarded earlier ideas, but it is also littered with grand constructions which had their brief day only to be thrown on the scrap heap later. What, for example, has happened to the "stationary state" or to the "progressive misery of the working class"? Of course, there will always be some to lend a new interpretation to old ideas in order to rescue them from oblivion, even though their original authors would never have dreamt of these new ways of presenting their work. Thus, the trouble is — and this applies more to the more speculative branches of economics than to the more abstract analyses — that while not every new-fangled, fanciful socioeconomic idea deserves serious examination, the worth of those that appear to do so (perhaps consumers' choice is as important here as the free marketeers claim and prima facie acceptance can have the validity of *vox populi!*) often cannot be established until long after they have appeared. I am by no means arguing that no discrimination can be practiced, only that a certain caution is in any event indicated. But what I do insist on is that the Galbraithian concepts are not simply to be brushed aside on the grounds that they are not derived from the simplest propositions of, say, rational expectations theory, or because they clearly are not imbued with a wholehearted belief in the beneficence of unbridled free-market forces, or because other eminent economists have preferred to devote their intellectual labors to more abstract theorizing.

Thus, well beyond the particular case of the standing of Galbraith's work in contemporary economic theory and discussion, some attitudes to it have at least had the merit of showing how many basic questions of scope, method, and indeed purpose of economic inquiry are still unresolved. To one who started to study the subject sixty-three years ago, it comes almost as a shock to find that some of the conundrums that were already hoary in his undergraduate years could still form, and indeed do form, lively topics of controversy. The old question whether economics, as distinct from the old political economy, should and can be a positive (i.e., ethically neutral) science — hence virtually a branch of mathematics, whether mathematical symbols are used or not — or whether it should be, and inescapably had to be normative (i.e., one in which moral desiderata are integrated into its logical process), is still very much alive, even if it is not always explicitly recognized.

A recent study of Keynes, for example (*Keynes's Vision* by Athol Fitzgibbons) argues cogently that Keynes's economics cannot be fully understood without accepting that it is inextricably linked with ethics and politics (and also with Keynes's views on probability, i.e., in this connection, uncertainty). This question of the inclusion of ethical desiderata, which may, of course, change over time, leads naturally on to the question of what part the state (or, more broadly, authority) should play and, furthermore, what the actual economic organization and, therefore, the power of nonstate business structures, is at any one time. Since this is inevitably a topic of not only intellectual debate, but also, and more acutely, political controversy, it is understandable that the question is often elided rather than met head-on, because to do so may not lead to what is politically most acceptable at any one time. Moreover, the question is greatly complicated by past history, which has left its barnacles (very different for different parts within the world), around social institutions, including attitudes within the contemporary scene.

While the progress, in technical terms, of more abstract, positive theory has been remarkable in the last four or five decades, the attempts to integrate "welfare economics" into it have, despite a few outstanding and remarkably courageous efforts, not yet produced convincing results. Nor can it be said with confidence that economics is clearly on the road to an early achievement of a kind of economic technology based on "pure" economic science. Nevertheless, even if one doubted the possibility of ultimately achieving an ideal integration of politics and economics, it would be wrong to lapse into a kind of obscurantism. Keynes, incidentally, did not doubt it, or at least did not doubt that economics could produce a solution to the economic problem as such, which in a celebrated phrase (of 1932) quoted by Galbraith, he did not regard "as the permanent problem of the human race." He thought that economists could eventually become — and come to be regarded — as "humble, competent people, on a level with dentists."

As Galbraith rightly points out, this prediction has not proved correct. Saying this leads Galbraith to expand on a familiar theme, the role of the present structure of business enterprise, the inherent opposition of business and government, the resulting triumph in some advanced countries of an extreme free-market policy, the decreasing importance of the old theories of production and distribution, of the level of prices and of wages and the much greater importance that will be attached in future to unemployment or loss of employment. In this respect, he reaches in his last book the somewhat surprising conclusion (surprising, partly, because it corresponds to a theory enunciated a few years ago by the present British chancellor of the Exchequer!), namely that "Unemployment in the past has been seen, overwhelmingly, as a macroeconomic problem, something caused or remedied by the overall design and management of fiscal and monetary policy. This also will cease to be so." Microeconomic factors, the performance of particular industries and markets, are the causes of, and the areas of remedy for, the overall performance of the economy, particularly as regards security of employment.

Somewhat paradoxically, this does not lead Galbraith to rely more on the invisible hand, but rather to a more emphatic assertion that "the separation of economics from politics and political motivation is a sterile thing; it is also a cover for the reality of economic power and motivation." His hope that the two may be reunited in order to form again "the larger discipline of political economy" may be shared by all who have regarded this nearly three-hundred-year-old intellectual discipline as ultimately having to respond to Bacon's injunction of having "a tendency to use."

Paul A. Samuelson

Galbraith as Artist
and Scientist

1

Years ago in a pastoral lecture to brethren in the economics game, I said that whereas non-economists may take Kenneth Galbraith too seriously, we insiders pay Galbraith too little attention. As usual in my writings, I may have been only half right.

Certainly students come into our freshman classes already knowing the name of John Kenneth Galbraith — his *Affluent Society* and *New Industrial State*. If Shelley was right that poets are the unacknowledged legislators for the world, then he who writes society's legends is even more important than those who draft its laws, charters, and Ph.D. dissertations. Long before Vilfredo Pareto reaches students' minds with the doctrines of efficiency and deadweight loss, John Kenneth has already been there with his gestalt of the Fortune-500 corporation.

John Jay Chapman opined that what a man from Mars would observe on earth came closer to a Wagnerian opera than an Emerson essay. Certainly what the Martian saw in earthly markets would look less like a Walras-Debreu system of equilibrium than a Galbraith-Schumpeter picture of corporate bureaucracy.

Even a new doctor of philosophy from Chicago labors in the vineyard to find proper microfoundations for macroeconomics. Those are code words for dissatisfaction with the paradigm of perfect auction markets of purely competitive type. The National Bureau of Economic Research, from its aerie on holy ground halfway between Harvard and MIT, issues forth each year a hundred manuscripts testing the hypothesis of rational expectationism and scarcely a one fails to reject its null hypothesis.

You will conclude, "Galbraith has won out in the Darwinian struggle for survival of ideas." It would be naive to think so, and would betray a lack of sophisticated understanding of how Kuhnian science develops.

Sinclair Lewis recirculated the words, "When fascism comes to America, it will come in the guise of anti-fascism." Similarly, orthodox mainstream economics arrives at its own version of Galbraithism without ever admitting agreement to his contentions. Indeed, if the simple truth were told, the process of absorption is genuinely unself-conscious and non-Machiavellian.

How is this possible? Very easily, and you can count the many ways. A George Stigler is hardly a Galbraithian. Rather he is a card-carrying founder of the Second Chicago School — not the First Chicago School of Frank Knight, Henry Simons, and Jacob Viner, but that of Aaron Director, Milton Friedman, and George Stigler. When you read Stigler's fascinating and breezy autobiography, *Memoirs of an Unregulated Economist,* you learn that his own most important contribution to economic science involved discovery of the crucial role for markets of "information." Prices fail to be glued to marginal costs because of the costs connected with search and information. We are carried back, not to the Jevons and Walras *Weltanschauung* of competitive capitalism, but rather to the vision of Carl Menger and Kenneth Galbraith!

When I walked into Joseph Schumpeter's classroom in 1935, he described the real world in non-Walrasian terms. At that period he believed that General Motors reigned on borrowed time. By the time of his death in 1950, Schumpeter had changed his vision: General Motors and General Electric had mastered the technology of staying on top, but the deviations of their behavior from Marshall-Cournot equality of marginal cost and price was of secondary importance. If competition was imperfect, it was workably efficient. Zealous trust-busting would do more harm than good. The label on the Pepsi Cola bottle is not that on the Coca-Cola bottle, and the labels on the Schumpeter-Stigler goatskins do not carry the letters JKG; still the wines are of the same vintage and demonstrably different from the Walras-Debreu grapes.

Perhaps the ultimate triumph is when your target is converted without realization.

2

Needless to say, the notions of JKG have altered exogenously and also in response to the findings of mainstream economics.

Affluence is seen to be less imminent than in the 1950s. Wasteful *public* expenditure remains a problem. Countervailing power from downstream and upstream competitors is seen to be secondary to rivalry by rivals. K-Mart has trimmed Sears down to size more than have any unions of retail clerks or retail clients. Trade union power, and that of their top officials, has been limited more by imitative manufacturing in the Pacific Basin than by Taft-Hartley and anti-labor legislation. Internationalization of markets has done more to keep competition workable than has the promotion of antitrust regulation. Just after Schumpeter began to believe in the permanency of corporate residents on the top floors of capitalism's hotel, every oligopolist began to compete in every other oligopolist's markets domestically and abroad. If a Paul Sweezy doubted in the prewar world that a fifth rival to the existing steel giants could secure the needed initial finance, at century's end viability obtains for innumerable small-scale producers of steel in electric furnaces and with nonunion labor. The members of the class of Galbraithian technocrats alternately cringe at the power of the purse and the ballot box and tyrannize their subordinates. Each new edition of my *Economics* and the Samuelson-Nordhaus *Economics* has had to move further away from the Berle-Means paradigm of corporate-bureaucrats-in-the-saddle and shareowners-*sans*-power. A Harold McGraw shivers when a Boone Pickens is on the prowl. Minority battles minority, and uneasy sleeps the head that wears the corporate crown. Investment bankers no longer run the roost as in days of yore, but they are back in the Temple to pick up fees putting the cogs together and taking them apart.

3

Had Schumpeter lived to observe the four decades after 1950, I suspect he would have moved at least a small way back toward his earlier view on how limited are the powers of the giant corporations. In any case, I believe that Galbraith would do well to realize how much like constitutional monarchs his dinosaurs are: they reign only so long as they do not rule. The history museums are full of the fossil bones of Montgomery Ward, International Harvester, American-Nash-Studebaker Motors; GE of today has only a historical connection with the General Electric that used to make our fans, toasters, and turbines. When I gently protest that JKG lacks proper respect for the market, I refer not at all to his failure to worship Adam Smith's Invisible Hand and Pareto's elimination of deadweight loss. All that concerns ideology, and it is the bigger game of positivistic science that my gunsights are trained upon.

Let me connect up, as they say in court, with Gorbachev's attempted *perestroika* (restructuring) for the Soviet Union. Youngsters of my generation used to read the debate between Lerner-Lange and Von Mises on economic planning in a socialist state. We decided that L-L won decisively. Mises erred logically and empirically in denying that economic optimality could be even defined in the absence of markets (a position already refuted by Barone, Pareto, Wicksell, and Fred Taylor). By instructing bureaucrats to *play the game* of being price takers in auction markets, a totalitarian state could equal or surpass the efficiency of laissez-faire capitalism, achieving all the needed equalities between prices and marginal costs (and, indeed, relative marginal utilities).

That was the state of the debate in, say, 1939. But by 1989 connoisseurs realize that it was really Hayek and Schumpeter who were the winners of the debate. Even if the constant-returns-to-scale conditions conducive to perfect competition were fulfilled in the Communist state — a contra-factual premise — Lerner-Lange need to address a problem they have ignored: how are the bureaucrats to be motivated to actually do what L-L's rules of the game want them to do? *Sed quis custodiet ipsos Custodes?* Why shouldn't they use the monopoly powers L-L admit *they* always have? Why expect them to ignore such powers? This game-theoretic line of argument leads remorselessly toward having the planners not *play-act* the game of market competition but actually instead be the entrepreneurs who personally risk losses and seek gains.

At this point Hayek plays his trump card: knowledge is incomplete, fragmented, and ever-changing. Only with free entry of any would-be rival can *dynamic intertemporal*–Pareto efficiency be approximated and maintained. A Wriston may be as fallible as a Lysenko, but no one needs permission in a market mechanism to slay a Sewall Avery or a Walter Wriston; the jungle of bureaucracy and politics has its own Darwinian processes, but *there is no Bergsonian theorem that its mechanisms are eliminative of deadweight loss*. Lenin, on the eve of the October Revolution, believed wrongly that scarcity would wither away if man's institutions were not vile; only "the rule of three" would be needed to unleash technology's abundance once capitalism's centralized bastions fell to the revolutionists; "electricity plus democracy equals communism" is his romantic formula for a brave new world in which gold would be relegated to the construction of toilet seats. Eight decades later an economist in Hungary or East Germany, to say nothing of Moscow or Beijing, will despair that such romanticism was once taken seriously. Henry George, Bernard Shaw, and Joan Robinson imagined that whatever the problems of creating the golden-rule stationary state, once created it could maintain itself with all returns to property expropriated for the workers. Reality is more stubborn. As with the second law of thermodynamics, Schumpeter's stationary state runs down into disorder from the first instant of its creation. No one-time winding of the clock can outlast the day of its birth.

A real-thing (rather than a play-acting) Lerner-Lange system makes socialism reap the virtues of markets only by its reverting back to becoming capitalism. Gorbachev and Deng may not desire unemployment, bankruptcies, and inflation, but that is the road logic is taking them down.

Schumpeter spoke unemotionally of capitalism as "creative destruction." That is a euphemism for the system's cutting its losses. When we observe South Korea, Taiwan, and Singapore in the 1970s — and the rise and fall and persistence of the Chicago Boys in Chile during the 1980s — we realize that *glasnost* is no causal condition for *perestroika;* perhaps it is even the reverse. Demand-pull suppressed inflation is the specific disease of the halfway house between mindless "centralized planning" and mindless "free markets."

Logically, there is a way out of the dilemma. But it is not a prospect pleasing to Marx, Engels, Lenin, Trotsky, Mao, or even Beatrice Webb. And it would come as something of an anticlimax to Schumpeter and Galbraith — but not to Franklin Roosevelt or Maynard Keynes.

I refer to the mixed economy of the mainstream economists. For most of the year's work it relies on the market and not on governmental factories or planning agencies. But the extremes of laissez-faire inequality are tempered by the mutual reinsurance transfer payments of the fiscal-welfare system. And the extremes of macroeconomic instability are attenuated by discretionary central-bank and budget policies. (Robert Lucas has a statute in its Pantheon, not because rational expectations are rational or realistic, but because the constraints on policy ambitions are real, systematically changing, and need studying!)

Shaw said the trouble with capitalism is that, like Christianity, it has never really been tried. I have to admit that the trouble with the New Deal is that the citizenry do not display a consistent passion for achieving their New Jerusalem and that economic science lacks full understanding of its entailed trade-offs.

4

Political economy is an art as well as a science. John Kenneth Galbraith has always been a creative artist in formulating theories of the social world. His fabrications constitute the stuff of economic science.

II

ECONOMIC STRUCTURE
AND POLICIES

Walter Adams and James W. Brock

Power, Planning, Public Purpose

No ECONOMIST in the twentieth century, with the possible exception of Thorstein Veblen, has contributed a more trenchant dissection of economic orthodoxy than John Kenneth Galbraith. In his analysis of both neo-classical and neo-Keynesian dogma, he has laid bare the questionable assumptions on which they are based — assumptions by which power, and therewith political content, is removed from the study of our discipline. In so doing — in eliding power and thus making economics a nonpolitical subject — modern theory, he points out, has destroyed its relation with the real world and sacrificed its validity and usefulness (JKG, 1973b, p. 2).

With the pervasive role of the large corporation in advanced industrial society, Galbraith shows us, it is no longer admissible to base economic theorizing on the simplistic assumptions that (1) the business firm is subordinate to the instruction of the market, and that (2) the state is subordinate to the instruction of the citizen. Appeal to the evidence of the eye, says Galbraith, should be sufficient to persuade us that "the modern corporation either by itself or in conjunction with others has extensive influence over its prices and its major costs," on the one hand, and that it "has a compelling position in the modern state," on the other (JKG, 1973b, pp. 4, 5). Moreover, the large corporation, with its "power over markets, power in the community, power over the state, [and] power over belief," is more than an economic institution. It is also "a political instrument, different in form and degree but not in kind from the state itself." To pretend that the market is the guiding force of economic activity "is not merely to avoid the reality. It is to disguise the reality" — for the benefit of "the institutions whose power we so disguise" (JKG, 1973b, p. 6).

In short, as Galbraith demonstrates, the country's very largest corporations constitute a comprehensive planning system that supersedes the function of the market and rivals the power of the state.

Having exposed this concentration of vast discretionary power, however, Galbraith does more. He suggests that, realistically, matters cannot be otherwise. Why? Because in a modern industrial economy like the United States, the large corporation alone affords the intricately organized combination of specialized skill, talent, and intelligence required to carry out society's central economic planning function. The fragmented, decentralized competitive market is singularly ill suited to the task. So too is the entrepreneur. Decisive power, Galbraith argues, is no longer "exercised by capital but by organization, not by the capitalist but by the industrial bureaucrat." Bureaucratic organization, the "technostructure," is in control of the social planning process — a phenomenon Galbraith deems "inescapable in a world of advanced industrial technology [and] large-volume industrial production" (JKG, 1978, p. xvi). And in performing this function, Galbraith believes, "the most obvious requirement is large size" (JKG, 1978, p. 77). Thus, firms like General Motors, Exxon, and IBM are big, not primarily to attain economies of scale or to exercise monopoly but to engage in effective planning. "And for this planning — control of supply, control of demand, provision of capital, minimization of risk — there is no clear upper limit to the desirable size. It could be," he concludes, "that the bigger the better" (JKG, 1978, p. 81).

This observation does not mean that Galbraith would grant industrial giants untrammeled license to roam the Darwinian jungle. In fact, he is an inveterate advocate of price and wage controls in the oligopolistic industries which make up the "planning system." He notes, for example, that in an economy dedicated to providing full employment, the "spiral of wage and price increases is an organic feature of the planning system" (JKG, 1978, p. 258) and insists that the "obvious remedy for the wage-price spiral is to regulate prices and wages by public authority" (p. 259). He repeatedly points out that "since the [planning] system is unstable at full employment, there is no alternative to control. However regretted, it is inescapable" (p. 264). And again: "The planning system must, by its nature, be subject to external restraint on its prices" (p. 262). On this point, Galbraith has been consistent and uncompromising over the years. (See, for example, JKG, 1952a, p. 205; JKG, 1952b, pp. 63–71; JKG, 1973a, p. 194; Galbraith and Menshikov, p. 94.)

This nevertheless leaves some unanswered questions. Are mammoth corporations the adroit planners they are commonly believed to be? What is the quality of their planning and their economic performance? If mistakes are made, what mechanism is in place to correct them? At whose cost? To whom is the planning bureaucracy accountable, and how can it be made accountable? What assurance is there that this private planning system (a form of private socialism) will harmonize with the public purpose? And, finally, is this bureaucratic corporate bigness complex the inescapable price of operating a modern economy based on "advanced industrial technology" and "large-volume industrial production"?

I. Private Planning and Economic Performance

In exploring these issues, and in deference to Galbraith's methodological prescriptions, it is instructive to "appeal to the evidence of the eye. And the evidence of the eye is assuredly there" (JKG, 1978, p. xiv). But does the evidence support a policy of benign tolerance toward corporate concentration and fatalistic acceptance of private planning?

1. *The Automobile Industry.* Long dominated by a triopoly of horizontally, vertically, conglomerately, and internationally integrated giants — ranking among the very largest industrial corporations not only in the United States but in the world — the technostructure in the auto industry is hardly a deus ex machina. It has distinguished itself neither by its sagacious foresight nor by its intelligent long-run planning nor by its technological acumen. It has congentially ignored, or fatuously dismissed, fundamental market developments. It has consistently lagged, not led, in technological innovation. Its reluctance to face facts, much less to anticipate them, has confronted the industry — and the country — with a series of recurring crises (Adams and Brock, 1987, pp. 38–41, 60–62, 66–74).

With respect to fuel economy, for example, the automobile triopoly showed little concern for the finite nature of petroleum supplies or the declining fuel efficiency of its cars. It ignored warnings of industry insiders (like the director of Ford's science laboratory), voiced some two decades before the first OPEC oil crisis, that "if there is any industrial area in the U.S. where an important new idea is absolutely necessary for survival, it is in the automobile industry. The oil prospects for the world are so very dim that this largest of all American industries must have an important, original, inspired breakthrough sometime within the next 25 years. . . . What we must have is something so new, so radical, and so unanticipated that it would be folly to compartmentalize our thinking into how to go about pursuing this."

The auto technocracy was not impressed by such prescient admonitions. Asked in 1958 what steps his organization was taking in fuel economy, the general manager of General Motors' Buick division replied: "Oh, we're helping the gas companies, the same as our competitors." The industry refused to develop smaller, more fuel-efficient cars, and denigrated Volkswagen beetle buyers as "eccentrics." It merrily persisted in building ever larger gas guzzlers so that, by 1973, it could boast of a technological milestone: its fleet that year attained an average fuel efficiency of thirteen miles per gallon! Months before the first OPEC oil embargo, and amidst mounting national concern, GM continued to dismiss the problem, suggesting that nuclear power plants were a good way of dealing with America's fuel consumption "question." As late as 1979, shortly before the overthrow of the shah of Iran and the onset of the nation's second oil crisis in six years, General Motors still proclaimed that auto "fuel economy standards are not necessary and are not good for America."

The Big Three's record in automotive smog emissions was equally unimpressive. Again, their initial response was to deny the existence of a problem. "Waste vapors are dissipated in the atmosphere quickly and do not represent an air-pollution problem," Ford instructed Los Angeles officials in 1953. "The fine automotive power plants which modern-day engineers design do not 'smoke.'" Later, as public concern mounted, the Big Three formed a cartel to eliminate competition among themselves in developing pollution control technology. When government pressure finally forced the oligopoly to respond, the technostructure opted for costly, complicated catalytic converters — a decision described by the National Academy of Science as "the most disadvantageous with respect to first cost, fuel economy, maintainability, and durability." Of the industry's planning, the Academy said: "It is unfortunate that the automobile industry did not seriously undertake such a [pollution control] program on its own volition until it was subjected to governmental pressure. A relatively modest investment, over the past decade, in developmental programs related to emission control could have precluded the crisis that now prevails in the industry and the nation. The current crash programs of the major manufacturers," the Academy concluded, "have turned out to be expensive and, in retrospect, not well planned."

Suffering from an acute case of "Grosse Pointe myopia," and unable to see beyond their hood ornaments, the U.S. auto technocracy also fell behind its foreign competitors in operating efficiency, plant productivity, product quality, and new product technology (Yates, pp. 77–109, 149). The industry eventually paid a price for its delinquent performance and desultory planning, but so did the public at large: a torrent of fuel-efficient imports which captured roughly 30 percent of the U.S. market, and massive plant closings and layoffs which reverberated throughout the economy and aggravated the worst economic downturn since the Great Depression.

Scarcely a record to inspire confidence in private planning by an oligopolistic technostructure!

2. *The Steel Industry.* Here, as in autos, the technostructure is hardly the prototype of organized intelligence attuned to market developments, digesting information with alacrity, operating at the frontiers of technology, and judiciously anticipating the future. Instead, Big Steel has for decades been afflicted with the inefficiencies, the technical backwardness, and the bureaucratic dry-rot symptomatic of excessive organizational size. Like the auto oligopoly, Big Steel has perennially lagged, not led, in innovation — with deleterious consequences for the industry and the nation (Adams and Brock, 1987, pp. 34–38, 57–59, 263–270).

The economic infirmities of oligopoly giantism emerged early in the industry's history. "We are today something like five years behind Germany in iron and steel metallurgy," *Engineering News* reported in 1911. The main reason, the magazine suggested, was "the wholesale consolidation which has taken place in American industry. A huge organization is too clumsy to take up the development of an original idea. With the market closely controlled and profits certain by following standard methods, those who control our trusts do not want the bother of developing anything new" (Brandeis, pp. 150–51).

Twenty years later, in the 1930s, a management consulting firm retained by U.S. Steel to conduct an internal efficiency study found the nation's largest steelmaker to be "a big, sprawling, inert giant, whose production operations were improperly coordinated; suffering from a lack of a long-run planning agency; relying on an antiquated system of cost accounting; with an inadequate knowledge of the costs or the relative profitability of the many thousands of items it sold; with production and cost standards generally below those considered everyday practice in other industries; with inadequate knowledge of its domestic markets and no clear appreciation of its opportunities in foreign markets . . ."

The industry's subsequent performance did not reverse this pattern. In the postwar era, Big Steel (in conjunction with Big Labor) leisurely played the price-wage-price escalation game (Galbraith and Menshikov, p. 94). It became a powerful engine of cost-push inflation in the economy. It disregarded the emergence of foreign competition as well as the growth of substitute materials like aluminum and plastics.

Most notably, Big Steel demonstrated a marked aversion to innovation. It cavalierly dismissed the oxygen furnace — a technological breakthrough that offered per-ton operating cost savings of 40 percent, per-ton capital cost savings of 60 percent, and a 90 percent reduction in tap-to-tap times between pourings. This innovation was widely adopted by smaller U.S. firms in the 1950s, while Big Steel blithely constructed 40 million tons of antiquated open-hearth facilities — an investment that *Fortune* pointed out was "obsolete when it was built" and that by installing it Big Steel had "prepared itself for dying."

The steel giants responded in like fashion to the advent of continuous casting. This technological advance — which by-passes the laborious ingot-pouring process, as well as the energy-intensive reheating of ingots and primary rolling — was pioneered in the United States, not by Big Steel but by a small firm (Roanoke Electric) in

1962. Other smaller steel firms followed so that, by 1968, firms with roughly 3 percent of the nation's steel capacity accounted for 90 percent of continuously cast production. By 1978, when small firms were continuously casting more than 50 percent of their output, Big Steel's rate was still only 11 percent. Inevitably, the American industry fell significantly behind its Japanese and European rivals.

The steel oligopoly lost export markets abroad and became increasingly vulnerable to import competition at home. In the 1950s, the United States exported about four times as much steel as it imported. By 1968, the situation was reversed, with imports exceeding exports by a margin of 8 to 1. The share of foreign competitors in the U.S. market steadily escalated — from 1 percent in 1956 to 17 percent in 1968; eventually it reached 27 percent in 1984.

By the 1980s, the steel technocracy was generating financial losses of billions of dollars, as well as mass plant closings and job layoffs. It had reduced employment in the industry to less than 200,000 (the lowest level since records began to be kept in 1933 and far below average employment levels of 450,000 in the 1970s). It was decimating steelmaking communities across the country. And in 1986, in spite of its successive mergers with three major steel producers (Jones & Laughlin, Youngstown Sheet & Tube, and Republic), the nation's second largest steel concern (LTV) lost $3.3 billion and then collapsed into bankruptcy.[1] Merger-induced size had failed to assure either production efficiency or international competitiveness.

Finally, it is noteworthy that small firm size in steel does *not* seem to necessitate turning back the technological clock. While Big Steel has foundered, "mini-mill" steel firms have succeeded spectacularly. These mini-mills are efficient, sophisticated, and hyper-advanced. They are specialized, nonintegrated, and highly profit-

---

1. Conglomerate expansionism compounded the steel oligopoly's problems. Armco Steel has suffered substantial losses in its diversified operations, including a cumulative half-billion dollar loss from its foray into insurance underwriting (*Business Week*, February 1, 1988, p. 48). National Steel's diversification into oil, pharmaceutical distribution, and five-and-dime retailing (Ben Franklin stores) is foundering (*Wall Street Journal*, June 30, 1988, p. 24). And the U.S. Steel Corporation expended $9 billion buying oil companies in the early 1980s — on the eve of the worldwide collapse of oil prices.

able. Their small size facilitates, rather than impedes, technological innovation. They have captured large shares of the steel markets in which they compete, not only from the domestic oligopoly but from such supposedly invincible producers as "Japan Inc." Their success raises the pragmatic question whether the decentralized competitive market might not be a better instrument for intelligently utilizing society's resources than planning under the aegis of the steel giants.

3. *The Petroleum Industry.* As described by one Congressional committee, the petroleum industry constitutes a "planning system which operates on an essentially global scale," commanding "extraordinary financial and physical resources greater than those of most industries and many nation states" (Senate Subcommittee on Oil, p. 1597). It is dominated by a handful of majors (including the multinational Seven Sisters) who are vertically integrated in the production, refining, transportation, and marketing of crude oil and refined petroleum products. These majors are intricately interlinked with one another through a web of joint production ventures, joint bidding arrangements, joint ownership and operation of pipelines, product exchange agreements, intercorporate stockholdings, and interlocking directorships. They are also diversified energy conglomerates, owning at least half the nation's coal reserves, nearly half its proved uranium reserves, and directly or indirectly controlling 90 percent of the solar energy field.

Toward what ends has this corporate planning system been directed? Have its objectives been congruent with the public purpose? In particular, has private planning power operated to ameliorate the country's precarious dependence on geopolitically volatile foreign oil supplies? Has it promoted national energy security?

The record is not reassuring. Big Oil has lobbied for import restraints that depleted the nation's dwindling domestic crude oil reserves, and that left the country more (not less) vulnerable to embargoes. In addition, Big Oil has stifled, rather than promoted, alternative fuel technologies that might have lessened American dependence on oil — presumably because alternative fuels would have undermined the majors' oligopoly control.

In the 1950s, for example, U.S. oil giants lobbied for, and obtained, government quotas on foreign oil imports into the American market. These quotas, in place from 1957 until 1973, established a convenient price floor for the integrated majors. But Big

Oil's planning produced far more adverse consequences over the longer run: the quotas encouraged consumption of domestic oil reserves at an artificially accelerated rate while keeping low-cost, readily available foreign supplies from the U.S. market. Doubtless, this was pecuniarily palatable to the oligopoly. But as a result, the United States grew *less* self-sufficient in petroleum and became *more* vulnerable to the oil embargoes and crises of the 1970s. If anything, the private planning system had exacerbated the nation's energy *in*security.

Big Oil has also suppressed the development of alternative fuels technology (Adams and Brock, 1987, pp. 76–78). In the 1920s, for example, the German chemical combine IG Farben made a spectacular breakthrough, enabling it to produce synthetic gasoline from coal. A Standard Oil executive, dispatched to Germany to investigate, reported: "Based upon my observations and discussion today, I think that this matter is the most important which has ever faced the company since [its 1911 antitrust] dissolution . . . [Farben] can make high grade motor fuel from lignite and other low quality coals. . . . This means absolutely the independence of Europe on the matter of gasoline supply." He expressed the fear that "straight price competition is all that is left."

The petroleum technocracy deftly quashed this technological threat. Pursuant to a "marriage" agreement, the oil oligopoly obtained worldwide control (except for Germany) of Farben's "hydrogenation processes and any future [Farben] processes for making synthetic products having similar uses to those of customary petroleum refinery products." The oligopoly's goal was something other than innovating synthetic fuels technology at the expense of its extensive crude holdings. According to a Twentieth Century Fund study, the oligopoly's subsequent behavior "shows clearly that its main object in acquiring them was to strengthen its control over the oil industry. . . . Standard and Shell did little to encourage widespread synthetic production of liquid fuels and lubricants from coal." Former Standard Oil president Walter Teagle admitted as much in an internal corporate document. "There is little doubt in our minds," he stated, "but what, if other than oil companies had dominated the situation, the management's conduct of the business would have been along lines better calculated to secure the maximum return on the capital invested."

Suppression of alternative energy technologies apparently continues to characterize Big Oil's planning. In a document recently uncovered by Canadian antitrust authorities, an official of Humble (an Exxon subsidiary) frankly concedes the importance of forestalling synthetic fuel development:

> It is therefore desirable for Humble to do research work on shale and coal to know where the processes are headed. . . .
> In the meantime, it should not itself initiate commercial production, or take other action or make announcements that would motivate other companies to initiate commercial production or even development.
> It is felt that there is a fair amount of mass psychology in the industry and that, while many companies would prefer to go slow because of their domestic crude interests . . . they would feel compelled to start plants if others did and particularly so if a company with the stature of Humble did.

The name of the game, it seems, is anything but technological innovation and the public purpose.

4. *Nuclear Electric Power.* The planning system in nuclear power dates from the end of World War II, when a centralized government/business technocracy was assembled for the commercial exploitation of wartime atomic technology.

Government planning power was concentrated in the Joint Committee on Atomic Energy in Congress and the U.S. Atomic Energy Commission. Corporate participation also was highly concentrated: "Just four companies — Westinghouse, General Electric, Combustion Engineering, and the Babcock and Wilcox subsidiary of McDermott — have supplied virtually every nuclear reactor ever purchased by U.S. electrical utilities. The same four, plus Exxon, completely control the market for ready-to-use nuclear fuel. Three giant construction firms — Bechtel, Stone and Webster, and the United Engineers and Constructors division of Raytheon — have built more than 75 percent of America's nuclear power plants. Five companies, including oil companies Gulf, Kerr-McGee, and the Conoco subsidiary of du Pont, own almost half of the nation's uranium reserves. Nearly 70 percent of U.S. uranium-milling capacity belongs to Exxon, Atlantic Richfield, Kerr-McGee, the [former] Utah International subsidiary of General Electric, and United Nuclear" (Hertsgaard, p. 104).

This government-industry planning complex acted largely autonomously in mapping a nuclear future for the country. It expended billions of public and private funds promoting nuclear power. It was insulated by statute from liability and risk. In the main, it functioned in secrecy. Overall, it operated without effective checks or balances, either from market forces, or from informed public oversight (Adams and Brock, 1987, pp. 274–80).

And with what results? In spite of four decades of public subsidization, amounting to $54 billion or more, nuclear power is an inefficient electric power source. Even if these subsidies are ignored and the costs of nuclear power understated by approximately one half, the electric industry's own research institute admits that "the average new nuclear plant coming on line between 1985 and 1992 will produce electricity at a cost that is 25 percent to 50 percent higher than the typical new coal plant." Some of these plants (should they ever become operational) will produce electricity at a cost equivalent to oil priced at $130 per barrel.

The industry's construction incompetence is legendary. Eighty-four percent of the nuclear plants built in recent years have eventually cost at least twice as much as initially estimated. For 30 percent of them, actual costs have exceeded initial estimates by a factor of four. The technocracy has boldly built plants backwards and on geologic fault lines.

Scores of plants have simply been abandoned. As of 1982, one hundred nuclear power plants, representing aggregate investments of $10 billion, had been deserted as nonviable. Other plants in various stages of construction, but vulnerable to abandonment, represent additional investments of $4.5 to $8.1 billion.

The nuclear power debacle has also been expensive in opportunity cost terms. Billions of dollars have been spent that could have been devoted to more promising, less risky alternatives, like conservation and solar power. Also significant is the fact that the safe disposal of radioactive wastes — which remain toxic for 250,000 years or more — never played a prominent part in the industry's planning. It is a problem that remains unresolved to this day.

In all, the industry's performance, *Forbes* says, "ranks as the largest managerial disaster in business history, a disaster on a monumental scale. The utility industry has already invested $125 billion in nuclear power, with an additional $140 billion to come before the decade is out, and only the blind, or the biased, can now think that most of the money has been well spent" (*Forbes,* February 11, 1985).

Here, then, has been planning. But planning for what? With what consequences? For whom? At what cost? With what accountability to the public interest?

5. *Conglomerate Planning and Merger Mania.* Does the giant conglomerate firm, centrally directing an empire of unrelated operations, mark a higher stage of evolution in technocratic planning? Has it distributed technocratic talents across markets, industries, and sectors of the economy? Is it superior to competitive capital markets in generating and allocating funds? Does conglomeratism and, more generally, merger and acquisition mania, promote a more intelligent utilization of society's resources?

The evidence suggests, and Galbraith now agrees, that it does not. Corporations like ITT and Gulf & Western, which gorged themselves on conglomerate mergers in the 1960s and 1970s, and which grew to huge proportions, have recently divested scores of previously acquired businesses. ITT, for example, has sold off ninety-five operations (including an oil and gas firm, Canadian timberlands, Continental Baking, and soda bottling). It has shrunk in employment size by two-thirds; its economic and financial performance has improved substantially in the wake of its deconglomeration strategy. Gulf & Western, another hyperactive conglomerateur of the 1960s, has divested more than sixty businesses, ranging from sugar and zinc-mining operations, to cigar production and horse-racing tracks. General Mills has sold off some twenty-six businesses following a loss-ridden conglomerate adventure that spanned restaurants, Play-Doh, and costume jewelry. Transamerica — which one analyst cites as proof "that if you diversify enough you can keep your earnings low" — has done the same.

Likewise, Big Oil has struggled to escape from its adventure in conglomerate expansionism: Mobil Oil has finally found a buyer for its money-losing Montgomery Ward subsidiary; Exxon has written off hundreds of millions of dollars of investments in Reliance Electric and office equipment systems; Arco has divested Anaconda (the nation's largest copper company); Sohio has dismembered Kennecott (the second largest copper company); Amoco has spun off Cyprus Mines (yet another copper producer); Schlumberger has sold Fairchild Semiconductor (and absorbed a $200 million write-off in this failed diversification effort); and Sun Oil has also divested a number of non-oil acquisitions.

These failures of the conglomerate planning system are not isolated. They are corroborated by a plethora of generalized statistical investigations. For example, Ravenscraft and Scherer conclude
in their recent study that for acquisition-active conglomerates,
"Investors got less return on average with more risk" (Ravenscraft
and Scherer, p. 210). A McKinsey & Company analysis of the record of fifty-six large firms over the period 1972–1983 finds that
most (thirty-nine of fifty-six) of the firms that embarked on diversification programs failed, and that the likelihood of failure is
greatest for large unrelated mergers and acquisitions (*Mergers and
Acquisitions*, May–June 1987, p. 13). Especially revealing is Porter's
recent analysis, in which he examined the merger and diversification record of thirty-three large, prestigious U.S. firms over the
1950–1986 period. He found that "on average corporations divested more than half their acquisitions in new industries and more
than 60% of their acquisitions in entirely new fields. Fourteen
companies left more than 70% of all the acquisitions they had made
in new fields. The track record in unrelated acquisitions is even
worse — the average divestment rate is a startling 74% . . . Of the
comparatively few divestments where the company disclosed a loss
or a gain, the divestment resulted in a reported loss in more than
half the cases" (Porter, pp. 45, 47). Specific failure rates include
ITT (52 percent), Exxon (62 percent), General Foods (63 percent), General Electric (65 percent), Xerox (71 percent), and CBS
(87 percent). In all, it is a performance Porter characterizes as "dis-
mal."

Nor are these failures limited to conglomerate mergers. They
are typical of mergers and acquisitions generally, whether horizontal, vertical, or conglomerate. Ravenscraft and Scherer, for
example, report that the average merger (of every variety) is followed by deteriorating profit performance, that these productivity
and efficiency losses cast doubt on the efficiency-enhancing faith
in mergers, and that there is no credible evidence that mergers
enhance R&D and technological innovation (Ravenscraft and
Scherer, pp. 121, 212, 224). Summarizing his exhaustive survey of
the statistical evidence, Dennis C. Mueller finds no support for the
notion that mergers promote good economic performance (Mueller, p. 259). And Murray Weidenbaum reports that "the widely
held belief that shareholders generally benefit from takeovers does

not hold up to serious analysis" (Weidenbaum and Vogt, p. 57).

The public purpose is not unaffected. Not only does deal-mania directly undermine corporate performance; it also imposes a sizable opportunity cost burden on the economy. Two decades of managerial energies devoted to playing the merger and takeover game (organizing raids, designing golden parachutes, and devising poison pills and PAC-man defenses) are, at the same time, two decades during which management attention has been diverted from the critical job of building *new* plants, bringing out *new* products, investing in *new* state-of-the-art production techniques, and creating *new* jobs. Hundreds of billions spent on shuffling paper ownership shares are, at the same time, hundreds of billions *not* spent on productivity-enhancing investments to restore U.S. competitiveness. So, too, the billions absorbed in the legal fees and investment banking commissions generated by merger mania — expenses incurred at the initial corporate nuptials and again at the subsequent divorce proceedings — represent funds *not* plowed directly into the nation's industrial base. In 1986, the corporate planning system spent far more on mergers and acquisitions ($204 billion) than it did on R&D ($56 billion) and net new investment in plant and equipment ($81 billion) *combined* — a possibly unprecedented misallocation of resources at a time when the nation confronts withering foreign competition and record foreign trade deficits.

II. Private Planning and Public Purpose

Judging by the "evidence of the eye," giant oligopolies are not endowed with supereminent proficiency for planning. They are not the indefatigable engines of efficiency, technological innovation, and superior economic performance postulated by popular mythology. In their planning, they enjoy a comfortable immunity from both the dictates of the market and control by the state and exercise wide-ranging discretion without corresponding accountability to those whose lives are substantially conditioned by their decisions. They are (as Burke said of the East India Company) "states in the guise of merchants." And, there is no built-in mechanism to insure that the technostructure's private planning will necessarily or predictably conform to the public purpose.

Beyond these, however, is a more fundamental problem: Because these mega-giants are fallible, and because they are big, their misjudgments, misfeasances, and blunders are big too. Their failures are not only private mistakes, but social catastrophes. And this, in turn, creates troublesome and, at times, intractable public policy dilemmas.

In autos, for example, the imminent bankruptcy of Chrysler in 1979 — then the nation's tenth largest manufacturing concern, with plants and jobs throughout the country, which affected employment and production operations in a myriad of related industries — confronted the public with a painful choice. Should Chrysler be bailed out by government, even though smaller firms fail without receiving such privileged treatment, even though Chrysler's problems were mostly of its own making, and even though a public bailout would provide "flunk insurance" for poorly performing firms (if they are big enough and incompetent enough)? Or, alternatively, should Chrysler be allowed to fail, when to do so might produce potentially devastating effects on communities, states, and a weakening macroeconomy?[2]

Two years later, the entire U.S. automobile industry — afflicted with record imports, record financial losses, and the consequences of decades of delinquent performance — demanded a bailout in the form of government restraints on foreign competition. The industry thus confronted the country with an unpalatable public policy choice between protectionism, higher new-car prices, and a

---

2. Galbraith has repeatedly opposed the bailout of corporate giants from the consequences of their self-inflicted injury. Testifying on the proposed loan guarantee for the Lockheed Corporation, for example, he characterized such bailouts as a "reward for incompetence, extravagance, and mismanagement." He told the Senate Committee on Banking, Housing and Urban Affairs: "Even were I a socialist, I would oppose this guarantee. Lockheed gets much of its plant from the Government — including that in which the L-1011 is being built. It also gets most of its working capital from the Government and nearly all of its business from the Government. . . . Its cost overruns, in the past, have been extensively socialized. Only its profits have been really in the private sector. Unquestionably, this guarantee carries socialism further. But it is socialism not for society, but for a private corporation and its creditors. It is not the old-fashioned socialism for the poor, but the new-fashioned socialism for the rich."

Galbraith concluded that "if Lockheed is given this loan, it will be proof that, despite some recent criticism, the military-industrial complex is alive in Washington and doing well. It has the muscle not only to get the military business that it needs, but to be bailed out of its civilian misadventures as well" (Hearings, Emergency Loan Guarantee Legislation, 92nd Cong., 1st sess. [1971], pp. 857, 854–55, 856).

continuation of the counterproductive status quo on the one hand and the substantial shrinkage of a major domestic industry on the other.

In steel, the oligopoly's incessant lobbying for government import restraints, and for public bailouts from its self-inflicted wounds, has presented the country with a perennial public policy dilemma: should import competition be suppressed, when to do so may preserve some jobs and profits for Big Steel, but at the cost of higher steel prices that handicap steel-using U.S. firms, inflate their costs, erode their international competitiveness, and lead to job losses in these other important (and innocent) industries? Or should Big Steel be compelled to take responsibility for correcting its own performance deficiencies, without government succor, when to do so may condemn steelmaking communities to continuing economic hardship? What of the $12 billion in pension liabilities that the steel oligopoly now claims it cannot finance? Shall government subsidize Big Steel so that it can honor these obligations? Or shall steelworkers lose the benefits that they legitimately earned at the bargaining table and on which they had come to rely in their retirement planning?

In nuclear power, who will pay for the technocracy's multibillion dollar mistakes? Should the costs be passed on to utility customers in the form of sharply higher rates, when the customers are blameless, and when higher electricity prices may drive economic activity from affected states and localities? Should the costs be passed on to investors, in the form of financial losses, write-offs, and dividend eliminations? If so, might this not jeopardize the financial solvency of the firms and utilities? Or should the industry be bailed out by the public, and its losses and mistakes socialized? What of nuclear wastes? Shall communities and states be coerced to accept nuclear waste dumps that threaten not only their health and safety but that of generations to come? More generally, may not the country confront an industry-created Hobson's choice between nuclear power and (as a former Westinghouse chief executive puts it) "some tough alternatives. Alternatives like inflation, higher unemployment, no economic growth, and national insecurity?" (Hertsgaard, p. 6).

Of course, Galbraith is not oblivious of these problems. Nor does he condone the policies which gave rise to them. He recognizes, as did Oskar Lange fifty years earlier,[3] that the bureaucratic virus afflicts centralized planning in advanced industrial economies (Galbraith and Menshikov, 1988, pp. 38–39). The result of bureaucratization, especially in aging giants, he told a Congressional committee in 1981, "is that investment becomes cautious; that innovation acquires an aspect of danger . . . ; that the ability to adjust to changing circumstances dwindles; that the future is sacrificed to the near present . . . and that overall performance becomes increasingly mediocre" (JKG, 1982, p. 14). Nor does Galbraith naively presume that the private ends of corporate power are necessarily congruent with the public interest. He recognizes that the purposes of corporate planning power "are frequently different from those of the public" (JKG, 1979, p. 77).

In spite of his awareness of these problems, Galbraith nevertheless concludes — quite uncharacteristically — with a counsel of toleration. "I think we have to admit that there's no conceivable alternative to the large bureaucratic enterprise at the moment," he writes (Galbraith and Menshikov, p. 125). "As to the sclerotic tendencies of the large organizations and related shortcomings," he maintains, "the only answer is to recognize them. Adverse developments — bureaucratic stasis, personnel proliferation, surrender of thought — must be seen as wholly normal . . ." (JKG, 1988, p. 40). He would bow to what he considers inevitable, because "modern industrial planning requires and rewards great size" (JKG, 1978, p. 198). "It reflects, very simply, the accommodation of organization, capital and scale to major tasks. If you are going to build automobiles in the modern manner, bring oil from the Middle East or supply mainframe computers, the firm so engaged is not going to be small. Under either capitalism or socialism it makes no difference; the operating entity is going to be very large" (JKG, 1988, p. 38). Moreover, such size is indispensable for technological progress. The competition of the atomistic competitive model, with its

---

3. Even before he became chairman of Poland's socialist planning authority, Lange noted the innate tendency of centralized economic systems to stifle entrepreneurship. He warned "that *the real danger of socialism is . . . a bureaucratization of economic life*" and went on to point out that the same danger afflicts centralized planning and decision making under private-sector monopoly (Frederic M. Taylor and Oskar Lange, *On the Economic Theory of Socialism* [Minneapolis: University of Minnesota Press, 1938], pp. 109–10, emphasis in original).

pervasive checks and balances, makes this impossible; it "almost precludes technical development" (JKG, 1952a, p. 91). A return to control by the competitive market system, Galbraith concludes, is therefore unthinkable.

Of course, this does not imply that Galbraith would immunize private decision-making by the technostructure from thorough-going social control. He would be the last to embrace the simplistic laissez-faire, laissez-passer preachments of the Chicago School or the self-serving rationalizations of the apologists for private social-ism. He would merely maintain that corporate power "is inevitable and, *if subject to proper guidance and restraint,* can be socially useful" (JKG, 1979, p. 62, emphasis added). In short, he would insist — uncompromisingly — that direct social control of private planning is indispensable in effectuating the public purpose.

III. Conclusion

How then are we to resolve the dilemma of power, planning, and public purpose? Perhaps, as the evidence suggests, decentraliza-tion of corporate power and control is possible *without* significant loss of production efficiency, technological progress, and interna-tional competitiveness. Perhaps the harsh trade-off between per-vasive corporate concentration (and efficiency) on the one hand and a decentralized market system (and lackluster performance) on the other has been exaggerated.

Significantly, there is currently emerging a worldwide disillu-sionment with organizational giantism. In the United States, Rich-ard G. Darman (deputy secretary of the Treasury in the Reagan administration and President Bush's director of the Office of Man-agement and Budget) has bemoaned the curse of "corpocracy," which he defines as "large-scale corporate America's tendency to be like the government bureaucracy that corporate executives love to malign: bloated, risk-averse, inefficient and unimaginative." Prominent business periodicals are filled with articles carrying such revealing titles as "Small Is Beautiful Now in Manufacturing," "Big Goes Bust," "Big Won't Work," "Do Mergers Really Work? Not Very Often," and "Soap and Pastrami Don't Mix." Some progres-sive corporate executives now maintain that "bigness is not a sign of strength. In fact, just the opposite is true" (*Business Week*, July

1, 1985, p. 53). They argue that "most of the classical justifications of large size have proved to be of minimal value, or counter-productive, or fallacious" (*Fortune,* February 29, 1988, p. 34). An accumulating body of evidence suggests (as Tom Peters puts it) that what "has been the most venerated tradition in American economics, or, indeed, the American psyche — that big is good; bigger is better; biggest is best — isn't so. It wasn't so. And it surely won't be so in the future" (Peters, p. 20). Aware of the recent excesses of *uncontrolled* bigness, Galbraith would hardly disagree.

In Western Europe, economic analysts and policy makers also are increasingly questioning the bigness mystique (Adams and Brock, 1988). They are struggling to extricate themselves from the burdens and the poor performance of the corporate bigness complexes they fashioned in the 1960s. They are discovering, according to Paul Geroski and Alexis Jacquemin, that the "super-firms did not give rise to a new competitive efficiency in Europe" and that "by creating a group of firms with sufficient market power to be considerably sheltered from the forces of market selection, the policy may have left Europe with a population of sleepy industrial giants who were ill-equipped to meet the challenge of the 1970s and 1980s" (Geroski and Jacquemin, p. 175; see also Galbraith and Menshikov, p. 55). They are recognizing that the traumas and bailout dilemmas they now face are the product of past policies that encouraged excessive corporate size and high market concentration, in the attempt to create "national champions" — champions which, in retrospect, too often turned into *canards boiteux* (lame ducks). What Gibbon said of the Roman legions in the declining days of the empire may well apply to these chosen instruments: "their vices were inherent, their victories were accidental, and their costly maintenance exhausted the substance of a state which they were unable to defend" (Gibbon, p. 776).

Even the most stalwart advocates of centralized economic planning, the Soviet Union and China, are now embarked on an apparently revolutionary reorganization of their industrial structures. In the process of that *perestroika,* they are striving to break down concentration and decentralize decision making in order to obtain better economic performance [Galbraith and Menshikov, 1988]. It is a task that will not be easy.

Nor will it be easy to reform the structure of the corporate planning system which dominates the American economy. Such attempts are inherently fraught with nettlesome problems in political economy. As Galbraith incisively observes, "The state is the prime object of economic power capture. Yet on all the matters [of social planning] remedial action lies with the state. The fox is powerful in the management of the coop. To this management the chickens must look for redress" (JKG 1973*b*, p. 10). It is a perennial dilemma for anyone intent on inducing structural change or designing a regulatory system that serves the public purpose.

REFERENCES

Adams, Walter, and James W. Brock. *The Bigness Complex.* New York: Pantheon Books, 1987.

———. "The Bigness Mystique and the Merger Policy Debate: An International Perspective," *Northwestern Journal of International Law and Business* 9 (Spring, 1988).

Brandeis, Louis D. *Other People's Money.* New York: Frederick A. Stokes, 1940.

Galbraith, John K. *American Capitalism.* Boston: Houghton Mifflin, 1952*a*.

———. *A Theory of Price Control.* Cambridge: Harvard University Press, 1952*b*.

———. *Economics and the Public Purpose.* Boston: Houghton Mifflin, 1973*a*.

———. "Power and the Useful Economist," *American Economic Review* 63 (March, 1973*b*): 1–11.

———. *The New Industrial State,* 3rd. ed. Boston: Houghton Mifflin, 1978.

———. *Annals of an Abiding Liberal.* Boston: Houghton Mifflin, 1979.

———. "The Aging and Bureaucratic Process in the Private Corporation" in *Corporate Initiative.* Oversight Hearings, Subcommittee on Monopolies and Commercial Law, Committee on the Judiciary, House of Representatives, 97th Cong., 1st sess. Washington, D.C.: U. S. Government Printing Office, 1982.

———. "The New, Improved Industrial State," *Business Month* (January 1988): 38–40.

Galbraith, John K., and Stanislav Menshikov. *Capitalism, Communism and Coexistence.* Boston: Houghton Mifflin, 1988.

Geroski, Paul A., and Alexis Jacquemin. "Industrial Change, Barriers to Mobility, and European Industrial Policy," *Economic Policy* (November 1985): 170–203.

Gibbon, Edward. *The Decline and Fall of the Roman Empire.* New York: The Modern Library.

Hertsgaard, Mark. *Nuclear Inc.* New York: Pantheon, 1983.

Mueller, Dennis C. "Mergers and Market Share," *Review of Economics and Statistics* 67 (May 1985): 259–67.

Peters, Tom. *Thriving on Chaos.* New York: Knopf, 1987.

Porter, Michael E. "From Competitive Advantage to Corporate Strategy," *Harvard Business Review* (May–June 1987): 43–59.

Ravenscraft, David J., and F. M. Scherer. *Mergers, Sell-Offs, and Economic Efficiency.* Washington, D.C: Brookings Institution, 1987.

Special Subcommittee on Integrated Oil Operations, U.S. Senate. *Market Performance in the Petroleum Industry: Hearings.* Part 5, 93rd Cong., 2d sess., 1974.

Weidenbaum, Murray, and Steven Vogt. "The Pot versus the Kettle." *Challenge* (Sept./Oct. 1987).

Yates, Brock. *The Decline and Fall of the American Automobile Industry.* New York: Vintage, 1983.

Henry S. Reuss

Reuniting Economics
with Politics

Economics does not usefully exist apart from politics. . . . No
volume on the history of economics can conclude without the hope
that the subject will be reunited with politics to form again the
large discipline of political economy.

Galbraith, *Economics in Perspective,* 1987

THE WRITER, a politician who has dabbled in economics, shares
the hope for a return to a political economy of our honoree, an
economist who has dabbled in politics.

Ken Galbraith's indictment is plain. In the past two decades, both
the course of economics and the eminence of its practitioners has
declined.

This is not Galbraith's fault. In twenty-five books, hundreds of
articles, and thousands of pages of testimony, he has spelled out
his economic recipe:

- a whiff of Maynard Keynes and Alvin Hansen in fiscal policy —
  adjust taxes and spending depending on whether unemployment or inflation is the principal threat
- a pinch of Jim Tobin in monetary policy — the level of interest
  rates and the availability of credit are more important targets
  than the money supply
- copious grindings of governmental microeconomics — an Aus-
  trian-style wage-price policy to avoid having to fight inflation by
  macroeconomic measures alone; a Euro-Japanese credit conser-

vation policy to discourage wasteful uses of credit; a Franco–
Pacific Rim industrial policy to foster those activities best suited
for survival in an interdependent world

All these Galbraithian economic policies require government for
their implementation, as opposed to those systems which would
shunt off most of the hard work to the free market. The Keynesians enlisted government for their spending and taxing functions,
but they regarded monetary policy as relatively unimportant and
were willing, in a Munich-like concession, to yield to the free-market lobby and to stay out of governmental microeconomics. The
monetarists were quite willing to use governmental monetary policy for their monetary ends, but they regarded fiscal policy as unimportant and bitterly opposed any governmental intrusion into
free-market microeconomics.

The Record of Two Decades

Only the Galbraithian synthesis, to which (incidentally) I adhere,
asks for wise governmental activity across the board — in fiscal
policy, in monetary policy, in microeconomic policy, and in international economic policy.

For the past two decades, so runs our complaint, U.S. governmental activity has more often than not been *un*wise.

Fiscal policy since 1981 — increasing spending, particularly for
the military, while reducing taxes — has through its incredible deficits brought about an America of grave social tensions at home
and diminished respect abroad.

Monetary policy — too loose in 1972–1973, too tight in 1974–
1975, too loose in 1977–1978, too tight in 1980–1982, and always
shielded from democratic accountability, contributed mildly to inflation and hugely to unemployment.

Microeconomic policy, such as it was, was worse than useless. It
was either wrong-headed (witness an industrial policy that concentrated on the military-industrial complex), poorly administered and
quickly withdrawn (witness the brief 1971–1972 Nixon incomes
policy), or nonexistent (witness the disdain for credit conservation
while enormous shares of the nation's scarce credit were diverted

to speculation in the stock and futures markets, corporate take-overs, and attempts to corner commodities markets).

The trouble with our performance in the last twenty years has not been the dearth of sensible economic ideas: there they were all the time, on the table. Nor is the blame to be put entirely on the political actors: there were always a few philosopher kings on hand, however frustrated. Nor yet is the fault to be laid on the voters: how were *they* to resolve the legislative-executive deadlock, to pierce the ectoplasm of the Federal Reserve, to perceive Economic Truth amid the discord of self-interested advice?

No, the failure of our economics in the last twenty years is due primarily to shortcomings in our political structure. The fact is that our leaders in the last generation have been the best educated in our history and that advances in communications have made public scrutiny closer than at any earlier time. Rather than curse the darkness of our politicians and our public, therefore, let us take a closer look at our political structure. Let us ask whether that structure is really adequate to fulfil its role as the equal partner with economics in a successful *political* economy.

I doubt that it is.

How Political Structure Frustrates Economics

In fiscal policy, since 1981 the administration and at least one house of the Congress have been controlled by different parties. Each branch blames the other for the continuing failure to bring the budget under control. Yet the governmental deadlock, the root of our domestic and foreign deficits, has persisted to the brink of disaster.

In monetary policy, alone among the world's democracies our institutions keep policy insulated from democratic control. Though the Federal Reserve is "independent" from the executive, the executive can and does manipulate the Fed in ways for which it escapes accountability. The Fed's seven-person Board of Governors is so large and amorphous that accountability is impossible. For the most important monetary tool, open-market operations, the voice of officialdom is diluted by the presence on the Open Market Committee of five private citizens genially selected by commercial bankers, whose interests are by no means necessarily identical with those of the public.

In microeconomic policy, and in the coordination of all economic policies, the nation lacks an authoritative institutional voice. The Council of Economic Advisers speaks for the President, and the Joint Economic Committee and various other committees for the Congress. But under our political system of separation of powers, there is no one equipped to speak for the broad public interest, as is, say, the Economic Council in the Federal Republic of Germany. The result, to put it plainly, is mush. And in international economics, the industrial democracies lack an institution that can speak authoritatively for the common interest that must be weighed along with the narrow national interests of those who assemble every year at the summit.

Let us now look in more detail at how our political structure frustrates sensible economics, and at what a political economist, upset that the best-laid economic schemes nowadays gang aft agley, might suggest to improve that structure.

Fiscal Policy: The Deficit Deadlock

Consider, first, fiscal policy. The tendency of our government to deadlock and stasis has grown in the last twenty years in tandem — and not by coincidence — with its loss of control over the fisc.

In large part, stalemate stems from split party control between the President and Congress. The Founders deliberately chose the checks and balances inherent in divided but shared powers — legislate, filibuster, veto, override, declare unconstitutional — in order to forestall the tyranny that might ensue if all powers were lodged in one branch, as under the parliamentary system. They were also opposed to political parties as divisive "factions," as James Madison called them, and made no mention of them in the Constitution.

But the Founders shortly discovered that something was needed to achieve coordination between the polarized Congress and President. So they promptly, with Madison in the lead, created national political parties — Hamilton's and Adams's Federalists versus Jefferson's and Madison's Democratic-Republicans. The President became the *de facto* leader of his congressional majority.

For a century and a half, the party system acted as a centripetal harmonizer for a centrifugal system of checks and balances. Up to 1900 a newly elected President, except for Fillmore, Hayes, and Cleveland, always had a majority of his own party in Congress. Through 1950 there was one-party government, executive and legislature, more than 75 percent of the time. Only with Eisenhower in 1956 did an incoming President face a Congress with both parties in hostile hands. In the crucial last twenty years, there has been one-party government only 20 percent of the time. In 1900 only 4 percent of congressional districts elected a President and a congressman of different parties; in 1984, 45 percent did so.

Today's divided governments coincide with the decline of our political parties. That decline, probably irreversible, stems from many causes. The now almost universal open primary means that the power of nomination passes from party leaders, otherwise known as "bosses" in smoke-filled rooms, to the electorate. That staple of party power, patronage, went out with advancing civil service. That other staple, the political Thanksgiving turkey or January scoop of coal to induce loyalty on Election Day, fell victim to public welfare.

Cohesion between President and Congress was further weakened by the rise in cost of political campaigns and by the substitution of special-interest political action committees for party treasuries as an important source of campaign funds. TV, radio, direct computerized mailings, and professional campaign assistance are all prodigiously expensive. In 1986, $400 million was spent on congressional campaigns alone. To make matters worse, the Supreme Court in *Buckley* v. *Valeo,* 1976, held that Congress may not constitutionally impose any overall limits whatever on what may be spent in a congressional campaign. Contributors prefer to contribute directly, or through a Political Action Committee, to the candidate so as to give the message undiluted. Their recipients no longer need, nor much heed, the party.

Finally, ballot-splitting has become a popular American pastime. With the programs of the parties no longer generating much confidence in the voter, why not split your ticket and at least obtain an insurance policy against being too badly put upon? Indeed, recent polls indicate that Americans at one and the same time demand a wide variety of governmental services, a view usually associated

with the Democrats, and believe their federal government too big
and too intrusive, a view usually associated with the Republicans.
Accordingly, they've been voting recently for a Republican for
President and Democrats for Congress.

Nowhere is the failure of deadlock-prone government more de-
structive than on the budget question. For even if fiscal control
were imposed tomorrow, lasting damage will have been visited upon
the economy.

A Special Election to Resolve Deadlocks

What could be done to lessen our propensity toward deadlock?
Modern economists have deservedly won laurels for working up
economic concepts of the multiplier, input-output analysis, the
wage-price guidepost, the penalty asset reserve requirement. Why
shouldn't a political economist equally put his mind on political
concepts of how to make fiscal policy work in a democracy?

The proposal I am about to make — for involving the electorate
in democratic deadlock-resolving under our system of separated
but shared powers — is presented not so much to elicit approval
as to suggest one approach that political economy might take.

The proposal is for a constitutional amendment which would
make possible a special election for new terms for President and
Congress where a serious stalemate persists. Such a national election could be called either by the President or by either house. If
this were deemed too destabilizing, both houses of Congress could
be required as the caller of the special election; or a vote by an
extraordinary majority could be stipulated; or the special election
could be restricted to the second and third years of a four-year
term.

Whatever the details, the threat of a special election could put
both parties to the deadlock under pressure either to compromise
or to refine their side of the question into an issue for the voters at
the upcoming special election.

It would be tidier if this amendment could be accompanied by
another amendment changing House terms to four years, running
at the same time as the President, and the Senate to eight years,
with half the candidates running in presidential years. True, this
would eliminate the present off-year congressional election, which

often simply makes the deadlock worse. But the availability of a special election *if needed* arguably compensates for the elimination. Another amendment — which should be made in any event — would repeal the Twenty-second Amendment, which restricts the President to two terms.

The proposal would by no means impose a parliamentary system, with its legislative supremacy. President and Congress would continue to be separately elected, and the voters could still split their ballots if they wished.

Suppose the proposed system had been in effect in the eighties. I believe that at some point public opinion would have compelled the Democrats, as the loyal opposition, to pull themselves together and in a coherent way to challenge Reaganomics. Both parties would have had to hold out a party platform and a tentative party presidential candidate and to be ready for a short election campaign, such as ninety days — not a bad idea in itself. Now, it is perfectly possible that the voters in this hypothetical election might have returned Ronald Reagan. But then the responsibility would have rested not in their movie stars, but in themselves.

We are still celebrating the bicentennial of our constitutional system. Part of that system is the power of amendment — what Jefferson had in mind when he said, "Each generation has the right to choose for itself that form of government it believes most promotive of its own happiness." To consider constitutional changes that would make a more perfect Union does honor to the Founding Fathers.

Making the Monetary Mechanism More Democratic and Accountable

Another area where political structure collides with sensible economics is our monetary policy mechanism. The Federal Reserve possesses at least three grave structural defects.

The first is its seven-person Board of Governors. This is simply too many. Hardly anyone can reel off the names of the members. Where so many are responsible, responsibility cannot be fixed. The statute setting up the system should be amended by cutting down the membership to no more than three, or, better, to one, as in almost every other major central bank.

A second defect is the presence on the twelve-member Open Market Committee, which conducts the most important monetary operation, of five presidents of the regional Federal Reserve banks. It is ridiculous that the five consist of one representative, always, of the New York Fed; one representative, every other year, of the Cleveland and Chicago Feds; and one representative, every third year, of those lower orders, the Feds of Boston, Philadelphia, Richmond, Atlanta, Dallas, St. Louis, Minneapolis, Kansas City, and San Francisco.

These representatives are selected by the member commercial banks of each district and are not public officials at all. Incidentally, this violates the mandate of Article II, Section 2, Clause 2 of the Constitution providing that "officers of the United States" must be appointed by the President and confirmed by the Senate. Yet here they are, voting in 1981 and 1982 for open-market policies which threw three million Americans out of work, without such appointment and confirmation. Other congressmen and I over the years have blunted our spears in federal court litigation we brought to have the Open Market Committee deprivatized. The courts, bless them, held we lacked legal standing to sue, and that we should get Congress to change the present law if we didn't like it — something easier said than done.

A proper Federal Reserve reform act would eliminate the non-officer members from official decision-making, though carefully preserving their opportunity to give advice.

The third Federal Reserve defect has to do with the abuse of its much-touted independence. The Fed, as a creature of Congress, is subject to its ultimate control, although Congress wisely leaves it to its own day-to-day operations.

The Fed, however, has traditionally been independent of the executive. I am still not convinced that ending "independence" and making the Fed part of the Treasury would be wise. But "independence" has frequently been used by both the Fed and the executive as a sort of shell game to escape responsibility. This is inevitable under the present practice whereby administrations give the Fed private "hints" on how to conduct its monetary affairs.

Some examples are instructive. During the great Treasury-Fed feud of 1951 about whether the Fed had to support the Treasury bond market, President Truman had a dramatic secret meeting with the Fed at the White House, after which the White House issued a press release thanking the Fed for pledging "its support to President Truman to maintain the stability of government securities." The Fed promptly leaked a denial. Nobody was edified.

In 1982 President Reagan called Fed chairman Paul Volcker to the White House for a private consultation, allegedly to request a further bout of tight money. In the fall of 1987 the Fed kept getting two conflicting messages from the administration: from the Council of Economic Advisers, to tighten money, and from the Treasury, to loosen money. And in February 1988, Fed chairman Alan Greenspan complained to Congress about Assistant Treasury Secretary Michael Darby's sending to Fed officials on the eve of a monetary meeting a warning against a decline in M2, one of the monetarists' guiding stars.

Of course, monetary policy is a legitimate concern of the Administration. But when it states its views, they should be on the record, not an off-stage mutter. A Federal Reserve reform act might thus well provide that the President should state in writing, for the published record of every Open Market Committee meeting, the administration's position on current important monetary action. Then the Fed could follow or dissent as it wished. But at least the public could hold its servants accountable.

A Truly Independent Economic Council

A third area of political economy also needs attention. The Council of Economic Advisers, whatever its 1946 congressional sponsors may have envisaged as its independent role, has long since become a mere economic arm of the administration. The Council, and its staff, are certainly needed. But perhaps the time has come to rename it, or them, as the President's Economic Adviser, and to set up a nonpartisan, independent, long-term-or-for-life Council on Political Economy. Its three or five members could be appointed, say, one to a President, with congressional confirmation by both houses as in the case of a successor vice president under the Twenty-fifth Amendment. Qualifications would be ability, stature as political economists, and integrity. Its members could hold outside positions not involving a conflict. Its duty would be to report to the public in timely fashion on the economic state of the nation. One could hope that its lofty pulpit would enable it to speak truly of new economic fads which in the future may be offered as successors to old ones like free silver, the commodity dollar, supply-side economics, rational expectations, and monetarism.

A Voice for the Common Interest
in International Economics

Nowhere is the political structure more inadequate than in international economics. For a decade now, the leaders of the great industrialized democracies — Britain, France, Germany, Italy, Japan, Canada, the United States — have been meeting at annual economic summits to consider the problems of growth, trade, money, and aid. Nothing much has come from it. The United States insists on its right to stand tall by having the rest of the world prop it up; Japan wants to continue its export surpluses forever; Germany remembers its 1923 inflation; France still likes gold; conservative Ottawa is reluctant to criticize conservative Washington. But no one speaks for the common interest, as opposed to the narrow interests of each nation.

One way of energizing the international political economy would be to link the Summits with an invigorated Organization for Economic Cooperation and Development. Founded in 1961, and with the twenty-three industrialized democracies as its members, the OECD is long on economic savvy but short on influence. Why not give it an organic link to the annual Summits; endow it with a commission of three or five distinguished and disinterested political economists from the member nations able to make public recommendations for the common good to the summiteers; fortify it with a consultative assembly of parliamentarians from the member countries to debate economic issues and thus contribute to public education? Some "adaptive reuse," as for other historic structures, may be just what the OECD needs.

As Galbraith has been pointing out, the problems of political economy have fallen unattended between economics and politics. The time for a new synthesis is now.

William G. Shepherd [1]

On the Nature of Monopoly

GALBRAITH'S DISCUSSIONS of economic power are an important part of his contribution to economics. The work may not appear to fit neatly within the mainstream field of "industrial organization," but I will show here that his ideas do fit well within that research tradition.

They also continue to influence the wider public debates about power in the U.S. economy. Galbraith has stressed that large corporations often influence or control their markets. The power is not unlimited: in 1952 he advanced the concept of "countervailing power," by which large buyers or suppliers may neutralize the market power held by large oligopoly firms. He has also emphasized the "techno-structure," at the core of the military-industrial complex. He has urged that public enterprise be developed further, to mitigate the effects of private power. And he has warned that ideas and research should not be limited to the bounds set by neoclassical analysis and "arcane" theorizing.

In the meantime, since 1970 three "new IO theory" schools have emerged: (1) a neo-Chicago-UCLA School, which focuses on three "efficient-structure" hypotheses, (2) "contestability" theory, an extreme case within the wider study of entry and barriers, and (3) short-run Cournot-Nash modeling of duopolies. Their exponents have sought to lead the field, and U.S. policies, in precisely the opposite directions from those favored by Galbraith and others in the mainstream.

The new schools have both enhanced and weakened the mainstream field, in various specific ways which this paper will assess.

Even more confidently than in the 1890s, 1920s, and 1950s, eminent analysts have developed an apologetics for monopoly power. The claim is that monopoly's scope is minor and its effects are beneficial, not harmful.

In fact, "new IO theory" is really a separate, parallel field, a branch of neoclassical theory.[2] It explores special cases and pure models, as distinct from the mainstream of complex market conditions. Its authors have claimed that "new IO theory" displaces the established mainstream field. Instead, much of it is like academic music, which pursues formalism and exotic variations, isolated from the vast flow of classical and popular music.

Galbraith and the mainstream can usefully be assessed in comparison with the "new IO theory" schools. I will note several weaknesses of those "new" ideas, along with some strengths. The neo-Chicago–UCLA "efficiency hypotheses" are assessed in sections III and IV, and entry barriers and "contestability" are treated in section V. But first, section I restates the nature of effective competition as a process, and section II summarizes the main lines of the mainstream field as it had developed for over a century.

I. Effective Competition

1. The Role of Competitive Parity

For a century the field has debated the nature of effective competition. Are two firms enough, as some neo-Chicago–UCLA analysts say? Does "perfect contestability" nullify monopoly, so that *one* firm is enough? Or is effective competition just a comparison of costs, as in many duopoly models?

Effective competition is actually much more complex, and its effects occur in several dimensions rather than just the static efficiency covered in most "new IO theory." Among the many forms and degrees of competition, many are ineffective.

Effective competition requires strong mutual pressure applied among comparable rivals on a basis of *competitive parity*.[3] At each point in the sequence of competitive episodes, the numerous rivals can apply the same array of competitive devices, and they each have approximately the same prospects of winning in each episode. All firms can assert and defend themselves effectively.[4]

Each firm seeks to defeat all of its competitors, of course, but its

FIGURE 1

FIGURE 1

*The basic relationship between market share
and profit rate.*

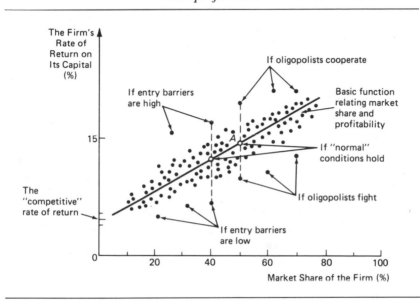

impacts are absorbed by the totality of competitors, without causing any efficient ones to fail. Each competitive episode may be highly
complex, but winning occurs only by superior performance. The
structure of rewards is embodied in differential rates of profitability, as shown by the function relating rates of return on assets to
market shares (let us call it the MS-RR function). As illustrated in
Figure 1, it has been confirmed by extensive research since 1970.

Competitive parity is therefore fundamental for effective competition in markets, as is also true in sports competition.[5] But while
sports leagues minutely control the competitive setting with extreme thoroughness so as to assure parity, some "new IO" theorists
appear to be indifferent to parity in real markets.

2. Market Dominance as Ineffective Competition

"Competition" between mismatched firms can be as meaningless
as it is between mismatched athletes and teams.

In general, *market dominance prevents effective competition,* because parity is absent and firms are mismatched. The leading firm has over 40 to 50 percent of the market, and there is no close rival.[6] The dominant firm can eliminate any small rival it chooses, at any given time, or possibly all of them. This power is, of course, much greater than whatever the little rivals possess.

That is because the dominant firm can deploy competitive weapons which are unavailable to the little rivals. Dominant firms face only light pressure, and they are not forced to perform well, while small rivals face extreme pressure and risk. Therefore, competition is ineffective and performance is inferior.

3. An Unstable Process?

Moreover, the imbalance may continue or accentuate, rather than correct itself. *Effective competition may be an unstable case.* The MS-RR function links the reward structure to market structure. If it is robust, with high profit yields to increases in market share, then it can generate dominance. Each period's profits expand the firm's abilities to defeat competitors in later periods. By a ratchet effect, a steep MS-RR function makes competition more prone to degenerate toward monopoly, even if there are no underlying economies of scale or superior efficiency.

Against this cumulation toward dominance, there are several important constraints. For one, all firms are trying for monopoly at the same time, and so they may collectively constrain each other: that, precisely, is effective competition.

More broadly, there is a *general process of decay,* which erodes high market shares. My own estimates are that market shares above 60 percent tend to decline at about one point per year, on average, while Paul Geroski puts the rate at only about one-half point per year. The decay is real, but rather slow.

Another constraint is *technical diseconomies of scale.* Estimates which *don't* filter out pecuniary economies suggest that there are wide ranges of constant costs in many industries. If there are significant *pecuniary* economies, then genuine diseconomies may be significant.

The third constraint is the dominant firm's own tendency toward *X-inefficiency and a retardation of innovation.* That will reinforce the tendency toward the erosion of dominance.

Each actual market structure, at each moment, therefore exists in a state of tension, as each firm makes choices guided by the marginal yields and penalties of additional market share. Effective competition is defined mainly by market shares, which indicate the *state* of competitive parity among a significant number of rivals, at each moment. The *process* of effective competition requires renewing this parity for successive episodes.

Unfortunately, the neo-Chicago–UCLA and "contestability" schools have focused mainly on cases of ineffective competition, as I will discuss soon.

II. The Mainstream Field

But first, I need to review briefly the mainstream field. The common "new IO" myth is that the field in 1970 was still primitive, merely "descriptive," and embodying only a simple-minded "structuralism." Since about 1970, the myth goes, "new IO theory" has rescued the field from its own vacuity.

That is quite wrong: nearly a century of extensive research had accumulated a thorough, vigorous, often sophisticated assemblage of research, and the work has continued. Of course, there were many unsettled issues as of 1970, and much less formalism than the "new IO theory." But there was also a massive volume and variety of debate and evidence, some of it quite sophisticated. Nowadays, when "new IO" papers mainly cite each other and seem ignorant of virtually every source before 1970, it is important to cure the amnesia that has gripped much of the field. Only by ignoring the mainstream field can the current "new IO theorists" offer their "insights" as important new discoveries.

1. Beginnings
The modern study of competition and monopoly began in the 1880s.[7] Its concepts began to be deeply and firmly set with work by John Bates Clark, Henry Carter Adams, Richard T. Ely, and Charles J. Bullock, among many others. Most of the current ideas at the center of the field — degrees of monopoly, actual and potential competition, the efficiency and other effects of monopoly, economies and diseconomies of scale, oligopoly, price discrimina-

tion, first-mover advantages, the importance of innovation, dynamic processes, overhead costs, risk and uncertainty — had been discussed extensively by 1925. American economists (Clark, Ely, Adams, Bullock, Frank H. Knight, J. M. Clark and others) had advanced the literature far, and the concepts had been applied to a large number of major industries.[8]

The 1930s initiated more complex theoretical study (e.g., Chamberlin, Robinson, Neumann and Morgenstern), extensive statistical research of concentration, costs and profits, the TNEC investigations of 1939–1941, and the formation of the field's basic conceptual design. Structure was seen as influencing behavior and performance, though not rigidly or hermetically.

Stocking and Watkins assembled detailed assessments of cartels and monopoly conditions, both in foreign and domestic markets. Fritz Machlup (1952, 1952) published comprehensive, sophisticated assessments of monopoly, strategic actions, and public policies. By the early 1950s, Stigler (1955) could assemble a wide range of scholarship on major branches of the field, including Adelman's path-breaking evaluation of vertical integration. Joe S. Bain's work on barriers emerged in 1956, Simon Whitney surveyed some twenty industries in 1958, and Kaysen and Turner in 1959 provided comprehensive, subtle analysis of the tight-oligopoly problem. Many case studies had accumulated, both by treatises and antitrust cases.

The 1960s brought many broad-scale econometric studies of structure and performance, by Weiss, myself, Scherer, Comanor and Wilson, and others. Williamson led the development of micro-micro aspects of firm behavior. Leibenstein's X-efficiency concept debuted in 1966. Edwin Mansfield and his associates prepared extensive studies of innovation, and Scherer's work in the mid-1960s was important (see the collection of his papers in Scherer, 1986). Scherer's survey treatise on the entire field appeared in 1970. Moreover, public-utility economics — with lengthy study of profit and price-cost criteria — had undergone sharp changes in the 1960s, and Alfred E. Kahn's classic volumes on it appeared in 1971.

In short, there was a large accumulation of knowledge and technical skills, combining theory, econometrics, cases, and policy issues. There was vigorous debate among many schools and research methodologies, and no orthodoxy prevailed. Meanwhile, antitrust and regulatory policies were mostly moderate (for example, the prospect of a Bell System divestiture was scarcely conceivable, and the deregulation of railroads and airlines was only a faint hope).[9]

2. Main Lessons

The mainstream learning can be summarized as follows:

a. *Competition promotes several main values,* including (1) X-efficiency, (2) Innovation, (3) *Competition itself as a process,* (4) Fairness, and (5) Freedom of choice.[10] Any limitation of normative analysis to just static efficiency is arbitrary and narrow.

b. *Causation runs mainly from structure to behavior to performance.* The partial MS-RR relationship, as illustrated in Figure 1, has been amply confirmed in many statistical settings. Much of it reflects market imperfections and market power, as dominant firms use price discrimination and other techniques to generate excess returns. It takes only moderate conditions of demand elasticity for price discrimination to yield high average rates of return.[11]

But random elements are large, and differential performance can influence structure in some cases. Also, much of the scatter around the MS-RR regression reflects the varieties of oligopoly structure and behavior, as well as entry behavior, as Figure 1 indicates. In the recent flood of oligopoly theory, determinate results are achieved only by adopting short-run Cournot-Nash assumptions and focusing on static efficiency. That severely restricts the generality of the results.

c. *High market shares can come from many types of market imperfections, as well as superior efficiency.* Mainstream research demonstrated a wide array of imperfections, as codified concisely in Table 1. They permit average or inferior firms to obtain dominance.

A robust MS-RR function sets a presumption that monopoly power, reflecting the imperfections, is the main cause. It can be overcome by positive evidence that scale economies or superior performance are sufficiently large.

d. *Potential competition is usually a peripheral matter,* with less significance than conditions of direct competition inside the market. Exceptional cases (such as a small market overshadowed by a known, very large, and powerful potential entrant) are rare and usually unimportant.

TABLE 1

Nine Categories of Market Imperfections

1. *Pecuniary gains* may arise from access to cheaper inputs, including capital, permitting supra-normal profits not based on technical economies.
2. *Irrationalities, lags, and uncertainties* may exist among producers and/or consumers, permitting strategic advantages not attributable to economic efficiency.
3. *Consumer loyalties* may be instilled or accentuated by advertising and other marketing activities, which alter buyers' preferences.
4. *Markets may be segmented,* so that price discrimination can be used to extend and sustain monopoly power. Segmentation violates the single-good, single-price assumptions of the pure-market case. It can prevent effective competition by rivals in the whole of the market.
5. *Differences in access to knowledge* may skew the pattern of innovation. Dominant firms may influence the flows of knowledge about technology so as to limit their rivals' innovation.
6. *Controls on key inputs* (ores, locations, specific personnel) may be held and used so as to exclude competitors.
7. *Barriers to new competition* may occur naturally or be developed artificially, both at the market's edges and within the market.
8. *Strategic actions* of many kinds, including threats, may be used to gain and defend monopoly positions. They may create non-efficiency advantages or merely exploit existing ones.
9. *Transactions costs and "asset specificity"* may be large enough to impair perfect adjustment processes.

Mainstream research since 1970 has been extensive, including a renewed focus on market share as a main indicator of market power.[12] Other important research directions include Scherer and associates on the economies of scale, Williamson on transactions costs, Leibenstein and others on X-efficiency, Michael Porter on enterprises' competitive strategies, many econometric studies of profitability and structure, Dennis Mueller and Ravenscraft and Scherer on mergers, my assessment of the trend of competition, and scores of case studies.[13]

3. Galbraith

As for Galbraith, his position in this mainstream flow is among those stressing that market power is large, especially in the case of large oligopolists which control their markets. Demand is manipulated and stabilized by the producers in their own interests. Countervailing power can develop to neutralize this power, but it fails to do so in many sectors, especially the weapons sector.

Galbraith also speaks of a dual economy, in which large firms have power but little ones don't. Research suggests that there are important exceptions to this: large firms have little power if they are in large, loosely oligopolistic industries, and many small firms hold petty monopoly power in small, local markets.

In part, events have changed the situation since the 1950s, when U.S. corporate power was at its most extensive. Tight oligopoly has shrunk by half since then, and many large firms have encountered un-Galbraithian turbulence.[14] But much of this change occurred precisely because U.S. firms' market power had led them into inefficiency and slowed innovation, which invited the corrective of massive import competition. The initial analysis of market power was correct, and substantial amounts of market power still remain.

In all, Galbraith's views are probably correct for about 85 percent of the economy. That is a higher rating of relevance than is achieved by the "new IO" schools which are reviewed in the next sections. Moreover, Galbraith has relied on realistic judgment applied to the central problems rather than solely on formal theory, applied as an exercise to obtain "insights."

III. The Three "New IO Theory" Schools

Now compare the three strands of "new IO theory," which have emerged since 1970. Their perfect-market assumptions diverge from mainstream industrial organization, where market *impurities* are the central research problem.

1. Neo-Chicago–UCLA

In the 1950s, the neo-Chicagoans, led by George Stigler, Aaron Director, and Ronald Coase, reversed the original Chicago School's sophisticated, pessimistic realism to a new basis of dogmatic free-market optimism.[15] After 1970, Harold Demsetz at UCLA and others carried it further. The full neo-Chicago–UCLA position, developed primarily by Demsetz, Brozen, McGee and Peltzman, involves one factual claim plus three categorical hypotheses.[16] The factual claim is that monopoly is rare, weak, and transient. The hypotheses are:

Hypothesis 1: Dominance arises only from superior efficiency. Therefore, *causation runs from performance to structure:* superior innovation or management gives a firm higher profits and, incidentally, market dominance. The mainstream structure-to-performance logic is therefore reversed to a performance-to-structure direction. Higher concentration is advocated, because any monopoly harms from it will be offset by efficiency benefits.

Hypothesis 2: Because all concentration represents superior efficiency, the only remaining kind of genuine monopoly power is collusion among oligopolists. The only monopolizing actions are ones which "facilitate collusion." Yet that collusion is weak and transient, collapsing quickly from internal conflicts and cheating.

Hypothesis 3: Monopolists do not obtain monopoly profits, because they must spend heavily in advance on costly monopoly-seeking activities. Once the monopoly position is obtained, then only rent can be captured rather than monopoly profits.

A Series of Defeats. These views gained a certain degree of popularity in the 1980s, particularly among officials in the Reagan administration.[17] But oddly enough, they actually represent a last resort, after a series of defeats by the neo-Chicago–UCLA School on each major issue since the 1950s.

First, Stigler and others said in the early 1950s that competition was nearly ubiquitous in the U.S. economy.[18] That was disproven.[19] Then they asserted that any actual monopoly power will tend to decay rapidly.[20] That was shown to be an exaggeration.[21]

They said that the economies of scale were large enough to justify most important cases of market dominance.[22] Bain, Scherer, Pratten, Weiss, and others disproved that general claim.[23] Neo-Chicagoans also tried to deny that market structure is related to profitability, because concentration ratios relate only loosely to price-cost margins.[24] But econometric research soon showed that individual market shares are strongly related to profit rates and other measures of monopoly gains.[25]

Finally, neo-Chicago–UCLA writers hazarded a kind of last-resort idea. Demsetz, McGee, and Brozen suggested Hypotheses 1 and 2, and Posner (following Tullock) offered Hypothesis 3. Robert Bork and others cast them as absolutes. Each hypothesis may apply in some degree so some markets, but these *possibilities* came to be stated as *certainties*.[26]

2. Contestability

The field's interest in potential competition began in the 1880s, with John Bates Clark, who by 1901 stressed that potential competition was the crucial condition restraining monopolies.[27] Much later (in 1956), Bain developed the topic in detail, followed by numerous others. An extreme theoretical case was advanced in 1982 by the "contestability" group, led by William J. Baumol.[28] In markets with ultra-free entry, the power of potential entry wholly supersedes the market's internal conditions (of structure, behavior, and performance) in guaranteeing an efficient outcome. Their centerpiece case is the entry-nullified pure monopoly.

3. Duopoly Modeling and Strategic Analysis

The new-wave oligopoly modeling is commonly based on short-run Cournot-Nash assumptions, using strictly static consumer-surplus normative criteria. It relies on pure theory, with little or no empirical testing or fitting to real cases. It focuses on issues which can be framed in determinate models, usually in a short-run context.[29] It assumes that the firms' choices are strictly independent, rather than cooperative.

Taken together, these three "new IO" lines of theory have provided advances in technique. But there are costs. "New IO" theory is claimed to replace mainstream research rather than to complement it. Theorists now teach "IO Theory" under the name of "industrial organization" in many departments. The theories are virtually untested against real markets or business experience.

The "new IO" schools not only ignore the field's research content, they also tend to deny that monopoly is important. Such "new" apologetics for monopoly have risen and ebbed before: in the 1890s, led by defenders of the new trusts; in the 1920s, and in the 1950s. Each time a "new" learning was asserted, but it primarily restated the interests of large firms. The recent "new IO" schools have been technically more formidable, but their effect is largely the same as before.

Some of the "new IO" analysis arose from activity sponsored by large US companies (e.g., IBM and AT&T), which were resisting antitrust challenges.[30] The defensive technique was to attack the mainstream concepts of competition and monopoly, profitability criteria, and other standard concepts.

Their partisan background need not disqualify the ideas, which should be judged on their merits. But they do suggest why monopoly-defending doctrines have been vigorously advanced.

IV. Evaluating the
Neo-Chicago–UCLA Hypotheses

The issue is whether the three hypotheses explain all market shares rather than just some or a few. Consider first one deductive point, and then (briefly) some evidence.

1. Logic: Pure Assumptions and Internal Conflicts

The basic neo-Chicago–UCLA assumptions are pure. Perfect-market conditions are assumed, including perfect knowledge and foreknowledge and instant, frictionless adjustment in single-product, single-price markets. All of the imperfections listed in Table 1 are assumed away. Accordingly, all three hypotheses are valid, but as tautologies. Instead of explaining the degree of superiority, the hypothesis merely assumes that it is complete.

Even more seriously, there is a fallacy at the core of Hypothesis 1, which also infects Hypothesis 2. Superior performance can explain market dominance only if the superiority lasts for significant intervals of time, while the superior firm prospers, grows, and gains dominance. If the firm's superiority does not persist for these sustained intervals, then superior efficiency cannot be explained by the creation of dominance.

Yet that persistence creates a logical conflict, *because any significant persistence is excluded by the ideal-market assumptions underlying the hypothesis.* Innate superiority is subject to immediate, total elimination by the ideal market process itself. Superiority can be sustained only if there are imperfections, such as those in Table 1!

Superiority is eliminated in two main ways. First, market competition bids up the prices of superior factors or hires them away so that cost differences cease to exist. Second, superior products and processes are immediately matched or copied by other firms.

Therefore, the efficient-structure hypothesis contains a fallacy. Superiority can create dominance if market processes are *imperfect.* Yet imperfections have been assumed away. Either there are imperfections or there aren't. The efficient-structure theorists have been trying to have it both ways, but that makes their hypothesis vacuous. The basic issues of monopoly's effects and of performance-to-structure causation require careful research, not tautological, flawed theory.

By the same logic, Hypothesis 2 is also vacuous. Monopoly positions can reflect nonefficiency causes and have distorting effects. In fact, multifirm collusion is only a diluted form of single-firm dominance; collusion cannot have stronger effects than dominance, and it will commonly have weaker effects. Collusion is prey to disintegrative forces, while the dominant firm's unified control is tighter, and its effects can be more thorough, complex, and refined. Dominant firms' structures of discriminatory prices and strategic actions are more precise and complete.

Therefore, collusion is not the exclusive form of monopoly power, but rather the lesser, weaker form.

As for Hypothesis 3, I have space only to note that an advance dissipation of precisely all monopoly profits would be a fluke. The research question remains how large that effect is, and there has been virtually no supporting evidence that it is important.

2. Some Evidence

Turning to evidence on Hypotheses 1 and 2, a brief comment on some basic evidence may be helpful.[31] The evidence is mainly the familiar regressions of large U.S. corporation profit rates against various elements of market structure. A number of colleagues and I have been developing and retesting these patterns since 1970, and they are now recognized to be well established.

The debate has been mainly about their meaning: what proportions of monopoly power versus efficiency does the MS-RR function reflect?[32] In the great variety of case evidence (e.g., IBM, Eastman Kodak, Kellogg's) sustained superiority explains only a minority of dominance in important markets. Imperfections and monopolizing actions are probably important.

The presumption, therefore, is that much, perhaps most, of the estimated MS-RR functions represents market power. Recent regressions in Table 2 can serve to illustrate; they cover large U.S. manufacturing corporations during 1960–1969.[33] Some more recent preliminary results for 1980–1984 are given in Table 3.[34] Profitability is represented both by reported rates of return on equity capital (lines 1, 2, 3, 4, and 5 in Table 2), and by the estimated ratio of the market value of company stock to its book value (Tobin's q). Both measures give similar econometric results.

The focus is on line 2 in Table 2 and lines 1 and 3 in Table 3. Market share has a substantial slope and high statistical significance, while four-firm concentration's coefficient is not significant. If the strict Chicago School assumptions hold, then the evidence is not inconsistent with both Hypotheses 1 and 2. But of course it cannot "prove" the validity of Hypothesis 1.

More probably, the market-share coefficient reflects significant monopoly effects, while collusion plays an insignificant additional role. Dominance would therefore be the prime form of monopoly power, while collusion is much weaker.

Barriers, meanwhile, play a secondary role. At most, high barriers may enhance profit rates by about three points (the coefficient under "High Barriers"), but that is much smaller than dominance, which can add twelve to seventeen points to profit rates.

In short, only by extreme and implausible assumptions could these results be said to support the neo-Chicago–UCLA hypotheses. As further empirical testing continues, startling new evidence might emerge to reverse the weight of mainstream findings. But so far the evidence in that direction is minor.

V. Potential Entry and Barriers, Including "Contestability"

Baumol, Willig, and others present "contestability" theory as replacing the mainstream's core concepts, and they have testified in important antitrust and regulatory cases that the theory is widely accepted and can settle practical issues decisively. Is "contestability" merely a "new IO theory," or might it revolutionize the mainstream field or at least enter it? The main issues it raises may be familiar by now, but I find that two points (a logical flaw and robustness) need more comment.

TABLE 2
Regression Analysis of Profitability and q, 117 Large U.S. Industrial Corporations, 1960–1969 [a]

Regression Number	Dependent Variable	Constant Term	Market Share M	Concentration C	Group $(G–M)$	Log of Asset Size	Advertising/ Sales Ratio	Barriers Medium	Barriers High	Growth	Correct R^2 (F value)
1	Profit Rate (π)	+7.69 (3.21)	+0.24 (8.42)		+0.04 (1.55)	-0.56 (1.79)	+0.26 (3.98)			+0.51 (2.09)	0.573 (32.18)
1q	q Ratio	+1.09 (1.42)	+0.06 (7.05)		+0.01 (0.79)	-0.19 (1.94)	+0.09 (4.09)			+0.27 (3.48)	0.558 (30.28)
2	π	+7.69 (3.21)	+0.20 (6.27)	+0.04 (1.55)		-0.56 (1.79)	+0.26 (3.98)			+0.51 (2.09)	0.573 (32.18)
2q	q	+1.09 (1.42)	+0.06 (5.64)	+0.01 (0.79)		-0.19 (1.94)	+0.09 (4.09)			+0.27 (3.48)	0.558 (30.28)
3	π	+3.77 (2.38)	-0.23 (6.71)	+0.02 (0.74)				+1.76 (1.88)	+2.99 (2.32)	+0.51 (1.95)	0.516 (25.70)
3q	q	-0.21 (0.41)	-0.07 (5.96)	+0.004 (0.41)				+0.26 (0.86)	+0.59 (1.40)	+0.27 (3.21)	0.475 (21.96)

Independent Variables

[a] The t-ratios are shown in parentheses. Profitability is the rate of return on book equity.
Source: adapted from Shepherd, "Tobin's q," 1986, Table 1.

TABLE 3

Structural Regressions, 95 Large U.S. Industrial Corporations, 1980–1984. Independent variable: average rate of return on equity for the designated period.[a]

Constant Term	Market Share	4-Firm Con-centration	Log of Assets	Ad/Sales Ratio	Barriers			
					High	Medium	Growth	R^2
1980–1984								
11.6	.303	−.011	−.479	.300			.962	
(3.66)	(6.98)	(−.33)	(−2.06)	(3.62)			(3.10)	.53
1980–1984								
8.0	.300	−.066			3.88	2.91	1.19	
(3.60)	(6.54)	(−1.66)			(2.67)	(2.57)	(3.57)	.49
1982–1984								
12.7	.334	−.027	−1.66	.333			.535	
(3.53)	(6.78)	(−.71)	(−2.03)	(3.55)			(1.52)	.48

[a] t-ratios are in parentheses. Ratios of 2.4 are significant at the 1 percent level.

Source: regressions by the author, using data prepared as in Shepherd, "Tobin's q," 1986.

In a "contestable" market, there is perfectly free entry *and exit* (a better term for the situation is "ultra-free entry"). Potential entry strictly controls the firm or firms already inside the market, so that not even a complete monopolist can raise its price above minimum cost without provoking total displacement by an entrant. By assumption, even a monopolist will adopt competitive behavior. Dominance ceases to be a problem, because it is assumed away.

1. Problems of Barriers and Potential Competition

Ultra-free entry is nested within the larger — and currently popular — subfield focusing on entry barriers. That subfield suffers from problems of definition and measurement which are more severe than is generally admitted. In order to consider "contestability" adequately, I will first review these wider problems.

Potential competition is a value-laden topic, because it inher-

TABLE 4

Common Causes of Entry Barriers

I. Exogenous: economic (intrinsic) causes of barriers

1. Capital requirements (related to plant and firm size, and to capital intensity)
2. Economies of scale (from both technical and pecuniary causes)
3. Product differentiation (occurring naturally among products)
4. Absolute cost advantages (from many possible causes, including differential wage rates)
5. Diversification (giving the possibility of massing and redeploying resources among branches)
6. Research and development intensity
7. High durability of firm-specific capital (giving rise to sunk costs, which make entry more risky)
8. Vertical integration (which may require entry to occur on two or more levels at once)

II. Endogenous: voluntary and strategic causes of barriers

1. Retaliation and preemptive actions (by the use of price or other devices. This category is large and varied.)
2. Excess capacity (as a basis for effective retaliation, or for threats of retaliation)
3. Selling expenses, including advertising (to increase the degree of product differentiation)
4. Patents (which provide exclusive control over technology)
5. Control over other strategic resources (such as ores, locations, specific talents, etc.)
6. "Packing the product space" (in industries with high product differentiation, as in the U.S. cereals industry)

ently diverts attention from actual competition (and monopoly) inside the market. For nearly a century, beginning with J. B. Clark, it has provided a way to minimize the importance of monopoly power.

There are four serious, possibly fatal, research questions.

(1) What Causes Barriers? The very nature of barriers is confusing. More than a dozen possible causes of barriers have been advanced, all of them plausible and possibly important. They are in two main categories, as grouped in Table 4: (I) *Exogenous* condi-

tions, which are intrinsic to the underlying conditions of the market and therefore outside the leading firms' control, and (II) *endogenous* conditions and strategic actions, which are governed by the dominant firm's own voluntary choices.

As Bain stressed, exogenous conditions are embedded in the nature of each industry, and they are governed by technology and demand. Endogenous "barriers" are entirely different, because they depend strictly on the voluntary choices made by the established firm. The firm can create barriers simply by electing (or merely threatening) to take severe actions against an entrant. Far from being concrete and lasting, those "barriers" are evanescent.

Such voluntary "barriers" are not really barriers at all. They merely reflect and express the degree of imperfections inhering in the market, which the dominant firm can exploit *against existing rivals as well as against any possible entrants.* Caves and Porter's concept of "mobility barriers" recognizes this point.[35] If those imperfections are large, then these supposed components of entry barriers will be high. But that is just semantics; imperfections will continue to exist as they are whether we call them barriers or imperfections.

So the question remains: how large are the imperfections, and can they be exploited by a leading firm? If they are significant at all, then barriers will be substantial strictly because of strategic actions by the established firm, even apart from any intrinsic, underlying causes of barriers. But such barriers also inhibit existing small rivals, and so it may not be meaningful to conceptualize them separately as barriers.

(2) Can Barriers Be Measured? Barriers cannot yet be measured with any reliability, thirty-two years after Bain's *Barriers,* and it seems unlikely that they ever will be. The strategic "barriers" are as fluid as quicksilver, while the exogenous elements of barriers are also extremely difficult to specify and measure. The eight such elements noted in Table 4 cannot be measured on well-defined scales.

Moreover, combining the elements into total estimates of barriers "height" is still a black art, not a scientific method. Should the elements be added to each other, or is each one independently sufficient to create a high barrier? Do two medium-strong elements create a high barrier? Or should the elements be multiplied by each other in some fashion, because they are strongly reinforcing?

After three decades, this question is largely untouched in the literature. Few systematic studies of actual barriers have been done, and they have not addressed or begun to solve those problems.[36] Barriers are still "estimated" as being merely "high," "medium," or "low," based largely on educated judgment. That is the source of the estimates used in Tables 2 and 3. Only limited reliance can be placed on those estimates. By Kelvin's rule, such a vague "phenomenon" does not clearly exist. Nor is there much serious research now being given to solve this inability to measure barriers.

(3) Can Potential Entrants Be Identified? The pool of potential entrants is an important determinant of entry's force. If there are few candidates in the wings, or only weak ones, then entry may exert little pressure even if barriers are low.

Yet virtually no research has been done to develop methods for identifying and assessing potential entrants.

(4) How does Entry Take Effect? Entry has been accorded a kind of special glamor. Fear of entry is said by a number of colleagues to supersede the normal fear and impacts among existing rivals.

Instead, entry should be subsumed under actual competition, because *new entry only affects existing firms by taking away their market share.* Indeed, that is the correct technical definition of the scope of entry: the loss of market share by existing firms. But that also defines the impacts of competition among existing firms. Entry is therefore merely a secondary, indirect subcategory of the common form of actual competition within the market. Rather than replace market share as the focus, entry is subsumed under it.

Taken altogether, the entry literature has involved a detour away from mainstream market conditions, built on technical illusions of newness and importance. Attention has been displaced from clear, concrete, and important patterns of actual competition to obscure notions of potential competition.

Together, entry and oligopoly have reinforced each other as detours away from a focused analysis of real market power. There is a need to recognize the continuing importance of market shares in suggesting the likely degrees of competition and performance.

2. Ultra-free Entry ("Contestability")

As a special case of entry, "contestability" shares these problems. It also contains several of its own, which so far have prevented it from illuminating important markets.

I will note here only two points.

First, the theory is logically defective at its core: its key assumptions are mutually exclusive. The theory assumes that an entrant is so small that the existing firm will not bother to react to it at all. That permits the crucial Cournot-Nash assumption that no timely response occurs so that entry is absolute. But for such absolute entry to occur, the entrant must enter on a large scale, especially if it is replacing a monopolist.

The assumptions are contradictory: entry cannot simultaneously be both trivial and total. The assumptions can be valid for highly competitive industries, where the existing firms are small and numerous. But in those markets, competition is effective already. Ultra-free entry adds little to conventional theory. But for the monopoly case, the two assumptions are fatally flawed. The showpiece nullified-monopoly result is vacuous.

I advanced this point in 1984, but Baumol, Panzar, and Willig made no response, and they have not addressed the problem since. Whether such a crippled theory merits the continuing self-praise they give it is a matter of some moment.

Second, the theory is not robust. Using competitive theory, one can examine intermediate degrees of monopoly by weighing market shares, concentration, pricing and other behavior, and profits. The impacts of competition occur over a wide range of market shares: the theory is robust.

In contrast, ultra-free entry appears to apply only in the pure case, where the three assumptions hold perfectly.

At first the Baumol group said that the theory might be robust in "almost contestable" markets, even with significant deviations from the assumptions. But research by Schwartz (1986) and others has largely established that robustness does not exist. Prices tend to rise to the monopoly level even when sunk costs are still small. Ultra-free entry apparently remains a pure theory, part of "new IO theory" rather than the mainstream field.

Other problems (such as the exclusive focus on static efficiency, ignoring innovation) are discussed elsewhere. After six years, the mainstream research results arising from the theory are still modest. Accordingly, the theory seems likely to remain as a theoretical *curiosum.*

Real Cases? (1) *Petty Monopolists in Local Markets.* "Contestability" offers some insight when a small market faces the probable entry of a powerful firm; examples include a small-town hotel or lumber yard fearing entry by a large national chain. Such petty monopolists may stay close to competitive pricing.

Local monopolists in hotels, restaurants, clothing stores, and other retail markets are therefore the natural focus for mainstream research on ultra-free entry. But they are not the core industries of the national economy, with major dominant firms. Moreover, the familiar analysis of free entry developed in the 1950s by Bain has given the same insights for three decades.

(2) *Imports* may also fit contestability. If the country is small and the volumes of foreign goods are large, then domestic monopolists may be displaced rapidly, even totally, by imports.

Yet the relevance to ultra-free entry is limited. The outside producer does not fully *enter* the market by creating new production capacity. Only its products enter the market, often by small degrees. Moreover, "exit" means merely a decline in the amounts shipped in, not a genuine closure of capacity.

VI. In Conclusion

This review of mainstream research is not intended to understate the value of creative theory nor overstate the mainstream achievements. Knowledge of competition's nature and effects is still so embarrassingly limited that every promising research opportunity may be important.

But there can be detours, amnesia, and "new" ideas which do not add to knowledge. Intellectual progress occurs as new ideas are weighed skeptically and assimilated. That "new IO theory" is less valuable than its authors claim is entirely natural; that it may on balance have decreased understanding of the world is entirely possible. Galbraith's skepticism of all "wisdom," conventional and unconventional, new and old, is an apt guide.

Altogether, the main issues in this field are little changed from earlier decades. Monopoly is still defined in part by market shares, and its various social harms can be significant. Many recent "new" concepts have long been familiar, and some have (so far) tended to displace scientific knowledge rather than enhance it.

Will the mainstream field and "new IO theory" continue to develop separately? That depends mainly on whether the new IO theorists offer concepts that are internally consistent and can be fitted to the main conditions of real markets. The efficiency-school hypotheses are not provable in their axiomatic forms, but research on the sources of dominance could be extremely valuable. Contestability appears to be less amenable to empirical verification, but perhaps it can be modified to bring it into the mainstream. Duopoly modeling may eventually be fitted to real cases, but so far many of the methods and "insights" have been formalistic rather than verifiable, just special cases giving "insights."

Research is particularly needed on the nature of effective competition, including parity among rivals. Is effective competition a specialized, unstable case? Is virtuous dominance a common fact? This involves the MS-RR function, the economies and diseconomies of scale, the rate of decay of high market shares, and the relative role of superior performance in causing high market shares.

These are the old, core issues, still requiring conceptual and empirical research. They need, along with other tools, the unconventional wisdom exemplified by Galbraith, in this field as in many others.

NOTES

1. I am indebted to William J. Baumol, Kenneth D. Boyer, Richard E. Caves, William S. Comanor, Jacques de Bandt, Henry W. de Jong, Donald J. Dewey, Eleanor M. Fox, J. Denys Gribbin, John S. Heywood, Takeo Nakao, and Don E. Waldman for discussions on these issues. I have also benefited from seminar participants at the University of Amsterdam, the University of Chicago, the University of Massachusetts, the University of Michigan, the University of Nice and the Mediterranean Summer School on Industrial Economics, the University of Southern California, and the session on this topic at the American Economic Association meetings in December 1988. Research support from the University of Massachusetts is gratefully acknowledged. This paper draws on my "On the Core Concepts of Industrial Economics," in Henry W. de Jong and William G. Shepherd, eds, *Mainstreams of Industrial Organization*, 2 vols (Dordrecht: Kluwer Academic Publishers, 1987); "Three 'Efficiency-School' Hypotheses about Market Power," *Antitrust Bulletin* 33 (Summer 1988): 395–415; and *Effective Competition*, in preparation. Several of the points are expressed in similar language in "Potential Competition versus Actual Competition," *Administrative Law Review* 1990 (in prep).

2. For recent summaries of "new IO theory," see especially Jean Tirole, *The Theory of Industrial Organization*, (Cambridge, Mass.: MIT Press, 1988); William J. Baumol, John C. Panzar, and Robert D. Willig, *Contestable Markets and the Theory of Industrial Structure* (San Diego: Harcourt Brace Jovanovich, 1982); Michael Waterson, *Eco-*

nomic Theory of Industry (Cambridge: Cambridge University Press, 1984); William Sharkey, *The Theory of Natural Monopoly* (Cambridge: Cambridge University Press, 1982); Lester Telser, *Theories of Competition* (Amsterdam: North Holland, 1988); Joseph E. Stiglitz and C. Frank Mathewson, *New Developments in the Analysis of Market Structure* (Cambridge, Mass.: MIT Press, 1986); and Alexis Jacquemin, *The New Industrial Organization* (Cambridge, Mass.: MIT Press, 1987).

3. The standard dictionary definitions of "competition" refer to rivalry among comparable competitors. In the industrial organization literature, see Joe S. Bain, *Industrial Organization*, 2nd. ed. (New York: John Wiley, 1968); George J. Stigler, *The Organization of Industry* (Homewood, Ill.: Richard D. Irwin, 1968); W. G. Shepherd, *The Economics of Industrial Organization*, 3d ed. (Englewood Cliffs, N.J.: Prentice-Hall, 1990); and F. M. Scherer, *Industrial Market Structure and Economic Performance*, 2nd. ed. (Boston: Houghton Mifflin, 1990).

4. See my "Assessing 'Predatory' Actions by Market Shares and Selectivity," *Antitrust Bulletin* 31 (Spring 1986): 1–28, and the sources in Scherer, *Industrial Market Structure*, pp. 335–40.

5. In sports, parity is absolutely fundamental and tightly regulated. Competitors are divided rigidly into leagues so that mismatches do not occur (e.g., heavyweights versus flyweights, or high school versus professional teams). Sports leagues develop elaborate internal structures and rules of the game, intended precisely to maintain parity among the athletes or teams during the competitive process. These rules are frequently adjusted as needed, because unbalanced contests lack mutual pressure: competition ceases to occur meaningfully.

6. Market dominance was a prominent topic from 1900 to 1920, following the great trust merger wave and the ensuing investigations and antitrust actions. It fell into neglect after 1920, as actions ceased and the 1930s turned the field to oligopoly. On the rather sparse recent literature on dominance, see Scherer, *Industrial Market Structure and Economic Performance;* Shepherd, *The Treatment of Market Power* (New York: Columbia University Press, 1975); Dennis C. Mueller, *Profits in the Long Run* (New York: Cambridge University Press, 1986); and Donald Hay and John Vickers, eds., *The Economics of Market Dominance* (Oxford: Basil Blackwell, 1987).

7. See John Bates Clark, "The Limits of Competition," *Political Science Quarterly* 2 (1887): 45–61; Henry C. Adams, "Trusts," in *American Economic Association, Papers and Proceedings* 5 (December 1903): 91–107; Richard T. Ely, *Monopolies and Trusts* (New York: Macmillan, 1900); Charles J. Bullock, "Trust Literature: A Survey and Criticism," *Quarterly Journal of Economics* 15 (February 1901): 167–217; Alfred Marshall, *Industry and Trade* (London: Macmillan, 1920); Frank H. Knight, *Risk, Uncertainty and Profit* (New York: Harper & Row, 1921); John M. Clark, *Studies in the Economics of Overhead Costs* (New York: Macmillan, 1922); Edward H. Chamberlin, *The Theory of Monopolistic Competition* (Cambridge, Mass.: Harvard University Press, 1933 (8th ed., 1962); Joan Robinson, *The Economics of Imperfect Competition* (London: Macmillan, 1933); and A. A. Berle and Gardiner C. Means, *The Modern Corporation and Private Property* (New York: Macmillan, 1932).

From the 1940s on, William J. Fellner, *Competition Among the Few* (New York: Knopf, 1949); Morris A. Adelman, "The Measurement of Industrial Concentration," *Review of Economics and Statistics* 33 (November 1951): 269–96; Fritz Machlup, *The Political Economy of Monopoly* and *The Economics of Sellers' Competition* (both Baltimore: Johns Hopkins Press, 1952); George J. Stigler, ed., *Business Concentration and Price Policy* (Princeton: Princeton University Press, 1955); Joe S. Bain, *Barriers to New Competition* (Cambridge, Mass.: Harvard University Press, 1956); Edward S. Mason, *Economic Concentration and the Monopoly Problem* (Cambridge, Mass.: Harvard University Press, 1957); Morris A. Adelman, *A & P: A Study in Price-Cost*

Behavior and Public Policy (Cambridge, Mass.: Harvard University Press, 1959); Carl Kaysen and Donald F. Turner, *Antitrust Policy: An Economic and Legal Analysis* (Cambridge, Mass.: Harvard University Press, 1959); Martin Shubik, *Strategy and Market Structure* (New York: Wiley, 1959); Almarin Phillips, *Market Structure, Organization and Performance* (Cambridge, Mass.: Harvard University Press, 1962); Edwin Mansfield, *The Economics of Technological Change* (New York: Norton, 1968); and F. M. Scherer's articles, reprinted later in *Innovation and Progress in Schumpeterian Perspective* (Cambridge, Mass.: MIT Press, 1986).

More recent excellent mainstream research is exemplified by Mueller, *Profits in the Long Run,* 1986, and Hay and Vickers, *Economics of Market Dominance,* 1987.

8. Major studies and antitrust actions occurred in the first wave of Sherman Act Section 2 cases, toward Standard Oil, American Tobacco, U.S. Steel, Du Pont gunpowder, International Harvester, the meat-packer oligopoly ALCOA, and even AT&T.

9. Demsetz has noted that there were proposals to deconcentrate a number of industries in the 1968–1975 period, which appeared to pose a radical threat to industrial interests. Yet those never came near to being applied, and the neo-Chicago–UCLA reaction was far out of proportion to them.

   In contrast to the moderacy of 1960s policies, extremism has been common since 1980; see Eleanor M. Fox and Lawrence A. Sullivan, "Antitrust — Retrospective and Prospective: Where Are We Coming From? Where Are We Going?" *New York University Law Review* 62 (November 1987): 936–88, and Eleanor M. Fox, "Chairman Miller, The Federal Trade Commission, Economics, and *Rashomon,*" *Law and Contemporary Problems* 50 (Autumn 1987): 33–56.

10. I stress that competition itself is an important value, though many recent theorists have denied it. From neo-Chicago–UCLA analysts, the denial is ironic, because they portray themselves as defenders of competition. Instead, their doctrines defend monopoly and discard the value of competition.

11. This is shown in my "Monopoly Profits and Economies of Scale," in John V. Craven, ed., *Industrial Organization, Antitrust and Public Policy* (Boston: Kluwer Nijhoff, 1982).

12. See, for example, Darius Gaskins, "Dynamic Limit Pricing: Optimal Pricing under Threat of Entry," *Journal of Economic Theory* 3 (1971): 306–22; William G. Shepherd, "The Elements of Market Structure," *Review of Economics and Statistics* 54 (February 1972): 25–37; Shepherd, *The Treatment of Market Power,* chapter 4; Shepherd, "Tobin's q and the Structure-Performance Relationship: Comment," *American Economic Review* 76 (December 1986): 1205–10; and Hay and Vickers, *Economics of Market Dominance,* 1987, including especially Paul Geroski's chapter, "Do Dominant Firms Decline?" pp. 143–67.

13. On economies of scale, see F. M. Scherer et al., *The Economics of Multiplant Operation* (Cambridge, Mass.: Harvard University Press, 1975); and Leonard W. Weiss, "Optimal Plant Size and the Extent of Suboptimal Capacity," in Robert T. Masson and P. David Qualls, eds., *Essays on Industrial Organization in Honor of Joe S. Bain* (Cambridge, Mass.: Ballinger, 1976). On transaction costs, see Oliver E. Williamson, *Markets and Hierarchies* (New York: Free Press, 1975). On X-efficiency, see Harvey J. Leibenstein, *Beyond Economic Man* (Cambridge, Mass.: Harvard University Press, 1976). On competitive strategies, see Michael E. Porter, *Competitive Strategy: Techniques for Analyzing Industries and Competitors* (New York: Free Press, 1980); and Porter, *Competitive Advantage: Creating and Sustaining Superior Performance* (New York: Free Press, 1985). For summaries of profitability and structure studies, see Scherer, *Industrial Market Structure,* chapter 9; Shepherd, *Economics of Industrial Organization,* chapter 4; and Stephen Martin, *Industrial Economics* (New York: Macmillan, 1988), chapter 7. On mergers, see Dennis C. Mueller, ed., *The Determinants and Effects of*

Mergers: An International Comparison (Cambridge, Mass.: Oelgeschlager, Gunn and Hain, 1980); and David J. Ravenscraft and F. M. Scherer, *Mergers, Sell-offs and Economic Efficiency* (Washington, D.C.: Brookings Institution, 1987). On the trend of competition, see my "Causes of Increased Competition in the U.S. Economy, 1939–1980," *Review of Economics and Statistics* 64 (November 1982): 614–20. Examples of case studies include Zoltan Acs, *The Changing Structure of the U.S. Economy: Lessons from the Steel Industry* (New York: Praeger, 1984): Elizabeth E. Bailey, David R. Graham, and Daniel P. Kaplan, *Deregulating the Airlines* (Cambridge, Mass.: MIT Press, 1985); Gerald W. Brock, *The U.S. Computer Industry* (Cambridge, Mass.: Ballinger, 1975); Kerry Cooper and Donald Fraser, *Banking Deregulation and the New Competition in Financial Services* (Cambridge, Mass.: Ballinger, 1984); Robert Crandall, *The U.S. Steel Industry in Recurrent Crisis* (Washington, D.C.: Brookings Institution, 1982); Andrew F. Daughety, ed., *Analytical Studies in Transport Economics* (Cambridge: Cambridge University Press, 1985); Richard Thomas DeLamarter, *Big Blue: IBM's Use and Abuse of Power* (New York: Dodd, Mead, 1986); David S. Evans, ed., *Breaking Up Bell* (Amsterdam: North Holland, 1983); Franklin M. Fisher, John J. McGowan, and Joen E. Greenwood, *Folded, Spindled, and Mutilated: Economic Analysis and U.S. v. IBM* (Cambridge, Mass.: MIT Press, 1983).

Also Paul M. Joskow and Richard Schmalensee, *Markets for Power* (Cambridge, Mass.: MIT Press, 1986); Paul W. MacAvoy, *Crude Oil Prices* (Cambridge, Mass.: Ballinger, 1982); John R. Meyer and Clinton V. Oster, *Deregulation and the New Airline Entrepreneurs* (Cambridge, Mass.: MIT Press, 1984); Roger G. Noll, ed., *Government and the Sports Business*, rev. ed. (Washington, D.C.: Brookings Institution, 1985); Stephen A. Rhoades, *Power, Empire Building, and Mergers* (Lexington, Mass.: D.C. Heath, Lexington Books, 1983); Anthony Saunders and Lawrence J. White, *Technology and the Regulation of Financial Markets* (Lexington, Mass.: Lexington Books, 1986); Steven A. Schneider, *The Oil Price Revolution* (Baltimore: Johns Hopkins Press, 1983); Harry M. Shooshan, ed., *Disconnecting Bell: The Impact of AT&T Divestiture* (New York: Pergamon Press, 1984); J. Tunstall, *Disconnecting Parties* (New York: McGraw-Hill, 1985); Leonard W. Weiss and Michael W. Klass, eds., *Regulatory Reform: What Really Happened* (Boston: Little, Brown, 1986).

14. See my "Causes of Increased Competition in the U.S. Economy, 1939–1980," *Review of Economics and Statistics* 64 (November 1982): 613–26.

15. The original Chicago School members in the 1920s and 1930s with interests in competitive issues were Frank H. Knight, Henry C. Simons, and Jacob Viner. They were deeply opposed to monopoly of every kind, which they saw as endemic and harmful. See especially Simons, *Economic Policy for a Free Society* (Chicago: University of Chicago Press, 1948).

16. Leading writings include Stigler, *Organization of Industry*, 1968; Yale Brozen, "The Antitrust Task Force Deconcentration Recommendation," *Journal of Law and Economics* 13 (October 1970): 279–92; Brozen, *Concentration, Mergers and Public Policy* (New York: Macmillan, 1982); John S. McGee, *In Defense of Industrial Concentration* (Seattle: University of Washington Press, 1971); Harold Demsetz, "Industry Structure, Market Rivalry, and Public Policy," *Journal of Law and Economics* (April 1973): 1–9; Demsetz, "Two Systems of Belief about Monopoly," in Harvey J. Goldschmid, H. Michael Mann, and J. Fred Weston, eds., *Industrial Concentration: The New Learning* (Boston: Little, Brown, 1974); McGee, *Industrial Organization* (Englewood Cliffs, N.J.: Prentice-Hall, 1988); McGee, "Predatory Pricing Revisited," *Journal of Law and Economics* 23 (October 1980): 289–330; Sam Peltzman, "The Gains and Losses from Industrial Concentration," *Journal of Law and Economics* 20 (October 1977): 229–63; John Carter, "Collusion, Efficiency and Antitrust," *Journal of Law and Economics* 21 (October 1978): 435–44; and Richard A. Posner, "The Social Costs of

186   *William G. Shepherd*

Monopoly and Regulation," *Journal of Political Economy* (August 1976): 807–27.

For the more extreme versions, see Robert H. Bork, *The Antitrust Paradox* (New York: Basic Books, 1978); Dominick T. Armentano, *Antitrust and Monopoly: Anatomy of a Policy Failure* (New York: Wiley, 1982); Richard H. Fink, "General and Partial Equilibrium in Bork's Antitrust Analysis," *Contemporary Policy Issues* 3 (Winter 1984–85); Jack High, "Economics and Antitrust: Bork's Contributions — Introduction," *Contemporary Policy Issues* 3 (Winter 1984–85); and M. Bruce Johnson, "Can Economic Analysis Give Better Guidance to Antitrust Policy?" *Economic Inquiry* 1 (January 1983).

The main papers have appeared primarily in one Chicago journal (the *Journal of Law and Economics*) rather than a variety of leading mainstream journals.

For a parallel view, see also Franklin M. Fisher, "On the Misuse of Accounting Rates of Return to Infer Monopoly Profits," *American Economic Review* 73 (March 1983): 82–92; and Fisher, McGowan, and Greenwood, *Folded, Spindled and Mutilated*, 1983.

17. As Fox and Sullivan note, the view has prevailed only in the Reagan administration rather than in the research community, where it is still a (vigorous) minority; see Fox and Sullivan, "Antitrust," 1987. See also Richard Schmalensee, "Collusion versus Differential Efficiency: Testing Alternative Hypotheses," *Journal of Industrial Economics* 34 (June 1987): 399–425; Ioannes N. Kessides, "Internal vs. External Market Conditions and Firm Profitability: An Exploratory Model," Working Paper, Department of Economics, University of Maryland, December 1987; and W. G. Shepherd, "Three 'Efficiency School' Hypotheses about Market Power," 1988.

18. For example, see George J. Stigler, *Five Lectures on Economic Problems* (London: Longmans Green, 1949), and G. Warren Nutter, *The Extent of Enterprise Monopoly in the United States: 1899–1939* (Chicago: University of Chicago Press, 1951).

19. See Bain, *Industrial Organization*, 1968; Walter Adams, ed., *The Structure of American Industry* (New York: Macmillan, 1955); W. G. Shepherd, *Market Power and Economic Welfare* (New York: Random House, 1970); and John M. Blair, *Economic Concentration.* (New York: Harcourt Brace Jovanovich, 1972).

20. See, for example, Stigler, *Organization of Industry,* 1968; and Michael Gort, "Analysis of Stability and Change in Market Shares," *Journal of Political Economy* 71 (February 1963): 51–61.

21. See Blair, *Economic Concentration;* Shepherd, *Market Power and Economic Welfare;* Scherer, *Industrial Market Structure and Economic Performance.*

22. See George J. Stigler, "The Economies of Scale" *Journal of Law and Economics* 1 (October 1958): 54–71; Stigler, *Organization of Industry,* 1968; Sam Peltzman, "Gains and Losses," 1977; Bork, *Antitrust Paradox,* 1978.

23. See Scherer, *Industrial Market Structure and Economic Performance,* 1980, especially the review and summary of data on pp. 91–118.

24. The low correlation would reflect both measurement errors and the innate complexity of any concentration-price relationship (because any given concentration ratio is consistent with many varieties of structure among the leading four firms).

25. Attention originally focused on 4-firm concentration ratios; see Leonard W. Weiss's survey chapter of concentration-profits patterns, in Goldschmid, Mann, and Weston, *Industrial Concentration,* 1974.

On more complete structural models, including market share, concentration, and entry barriers, see my "The Elements of Market Structure," *Review of Economics and Statistics* 54 (February 1972): 25–37; W. G. Shepherd, "Tobin's q," 1986; David J. Ravenscraft, "Structure-Profit Relationships at the Line of Business and Industry Level," *Review of Economics and Statistics* 65 (February 1983): 22–31; and Mueller, *Profits in the Long Run,* 1986.

26. The main empirical work supporting these points is in Demsetz, "Industry Structure," 1973; Peltzman, "Gains and Losses," 1977; and Michael Smirlock et al. "Tobin's *q* and the Structure-Performance Relationship," *American Economic Review* 74 (December 1984): 1051–60. See Scherer, *Industrial Market Structure and Economic Performance,* 1980, pp. 289–90, and my "Tobin's *q*," 1986.

27. See especially Clark, "Limits of Competition," 1887; and Clark, *The Control of Trusts,* (New York: Macmillan, 1901). See also the illuminating review by Philip Williams, "John Bates Clark and Antitrust: A Leader of Progressive Economists," Working Paper, Department of Economics, University of Melbourne, 1985.

28. See especially Baumol, Panzar, and Willig, *Contestable Markets and the Theory of Industrial Structure,* 1982. For further praise of the theory, see Baumol and Willig, "Contestability: Developments Since the Book," *Oxford Economic Papers,* November 1986, Special Supplement.

29. The limits of the short-run framework are evident even in recent supportive reviews of the approach, such as in Tirole, *Theory of Industrial Organization,* 1988; Stiglitz and Mathewson, *New Developments in the Analysis of Market Structure,* 1986, and Jacquemin, *New Industrial Organization,* 1987.

30. For IBM, Franklin M. Fisher and his associates led the economic defense team; their approach is presented in Fisher et al., *Folded, Spindled and Mutilated,* 1983. See also Fisher, James W. McKie, and Richard B. Mancke, *IBM and the U.S. Data Processing Industry: An Economic History* (New York: Praeger, 1983).

   For AT&T, William Baumol, Robert Willig, Paul MacAvoy, John Panzar, and perhaps twenty-five others provided research, new concepts, and direct testimony. See Baumol, Panzar, and Willig, *Contestable Markets,* 1982, and Baumol and Willig, "Contestability," 1986, and other papers by their group cited in those sources.

31. The empirical support for Hypothesis 1 is mainly Peltzman, "Gains and Losses," 1977. On Hypothesis 2, see Carter, "Collusion, Efficiency, and Antitrust," 1978, and Smirlock et al., "Tobin's *q* and the Structure-Performance Relationship," 1984.

   For a rejection of Peltzman's evidence, see F. M. Scherer, "The Causes and Consequences of Rising Industrial Concentration," *Journal of Law and Economics* 22 (April 1979): 191–208. On Smirlock et al., see my "Tobin's *q*," 1986.

32. Of course, MS-RR may also reflect mere coincidence or random factors. But the task is to determine how large those components are, not just that they *might* exist.

33. They are from my "Tobin's *q*," 1986.

34. These are unpublished regressions, based on methods of estimating structural elements and using profit sources which are identical to those in my "Elements of Market Structure," 1972; and "Tobin's *q*," 1986.

35. Richard E. Caves and Michael E. Porter, "From Entry Barriers to Mobility Barriers," *Quarterly Journal of Economics* (May 1977): 241–61.

36. Bain, *Barriers to New Competition,* 1956, and Mann tried to include several elements; see H. Michael Mann, "Seller Concentration, Barriers to Entry and Rates of Return in Thirty Industries, 1950–1960," *Review of Economics and Statistics* (August 1966): 296–307.

   But the data were often roughly estimated and there was no general, objective formula or technique for combining them. To say that is not to criticize; the estimates were probably about as good as can be made.

Lester C. Thurow

Putting Capitalists
Back into Capitalism

A SUCCESSFUL ECONOMY is one that generates a rising real standard of living for its citizens. Yet after correcting for inflation, real hourly wage rates are back to where they were in 1968. Since their peak in 1972 real hourly wages have fallen 7 percent. The trend continues. In 1987, hourly wages fell 1 percent.[1] Never before in American history has there been a fifteen-year period of time with falling wages.

The key to a rising standard of living is increased productivity — the production of more goods and services per hour of work. If that does not occur, standards of living cannot rise.

In the American system, private business is responsible for raising productivity. If it isn't rising at a healthy rate, American business is failing to do its job.

The failure is evident. In the past ten years (1977–1987) productivity grew at an annual rate of 0.8 percent, and in 1987 the rate was only 0.8 percent.[2] Short-term and long-term trends are consistent. In contrast, productivity grew at more than 3 percent in the 1950s and 1960s and is growing at a healthy 3 to 4 percent in the rest of the industrial world.[3] America's current productivity performance is simply not world class.

With slow productivity growth, some extra output is being created, but market division of that output has led to falling wages for production or nonsupervisory workers (the workers covered in the Department of Labor's data on wages) and rising wages for managers. Renewed class warfare is one answer to this distribution problem, but a far better answer is to restructure the American economy to restore a healthy productivity growth.

Meanwhile, the whole global picture has been transformed. Instead of enjoying trade surpluses and the benefits of being the world's largest net creditor nation, the United States now suffers from large trade deficits ($160 billion in 1987) and has to bear the costs of being the world's largest net debtor ($500 billion at the beginning of 1989).[4]

American wages have already slipped below those in Japan or West Germany and can only slip farther as the dollar falls to the levels necessary to balance America's international accounts.[5] With lower wages, management's excuses for failure are gone. If American firms still cannot compete, the failure cannot be blamed on wage rates that are out of line. Wages are both falling and below those in our most advanced industrial competitors. If Americans cannot compete, something is wrong with management.

Yet all too often American firms cannot compete. If one wants steel rolled to the highest tolerances, silica with the least impurities, or robots with the greatest precision, one simply does not buy American. The result is a trade deficit that improves with painful slowness despite an ever lower dollar.

Current events would seem to indicate that some key ingredient must be missing from American capitalism.

The Missing Ingredient

America is rich in financial investors of every size and variety, from the man on the street to the giant pension funds to the get-rich-quick speculators and the takeover artists. We have more corporate managers than we know what to do with — in recent years, managers and executives have been growing far faster than output (in 1987 the number of managers on American payrolls grew by 5.3 percent while the GNP was only growing by 3.4 percent).[6]

What we lack are genuine, old-style capitalists — those big investors of yesteryear who had often invented the technologies they were managing and whose personal wealth was inextricably linked to the destiny of their giant companies. We miss them. Men like

Henry Ford and Thomas J. Watson of IBM are at the heart of the
system that produced the greatest economic power and the highest
standard of living in history. America desperately needs their energy and their staying power today. Without them our corporations have been losing their dominant positions in world markets
and their vitality.

Put bluntly, American capitalism needs a heart transplant. The
financial traders who have become the heart of American capitalism need to be taken out and replaced by real capitalists who can
become the heart of an industrial rebirth.

Old-fashioned corporations were run by individual capitalists —
a shareholder with enough stock to dominate the board of directors and to dictate policy: a shareholder who was usually also the
chief executive officer. He was in control and locked in. Both factors are vital.

Owning a majority of controlling interest, the old-fashioned
capitalist did not have to concentrate his attention on reshuffling
financial assets to fight off the raids of the financial vikings. He
was an industrialist who made his living by producing new products or by producing old products more cheaply. He was in control.

But he was also locked into his corporation. He couldn't look to
get rich by selling out for a quick profit — dumping his large stock
holdings on the market would simply depress its price and cost
him his job as one of the captains of American industry. His wealth,
job, ego, and prestige were all locked up with the success or failure
of his corporation. He had no choice but to work to improve the
long-run efficiency and productivity of his company.

Today, with very few exceptions, the stock of America's large
corporations is held by financial institutions like pension funds,
foundations, or mutual funds, not by large individual shareholders. These financial institutions by law cannot become real capitalists who control what they own. They are limited by law in how
many of their assets they can put in any one company, how much
of any one company they can own, and how actively they can in-
tervene in the decision making of companies where they own stock.
By law they are forced to be traders and speculators. By law they
cannot be active builders who seek to strengthen a company's long-
run competitive position.

There are, of course, a few families and individuals who control large public companies. Each generation has its founding fathers, such as An Wang at the Wang Corporation or Ken Olsen at the Digital Equipment Corporation, and there are always a few children of the founding fathers who continue the family tradition of hands-on control. But by far the majority of our big corporations lack such dominant shareholders.[7] In the absence of dominant shareholders, corporations are effectively run by their professional managers.

Minority shareholders and professional managers have an agenda very different from that of the dominant capitalist. Minority shareholders are short-term traders. Since they do not have the clout to change business decisions, strategies, or incumbent managers with their voting power, they can only enhance their wealth by buying and selling shares based upon what they think is going to happen to short-term profits. As a result earnings per share, judged on a quarterly basis, becomes the dominant factor determining whether the institutional investors will keep a stock or sell it off, sending its price plummeting or soaring. Hundreds of millions of shares change hands every day in a game that has nothing to do with beliefs about long-term success or failure or with plans to convert failure into success.

Unlike founding fathers, the chief executive officers of large corporations usually reach that exalted position just a few years before they retire. Long-run careers at the top are very unusual. As a short-term CEO they not surprisingly organize compensation packages that emphasize bonuses and salaries keyed not to long-term performance but to current profits or sales. Their short-run compensation packages are completely congruent with the short-run perspective of their short-run shareholders. Neither the manager nor the shareholder expects to be around very long.

For both managers and minority shareholders mergers and acquisitions — the takeover game — represent an almost irresistible path to glory. The managers of acquiring companies can double sales and profits (and hence their own salaries and bonuses that are tied to those sales and profits) with a stroke of a pen — without risking a cent of their own personal money. If the firm were to home-grow its own economic crop of new or cheaper products, the crop probably wouldn't ripen before the incumbent manager retires. Empires can be quickly built in the merger wars.

Those who rise to the top from finance, a large fraction of American CEOs, may in fact know far more about fighting the financial wars than they know about running their own production facilities. It is what they are good at. It is what they have been trained to do. Attack or be attacked! Some managers lose in the takeover games, but those on the losing side have the solace of multimillion-dollar golden parachutes.

For minority shareholders, the takeover game is simply the best moneymaking game in town. Opportunities exist to make a lot of money quick. It is far better than the normal uncertain ups and downs of the stock market. No matter which takeover artist wins, they win. Moreover, the laws are often written so that institutional investors must sell whenever a takeover artist offers them more than the current stock market value. A pension fund that did not sell out in such a situation could be sued for not living up to its fiduciary responsibilities to maximize stock-market values for the benefit of future pension recipients. To look to the long run and ignore the short run is often actually illegal in the American system.

The Forgotten Lessons of History

In the dicta of Adam Smith, the individual search for profits would always promote the nation's economic growth. But in practice a problem developed. Too often Adam Smith's "invisible hand" became the hand of a pickpocket. Free unfettered markets have many virtues, but they have a habit of discovering very profitable — but nonproductive — activities. Practical experience teaches us that profit maximizing often does not necessarily lead to output maximizing.

When the nineteenth-century railroads attempted to use their monopoly over the means of transportation to divert the fruits of others' (often farmers') productive energies to themselves by setting transportation prices that would extract monopoly rents, the United States invented the Interstate Commerce Commission to refocus the attention of railroad entrepreneurs back on running better railroads rather than extracting monopoly rents from the rest of society. The railroad barons were profit maximizing, but their profit maximizing did not lead to a larger economic pie. Quite the reverse, it led to a smaller economic pie. Without the pricing regulations of the Interstate Commerce Commission, there was simply more money to be made redistributing the existing income than there was to be made in expanding the economy with a better transportation system.

Later the robber barons in steel, oil, and copper discovered the same facts of life. Man-made monopolies were as good as those made by technology. Establishing monopolies and raising prices were far more profitable than increasing efficiency or production. In engaging in these activities the corporation was fulfilling its private obligation to maximize profits and shareholder wealth, but it was not meeting its social obligation to be a vehicle for maximizing national growth and higher standards of living for everyone.

So society refocused the profit-making ambitions of these robber barons with the Sherman Act of 1890 to outlaw monopolies and the Clayton Act of 1914 to prevent mergers that would lessen competition. The new laws were designed to insure that the name of the game was not simply "make money" but "make money by building better or cheaper products."

As Americans have discovered in the past, it is often necessary to rearrange one's economy so that both institutions and individuals channel their talents and energies into activities that promote an expansion of output rather than into activities that either contract production or redistribute it from one person or institution to another.

In each of these historical cases, America successfully changed its institutional structure to refocus entrepreneurial energies where they ought to have been focused. But times change. What was called for at one point in time is not called for at another point in time. Societies decline when they get frozen into old rigid institutional forms that become counterproductive. Today's need is not more regulations or antitrust laws to prevent the exercise of monopoly powers. Quite the contrary.

But today we do need a similar refocusing. Our giant corporations, to whom the nation has entrusted the task of assuring economic growth, are failing in that goal. They are losing in the economic competition with foreign nations. They are chasing fast, easy increases in stock-market values instead of increased productivity and competitiveness. Once again, as in the nineteenth century, society must reformulate its rules of social organization to get its corporations back on track.

Deregulation, simply letting the market function without rules and regulations, doesn't work, since, as the robber barons of the nineteenth century demonstrated, there are all too often circumstances where the most profitable activities lead to actions that contract output and redistribution earnings. Left to themselves, unregulated markets will inevitably focus on these activities — as they are now doing in the financial merger wars. Mindless financial market deregulation has in fact helped make industry into a plaything for finance rather than helping finance service the needs of industrial expansion. Profit maximization (something that firms will automatically do with or without government regulations) is not a synonym for output expansion.

America is proving that capitalism without capitalists does not work. But we also have learned, or should have learned, from our nineteenth-century experiences with real capitalists that they must be boxed in to keep their attention focused on the national goals of higher growth and hence more income for everyone rather than on simply raising their own profits.

The time has come to make our rules and regulations consistent with the realities of modern technology and a competitive world economy. The Reagan administration talked about changing the antitrust laws to allow more mergers, to permit joint research and development in industries hurt by imports, and to loosen the restrictions on interlocking directorates. Changes are certainly needed. Present laws are often the equivalent of shooting oneself in the foot.

General Motors, for example, is permitted to engage in a joint venture with Toyota that will effectively attack Ford and Chrysler, whereas it would not be permitted to engage in a joint venture with Ford to repel the Japanese auto invasion. Antitrust limitations that apply to two American firms do not apply to an American and a Japanese firm, although there is now a worldwide, not a separable American, market for cars.

What has to be done, however, is not simple deregulation or minor changes in antitrust laws. The entire regulatory framework governing finance and industry must be altered so that the biggest profits and highest incomes are paid to those who expand productivity and output rather than to those who rejuggle financial assets.

To find out what, if anything, should replace today's rules and regulations one needs to look at today's industrial problems. The central problem is slow productivity growth. The financial vikings, today's counterpart to yesterday's robber barons, need to be reined in to refocus their attention on production rather than the privately very profitable financial wars, just as those earlier robber barons had to be refocused on production rather than monopoly profits.

No one doubts that more money can be made faster in merger or leveraged buy-out games than it can be made in production, just as no one doubts that the robber barons made more money than those who simply tried to build better products in the nineteenth century. What is privately profitable, however, need not be socially productive. The social problem is to reverse this situation so that the brightest individuals go into private production rather than private income redistribution.

When companies are acquired, the shareholders of the company being taken over are certainly enriched, but the economy has gained nothing. The productivity assets that it did have are still there — no bigger and no smaller. A redistributive activity rather than a productive activity has occurred.

Financial takeovers are always justified on the grounds that they will enhance productivity and competitiveness, but the promised leaner and meaner corporations do not seem to emerge. No one can know for sure how today's mergers will be performing fifteen years from now, but we do know that the mergers of the late 1960s and early 1970s have not led to firms with superior performance. Profits centers were bought and sold to reduce debts, but the various pieces ended up without improved performances. The whole process looks much like a random walk — some winners, some losers, but on average an average performance. Companies were often put back into financial play, but they seldom became world-class productivity performers. Spending a lifetime making the firms into world-class performers is simply not what the financial vikings have in mind.

If financial redeployments were, in fact, the route to higher productivity, the United States would have the highest and not the lowest rate of growth of productivity, for it has had by far the highest level of asset rearrangement. Precisely the opposite may occur. Firms end up loaded with debt. The result is fewer free funds to invest in new products, new processes, or research and development. Firms become financially weaker and more vulnerable to financial collapse in recessions. The first big test for the current merger wave will be the next American recession. Will they be able to survive a downturn in revenue given their needs to make huge interest payments? Until then we won't know if the current merger wave is viable, much less productive. Firms may also become more risk averse — less willing to bet the company on new activities — in the aftermath of merger activities. They cannot bet the company since the company has effectively already been bet.

Those who argue for the virtues of the takeover movement do so on the basis that it enriches the shareholders and that firms exist solely to serve the interests of the shareholders. There is no doubt that the enrichment part of the argument is true, but questions can be raised as to whether firms exist solely to serve the interests of the shareholders. If this view had been taken in the past, neither the antitrust laws nor the rules regulating railroads could have been adopted. There is no doubt that each of these activities enriched shareholders. Shareholders' rights, however, are not in fact paramount.

Private firms exist in our society because we have collectively decided that private firms are in general the best way to expand the output available to everyone, shareholder and nonshareholder alike. If private firms fail to serve this social function, they will either be abolished and replaced with something that will serve this social function or they will be redirected, as they have been in the past, with a new set of rules and regulations that, one hopes, once again sets them off on a productive path.

If one looks at foreign countries (Germany, Japan, France) with higher rates of productivity growth, none of them has America's numerous takeovers. There the fastest route to personal and corporate economic success is still in inventing new products before one's competitors or in making old products cheaper than one's competitors. Financial manipulation is not the fast track to personal or corporate success. A hyperactive merger movement is not necessary for economic success. Quite the contrary, the most activity occurs in the country with the slowest rate of growth of productivity in the industrial world — the United States.

What has to be re-created is a market where the biggest profits and highest incomes are paid to those who expand output. The robber barons took bread out of the mouths of babes in a very direct and overt manner. Their very directness was their undoing and led to their activities being proscribed. In contrast, today's financial manipulations look as if they are a variant of cannibalism — one big businessman eats another. If so, why should any of the rest of us care? The answer is that we should care. Just as yesterday's monopolistic activities lowered standards of living for many, so too do today's financial activities lower our future standards of living. Real talent is siphoned off into the most lucrative route to success — a route where money is made by rejuggling financial assets and redistributing income from one shareholder to another. The only real route to higher standards of living for all — expanded output — gets both ignored and harmed.

To make American industry work, real capitalists are going to have to be put back into the American economy. Once there, they then have to be boxed in so that their profit-making energies are focused on activities that raise productivity and output.

Realistically, this means creating institutional capitalists rather than expanding the supply of individual capitalists. Occasionally, brilliant entrepreneurs will come to the fore and nurture a corporation into one of America's largest, but within one or two generations that corporation, like the rest of American industry, will be without dominant shareholders. New start-ups are great. But new start-ups are not substitutes for giant corporations that retain their vitality. The new start-ups that we need most are precisely those that eventually become giant corporations. A small business that remains small is of limited value.

To put real capitalists back into American capitalism, today's short-term financial traders must be remade into tomorrow's long-term capitalistic builders. To do so, the legal limits that now prevent financial institutions from acquiring a dominant or majority shareholding position should be removed. Instead of preventing these institutions from becoming real capitalists, they should be encouraged to sit on the boards of directors of companies in which they invest, to actively hire and fire firm managers, and to worry about the strategies and investments that will make their companies (investments) successful.

Instead of being encouraged to remain liquid, they should be encouraged to get into situations from which they cannot extract themselves financially except through making the corporations in which they have invested successful. Instead of maintaining an arm's-length separation between finance and industry, they should be encouraged to become so entwined that their destinies cannot be separated. American finance should be put in an institutional straightjacket where it cannot succeed unless American industry succeeds.

Key to this is changing the regulations (mostly found in the Glass-Steagall banking law of 1933) that prevent American commercial banks from becoming merchant banks — banks that own and control industrial corporations. In much of the rest of the industrial world it is the merchant bankers who are the real institutional capitalists who make the system work.

When the Arabs threatened to buy a controlling interest in Mercedes-Benz a few years ago, the Deutsche Bank intervened on behalf of the German economy to buy a controlling interest. It controls the board of directors. It protects the managers of Mercedes-Benz from the raids of the financial vikings. It frees the managers from the tyranny of the stock market with its emphasis on quarterly profits. It helps plan corporate strategies and helps raise the money to carry out these strategies. But it also fires the managers if Mercedes-Benz slips in the auto market and prevents them from engaging in self-serving activities such as mergers or golden parachutes that do not enhance the company's long-term prospects.

Some of what were once America's most successful companies — General Electric, U.S. Steel, International Harvester — were founded by merchant bankers before that financial species was outlawed during the Great Depression. In recent years, small-scale merchant bankers have reappeared in the guise of venture capitalists. They play a vital role in helping companies get started, but when the companies become middle-sized and offer their shares for sale to the public, the venture capitalist drops out, sells his stock, and starts over again with a new company. Venture capital is not a substitute for large merchant banks.

Outside directors who own few if any shares are no substitution for outside directors with a controlling block of shares. The former are controlled by management; the latter control management.

Instead of legally being forced to be short-term speculative traders of shares, banks, insurance companies, and pension or mutual funds should be encouraged to become real institutional capitalists who succeed or fail based on their ability to grow healthy industrial corporations. Their attention should be refocused from something that is marginal to America's long-run success — the buying and selling of shares and the rearrangement of corporate financial assets — to something that is central to American success — the growth of productivity and output.

Historically, merchant banking was made illegal in the aftermath of the Great Depression since the public was looking for a personal scapegoat to blame for it — much as the public recently looked for someone to blame for the space shuttle disaster. The public found such a person in the merchant banker J. P. Morgan and adopted legislation designed to punish him for his supposed crimes. Economic historians now know that the Great Depression was caused by much more fundamental factors than the speculations of J. P. Morgan, but the rules that were adopted then still exist.[8]

Moreover, we should see to it that all dominant shareholders, institutional or individual, are locked in to their investments. While the ownership of a large block of shares constitutes a substantial lock-in (it is difficult to sell a substantial number of shares without depressing one's own stock price), this natural lock should be buttressed. Anyone who owns a dominant position in any company — say, 20 percent or more — should be forced to give the public one day's advance notice of their intention to sell any of their shares. Unless this announced sale could be explained to the satisfaction of the investing public on grounds other than expected future failure, any such notice would inevitably trigger a general rush to sell the stock before the major investor could sell, leaving the big investor to sell at much reduced prices. Like the old-time capitalists, he would think long and hard before trying to bail out of his company if it were having trouble. Instead, he would have a major incentive to minister to his sick company, designing the strategies necessary to return it to health.

To reinforce the distinction between traders and investors, the voting rights of equity shares should rise the longer those shares are held. Major investors subject to the 20 percent rule would become instant owners, but others would gain full voting rights only over some substantial period of time. No voting rights might be given those who have owned shares less than two years with full voting rights gradually restored over the next three years — in year three one third of a vote for each share held, in year four two thirds of a vote for each share held, and in year five a full vote for each share held. Stock traders could still be traders, getting rich by buying and selling shares, but those who were traders would not have ownership rights — the right to set a firm's strategy, the right to make decisions.

While the tyranny of the quarterly profit statement is probably exaggerated as a deterrent to good management, it should be repealed as a symbol of what needs to be done. Japan has gradually moved from quarterly to half year to annual profit reports. The same should be done in the United States. Having to operate in an environment of great short-term ignorance might also persuade some of today's short-term traders that they could make more money by becoming tomorrow's long-term investors.

Management by the numbers is a failure, and fewer numbers wouldn't hurt. It simply isn't true that more information is always better than less information. Managers should not be placed in a position where, if they incur expenses this quarter that will make future prospects better, they will be penalized with falling stock prices today. While this may not happen very often, too many managers believe that it will happen.

Not long ago, I was consulting for a firm that had a problem. Its cost-cutting program had substantially exceeded expectations, and it had made 50 percent more money in one quarter than it expected to make. This good news, learned too near the end of the quarter to be effectively hidden by creative accounting, was treated as a disaster. Management was sure that its stock would immediately rise on news of the record profits but then plunge in the next quarter when the firm could not duplicate the previous quarter's feat.

Today's laws also draw too sharp a distinction between loans and equity. To avoid the appearance of a conflict of interest, executives from banks, insurance companies, and other lenders are allowed to sit only on the boards of directors of those firms to which they have not lent major amounts of money. They are not supposed to be financially involved participants. But that flies in the face of reason. It is precisely the institutions that provide major long-term loans to companies that should be taking an active role in the strategic direction of these companies. They should be interested rather than disinterested directors. To bring this about, long-term loans should carry voting rights. A $100 million long-term loan might, for example, entitle a lender to half the voting rights of a $100 million long-term equity investment. Major lenders, like equity investors, should not be allowed to be absentee landlords.

While small firms always feel as if their "friendly" banker is breathing down their neck, bankers exert an influence in the management of major companies to which they have lent money only when the company is failing. How much better it would be to bring their expertise to bear earlier in the process to help keep the company from the mistakes that led to its financial weakness. Prevention is better than remediation.

The antitrust laws prohibiting interlocking directorates, joint research, and trading companies were all designed to prevent the rise of monopolistic industrial combines. The restrictions on joint research have been weakened and those on trading companies eliminated in recent years, but the intellectual beliefs behind these laws remain in much of our legal structure.[9] These beliefs hold that if the same people are planning strategy in different firms, if products are being developed jointly, or if different firms are selling their products through a common sales organization, the companies involved would not be totally separate competitive companies. Strategies might be coordinated, joint development might lead to joint production, the common sales force might come to dominate the producing companies — de facto mergers might occur, monopolies might be built.

True once upon a time, but irrelevant in today's world economy. The big industrial combines of Japan (the Mitsui group — twenty-three member firms, the Mitsubishi group — twenty-eight member firms, the Sumatomo group — twenty-one member firms, the Fuji group — twenty-nine member firms, the Sanwa group — thirty-nine member firms, the Dai-Ichi Kangin group — forty-five member firms) exist and cannot be put out of business by U.S. antitrust laws.[10] These groups typically own from 20 to 30 percent of each other's stock. American firms have to compete with those groups in America, in Japan, and in the rest of the world. They need to be able to form the same strategic alliances, the same self-help societies, the same joint strategies for conquering world markets. In today's world economy, American companies must have an equal arsenal of weapons at hand. Our laws and regulations must be drastically overhauled to give American firms a chance. America is now in a position where it must adjust its rules to conform to those of the rest of the world; the rest of the world is not going to conform to the specific rules that have evolved from a peculiar American history.

Of course, we must maintain some safeguards against the return of the robber-baron era, measures that would keep newly formed merchant banks, capitalistic mutual funds, and aggressive trading companies in line. No one would propose lifting the antitrust prohibitions on price fixing. And in fact we have some outside help in preventing such evils as price fixing. The realities of the world market today are such that our overseas competitors would undersell any American combine that tried to keep prices artificially high. If one is worried about price fixing, the government protection that must be offered to American companies that cannot compete at home or abroad is far worse than anything the companies could privately rig for themselves.

In any reformulation of the rules governing our industrial structure, one central goal must be kept in mind. Put real capitalists back in the driver's seat of the American corporation. Then box them in so that they have no choice but to improve their firm's, and hence the nation's, productivity and competitiveness if they want to be personally successful.

Without capitalists, American capitalism can only fail.

NOTES

1. Council of Economic Advisers, *Economic Indicators* (Washington, D.C.: Government Printing Office, September 1988), p. 15, and Council of Economic Advisers, *Economic Report of the President, 1986* (Washington, D.C.: Government Printing Office, 1986), p. 300.
2. *Economic Indicators*, p. 16, and *Economic Report of the President*, p. 303.
3. International Monetary Fund, *International Financial Statistics*, July 1988, pp. 240, 311.
4. *Economic Indicators*, p. 36.
5. "Labour Costs," *Economist*, August 6, 1988, p. 81.

6. U.S. Dept. of Labor, *Employment and Earnings* (Washington, D.C.: Government Printing Office, January 1988), p. 181.

7. In most publicly held firms, institutions now control 60 to 70 percent of the total shares.

8. Peter Temin, *Did Monetary Forces Cause the Great Depression?* (New York: Norton, 1976).

9. Trading companies have been legalized, but joint research still depends on the personal whims of those running the Justice Department.

10. Abegglen, James C., and George Stalk, Jr. *Raisha, the Japanese Corporation* (New York: Basic Books, 1985).

Shigeto Tsuru

The Political Economy of
Urban Land:
The Right of Property and
the "Price Revolution"

Land monopoly is not the only monopoly, but it is by far the greatest of monopolies. . . . it is a perpetual monopoly, and it is the mother of all other forms of monopoly.

— Winston Churchill

Introduction

It was no accident that social science as a professional discipline was born in the period of transition "from status to contract," giving ideological support to the evolution of the civil society. The period in question extended roughly from the Reformation to the French Revolution, and through this transition there was born a new social class which established its title to a full share in the control of the state. "In its ascent to power," Harold Laski wrote, "it broke down the barriers which . . . had made privilege a function of status, and associated the idea of rights with the tenure of land. To achieve its end, it effected a fundamental change in the legal relationships of men. Status was replaced by contract as the juridical foundation of society. . . . The control of politics by an aristocracy whose authority was built upon the tenure of land came to be shared with men whose influence was derived solely from the ownership of movable capital."[1]

But, of course, this historical transition was by no means a smooth affair. The inevitable conflict between the old feudal class and the burgeoning capitalist class gave birth, as a transitional solution, to an absolutist rule in a number of countries, e.g., Tudor and Stuart dynasties in England, the *ancien régime* in France, the rule which naturally called forth the emergence of ideologues for the civil society which was in a sense an antithesis of the absolutist state. Pioneers in this respect were, to give a few examples, Machiavelli (1469–1527) of Italy, Hobbes (1588–1679) and Locke (1632–1704) of England, and Montesquieu (1689–1755) and Rousseau (1712–1778) of France. We may add Adam Smith (1723–1790) as an economist. All of these ideologues more or less shared (1) the hypothesis of *natural* state, (2) the *rationalist* concept of social contract, and (3) the *secularism* for the status of political right.

Social science as science for the civil society thus came into existence. We may say that it consisted of three major branches: (1) political science as science of midwife of the civil society, (2) economics as science for analyzing the civil society, and (3) legal studies as science for maintenance of the order of the civil society. As social science evolved with this kind of division of labor in emphasis, what at the outset was dealt with in a synthetic manner by most ideologues became compartmentalized as a discipline, and each of the three branches soon embarked upon an independent career, so to speak. Although such a trend gave impetus to the efforts for integration of several branches of social science under the christening of "sociology," an irrepressible urge for specialization could not easily be reversed, and the compartmentalization of a professional discipline has increasingly sharpened itself so that now we are no longer surprised, for example, when we hear Charles Schultze, a former president of the American Economic Association, say, "When you dig deep down, economists are scared to death of being sociologists."[2] In particular, overmathematization of economic theory has been a target of criticism in recent years, and none other than Wassily Leontief, one of the profession's most notable mathematicians, wrote in a letter to *Science* magazine, "Page after page of professional economic journals is filled with mathematical formulas leading the reader from sets of more or less plausible but entirely arbitrary assumptions to precisely stated but irrelevant theoretical conclusions."[3]

Such is the state of "purification" of economics, one major branch of social science — a state of affairs over which one can hardly rejoice in the face of important, concrete tasks expected of social scientists today. It is the intention of this paper, as a contribution to the Galbraith *Festschrift,* to follow in Galbraith's footsteps by choosing a subject matter that conjoins constituent branches of social science, and to try to answer the challenge which he has thrown at us in the concluding chapter of his recent publication, to wit:

> The separation of economics from politics and political motivation is a sterile thing. It is also a cover for the reality of economic power and motivation. And it is a prime source of misjudgment and error in economic policy. No volume on the history of economics can conclude without the hope that the subject will be reunited with politics to form again the larger discipline of political economy.[4]

For the purpose at hand, I have chosen the topic of the right of property and urban land.

1. The Classical Case of Price Revolution

By "the price revolution" we usually understand the inordinate rise of prices in European countries during the early sixteenth century to the first half of the seventeenth. According to Earl J. Hamilton, "Early in the sixteenth century the trend of prices turned upward in Spain, first and most rapidly in Andalusia, and rose for a hundred years, with practically all troughs and peaks above the preceding ones. Andalusian prices more than doubled in the first half of the sixteenth century and more than quintupled by its close. Prices increased fourfold in New Castile, the region closest to Andalusia, and three and one-half-fold in Old Castile–Leon and in Valencia."[5] There is no doubt that "the chief cause of the Price Revolution . . . was the great increase in the money supply. . . . [In particular] it was the explosive rise in silver production after the conquests of Mexico and Peru; the discovery of the fabulous mines of Zacatecas, Guanajuato, and Potosí; and the introduction of the mercury amalgamation process of mining in the middle of the sixteenth century that generated the Price Revolution."[6]

It was noteworthy that in the process of this price revolution money wages lagged significantly, to the extent, for example, of only a one-fifth rise in England in the sixteenth century when prices were rising 150 percent. Keynes accepts this fact of wage lag to mean that "the greater part of the fruits of the economic progress and capital accumulation of the Elizabethan and Jacobean ages accrued to the profiteer rather than to the wage-earner,"[7] and he goes on to say that "never in the annals of the modern world has there existed so prolonged and so rich an opportunity for the business man, the speculator and the profiteer."[8]

So it was. It was characteristic of this classical instance of price revolution, caused by the exogenous disturbance of the balance between the metallic monetary stock and the supply of commodities, to have had the effect of bringing about a new *relative price structure*, in favor of profits against wages that contributed to the development of the modern capitalistic system.

To be sure, in the annals of economic vicissitudes of many countries there have occurred numerous instances of inflationary price rises comparable to, or often bigger in scale than, that of the "price revolution." Consider, for example, French hyperinflation in the 1790s under the assignats and mandats, the U.S. experience of greenbacks during the Civil War of 1861–1865, the astronomical inflation of Germany in the wake of the First World War, the hundredfold price rise in Japan between 1944 and 1949, and so forth. These instances, however, were cases of *general* price rise occasioned by abnormal imbalances of aggregate supply and demand and were allowed to occur through the uncontrolled or uncontrollable issue of inconvertible paper currency.

The case of the Spanish price revolution was distinctly different from these in that a more or less sudden and considerable shift in the relative price structure was caused by an exogenous single factor, whereas the major factors in the other cases were the excessive demand due to war and its concomitants and the unrestrained use of inconvertible paper money. Considering this contrast, we may speak of a "new price revolution" in connection with the so-called first oil shock of 1973–1974. The price of Middle East oil of standard quality rose within one year (January 1973 to January 1974) from $2.59 per barrel to $11.65 or four and one-half times.[9] Subsequent to this price rise of crude oil, wholesale price indexes of major advanced countries registered sudden upward trends almost without exception, as shown in the following table.

TABLE 1

The Rise in Wholesale Price Indexes
Compared with One Year Earlier (%)

	October 1973	July 1974
U.S.A.	16.5	20.4
U.K.	13.1	25.1
West Germany	6.8	15.6
France	16.9	25.8
Italy	20.6	41.3
Japan	19.1	34.2

Source: Yoshikazu Miyazaki, *Atarashii Kakaku-Kakumei* [A New Price Revolution], 1975, p. 117.

True, contributory to this inflationary trend were the consequences of the U.S. decision in August 1971 to abandon gold convertibility. Immediately following Nixon's announcement of this policy, the price of gold in the London market started to rise, registering $115.60 per ounce in July 1973 compared with $37.375 in 1970. And along with the price of gold the prices of various internationally traded commodities began surging upward, starting from the spring of 1972. Thus the Reuters Index of agricultural and mining products nearly doubled between June 1972 and June 1973. Still, the quadrupling of the oil price in 1973 was a major factor in the subsequent realignment of *relative price structure,* in which the cost of energy and raw materials began occupying a permanently greater share. It is for this reason that some economists have spoken of the oil-shock of 1973 and 1979 as marking the new price revolution. It is also noteworthy that in this case, as contrasted with the case of the classical price revolution, which provided a rich opportunity for the burgeoning capitalist class, the Third World — in particular, the OPEC countries — has been in a position to benefit by the development of their economies out of the centuries-long oppression and exploitation by advanced countries. The significance of price revolution in both cases, the classical and the latest, has lain in a historical shift in the power relations of enduring character.

2. Another Price Revolution?

With such power shifts in mind, some of us in Japan speak of a "price revolution" in connection with the extraordinary price rise of urban land in Japan in the recent decade, although the area concerned was only a region within a single country.

This real estate madness did not escape the attention of *The Economist*[10]: "If this page were a piece of prime Tokyo property, it would cost 1.8m yen (about $12,000) to buy. If, instead, this page had been part of a recent, headline-making property deal in the City of London it would have cost $3,400. Property, like much else in Japan, is outrageously expensive. On the basis of average land prices it would cost twice[11] as much to buy Japan as it would to buy the United States, even though Japan is one-twenty-fifth the size."

If we examine the history of price changes of urban landed property in Japan's postwar period, we find that there have been three distinct periods of upheaval: (1) 1960–1961, the period associated with the policy announcement of "The Income-Doubling Plan" (2) 1972–1974, the period associated with the so-called Archipelago Regeneration Boom, and (3) 1986–1988, the most recent period associated with Tokyo's emergence as an international financial center. A brief summary may be given on the scale of these upheavals. The useful index for this purpose is the one compiled by the Japan Real Estate Research Institute twice a year for land price — presumably actually transacted price — of urban districts.

A remarkable degree of out-of-balance inflation of land price for the first period can be clearly seen by contrasting that index with the wholesale price index, as both have the base of unity for September 1936 as follows.

TABLE 2

	Land Price of Urban Districts (National Average) (A)	Wholesale Price (B)	A/B
March 1956	346.1	333.0	1.04
March 1961	1,156.2	338.0	3.42
March 1966	2,368.0	352.8	6.71

The balance that can be observed in 1956 was markedly upset by 1961, and the imbalance grew by 1966 to the extent that the ratio between the two indexes widened to 6.7.

For the second period, wholesale prices also rose, but the gap between the two indexes kept on widening, as shown in the following statistics, which are continuations of the above:

TABLE 3

	Land Price (A)	Wholesale Price (B)	A/B
March 1970	4,328.7	399.9	10.82
March 1975	8,346.7	626.8	13.32

The similar trend of gap-widening in the latest period can be observed, but this time it is characteristic that the upheaval in land price has been recorded mainly in the Tokyo metropolitan area, and the evidence can be more adequately drawn forth from the official statistics of "posted land prices."[12] These have moved more or less in parallel, though lagging in upward movement, with the actually transacted prices, and the percentage annual rate of increase in the Tokyo metropolitan area has been as follows:

TABLE 4

	Residential areas	Commercial areas
Jan. 1986–Jan. 1987	21.5%	48.2%
Jan. 1987–Jan. 1988	68.6%	61.1%

By September 1987, the land-price index of the six largest cities, on the prewar basis, rose to 19,405 and the gap with the wholesale price index increased further to 26.81.

In summary, we may say that through the three periods of up-heaval between 1956 and 1987, the urban land price in general rose by 56 times while wholesale prices rose only 2.2 times. It is this extraordinary imbalance which induces us to speak of another price revolution. Here again, we have an out-of-balance rise in a *cost item* producing a shift in the *relative price structure* with manifold consequences in nearly all the spheres of socioeconomic activities. It is to be noted, however, that in contrast with the earlier price revolutions, in which an element of historically progressive shift was involved, this new price revolution in Japan has been decid-edly retrogressive in the sense that the consequent shift in the rel-ative price structure is in favor of the minority land-owning class. For this reason, some economists in Japan prefer to refer to this historic episode as "Price *Counter*revolution."

3. Are Private Property Rights "Inviolable?"

The 56-times rise in urban land price in thirty years (from 1956 to 1987) while wholesale prices rose by only 2.2 times is blatantly ex-orbitant as a phenomenon in a modern civilized society. There naturally arises a question: was the government indifferent to such an extraordinary development, and did it do little or nothing by way of putting a brake on and countering the trend?

Of course political leaders were aware of what was happening and were concerned with the possible outbreak of mass protest against this price counterrevolution, although many of the politi-cians in the ruling party[13] were no doubt its beneficiaries. The typical excuse given in justification of the "do-nothing" policy on the land-price upheaval was that "we can do nothing in breach of the constitutional clause guaranteeing the right to own property as 'inviolable,' " as was remarked in 1965 by Mr. Ichiro Kōno, a leading conservative politician who had served as Minister of Con-struction as well as Minister of Local Autonomous Bodies.[14]

True enough. Article 29 of the Constitution of Japan, promul-gated in November 1946, reads, "The right to own or to hold property is inviolable. Property rights shall be defined by law, in conformity with the public welfare. Private property may be taken for public use upon just compensation therefor." Basically, this clause repeats Article 27 of the prewar Constitution of Japan of 1889, excepting the sentence that speaks of "just compensation therefor." This "inviolability" concept goes back to the French Declaration of the rights of man (1789), in which the memorable phrase "un droit inviolable et sacré" appeared — the phrase that has been so often repeated in the capitalist world ever since. Jeremy Bentham, in particular among economists, defended the right of property as an aspect of natural rights, "a right which it is the business of law not to infringe but to secure."[15]

But it has been well said that "concepts of property are subject to the endless erosion of time" (Ernest Beaglehole).[16] And it was none other than the occupying authorities, under General Douglas MacArthur, who proposed in a draft constitution for Japan the following article:

> Article XXVIII. The ultimate fee to the land and to all natural resources reposes in the State as the collective representative of the people. Land and other natural resources are subject to the right of the State to take them, upon just compensation therefor, for the purpose of securing and promoting the conservation, development, utilization and control thereof.

This article was followed by another one saying that "ownership of property imposes obligations," which expression reminds one immediately of the oft-quoted clause in the West German Constitution (Article 14) to the effect that the property right involves certain obligations.

In the light of what was likely to happen in a country destined to be highly congested on a meager natural resource base with some six million repatriates coming home from battle areas of the Pacific War, the SCAP (Supreme Commander of Allied Powers) proposal that "the ultimate fee to the land and to all natural resources reposes in the State as the collective representative of the people" was remarkably prescient indeed. But the Japanese government, then under the conservative Yoshida cabinet, strongly resisted this SCAP proposal and succeeded finally in replacing it with the wording we now find in the Constitution.

Subsequently, however, heated discussion ensued among legal specialists in Japan, a discussion that centered on the question of what was meant by "the guaranteeing of the private property right." On the one hand, an opinion was expressed by Professor Teruhisa

Ishii, for example, to the effect that in Japan "the social and public-interest aspect of property rights" has not been sufficiently appreciated and that as a result the government authorities have been unnecessarily timid in restraining aberrant claims allegedly based on property rights. On the other hand, a pertinent point was made when Professor Masamichi Rōyama called attention to the fact that the economic value of properties is bound to change in accordance with the mutations of social structure and conditions, and that it is impossible to guarantee property rights as a "basic human right" independent of their quantitative dimensions. Japan's legal minds wrestled with this problem and finally arrived at the formulation on the content of property rights by Professor Sakae Wagatsuma, which came to be accepted by many of the specialists in the field. His proposal was to define "property rights" in Article 29 of the Constitution as "the right pertaining to that property which individuals have earned and accumulated through their own labor and/or capital in the conditions of free competition."[17]

From the standpoint of economists, this definition by Wagatsuma is highly restrictive. For one thing, in a modern society the conditions of *free competition* prevail only in very limited spheres of activities. More important, external factors (e.g., the increasingly social character of production that accompanies technological sophistication) create positive and negative effects for individuals. There are almost no isolated cases of individuals who can claim that they have "earned and accumulated (their property) through their own labor and/or capital" *alone*. This is especially evident in the case of an individual for whom a piece of land he had owned appreciated in value through, for example, the opening of a new railroad line nearby. The windfall gain in such a case could be as high as 300 percent of the initial value of the land within eight years, as the 1988 government White Paper on Construction has officially admitted. It is a commentary on this feverish situation that a transferrable membership deed for the Koganei Golf Course is priced at 400 million yen (approximately twice the lifetime earning of an ordinary salaried man) in the market, because the said golf course, situated fairly close to the urbanized area in Tokyo, is rumored to be undergoing liquidation in the near future for urban development. The windfall involved would be more than one thousand times the price forty years ago. It is clear enough that some kind of tax measure is called for to absorb this kind of windfall. We shall come back to this question later.

4. What Is Essential Is the Right of Utilization

Why was the private property right considered inviolable in the historical context of the development of modern society? That right, along with the right to subsist, was an essential component of civil rights in the evolutionary process of the society.

The modern civil society is a society in which a citizen maintains his own economic subsistence as commodity owner through exchanging his commodity. Therefore, his *right to subsist* as man is grounded on the *property right* in his capacity as a commodity owner. For those independent burghers (proprietor farmers, handicraftsmen, independent manufactory owners) for whom ownership and work process are united, it was clear enough that the guaranteeing of the property right was ipso facto the guaranteeing of the right to subsist, so the property right came naturally to be regarded as being as inviolable as basic human rights. The evolution of the capitalistic process, however, meant that "labor power" became a commodity embraced, as it were, within the domain of "private capital." As has been pointed out by economic historians, for labor power to become a commodity the sellers of labor power, i.e., laborers, had to become "free" in a double sense of the term: first, "free" in the sense that, not subservient to anyone, they could freely offer their labor power in the market, and second, "free" in the sense that they were separated from the ownership of the means of production and freed from the task of marketing the products of their labor. In other words, here arose the separation of ownership and labor. Not only did this separation mean that the property right of owners of the means of production became separated from the subsistence right of laborers who did not own the means of production, but it implied further an antagonistic relation of the two major classes: capital and labor.

Basically, this separation of the property right and the subsistence right has continued and further sharpened in the process of capitalistic development. But at the same time it should be pointed out that there do exist, even in highly developed capitalist societies today, a fairly large number of individual proprietors who are conducting small-scale business on the basis of ownership of a small piece of land and some instruments of production and trade. For such people it cannot be denied that the property right and the subsistence right are synonymously conjoined in the concept of human right. Conversely, in a country like Japan, where public ownership of land is meager, a property right independent of the subsistence right (e.g., that of capitalistic enterprise or parasitic landowners) is being claimed with a strong voice by a significant majority. Such a property right may be termed a "nonsubsistence property right," and, being unrelated to the basic human right, it should be subject to restraints in the interest of public welfare.

Even in the case of land ownership for which the nonsubsistence property right is claimed, what is essential is the right to the land's *utilization.* From the standpoint of a capitalist enterprise, for example, a rational interest in the use of a factor of production, such as labor power, is to be able to hire and fire the owner of that labor power, not to establish ownership of him as a slave. The same may be said of land as a factor of production. So long as the use is guaranteed on terms agreeable as to the duration and rent, a capitalist enterprise with its main interest in the production of commodities should find maintaining such an agreement less cumbersome than having to insist on the property right over the land it decides to own.

It can generally be stated (1) that the land policy, whether as regards agricultural or urban land, had best be oriented with its central emphasis on *the right of its utilization* and (2) that those who nowadays favor the principle of "inviolability" of the property right are those whose major interest is in an expected speculative gain from the owned land in their assets portfolios. This second point is especially pertinent to the recent land-price controversy in Japan.

5. The Components of Price Formation of Urban Land

Thus we are led naturally to the question: what are the components of price formation for urban land in present-day Japan?

As with any other object for sale, it may be said in the first instance that the price of land is a function of supply and demand. Supply of land, on the one hand, is often said to be fixed, depicted for the textbook purpose as a straight vertical line on the P-Q quadrant. But this would be a drastic simplification inasmuch as the relevant supply, aside from the possibility of creating new land through reclamation, is usually regional and of specific quality, whether for agricultural, residential, or commercial purposes. Demand, on the other hand, is generally a derived demand, and the imputed price offered is based on the value of products and the marginal productivity of the land concerned.

We can discuss the price formation of land in these terms, but we have to warn ourselves immediately that such discussion is premised on the productive use of land; that is to say, here is implied the right of utilization, not necessarily the property right as such. When the property right is the major concern, the holding of land for speculative purpose would be a normal pattern of behavior, and it is most likely, in the period when a sustained price rise is expected, that what is known as "reserved demand" will arise. Given the ratchet effect of land prices, this is a kind of speculative action, constituting demand for capital gains from the land: a piece of land is held in reserve, appearing as if a part of supply, but with the owner's intention of reaping capital gains sometime in the future. If such "reserved demand" is significantly large, demand as a whole exceeds genuine supply, and the pressure for a price rise becomes much stronger. The textbook version of the "economics of uncertainty" tells us that there could be a positive role accorded to speculators' action, since, through their behavior of buying cheap and selling dear, they may be helping to even out the price differences between regions or over time. This would be true in the case of speculators on commodities like grain or cocoa or financial instruments. Even land speculators might perform the function of improving the allocation of resources through their action if their action were based upon the expectation of a rising trend in income gains from the land concerned. But the speculative demand for urban land in Japan in recent decades, taken against the backdrop of a 56-fold rise in prices over thirty years, can hardly be justified as a reflection of a rising trend of genuine income gains.

Thus we come to a consideration of the components of price formation of urban land in recent Japan, in which the speculative element has to be set aside as an extraneous factor of significant size. It has been suggested by some experts, in the course of discussion on the alleged "inviolability" of the private property right to land, that the land price is like an onion with many layers and that it is necessary to peel off one layer after another before coming to the very core, which alone could be considered the object of private property right. The first and the biggest layer to be peeled off should be the speculative component in the price formation of urban land.

What, then, are other component layers, and which are the ones to be peeled off before we come to the core?

Suppose we start with a piece of land utilized for agricultural purpose but situated in the suburb of an expanding urban center. Demand for that piece of land is a derived demand reckoned from the demand for its products; its price reflects the market value of such products and could rise, if it rises at all, only *pari passu* with the rise in that market value. But once that piece of land becomes the object of urban development, various kinds of developmental cost are incurred, such as new roads, waterworks, sewerage facilities, and other public utilities. Before long, schools, hospitals, and public parks may also have to be constructed. These developmental costs are usually borne in the first instance by the local autonomous bodies (and in some cases by the national government) and are naturally reflected in the land price. If the base price as agricultural land were, for example, 1,000 yen per unit area, the price might go up to 1,500 yen in consequence of the development. Who pays for this difference of 500 yen depends on the regulatory systems and other conditions that are relevant in the region concerned. The difference may be absorbed in the form of a capital gains tax imposed on the seller, or it may be borne partly by an intermediate real estate dealer or again partly by the buyer, as in the case of sewerage facilities and public utilities. But in any case, this additional price component of 500 yen cannot be counted as a portion of the property right of the original owner of the agricultural land in question. In other words, here is one layer of the onion that has to be peeled off before reaching the core.

Another layer that has to be peeled off is the price rise due to the emergence of the external economy. A reference was made earlier to the case of a windfall gain obtained through an opening of a new railroad line. Such an occurrence has been quite common in postwar Japan, and many episodes have been reported of political insiders, privy to the planning of a new line, purchasing the strategic land area cheaply in advance and selling it after the plan is made public. What was originally priced at 1,000 yen per unit area could easily rise to 4,000 yen, as the official White Paper itself admitted. In such cases also, the original landowner is not in a position to claim the property right over the windfall that may come into his pocket. Even when the gain is not realized through sale of the land, a tax measure may be justified in the form of the land appreciation tax.

Thus it may be said that extra layers to be peeled off in order to reach to the core of the onion for the purpose of ascertaining the quantitative dimension of the private property right on land are (1) the part of the price rise that is due to speculative activities, (2) the part of the price rise that is due to the effect of the external economy, and (3) the part of the price rise that is a consequence of incurring necessary developmental costs.

6. Socioeconomic Consequences of Price Revolution in Urban Land

Before we take up the problem of how to deal with this price revolution (or price counterrevolution) in urban land, we may review briefly some of its socioeconomic consequences.

Earlier, we distinguished price revolution from an inflationary situation by pointing to a major change in the relative price structure and to a historical shift in the power relations of enduring character. There is no question that the price counterrevolution of recent Japan has brought about a major change in the relative price structure as the price of urban land increased by a factor of 56 while the wholesale price index has risen by a factor of only 2.2 over the last thirty years. True, this latest case of price revolution (or price counterrevolution) is different from the earlier ones in one significant respect, namely, that the price rise in question has been only *partially realized* for a limited number of landowning individuals and/or institutions, most of whom have held on to their land while the price has continued to soar. Individuals, who could not escape the near-current-price assessment by the tax office at the time of bequest, were often forced to sell a portion of the land in order to pay the inheritance tax. But in the case of business enterprises and other institutions, land, if kept unsold, remains in their asset account at the original book value, which is now about one thirtieth of the current realizable value in most cases. Thus, latent profit on land for corporations with capitalization of one billion yen or more is now estimated to amount to as much as 432 trillion yen,[18] an amount equivalent to 130 percent of the country's GNP. Many of those corporations of long historical standing have retained their surplus land area in the manner of liquid assets without revaluation, thus giving the impression of undervalued equity in the stock market. It was natural that their stocks invited high expectation of appreciation quite independently of the expected yield possibilities. Their prices in the current stock market are quoted at the level of twenty to even one hundred times the face value, giving a dividend yield in most cases of less than 1 percent. Such a situation has led to the inflating of latent profit on the held securities (which too are recorded at face value in the corporations' asset accounts) to the amount of 228 trillion yen for the same group of corporations as above. Adding this figure to the latent profit on land, estimated above, will give us the total of 660 trillion yen. If we were to introduce a measure of asset revaluation, as was done in the immediate postwar period in Japan, and levy a 10 percent tax on the latent profit, the resulting tax revenue would enable the government to redeem by one stroke the entire outstanding amount of the so-called deficit financing bonds.

There is something wrong here, something that smacks of a casino society, with special circumstantial favors redounding to the business sector, in particular to the financial, real estate, and construction branches and, by interest association, to many of the politicians in the conservative wing. Probably more than in any other period in the history of Japan, we are now afflicted by what Veblen would have called "pecuniary orgies in a respectable form."

One peculiar consequence of the current price counter revolution is the inversion of what normally happens when the price of a particular commodity shows an exceptional rise. At the time of price revolution occasioned by the 1973 oil shock, a strong stimulus was given in the direction of economizing measures on oil and developing substitute sources of energy. It cannot be denied that, in the case of the exceptional rise in the price of urban land, there also was a market stimulus for more intensive use of land (such as high-rise buildings) and the substitution of agricultural land in the suburbs for residential and commercial purposes. But these market responses were overshadowed by the opposite reaction of holding the unused or semiused land as "reserved demand" for speculative purposes. The net effect of the price rise has been the further intensifying of demand (including reserved demand) for urban land and the shrinking of its actual supply. The land used for cultivation in the suburbs, for example, which could most logically be converted for expanding urban development, has remained as tax-favored agricultural land waiting for more lucrative opportunities in the future; in other words, it has remained as a kind of reserved demand rather than as a source of supply.

Such being the case, rational use of urban land oriented toward public-welfare purposes has been severely constricted. Several concrete examples may be cited in this connection:

(1) Ordinary citizens' dreams of owning their own houses, however small, in a city like Tokyo are being crushed. The average total income of a college graduate over a lifetime of employment is estimated at present to be around 166 million yen, which would be barely sufficient to purchase a meager one-room condominium apartment of 500 square feet near the central area of Tokyo. Five times one's annual disposable fund, consisting of one's earnings, savings, and borrowed money, is said to be a standard measure for the purchase cost of one's house in the Western world. If this measure is applied to a regular salaried person in Japan, the amount comes to about 30 million yen — not enough to buy even one *tsubo* (6 feet by 6) of residential land in the heart of Tokyo.

(2) The price counterrevolution in this case is breeding flagrant instances of social inequity. This fact is most eloquently revealed in the list of "high-income earners" annually made public by the Internal Revenue Office. It used to be the case that this list typically was topped by business tycoons, but the picture has changed in the last few years in such a way that the top fifty on the list would consist almost entirely of the persons who sold their land for profit. Even for those individuals who have not realized capital gains on the land they own, the possibility of obtaining loans secured on

their landed property is greatly facilitated by the rise in the latent asset value. Thus, it cannot be denied that the income and asset distribution in Japan has undergone a significant shift through the recent price counterrevolution.

(3) A proposal, partly in the form of pressures from abroad, has recently been repeatedly advanced in Japan to reorient the country's macroeconomic policies in the direction of stimulating *internal* effective demand in lieu of export drive. Since the time of the Nakasone cabinet (November 1982–November 1987), the government has officially favored such a proposal and has tried to emphasize the expansion of public works — a major area for which the government could take initiative and pay for the cost. It was only to be expected, however, that the sphere of public works was precisely the type of activity for which the acquisition of land was usually essential and that the exorbitant price rise of land therefore stood as a major impediment to the scheduled fulfillment of many of the projects. Just to give one example, the completion of the so-called Metropolitan Loop Road No. 2 has been stalled for several years because of the difficulty of financing the purchase of a mere 1,350 meters (0.84 miles) between Toranomon and Shimbashi. The government has found itself unable to meet the cost of procurement of the needed land, which has now risen to the level of 428.7 billion yen or 99.7 percent of the total cost of construction. The National Land Agency announced in March 1987 that the completion of the project would be delayed 108 years if the price of the relevant land should continue to rise 4 percent annually. One recalls the popular Chinese adage "It's like waiting one hundred years for the waters in the Yellow River to clear."

Especially deficient in the city of Tokyo are provisions for pedestrian roads, parks and children's playgrounds. Here again, the authorities concerned are greatly handicapped in their efforts by the price counterrevolution in land. Somewhat related to the problem confronting construction projects for public purposes is the unprecedented appeal by a group of ambassadors in Tokyo (representing thirty-one countries) to the Japanese Foreign Office to do something about the land situation, which has become so constrictive that a few countries, e.g., Uganda, have already decided to close their embassies in Tokyo, and several others, e.g., Australia and Spain, have chosen to offer for sale a sizable portion of their embassy premises. It is a sad commentary on the nature of affluence in Japan that foreign emissaries are being pauperized.

(4) A longer-range consequence of price counterrevolution has been noted by those people who set store by the warm and sociable neighborliness of an urban community that is being increasingly broken up. Referring to the process of divesting a community life of its once fertile components through the centrifugal effect of the unconscionable price rise in land, a noted publicist has commented recently, "The familiar noodle shop and then another old friend the laundry-man disappeared from the street corner; and the vacant site left behind is now surrounded by barbed-wire entanglements through which the cold blasts sweep down from nowhere. . . . Abiding, tried-and-true neighbors are gone almost unnoticed, and in their place nondescript strangers come in, who do not even say 'hello' as we meet. . . . How can we ever bring back sanity to the city of Tokyo?"[19] This can hardly be said to be an exaggeration, as the sense of hollowness spreads here and there in the erstwhile sprightly corners of the downtown Tokyo. A grave enough consequence of the price counterrevolution in land indeed!

7. Outline of Measures to Cope with the Urban Land Problem

It is not proposed here to discuss in detail pros and cons of concrete measures that have been advanced from various quarters for the purpose of wrestling with, and if possible solving, the seemingly intractable problems related to the price counterrevolution in land prices in Japan recently. I have to be satisfied on this occasion with presenting a bare outline of measures called for in coping with them.

First of all, I should like to emphasize the importance of two basic premises for the entire discussion, both of which were mentioned earlier: (1) the property right, as such, on land is *not* inviolable, and the land policy should be oriented rather toward giving full recognition to the right of utilization, and (2) the antecedent to the urban land policy should be well-considered planning as regards what type of city we would like to have — planning in which constituent citizens participate in one way or another. It follows, then, that legal and regulatory frameworks have to be worked out for the implementation of these premises as practical guidelines for which public planning is indispensable.

Second, it is almost axiomatic that land policy planning by public bodies is greatly facilitated when, as was specified in the Land Commission Act (1967) of Great Britain, legislative backing is given to ensure that the right land be available at the right time for the implementation of national, regional, and local plans. For this purpose, a logical solution would be to give to an appropriate government body the power to buy land compulsorily at a price net of increase due to betterment. The compensation provision is a key to land acquisition by public bodies. One recalls in this connection a 1962 Italian attempt to create a self-financing program of municipal land acquisition for low-cost housing, according to which the land was to be acquired at prices prevailing two years prior to the time of the planning decision. This provision was subsequently declared unconstitutional, and a concessional compromise was made to allow for the market price rise during the interval between the date of the planning decision and that of actual compulsory purchase. In the case of Japan it has been customary in recent years that the time interval referred to above linger on for several years, during which time the official "posted prices" themselves frequently have more than doubled. Expansion of publicly owned land in urban areas is definitely called for in Japan now, but at the same time the compensation provision has to be drastically improved in the direction of minimizing windfall gains to private land owners.

Third, how could we halt or preferably push down, the inordinate price rise of urban land in Japan? Of the three major components of its price formation mentioned earlier, the speculative element is of special character inasmuch as it depends mainly on the expectation of a rising trend itself in land price and is most likely to become less important as the price becomes stabilized. What was called "reserved demand" will also be on the decline as the expectation of rising trend tends to be disappointed. As regards the price increase as a consequence of incurring necessary developmental costs, one kind or another of "betterment levy" could be introduced as has been done in a number of countries.

Generally speaking, a more direct instrument in this connection is a system of taxation, of which there are two major types: (1) real estate tax and (2) capital gains tax. In Japan, the former is at present based on the official valuation of land by the Ministry of Local Autonomous Bodies — the valuation which is, at most, no more than 40 percent of the market value at any time. The tax rate, too, is being kept so low that the effective rate as a ratio of the total tax revenue to the aggregate market value of land property for the country as a whole comes out to be only 0.15 percent.[20] As for the capital gains tax on land property, the present system in Japan (after the revision in September 1987) is fairly complex, granting various concessions and exemptions, but is on the whole relatively lenient to property holders of long standing (five years or longer). If, for example, capital gains (the sale price minus the earlier purchase price minus the costs incurred in transaction) are calculated to amount to 40 million yen or less, the flat rate of 20 percent is applied as tax liability.

The controversy has centered on the problem of which tax system should be given a greater emphasis as an effective instrument for combating the rising trend of urban land. On the one hand, there is a strong opinion expressed by a public finance specialist like Yukio Noguchi,[21] who favors the raising of tax rates on holding the property, thus encouraging presumably more rational factor mobility; on the other hand, the opposite opinion is heard among some leading theoretical economists, like Ryūtaro Komiya[22] and Ken'ichi Inada,[23] who are advocating a near 100 percent tax on realized capital gains along with a concomitant tax measure on nonrealized gains in land value. One theoretical point is involved in this controversy, i.e., the question of a "locked-in effect,"[24] or the effect of "locking in" a particular type of asset in the owner's portfolio on account of a specific tax measure on that asset. A critical point is how important such a locked-in effect will be in the case of urban land in Japan today. Komiya, for example, concludes that it is insignificant. I do not intend to discuss this rather complicated problem in detail here, but I myself have taken a position basically agreeing with Komiya while not denying the advisability of raising tax rates somewhat on holding the landed property.

The fourth major focus related to policy measures for coping with the current price counterrevolution is the suggested program of deconcentration of the metropolitan functions of Tokyo, which has experienced the exceptional price rise of land during recent years, allegedly as a result of the convergence of international financial activities in Tokyo. The government has proposed that each ministry should take steps to move at least one agency or bureau from Tokyo to a less-congested locality, but resistance to this idea is, as expected, very strong. However, a number of gigantic plans of constructing reclaimed islands in Tokyo Bay are being offered by private groups of experts, the most ambitious of which is the one by the Kishō Kurokawa group, which proposes to create a land area of 30 thousand hectares in Tokyo Bay in order to move over all the central ministries and the parliament and to construct a residential center for 5 million people. Such a plan dodges realistic problems which are inseparably associated with manifold functions indigenous to Tokyo Bay and cannot be taken seriously. Still, almost everyone agrees that the present centralization trend toward Tokyo has to be countered somehow and, if possible, reversed. Here again, certain tax measures may be in order, such as a special enterprise tax levied against additional acquisition of office space in the central part of Tokyo, a special surtax on employers proportional to the number of employees who commute to the city center by public transport systems, and the revoking of the exemption clause as regards the real estate tax on governmental and otherwise public institutions situated in Tokyo and so on.

As awareness of the need for an interdisciplinary approach has become increasingly keen in the analysis of complex phenomena presented by modern society, new nomenclatures are being coined to refer to the types of discipline which bridge two or more traditional disciplines in social science — such nomenclatures as "eco-sociology" (meaning ecological sociology), "Verhältniss Soziologie," "techno-economics." It is certainly welcome that, wrestling with a problem which by its very nature is interdisciplinary, a specialist in a particular field goes beyond his or her accustomed domain to delve deeply into an associated field as the problem at hand demands. It is true that we do have nowadays numerous problems that require close cooperation by specialists in traditionally compartmentalized disciplines, such as nuclear power and energy, environmental disruption, demography and urbanization, peaceful coexistence and deterrence, multinational corporations and sovereignty. It may be tempting to coin a new nomenclature for scientific endeavor which crosses the traditional borderline, but it seems to me that the established disciplines in social science have developed to the present stage through many years of refurbishing and renovation and that although in economics, for example, different schools do exist, often disagreeing pointedly on specific issues, the rich heritage and store of tested hypotheses, theoretical constructs, and empirical propositions have grown into a mature tree of knowledge, as it were, which can be depended on as a basis even for an inquiry of novel character. It is in this spirit that I have focused in this essay upon the problem of property right where legal principles and economic analysis interpenetrate each other as contiguous areas of discipline. Such an approach, however, could be subsumed, I believe, under the nomenclature of political economy. Thus the title of this essay.

NOTES

1. Harold Laski, *The Rise of Liberalism* (1936), pp. 1–2.
2. Quoted in Robert Kuttner, "The Poverty of Economics," *Atlantic Monthly* (February 1985), p. 76.
3. Quoted in Kuttner, p. 78.
4. J. K. Galbraith, *Economics in Perspective: A Critical History* (Boston: Houghton Mifflin, 1987), p. 299.
5. *International Encyclopedia of the Social Sciences,* Vol. 12 (1968), p. 473.
6. *International Encyclopedia of the Social Sciences,* p. 474.
7. J. M. Keynes, *A Treatise of Money,* Vol. II (1934), p. 158.
8. Keynes, p. 159.
9. The second oil shock of 1979–1980 witnessed the price rise from $13.34 per barrel in January 1979 to $32 in November 1980.
10. *The Economist,* 3, October 1987, p. 25.
11. The more correct multiple is 3.5 times on the basis of the exchange rate of 130 yen for a dollar. Tokyo's twenty-three-ward area alone would be equivalent in price to the whole of the United States.
12. Compiled by the National Land Agency once a year as of January 1 as "that price which is seen to prevail when the transaction is free and normal." The absolute level of these "posted prices" follows more or less the actually transacted price and is usually 70 to 80 percent of the latter. Officially, there are two other sets of land price that are compiled: one, called "route rates," by the Internal Revenue Agency as a benchmark for inheritance and gift taxes, and another, by the Ministry of Local Autonomous Bodies, for the basis of landed estate tax. Both of these are much lower in absolute terms, the former being anywhere from 50 to 60 percent

of the actually transacted price and the latter from 20 to 40 percent, depending on the area concerned.

13. It may be relevant to remind ourselves in this connection that the present Liberal-Democratic party came into existence as the result of a merger, in November 1955, of two conservative parties, and ever since then it has continued to remain as a government party in power for more than thirty years.

14. In a dialogue with Hideo Aragaki of the Asahi Shinbun for *Hōsō Asahi*, January 1965.

15. *Jeremy Bentham's Economic Writings*, Vol. I, ed. W. Stark (1952), p. 332.

16. *International Encyclopedia of the Social Sciences*, Vol. 12 (1968), p. 592.

17. *Proceedings of The 13th Plenary Session of the Constitutions Research Commission* (1958), p. 40.

18. *The Asahi Shimbun*, April, 24, 1988, p. 13.

19. Kazuyuki Hibino, *The Asahi Shimbun*, December 27, 1987, p. 1.

20. As estimated by Yukio Noguchi in *Ekonomisuto*, January 26, 1988, p. 14.

21. Noguchi, *Ekonomisuto*, pp. 12–17.

22. Ryūtaro Komiya, *Gendai Nihon Keizai Kenkyu* (Tokyo Daigaku Shuppankai, 1975), pp. 225–68.

23. Ken'ichi Inada, "Toshi to Tochi-Zeisei," *Sekai* (December 1987), pp. 123–36.

24. See Richard A. Musgrave, "Effects of Tax Policy on Private Capital Formation," in CMC, *Fiscal and Debt Management Policies* (Englewood Cliffs, N.J.: Prentice-Hall, 1963), pp. 96–99.

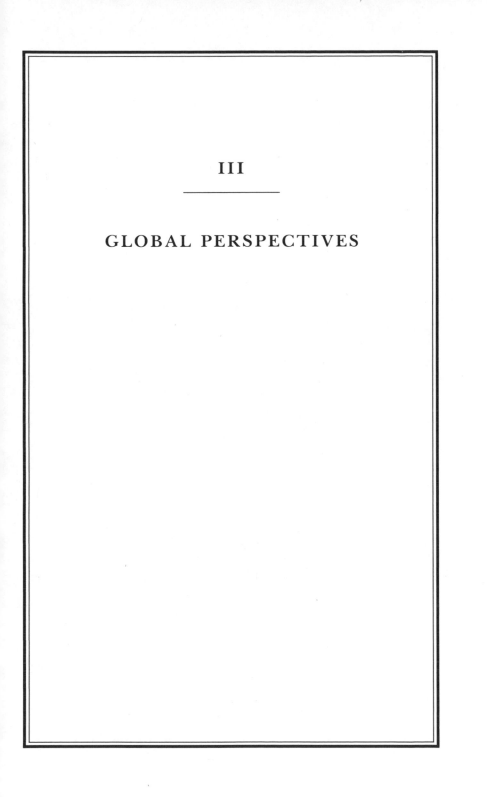

III

GLOBAL PERSPECTIVES

James K. Galbraith

Trade and the Planning System

THE RISE of international competition and the decline of the great American manufacturing corporation since 1967 are facts often cited by John Kenneth Galbraith's critics, who argue that they render the message of *The New Industrial State* obsolete. Galbraith himself concedes something to this point of view:

> . . . I did not see the development of the foreign, most notably the Japanese, competition to which [the corporation] would be subject. This is partly an aspect of the aging process. . . . No one can doubt that in our older industries this competition has substantially impaired the certainty and effectiveness of the planning process. (*New Industrial State*, 4th ed., 1985, pp. xxxi-xxxii)

This essay explores some aspects of the internationalization that lies behind the American corporation's decline in a way that is consistent with Galbraith's theory of the corporation and with compatible dissenting traditions. Beyond this, it will argue that certain unresolved mysteries of mainstream economics may perhaps be cracked by such an analysis. Two of these mysteries are the rapid expansion of U.S. exports in the late 1970s despite the decline of aggregate productivity growth and the rapid rise of inflation despite an absence of overtly inflationary macropolicy at the same time.

The discussion departs from neoclassical tradition in three cen-

The author would like to thank Stephen Marglin, Juliet Schor, Carol Heim, and other members of the Harvard-MIT Seminar on Non-neoclassical Economics for their comments.

tral respects, all identified with Galbraith, his predecessors, or his most important intellectual colleagues. The treatment of production follows Robinson (1956) and Salter (1969), within a macroeconomic accounting framework like that of Kalecki (1933). The motivation (or lack of it) attributed to the firm follows Galbraith (1967) as elucidated in an earlier article of mine (1984). The notions of historical process follow Veblen (1898) as reprised in Kaldor (1985). Each of these departures is explained below.

Structure of Production

Suppose that the economy consists, to expand slightly on the simplest Kalecki framework, of three productive sectors. The first of these produces capital goods for use in new plant and equipment; this sector uses highly skilled and well-paid labor; such equipment as it needs it builds itself. The second uses labor and capital goods to produce consumer goods. Finally, there is a sector using labor only to produce services. The sectors trade with each other to sell their product and satisfy their respective needs.

Suppose that, initially, the capital goods sector is just large enough, and growing just rapidly enough, to fill the demand for new capital goods of both goods sectors at their present rates of growth, and there is therefore neither excess supply nor shortage of capital goods. Wages in all sectors are just high enough to demand all consumer goods and service output at prevailing prices, and the consumer goods sector is just large enough to meet demand for wage goods generated at prevailing wages (workers do not save out of wages). Total profits are just large enough to buy needed capital goods at prevailing capital goods prices, and any maldistribution of profits between capital and consumers goods sectors is offset by lending from one to the other. Capitalists do not consume out of profits. No net profits are earned in services. Total profits therefore equal total investment, and total wages equal consumption. Growth has been going on for an indefinite time at a constant rate, and all the peculiar conditions for this, including stable expectations for future growth at the same rate, prevail. The economy is thus on a stable expansion path, or in a Robinsonian "Golden Age."

There is, at any given time, a "book of blueprints" from which alternative, discrete factor combinations for a given purpose may be chosen. Best practice technique is determined by the state of technology and by (current and expected) factor prices at the moment at which a blueprint is chosen. After that moment, factor combinations for that plant are (virtually) fixed. As techniques change, so do factor prices and least-cost factor combinations; these raise the comparative cost of older facilities (perhaps to the point of economic extinction) but cannot induce substantial factor substitution within them. Thus, at any time a spectrum of less efficient techniques coexists with the best practice.

Profit income as a whole is determined macroeconomically: "capitalists get what they spend." But to individual firms profit arrives mainly in the form of quasirents. And the manner in which quasi-rents are earned in the consumer and capital goods sectors is quite asymmetric. Differences of form and composition between the sectors and differences in their pricing strategies and in the effects of technical change dictate quite different patterns of quasirent distribution.

For a consumer good produced in mass fashion, you need a plant of a highly specific sort. An automobile factory is a matter of poured concrete and structural steel. It cannot be turned, in a car-buying recession, to some other use; indeed, it must be maintained as a car-producing entity or it will not survive at all. And if it does not survive, then a new car-building plant must be created to take its place before the rate of production of cars can again reach its former pace.[1]

To produce a capital good — whether a new computer or a jet aircraft — you need above all a reservoir of scientific and engineering talent, along with a store of precise but flexible tools and equipment. Capital goods are not made on mass assembly lines, and so the extreme specialization of the mass assembly line is usually not required.

For this reason, the difference between best and average practice technique is not so pronounced in the capital goods sector as in consumer goods. In computers or aircraft or structural engineering, virtually the whole industry moves forward with the cutting edge of technical change and older processes drop rapidly out of production. The marginal cost curve is comparatively flat (or even declining), up to the physical capacity limits of the best-practice technique, and there is no margin of second-best technique that is acceptable to purchasers in tight markets. Rents in this sector are earned in transient fashion by dynamic price discrimination. That is, the capital goods producer with a new technique to sell picks off early consumers at their high reservation prices and then moves down the demand curve as competition intensifies and cumulative sales increase. Success depends on maintaining a transient monopoly at least long enough to recover fixed costs; once imitators move in, price collapses to marginal costs. Typically, in practice the capital goods industry is a lottery: many aspire to be first to market, winner take all and the devil the hindmost.

Not so in consumer goods. There, new, best-practice factories are added to a stream of preexisting productive equipment. These produce common products by differing processes, and the final consumer is unaware of and (in general) indifferent to the vintage of the equipment on which his product was produced. Prices are set by unit costs of the least efficient facility that can be maintained in production. Hence the largest rents are earned by those companies with the most favorable technical profiles so long as there is a sharp contrast between costs at the best and worst facilities in the industry as a whole.

Motivation of the Firm

What does the corporation want? The neoclassical supposition that firms maximize profits is not so much wrong as overly vague. In the circumstances described, it fails to distinguish which alternative investment strategies in an uncertain world will be chosen, since any of several might be motivated *ex ante* by a *desire* to maximize profits. A more precise and more readily observable criterion is required. Specifically, as in Stackelberg models, the decision to invest can be either long-run profit-maximizing or profit- (and company-) destroying, depending on the (*ex ante* unknowable) reaction of other firms. Appreciating this, we can say more precisely that the corporation comes to behave in ways that emphasize industry-wide *stabilization:* control over the environment from technological development through sales becomes the crucial thing.

When substantial technical advances are made or new econo-

mies of scale achieved, competitive theory, based on profit maximization, seems to predict that all firms will try to move rapidly to
install the new and to scrap the old equipment. But actually such
events are treated by firms as the deepest sort of threat to existence. There is no reason why the industry's demand curve need
be sufficiently elastic to permit all existing firms, following major
technical change and investment, to sell all output at the new cost
structure. Nor can any particular firm be assured of maintaining
its place in the scramble. Nor indeed is there any reason why new
investment need be made by only *existing* firms: new corporate enterprise, free of the bonded debt and other ongoing obligations of
existing companies, may well be in a better position. The prospect
of a chaotic redisposition of industrial resources, of the Schumpeterian gale, hangs over technical planning like a cloud.

Yet we observe (as Galbraith did in 1967) that stable or only
gradually changing market shares is a feature of many industries
over quite long periods of time and across major technological
transitions. Shakeouts and other disruptive episodes do occur, but
they are occasional if not rare. This implies that the pattern of new
investments reflects the distribution of the existing capital stock,
and so that access to investable capital is also roughly proportion-
ate to existing capacity. Yet this can only be true if investment decisions are somehow coordinated, however imperfectly, across firms,
either by themselves or by an equally coordinated banking sector.
Some way has been found to avoid the scramble.

Stable competition in consumer goods sectors can be achieved if
major firms arrange to maintain similar production structures and
technical profiles. That is, each major enterprise must maintain
facilities of several vintages, approximately spanning the vintages
of the industry as a whole. In that case, the profitability of each
enterprise (and so, access to new capital) is affected in like fashion
by fluctuations of demand. The smallest viable firm size for the
long run is then determined not by the minimum efficient scale of
a single plant but by the minimum size required to maintain a rough
facsimile of the whole industry's technical profile. When this is
achieved, no one firm has an incentive to destroy the rent-yielding
cost-price profile, either by price cutting or by proceeding too ag-
gressively to the incorporation of new technology into productive
equipment. And this is the Planning System.

In an industry enjoying such an array of firms, it is in the individual interest of each to expand capacity at only the rate of growth of demand for the industry as a whole. To do less is a path to extinction: not only to lose market share, but also to become a comparatively high-cost producer and eventually to lose profitability. To do more is to risk comparable reaction by one's competition: a struggle for control of the leading edge and consequent collapse of the cost-price profile and of profits.

Thus, so long as the requisite information, about the rate of growth of demand at the prevailing cost and price structure, remains reasonably clear and accessible, firms will implicitly coordinate their investment decisions around that rate, in the interest of environmental control. This is something that firms within a single national economy and information market can often readily achieve. But, needless to say, in a competitive international environment maintaining conditions under which this stability is possible is a major feat. Because of the much higher cross-border cost of information, success in that environment is far from guaranteed and may be rare. The decline of the Planning System is nothing more nor less, ironically, than a failure of the transnational information market.

Cycles and Cumulative Causation

Even without trade, the Planning System is not free of instability. Business cycles occur in closed as well as open systems. To fix ideas, one may therefore ask, What are the consequences of instability for the evolution of industrial structure within a closed system?

This brings us to a third departure from neoclassical analysis, which is from the habit of thought that tends reflexively to decompose time series into cycle and trend and to focus with sequential exclusivity on one or the other. Sometimes, observed trends are conflated with the concept of long-run equilibrium, toward which the structure of formal models directs attention. Thus as Kaldor observed, the neoclassical analyst knows, or thinks he knows, more about the distant future (when disturbances subside and underlying properties emerge) than about immediate events.

Here we abjure the cycle/trend decomposition. Events are seen to build on each other in the short run, day by day, and the future becomes more uncertain, rather than less so, as one looks further ahead. When instabilities arise because certain chains of consequence cannot be sustained, these are primary or fundamental facts, and not ephemera overlaid over "underlying trends" that would be what they are even if unstable patterns of growth and decline somehow could be suppressed. The scientific exercise lies in seeking to understand the motor driving the process of cumulative causation and not in developing a theory of the direction (or indeed, average direction) taken by the car.

Now a slump can occur for any reason at all; all that is required is that confidence in future profitability is disrupted. Investment (the production of capital goods) then leads the way down, and so falls as a share of the value of all output (as does profit, since gross investment determines gross profits). Note that since confidence determines investment and investment determines profits, there is nothing whatever "irrational" about this process. Rational behavior for the investing businessman consists merely of coordinating one's thinking with everyone else's.

In the recovery, confidence soars and investment will lead the way back up. But even if investment makes a full recovery, the Golden Age growth path will not be regained. For the stream of production of consumer goods depends not on the flow of additions to capital but on the whole stock of fixed capital goods in existence at a given time, and this includes not only present investments but all of past investment that is still good to use.

To save costs in the recession, expenditures on maintenance are reduced. Further, relative factor prices may change, deepening the cost disadvantages of older equipment. Hence, not only does new capital equipment cease to enter the available pool, old capital equipment also makes an exit — there is scrapping. By the time of the trough, the capital stock will be well below its previous expansion path, and so the shock to output will have the cumulative character noted (but not explained) by Mankiw (1987).[2]

In the expansion, consumers' goods businesses first bring idle equipment they may still have available back into service. They then assess the rate of growth of consumer demand in relation to available equipment. Then they place orders with capital goods manufacturers (whether internal divisions of their own companies or independent suppliers) for new equipment.

Now, just as soon as new investment orders have been placed in anticipation of future capital needs, the sector which produces capital goods, which was the most severely idled in the recession, is back at full employment. Growth of *incomes* in the sector and in the whole economy is therefore very rapid. The recession has had little effect on the capacity of the capital goods sector to meet demand. Engineers and scientists and craftsmen and their tools rarely disappear so completely in the short period of a bust that they cannot be called back quickly in the ensuing boom. Politicians are moved to speak, as Reagan administration officials did frequently in 1983, of an "investment-led recovery."

With stalled income growth and unemployment, the growth of consumption too diminishes in the slump, and this obscures the developing situation. As recovery begins, there is still capacity in excess of need and so no immediate pressure on costs. The early stage of recovery is wonderful, just as Harrod's (1939) growth model predicted. But shortages lurk just over the horizon, in the ensuing recovery and boom.

Production takes time, and the growth of investment demand must happen before new capital equipment has actually been created and added to the stock. It is therefore inevitable that, within a short time, a rapidly rising demand for consumer goods will confront an as yet slowly rising supply.

Partly this may stimulate, as the neoclassical paradigm supposes, accelerated efforts to increase apparent productivity (intensity of work effort) and so, in effect, to move along the production function. These efforts will work to break bottlenecks, alleviate shortages, and bring products to the waiting consumers. But here the putty-clay nature of the consumer goods sector interposes a problem. Factors are not easily substitutable in existing consumers goods production. (If they were, why invest at all?) Some of the demand cannot be accommodated at prevailing prices in the short run.

In the neoclassical version of events, prices will rise in the consumer goods sector to clear that market, with few significant changes in any other markets. But in real life manufactured consumer goods prices do not rise to clear markets in the face of transitory shortage. Instead, prices are held constant (or rise only to the extent that underlying costs rise), backlogs appear, and demand flows elsewhere.

Therefore, in the closed-economy expansion there must generally be short run intersectoral displacement of demand. Specifically there will be substitution of *services* for *goods* in the consumption set. Rather than install an alarm, some apartment houses will hire a guard. Rather than buy a power lawnmower, I will hire a teenager. On the production track that would have occurred without recession consumers would, in each instance, have preferred the equipment. But they make do with the services. Factor substitution is occurring across rather than within productive sectors.

Again in the neoclassical version this phenomenon is transitory. Wages in the services sector will now rise, increasing supply, diminishing demand and restoring equilibrium as soon as the consumer goods that were wanted in the first place become available. But again real life is different. The supply of labor in the services sector is highly elastic when demand is rising so that wages do not need to rise much (if at all) to induce new supply. And once the supply is on the market, the effective demand for the consumers goods that services have replaced is no longer apparent. Therefore, the supply of such goods does not return to the level and growth track that would have prevailed without the recession.

These developments lead to a larger service sector, and to a smaller manufacturing sector, than would have been the case if no recession/expansion cycle had ever occurred. Some forced retirements, permanent layoffs, and displacements will occur. Within the manufacturing sector, the final result will be a new expansion path in which capital and consumer goods subsectors are once again in about the necessary proportions to each other. The economy will be more reliant on service activity, with its lower capital requirements, than it was before or than it would have been at the same average rate of growth but without the recession. Other things equal, the material standard of living will be lower. Now only technical change, embodied in new investments that may come on-line, can now assure rising living standards. Moreover, only a pattern of falling consumer goods prices relative to prices of services (as technique improves) can induce consumers to shift their patterns of demand back from services to goods.

Yet one curious effect of occasional recessions in this model is a more rapid pace of embodied technical advance than would otherwise have been the case. In the prolonged expansion, firms find ways to stretch the life of older equipment, all the more so as the expectation of an eventual recession grows, increasing the risks associated with being caught in a cash squeeze while a major investment project is underway. It takes a longer time for the requisite "room" to develop for a concerted advance to a new generation of technologies. Recessions clear the way.

Are recessions then required to unblock the path to technical progress? No: the sufficient requirement is merely vigorous competition and an adequate supply of "eager capital" willing to be risked on the lottery of innovation. Yet in a controlled environment in which consumer goods firms coordinate their new investments with a view to preserving industrial stability, recessions are useful to such firms as a coordinating device. They help to assure that all companies operating a given industrial process retire old techniques and advance to new ones in like fashion. Thus, relative profitability and market shares remain stable despite common fluctuations in gross profitability and sales. This reduces one critical element of uncertainty in the corporate life cycle, the risk of cutthroat, technology-based competition, which most threatens the survival of the corporation itself. In the closed economy, recessions reconcile rapid technical change with the Planning System.

In a word, the rate at which technical change is incorporated into the capital stock depends on two variables: the rate of scrapping of old capital and the expected rate of growth of demand. Recessions raise the rate of scrapping and have a nonlinear relationship with the expected rate of growth that depends on the expected frequency of future recessions.

That being so, one may speculate on an optimal frequency of recessions in a Planning System. In a completely stable macroenvironment (such as one might find under state socialism), the pace of technical advance (defined as the rate of reduction of unit production costs) is limited by the expected future growth of demand and by the rate of physical obsolescence of existing capital equipment. Recessions raise the obsolescence rate, and so (for a given pool of available techniques) the pace of cost reduction. But too frequent recessions can also slow the *expected* average growth rate of demand, depressing the expected profitability of new investment.

The trick of policy, therefore, must be to create an environment in which each succeeding recession is regarded for practical purposes as a one-time-only event, to be followed by a prolonged expansion in which all new capital investments (up to the full capacity of the capital goods sector for a sustained period) will be rewarded. It might be thought that in a world of rational long-run expectations such an environment is impossible. But rational expectations are not necessarily a problem. If the expansion is expected to be sufficiently long so that the losses from the next expected recession are heavily discounted, rational firms will be motivated to invest at a maximal rate even though they know that a new recession will happen at some time in the future. The key is that actual expansions be sufficiently long and that actual recessions be sufficiently infrequent.

Recession with Trade

Trade changes little in the scenario just described, so long as it is conducted predominantly between nations of the same general technological level, so long as all such nations are subject, at random, to economic instabilities and cycles of the same general size, and so long as all partake of a single Planning System.

But transnational information markets are, in fact, far from perfect. National entities keep secrets. Coordination across national lines is difficult. And internal business cycles vary across countries, making the synchronization of investment across national boundaries exceptionally difficult. Therefore, competing Planning Systems, each oriented primarily and by tradition to its own internal market, may develop. Free trade between such systems then enhances competition, assuring technical progress without the need for the purgative of recession. For this reason, trade may tend to dampen cyclical pressures, even though it increases structural instability. And resistance to international predation will arise in the form of nationalist and protectionist sentiment, at the very heart of the threatened system. In short, when trade between advanced entities places competing Planning Systems in conflict, the stability of both can be jeopardized and the political system may be called upon to restore order.

Suppose we now consider another aspect of trade, that which develops from the hierarchical character of scientific and technological accomplishment in the real world. Suppose specifically that there is one country that is capable of supplying the advanced capital goods necessary for internationally competitive production of goods for consumer use. Further, suppose that another country develops the capacity to produce consumer goods with capital goods that can be obtained from the advanced country.

We now have a trading system in which a Leading Technological Power (LTP) is facing an Intermediate Manufacturing Power (IMP). This is trade across national boundaries but within a single Planning System.

For the IMP to exist at all, the capital goods sector of the LTP must expand beyond the size required for the servicing of its own consumer goods sector. And the consumer goods sector of the LTP must shrink to make room for capital goods expansion. The LTP is now an exporter of capital equipment and an importer of consumer goods. This asymmetry creates another in the structure of incomes. The trade earnings of the IMP are essentially in the form of wage income and quasirents on consumers goods, while those of the LTP include the form of transient rents from the sale of advanced capital equipment. Since fewer workers are involved on the LTP side, their wage incomes (including returns on human capital) are naturally higher, so long as bilateral trade in the aggregate is balanced.

Now consider the recession initiated by tight policy in the LTP. As before, demand for consumer goods dips while that for replacement and expansion of capital equipment plummets. As before, this has little immediate effect on the permanent capacity of the capital goods industry. But, as before, the recession makes a serious dent in the permanent capacity, relative to full employment income, of the LTP's domestic consumer goods production. And, as before, in the recovery the demand for consumer goods begins after a time to outstrip the domestic supply.

What has happened, meantime, to capacity in the IMP? If the IMP were structurally exactly like the LTP, one might expect the recession to affect its own industrial capacity in the same way, so the cycle to leave the pattern of trade relations between the two is nearly unchanged.

But this structural similarity is not the case. The IMP's production facilities for manufactured consumer goods are newer than those of the LTP. They are for this reason alone less likely to be scrapped in the slump than their decrepit and depreciated counterparts in the advanced country. Whether the facilities are under the ownership of national enterprise or multinational corporations is immaterial to this point: structural stability across corporations does not imply structural stability across countries. Further, if the IMP government possesses any resources for intervention, these will be devoted to preserving the consumer goods export sectors. Such sectors are the most advanced available in the country and a principal earner of foreign exchange, whereas in the LTP competing consumer goods sectors are far from holding this position. And so in the slump the survival rates of existing capacity are likely to be higher in the IMP. Finally, even if existing consumer goods capacity in both countries were to be completely wiped out, new expansion afterward would go to the IMP, where even the highest wages for the best workers are lower than what must be paid in the LTP (and for labor that is not the best available and that may even be inferior to IMP labor).

In the aftermath of recession, then, the patterns of trade become deformed. Demand in the LTP for consumer goods rises rapidly, confronting a curtailed domestic supply. New orders are placed preponderantly with the IMP. Investors, seeing profit opportunities in the IMP, plan plant expansions there and place orders for new capital goods. These orders flow back to the LTP. Soon the share of trade is larger in both countries than it was before. The pace of technical change is again more rapid than it would have been without the recession, but now a significant share of the most advanced capacity produced in the LTP is being installed in the IMP rather than at home.

Therefore the LTP will come to enjoy an even larger share of income from rents in the capital goods sector than it did before.[3] But since capital goods are earning economic rents, they require fewer workers to earn enough to purchase from the IMP the same volume of consumer goods imports as were previously purchased from domestic workers. And, of course, these few workers do not want all the goods. So there is, in the LTP, a dual problem: more domestic workers left in unemployment than in the earlier situation and fewer workers remaining, however well paid, to demand the goods. The superfluous workers are displaced permanently from consumption goods manufacturing. Some of them will remain indefinitely on the public dole. But in the right climate of public policy most will be reabsorbed in the LTP service sector, taking secondary incomes paid, in effect, from the surplus earned in the sale of capital goods. This solves the problem: the LTP service workers generate just enough extra demand, in the aggregate, to keep up demand for IMP goods, close the trade circuit, and keep the system going.

Thus, trade can take either of two forms. Some of it occurs between competing Planning Systems; this type, we have seen, enhances competition and technical change by its own nature. On this hand, it may therefore remove some of the reasons for cyclical instability in the host economy. On the other hand, it is a threatening form of trade, for two Planning Systems undermine each other unless they can coordinate on precisely the points of investment and technical advance.

The other form is transnational trade within a simple Planning System. This type of trade is based on asymmetries in technological development, and it produces distortion in the composition of output in the more advanced economy. We may now explore possible implications of these distortions for surface phenomena, for big issues of macroeconomic perception. Two of these are, first, the measured rate of productivity growth, and, second, the rate of inflation. We shall see that the transition to asymmetric trade can be expected to play havoc with both.

Effect on Productivity Growth

At the time of apparent U.S. productivity crisis in the 1970s, both the measured rate of output growth (in the numerator) fell and the rate of labor input growth (in the denominator) rose compared to the 1960s. Parts of these developments have been well explained by Denison (1979), who has in particular delimited the small effects of increasing environmental and health and safety regulation, of rising energy prices, and of other commonly cited causes. However, most of the slowdown in productivity growth cannot be assigned to any of the causes Denison examines, nor are other, more econometric exercises more successful. Much mystery remains; Richard Nelson (1986) provides a recent, brief summing up. His verdict: "intellectual dissarray and confusion."

One might ask whether measurement difficulties occasioned by changes in the sectoral composition of output, in turn occasioned by asymmetric trade, may form part of the story.

General difficulties in the measurement of output and productivity growth in the presence of technical progress are well known.[4] A major imponderable occurs in the case where product rather than process change is the dominant form of technical progress and new products must be linked into existing indices of output. In the case of new products perceived to be enhanced versions of existing products (new generations of computers), the difficulty lies in assessing the degree of effective price reduction to associate with the quality change. In the case of products not previously in the index at all, an actual fall in real output may be registered, as the new product with low real input requirements (and market price) drives a high-cost competitor (perhaps in another SIC code and output subindex altogether) out of business. Both of these effects will tend to reduce measured growth of real output.

Given the comparable frequency of recessions, there may be no good reason to suppose that in the aggregate either process or product innovation was proceeding at a different rate in the 1950s, before the emergence of the IMPs, than in the 1970s.[5] Scientific progress was occurring and engineering talent was being applied to production problems in both periods, and so arguably there was a comparable distortion in the *level* of productivity in both. This would not itself affect the rate at which productivity changes and so cannot have caused the observed productivity growth slowdown.

But there is powerful reason to think that the trade deformations brought on by open-economy business cycles in the later period would precisely cause a change in measured productivity growth, even if the underlying rate of scientific progress had not changed.

The reason is that product change and redefinition is the more characteristic feature of capital goods industry, while process innovation is the more compelling and important characteristic in the production of consumer goods. In extreme cases (such as engineering and architectural blueprints), the capital goods sector effectively mimics the service sector. That is, it produces specialty products with no consistent price deflators, whose real output is therefore measured by real input quantities and whose measured productivity growth is therefore virtually zero almost by definition. And so, when a shift in shares of total production between capital and consumer goods occurs, the relative importance of unmeasured or undermeasured quality change will increase.[6] Measured output and productivity growth will then decline in comparison to the undistorted case before settling at a lower permanent rate defined by the new LTP sectoral mix.

In the particular case of the computer industry in the 1970s, the Bureau of Economic Analysis had assumed from 1969 to 1984 that the price of computers had remained unchanged. Thus, sales of computers in real terms could be measured by the dollar revenues of the computer producers. One could then compare this expanding "real" level of computer production with the expanding number of jobs in the business. Since the two were growing more or less in tandem, this led to the extraordinary conclusion that there hadn't been much productivity growth in the computer business.

In December 1985, the Bureau of Economic Analysis of the Department of Commerce published for the first time a special price index for computers (*Survey of Current Business*, 1985). On the basis of information supplied by IBM, the bureau calculated that the price of computers had, in fact, fallen about nine-fold from 1969 through 1984 (Cartright, 1986). The use of 1972 prices as the base year, then, resulted in measures of the "real quantity" of computer output that were higher by 102.4 *billion* 1972 dollars for 1984 than previously estimated. The gain disappears as the shift to the 1982 base year is made — but it would have been observed in the 1970s, and the apparent *aggregate* productivity crisis would have seemed less serious had the corrected price index and the old base year been in simultaneous use.[7]

Nor is this all. After internationalization, manufacturing employment in the consumer goods sector falls. Employment rises in (or near) the LTP's capital goods sector,[8] but for these well-paying jobs the former consumer goods worker is not likely to be qualified. He or she must perforce find a new home in the remaining sector, which is services,[9] which is also notorious for its slow, *mea-*

sured productivity growth. Here is a second, equally large or larger reason why measured aggregate productivity growth may fall with asymmetric trade.

There are consequences, too, for the household in the labor market. In the closed economy, the probability of recall in one's old industry remained high, and as new consumer goods were invented new types of industrial jobs would open up. By any principle of wage setting, consumer goods manufacturing jobs would pay well by national standards. That is, they would pay better than service jobs, while the classes of comparable employment that pay better (in capital goods manufacturing)[10] still would be small enough so as not strongly to affect the consumer goods workers' sense of comparative standing. In this environment the autoworker, and not the computer designer, defined the decent standard of working-class life. With a sufficient system of unemployment compensation, workers routinely maintained stable patterns of family consumption growth on the realized and expected income of the single wage earner.

In the open economy, the consumer goods producing jobs do not return so reliably once the recession is past. Workers on layoff find themselves stranded, and many must gradually give up on the hope of recall. Unemployment insurance eventually runs out. The very good jobs in the export sector that are created in the expansion are inaccessible. What remains are service jobs of varying quality that do not support, on their own, the former standard of material life.

For this reason, not only will primary workers be displaced to the service sector, "secondary" workers will flock into the labor market. They will do this first to assure continuity of living standards. Second, they will do it to provide some insurance against future unemployment and instability of family income. Third, they will do it to preserve relative standing. There is, in the new setting, intense competition from multiearner households for certain kinds of intrinsically scarce goods (for example, housing in neighborhoods with the best schools); such competition pressures even families whose own material conditions are untouched by unemployment or wage give-backs. Families that continue to rely on a single earner find themselves displaced downward in comparative living standards, unable to consume at rates they observe to be normal by watching their friends and neighbors. They too will send out wives and children to the service work force.

Were unpaid household labor counted in GNP, this phenomenon would yield a rise in measured productivity (Barrett and Bustillo 1987). But homework is not so counted, and the newly arrived labor-force participants are ill equipped with human and physical capital when compared with the mass of those already working outside the home. Here is a third large reason why the trade-deforming business cycle will tend to lower the measured rate of productivity growth.

Thus, with trade the business cycle may be expected to deform LTP social relations. The resulting society will include many more working people, at lower average hourly earnings, than the old one did. It will include a larger class of primary export earners with high average earnings than the old one did. It will include a smaller and shrinking class of import-competing consumers goods producers whose earnings, though high in relation to services, no longer define the social pinnacle achievable through work. It will enjoy a wider distribution of advanced equipment made available by an increase in the capacity of the capital goods sector.

In some respects, it will be a richer place, but it will be less secure. There will be more participants in the capital goods lottery. Having lost the internal control over technical development in the consumer goods sector previously supplied by domestic corporations, it will have a more complex macroeconomic policy problem. And it may suffer an apparent permanent slowdown of productivity growth if its scholars are too accustomed to viewing the production process in purely neoclassical terms. The Planning System, now spread over a North-South frontier, has less control and a weaker apparent performance at home.

Effects on Inflation

What are the consequences of the structural transition described above for inflationary pressures and for actual inflation?

In this framework prices are determined by costs. Therefore, rises in wages, or more completely an intensifying struggle for income shares (between wages and profits) inside the most developed countries, are the foundation and origin of inflationary pressures. It is pressure to pay higher money incomes (whether to capitalists or to workers) that brings on accommodating, and then expansionary, and then reckless, monetary policy behavior. It is pressure to increase real consumption that creates market conditions where supply shocks (cost increases external to the system under scrutiny) are prone to occur. To look at supply shocks as purely exogenous is, for the economist, simply to duck the issue, to dump the problem of the origins of inflation over into someone else's realm of study.

The distinction between shocks and mechanisms of propagation is nevertheless useful here. Shocks are the consequence of market pressures, due to changes in demand conditions or occasionally to abrupt changes in the climate of supply. A surge of grain prices, an oil embargo, and a rise of industrial wages in the capital goods sector are shocks to the stability of the price system, even though they may arise from prior developments within the advanced economies themselves.

Propagation mechanisms involve the lateral transfer of market-determined shocks to cost-determined prices. Formal indexing of wages to the cost of living is a propagation mechanism. So too is the informal use of reference wages to assure that pay relativities between capital and consumer goods producers are maintained, even though marketplace conditions would dictate that they diverge. When propagation mechanisms are strong, the echoes of an inflation shock can reverberate within an economic system long after the shock itself has come to an end.

Measured inflationary pressures arise, then, mainly when money wages demanded and paid to workers in the economy as a whole, on average, rise above the rate of measured productivity growth. At that point, pressures grow on the supply of consumer goods. The price response depends on the elasticity of supply. The prices of certain items (housing, oil, coffee, copper) may rise rapidly, while other prices (calculators, haircuts, theater tickets) may rise hardly at all. But in a large enough part of private business, a rise in costs and particularly in wage costs is followed by a rise in prices. And this then starts the acceleration of the wage-cost spiral whose self-perpetuating mechanics have been described by Wood (1979).

We may therefore focus on the determination of wages (and,

secondarily, of profits), rather than seek out perfidy in government or individual causes for each of a myriad of commodity price changes. What causes workers to seek wage increases above the measured rate of productivity growth? What prompts companies to grant such increases? What conditions can deter this behavior? And is there a difference to be expected between a closed and an open economy on this score?

The pertinent body of wage theory argues that workers care about their relative standing in the wage structure, in addition to accepted concerns with their absolute real income and purchasing power. This literature emphasizes the importance of patterns of wage bargaining, of reference wages, that set, for each group of workers, a standard or norm that becomes their point of comparison by which they judge whether, at any given stage in their working lives, they are doing well or poorly (Piore, ed., 1979). In this perception, then, workers have quite limited information about income standards on the national scale. They set their sights, and solve their information problems, by having reference to their local situation. And so an overlapping web of relations develops, providing each worker with just enough information to judge the settlement he or she is being offered. These webs or patterns of interdependence are known as "wage contours."

The existence of the wage contour does not suggest that workers are immune to economic pressures. Rather, the contours help explain how wage pressures spread. And they may help to explain how, in a period of structural transition, wage patterns may spread from one industry where they are appropriate to others with whom traditional wage-setting relations may exist but for whom appropriate market conditions are now, suddenly, wholly different.

In the closed economy, as we have seen, business cycles do not alter industrial structure in a dramatic way. They therefore also do not especially alter prevailing wage contours. In the recession, unemployment deepens, profits dive, and workers in the manufacturing sector, whether consumer or capital goods, sensibly withhold demands for rising wages. This enforced discipline spreads through the economic system, cost pressures slacken, and the inflationary pressure that existed beforehand tends to disappear.

In the expansion, confidence returns to labor gradually at first, but as time passes with increasing force. Workers gradually appreciate that the recession is over. And then it takes a few months to be sure that there will be no relapse. After that, as laid-off employees are called back and employment expands, those on the seniority ladder rise and their cultural distance from the margin of unemployment begins to grow. Within a few years, the worry of potential unemployment has receded. A few years more, and workers may well begin (with help from overoptimistic economists) to believe that the problem of recessions has itself been conquered. The temptation is irresistible, by this point, to demand a bigger share of company earnings. This is the ordinary mechanism of the Phillips curve, equally capable, in theory, of running backward as well as forward.

Trade-deforming business cycle expansions, we have seen, tend to drive the measured growth rate of productivity down. They should also be expected to drive up the militancy of labor.

As trade deformation proceeds, the technologically advanced capital goods sector of the LTP is expanding rapidly. The fact that measured productivity growth in this sector may be low in no way prevents the sector from paying, from needing to pay, very high and rising wages. High wages are necessary to attract highly skilled labor to the sector; they are feasible to the extent that there is quasi-rent income to be shared.

Such high wages reflect changing market conditions and not an intensification of the struggle for income shares as such. But consider their effect on the established wage contour. A wage explosion in one part of the contour inflicts a sharp relative loss on the other parts. This will be resisted. The autoworkers want what the airplane mechanics are getting. In many cases, the linkages run directly and strongly through the collective bargaining process. In others they run through coordinating mechanisms like retrospective cost-of-living adjustments in private wage contracts and in government transfer programs.

Deformation of the wage contour is thus a corollary of deformation of the industrial structure. It will generate a strong conflict over distributive shares that need not arise if trade deformation is not occurring. Whether inflation actually results is partly a matter of policy response. But there can be no doubt that the pressures to resolve incipient conflicts by accommodating all demands in monetary terms will be extremely strong. And so open economy business cycles will generate more inflationary pressure at every level of unemployment than their tame predecessors in the closed economy — pressures that can be offset only by exchange rate policies that maintain intense competitive pressure on the domestic consumer goods manufacturing sector and so exacerbate the trade deformation. Thus, they can explain why the Phillips curve shifts outward when structural change is under way.

It is, of course, possible for policy to resist the inflationary pressures that trade deformations add to the ordinary course of an economic expansion. In the 1980s, resistance has taken the form of policies that hold domestic costs down through foreign competitive pressure, maintained by an overvalued foreign currency exchange rate.[11] However, such a strategy cannot be sustained, for it runs in contradiction, in the medium term, to further expansion of capital goods industries. Imports, made cheap by the high currency, rise, but the exports to pay for them are lost to alternative foreign suppliers. The import expansion must then be financed by international debt. And if the capital goods industries are lost, then the debts incurred in an import-based antiinflation struggle must be paid in the long run with the depreciated coin of consumer rather than capital goods exports. To fight the inflationary pressures of an internationalized economy by maintaining an overvalued currency is thus a formula for regression in the hierarchy of international production.

Conclusions

Recessions and booms are not incidental events in the development of an integrated world economy. To the contrary, they are integral to that development so long as the Planning System finds them useful. There are severe human consequences for advanced country workers, political consequences stemming from destabilization of the price level, and perceptual consequences for the measurement of productivity growth. Yet recessions also raise the rate of embodied technological progress above its previous path and accelerate the installation of advanced technologies in developing countries. Indeed, they force the process along far more rapidly and violently than would otherwise be the case.

Internationalization assuredly destabilizes the Planning System. International information markets are imperfect, beset by barriers of language, culture, distrust, and frank disagreement on the appropriate pace of capacity growth. It is far harder to coordinate investment decisions across LTPs than to do so within the cozy confines of a tight oligopoly in one country. And so long as the Planning System is unstable, the Schumpeterian forces of technological change are more resilient and less dependent on macroeconomic cycles for their effective and rapid diffusion in the world economy.

Yet the Planning System can also develop across frontiers. Particularly, it reaches out to take advantage of cheap labor in developing regions. The New Industrial State re-creates itself transnationally. But as it does so, it loses its grip in its home base. Falling measured productivity growth and rising rates of inflation are in part the domestic symptoms of instability induced by the internationalization of the Planning System.

For macroeconomic policy, the internationalization of trade and of the Planning System will pose major problems both of perception and organization. Even a smoothly working internationalized Planning System can generate, we have seen, symptoms of apparent crisis — productivity growth and inflation. Can these be surmounted? Can an effective international macroeconomic policy be devised? Or will we see a failure of political institutions to meet the requirements of a transnational corporate structure and so a Planning System unable to stabilize itself? These questions remain pertinent, and, to the extent that they do, the underlying message of *The New Industrial State* is not at all obsolete.

NOTES

1. As Robert Heilbroner has pointed out to me, the specificity of capital goods is a major theme of Adolph Lowe, in *The Path of Economic Growth,* and largely neglected since.

2. It is instructive to compare Mankiw's formulation with Veblen's treatment of the same problem — "the metaphysics of normality and controlling principles" — in the same journal of eighty-nine years previously. The tendency of supposed equilibria to drift is now known in respectable circles by the fancy name of "hysteresis."

3. This is a judgment about the economics of the matter. Measured shares of profits and wages reflect accounting conventions that may not accurately capture the shift toward economic rents in national income — particularly a failure to measure returns to human capital as profit.

4. Theoretical issues in the measurement of quality change are surveyed in Griliches (1971). For a fundamental treatment of the practical issues, and particularly of the computer case, see Block (1985).

5. Though Block cites arguments why this may be the case. See also Piore and Sabel (1984).

6. This argument contrasts with one made by Krugman (1987), who argues that measured productivity of the remaining workers in an advanced country will rise when jobs of intermediate technical sophistication are exported to LDCs. This may be false even if the most advanced sectors do expand in the advanced country.

7. This technical irony in the computer case occurs when the base year for the price index is shifted to 1982. Then, the 1982 dollar value of computer sales (some $30-odd billion) becomes the real value of computer sales for that year. Deflating previous years' production now *reduces* the real estimates of output for those prior years, and so the "productivity gap" reemerges. But this raises an almost metaphysical question: is it more reasonable from the standpoint of measuring consumer welfare to regard a computer in, say, 1976 as an inferior version of the 1982 model or to think of the 1982 model as a vastly superior version of 1976? Clearly, had the new index been in use in 1976, the real measure of computer output would have been far higher than it was and the productivity growth gap would not have seemed nearly so serious as it did.

8. On this point, for measurement purposes census definitions of goods and service production are not completely satisfactory. There is a large "tail" of jobs in research, design, and consulting activities intimately associated with the production of capital goods. These jobs are classed as services, but they are, in fact, indispensable to capital goods manufacture and ought to be considered part of it. Thus, "producers services" as a share of all employment rose from 7.1 to 10.1 percent from 1960 to 1980, while durable and nondurable manufacturing fell from 15.5 to 10 percent. See Grubb and Wilson (1987).

9. Excluding the "tail" mentioned in the previous note.

10. Grubb and Wilson calculate that average wages in the advanced technological sector were $15,921 annually in 1980, as compared with average wages overall of $11,641.

11. In this, the Reagan administration is by no means unique. The United States ran a similar strategy on a much smaller scale in the late 1960s, and the European powers did so in the midseventies. Of the British experience since World War II, the late Nicholas Kaldor wrote in 1980:

> The main shortcoming of post-war "full employment policies" (in the British context) was that they regarded the problem of insufficient demand as if it had been mainly due to insufficient investment in relation to the amount of savings forthcoming at full employment, rather than of insufficient exports in relation to imports associated with full employment income. Hence the policy instruments were designed to generate "consumption-led" growth rather than "export-led" growth which, by its very nature, militated against a fast growth of productivity and involved policy-generated instabilities in response to balance-of-payments crises.

Of course, the prototype of such policies, and of their folly, lies in the destruction of British industrial competitiveness after Churchill, as Chancellor of the Exchequer, restored the pre–world war sterling parity in 1926.

REFERENCES

Barrett, Nancy, and Ines Bustillo. "Productivity Growth and Women's Labor Force Participation." 1987, mimeo.

Block, Fred. "Post-industrial Development and the Obsolescence of Economic Categories," *Politics and Society* 14, no. 1 (1985).

Bruno, Michael, and Jeffrey Sachs. *The Economics of Worldwide Stagflation.* Cambridge: Harvard University Press, 1985.

Cartright, David V. "Improved Deflation of Purchases of Computers." *Survey of Current Business* (March 1986): 7–10.

Denison, Edward. *Accounting for Slower Economic Growth.* Washington, D.C.: Brookings Institution, 1979.

Domar, Evsey. "Capital Expansion, Rate of Growth and Employment," *Econometrica* 14 (1946): 137–47.

Galbraith, James K. "Galbraith and the Theory of the Corporation." *Journal of Post-Keynesian Economics* 8, no. 1 (Fall 1984): 43–60.

Galbraith, John Kenneth. *The New Industrial State.* Boston: Houghton Mifflin, 1967.

Griliches, Zvi. *Price Indexes and Quality Change.* Cambridge: Harvard University Press, 1971.

Grubb, W. Norton, and Robert Wilson. "The Distribution of Wages and Salaries 1960–1980: The Contributions of Gender, Race, Sectoral Shifts and Regional Shifts," Lyndon B. Johnson School of Public Affairs Working Paper No 39, 1987.

Harrod, Roy. "An Essay in Dynamic Theory." *Economic Journal* 49 (1939): 14–33.

Kaldor, Nicholas. *Economics without Equilibrium.* Armonk, N.Y.: M. E. Sharpe, 1985.

——— "Memorandum by Professor Lord Kaldor," in *Memoranda on Monetary Policy.* House of Commons Treasury and Civil Service Committee. London: HMSO, July 17, 1980, p. 87.

Kalecki, Michael. "The Determinants of Profits" (1933). Reprinted in *Selected Essays in the Dynamics of the Capitalist Economy.* Cambridge: Cambridge University Press, 1971.

Krugman, Paul. "Slow Growth in Europe: Conceptual Issues," in Robert Lawrence and Charles Schultze, eds., *Barriers to European Economic Growth.* Washington, D.C.: Brookings Institution, 1987.

Mankiw, N. Gregory. "Are Output Fluctuations Transitory?" *Quarterly Journal of Economics* (November 1987).

Nelson, Richard R. "The Tension between Process Stories and Equilibrium Models: Analyzing the Productivity Growth Slowdown of the 1970s," in R. Langlois, ed., *Economics as a Process.* Cambridge: Cambridge University Press, 1986.

Pasinetti, Luigi. *Structural Change and Economic Growth.* Cambridge: Cambridge University Press, 1981.

Piore, Michael. ed. *Inflation and Unemployment: Institutionalist and Structuralist Views.* White Plains, N.Y.: M. E. Sharpe, 1979.

Piore, Michael, and Charles Sabel. *The Second Industrial Divide.* New York: Basic Books, 1984.

Robinson, Joan. *The Accumulation of Capital,* 3rd. ed. London: Macmillan, St. Martin's Press, 1969.

Salter, W. E. G. *Productivity and Technical Change*. Cambridge, Cambridge University Press, 1969.

Survey of Current Business. "A Note on the Revision of Producers' Durable Equipment." (December 1985): 16–17.

Veblen, Thorstein. "Why is Economics Not an Evolutionary Science?" *Quarterly Journal of Economics* 12 (July 1898).

Wood, Adrian. *A Theory of Pay*. Cambridge: Cambridge University Press,1978.

Mary Kaldor

The New Industrial State and the Cold War Revisited

I WAS RATHER DISTURBED to discover in an article by the well-known Hungarian economist Janos Kornai that those who oppose economic reform in Eastern Europe are known as "Galbraithian socialists."[1] Kornai assures his readers that "it may easily be that neither the members of the school nor Galbraith would be pleased." Nevertheless, he points out that these so-called Galbraithian socialists regularly cite *The New Industrial State* in order to argue that even under capitalism, markets are anachronistic and, therefore, that socialist countries should stick to central planning.

Today, in both East and West, the planning system described by Galbraith in *The New Industrial State* is in crisis. The response of neoconservatives in the West and official reformers in the East is to applaud, once again, the virtues of markets and deregulation. Galbraith's views are considered to be unfashionable and even reactionary.

And yet Galbraith was not defending the New Industrial State, nor was he predicting its permanence. He pointed out, rather wryly, that the new industrial state "has succeeded, tacitly, in excluding the notion that it is a transitory, which would be to say it is a somehow imperfect, phenomenon."[2] And in his concern about the dependence of the new industrial state on the manufacture of weapons of mass destruction, its neglect of aesthetic goals, and the subordination of the individual, he anticipated the preoccupations of the social movements that have emerged in the 1970s and 1980s (peace, the environment, civil liberties, personal politics). He was aware of the danger of growing state power but did not think that the answer was a return to the market. "The danger to liberty," he thought, "was in the subordination of belief to the needs of the industrial system."[3] Where he was, perhaps, overoptimistic was in the hope, shared, interestingly, at the time by intellectuals in Eastern Europe, that what he called the "educational and scientific estate" would come to play a progressive political role.

In this essay I shall focus on the relationship of the New Industrial State to the Cold War. Galbraith put forward two kinds of argument. First, he suggested that the New Industrial State required high levels of military spending. The industrial state needed the Cold War and its imagery just as the large corporation needed to create advertising images. Second, he predicted a convergence of the industrial systems in East and West. As the West became more dependent on planning, the East would place more emphasis on the autonomy of individual enterprises. And he hinted that this convergence might bring about an end to the Cold War. While he did think that alternatives to military spending were possible, he did not elaborate on how the contradiction between the convergence thesis and the dependence on military spending might be resolved.

I shall argue that the Cold War was, indeed, an essential dimension of the New Industrial State, as described by Galbraith. However, I would go further and argue that the convergence, which Galbraith and others observed in the 1960s, was, in fact, the consequence of the shared experience of both East and West of World War II and the Cold War. The two systems could be said to have been bound together through their joint participation in the war against Germany and, subsequently, their joint preparations to fight against each other. The faltering of the Cold War — the cycles of détente, renewed Cold War, and détente again — has accompanied the faltering of the planning system in both East and West. Whether we can expect in the future a renewed process of convergence around a reformed system of industrial planning or around a return to the market or diversity rather than convergence depends on political struggles now taking place, especially in Europe. In short, it depends on what replaces the Cold War.

I will explore this argument in relation to the West and to the East. But first, it is necessary to make some preliminary remarks about the analysis of war (or preparations for war) and the analysis of economies.

The Military Sector and the Economy

There is a marked similarity between strategic theory and economic theory. Both are attempts to reduce a complex web of social activities to logical concepts or models. Indeed, during the postwar period, strategic theorists have often borrowed the techniques of economists, like indifference curves, to set out their arguments. In both strategic theory and economics, there is also a tendency to get mesmerized by numbers. Because these social activities can be measured in financial flows and numbers of men or weapons, there is a tendency to construct theories which can be tested statistically and consequently to reduce what are, in effect, social or political debates to numerical comparison.

Clausewitz said that the study of war belongs neither to the realm of arts or of sciences but to the realm of social life.[4] And this is also true of economics. Both subjects deal with the relationships between organized groups of people — what Marxists call social relations. Economics has to do with the way people are organized for production and consumption of material goods. Strategic theory has to do with the way in which people are organized for war.

A central concern of both subjects is with what I shall term "regulation" — how to reconcile resources with requirements, supply with demand, or capability with need. The classical market is sometimes described as self-regulating. That is to say, it does not require the intervention of the state (in fact, of course, the state is required to guarantee the free movement of labor, capital, and goods, to set standards, and so forth). In the market system, prices are the signal of whether too much or too little is spent on the production of a particular product. The centrally planned systems can be described as systems of bureaucratic regulation. Bureaucrats administer prices and quantities to be produced. They receive signals in the form of shortages or unsold goods, but they do not necessarily have to heed those signals. In democratic societies, planners are likely to be more responsive to public signals than in authoritarian societies.

In war, fighting can be treated as a form of regulation. On the battlefield, weapons and strategies are tested out. Inefficient armed forces are punished by defeat, and those who have organized themselves efficiently are rewarded by victory. Clausewitz compared battle to the act of exchange in the marketplace.

In the Cold War, however, there is no fighting — only imaginary scenarios and training exercises. In this situation, the form of regulation is not so very different from a centrally planned system. The organization of production and the testing of weapons and strategies will be undertaken by military planners. They will receive some signals, as a result of wars in the Third World, for example, or the idiosyncracies of particular admirals or generals. But the absence of hot war in the central arenas of conflict (Europe and the Pacific) implies an inbuilt tendency to devote unnecessary resources to preparations for warfare. This is the sense in which I use the concept of "waste."

This argument has implications for our understanding of technical change, so central to Galbraith's thesis. In the modern period, both civil and military sectors of the economy have been characterized by more or less continuous technical change. By technical change, I mean a process by which new ideas or inventions are *assimilated* into social structures. As Galbraith argued, modern technology is not the product of individuals but of teams. How these teams are organized not just for research and development but also for production and use profoundly affects the nature of technology. By and large, social structures, i.e., ways of organizing people, are resistant to change. New ideas tend to be acceptable only if they leave the organization more or less intact. The market or the battle represents a form of outside pressure on the organization — a mechanism through which a mutual adaptation of social structures and ideas takes place. They are forms of experiment. In the absence of experiment, there is always a tendency toward inertia.

Understanding these different forms of regulation and what they imply for technical change is very important if we are to understand the evolution of different economies and their relationships to the military sector.

The Industrial State in the West

In *The New Industrial State,* Galbraith argues that high levels of military spending are necessary to maintain the level of final demand and to underwrite advanced technology, which requires large-scale mobilization of resources. He thought that military spending was particularly suitable for demand management because it was easier to adjust (especially upward) than either nonmilitary forms of public spending or taxation. The national security rationale was a bottomless sink. This argument was also expressed in NSC-68, the document which, shortly before the outbreak of the Korean War, advocated substantial increases in U.S. spending. Leon Keyserling, who was then Chairman of the Council for Economic Advisers, argued that the United States had to increase public spending to avoid a return to the prewar depression. He would have preferred social spending, but he recognized that increases in military spending were easier, politically, to implement.[5]

This Keynesian argument was echoed in Marxist literature during the 1950s and 1960s. Writers like Paul Baran and Paul Sweezy[6] and Michael Kidron[7] put forward the arms economy thesis — that capitalism needed armaments in order to survive. They drew their ideas less from Keynes than from Rosa Luxemburg and her argument about disproportionality — the tendency for Department I (the production of capital goods) to outstrip Department II (the production of consumer goods). In the last chapter of *The Accumulation of Capital,* entitled "Militarism as Province on Accumulation," she put forward two arguments as to why military spending was particularly suitable for resolving the problem of disproportionality. First, military spending is a form of waste spending, in the sense, *not* as described above of excessive spending for its purpose, but in the sense that it does not reenter the process for producing material goods as either capital or consumer goods. It can thus realize, i.e., buy, the output of Department I without expanding capacity. A second argument, which seems to have been her more important argument, was about imperialism. By bringing precapitalist modes of production into the sphere of capitalism, markets could be increased. This was the purpose of military spending.[8]

During the 1970s and 1980s, a new set of arguments has emerged which appear to refute the earlier arguments that capitalism needs military spending. The differing performance of the United States and the United Kingdom, on the one hand, and their erstwhile enemies, Japan and West Germany, on the other, has been noted and duly measured. The econometric work of Ron Smith and others shows rather convincingly that military spending as a share of GNP is inversely related to economic performance in advanced capitalist countries.[9] Smith himself initially argued that consumption (welfare plus private consumption) is a relatively stable share of GNP because of class competition and that, therefore, military spending competes with productive investment. However, this argument was predicated on a full-employment economy.

Seymour Melman and a series of writers in the 1980s[10] put the emphasis on productivity. Far from underwriting advanced technology, as Galbraith suggested, military spending absorbs a disproportionate share of scientific and technological resources which might otherwise be used for productive purposes. Moreover, military technology induces bad design and marketing habits. Melman suggests that arms enterprises are cost-maximizers rather than cost-minimizers because price is determined on a cost plus markup basis and the market is captive. Hence, high levels of military spending lead to a relative decline in the growth of productivity and in international competitiveness. This results in balance of trade deficits, unemployment, and inflation (as large oligopolistic corporations try to compensate for smaller markets).

My own view is that there is something in both arguments but that they apply at different levels of analysis and in different time periods. During the 1950s and 1960s, high levels of U.S. military spending did indeed maintain the level of aggregate demand both in the United States and in the world, thus stimulating high levels of employment and rapid rates of economic growth in advanced capitalist countries. Moreover, and this relates to the Marxist argument about imperialism and the argument put forward in revisionist histories of the Cold War,[11] the military alliance system constructed during the 1950s provided the underpinning for a global economic system dominated by the United States and the dollar. Today, this argument is even accepted by more orthodox writers. It is fashionable to argue that for economic stability, the world needs an hegemony; the United States was carrying on the important functions undertaken by Britain in the nineteenth century.[12]

Of course, the same result could have been, at least in theory, achieved in other ways — ways which might have avoided some of our current problems. The proposals of Keynes and Harry Dexter White for an international clearing union and a genuine international currency, combined with Roosevelt's ideas about self-determination and the role of the United Nations and a continuation of the New Deal domestically, also offered a solution to global economic problems. That this option was not adopted has to be explained in terms of the actual experience of World War II, which provided a solution to the Depression which was known to work. The Cold War reproduced the conditions of World War II — high levels of government spending, planning, a sense of solidarity against an external enemy — without the fighting and the tragedies.

This interpretation is illustrated by the role of Britain in the origins of the Cold War. Now that the relevant state papers of the period are publicly available, it is clear that Britain, and the British foreign secretary Ernest Bevin in particular, played a key role in persuading George Marshall and the U.S. administration that Germany should be divided, that Marshall aid should be provided to the non-Communist countries, and eventually that a Western alliance should be created which would ensure a permanent American military presence and a permanent flow of dollars to Western Europe. The British wanted to reproduce the Anglo-American wartime alliance in order to uphold the role of sterling, the British colonies, and Britain's occupation role in Germany.[13]

I do not want to suggest that the Soviet Union played no role in the evolution of the Cold War, that Stalinism would not have been imposed on Eastern Europe had it not been for the Cold War. On the contrary, I believe that orthodox historians are right when they claim that the roots of the Cold War in the East lie in the Soviet occupation of Eastern Europe in the early 1940s and in the bestial behavior of the Red Army. But I also accept George Kennan's argument that military containment was never an answer to the occupation of Eastern Europe.[14] There was never a military threat to Western Europe — Soviet forces, which understandably created apprehension, were, at least in the early period, largely garrison forces. The creation of NATO, however, did freeze the situation, did legitimize the Soviet presence in Eastern Europe, and did, I believe, slow down the de-Stalinization process as well as preclude the possibility of agreements about Germany or about troop withdrawals after Stalin's death.*

But if the Cold War reproduced certain elements of the World War II experience that contributed to postwar prosperity — high levels of spending, planning, domestic cohesion — it could not sustain wartime rates of technical change. Regulation by battle was replaced by bureaucratic regulation. In the war, military technology had drawn on the experience of new dynamic sectors which developed in the United States in the 1920s and 1930s, particularly the automobile industry. Churchill said that the war was won by the DC-3 and the bulldozer. And he was right. It was the combination of mass production and the internal combustion engine that won the war. Of course, the war stimulated other inventions which were more or less important after the war — radar, the computer, atomic energy. But the Cold War was never able to achieve the same momentum. Technical change became introverted, despite the devotion of growing amounts of scientific and technological talent, moving along a trajectory that least disturbed the social structure of the military sector (the hierarchy of armed services, the relationship with large and rather stable defense corporations). Elsewhere, I have termed this form of technical change which results in smaller and smaller improvements in performance for ever larger amounts of resources as "baroque."[15]

Thus, I would accept Melman's argument that high levels of military spending in the United States *did* slow down technical change in the civilian sector. Because of the form of regulation in the military sector — bureaucratic regulation with little restraint or outside pressure — technical change in the military sector became less and less relevant to civilian innovation. It became wasteful. Military technology did indeed divert resources and influence habits of design. The inverse relationship between spending on military research and development and international competitiveness in manufacturing is rather striking.[16]

---

*Kurt Schumacher, the General Secretary of the German Social Democratic party, referred bitterly to Konrad Adenauer as the "Chancellor of the Allies." He believed that the integration of the Western zones into a Western economic system and the creation of the Federal Republic was a way of abandoning the 18 million people living in the East Zone and condemning them to totalitarianism.

In other capitalist countries, where military spending was much lower, civilian innovation was more rapid, at least as measured in productivity growth or trade performance. These countries were not necessarily more market-oriented. They were characterized by large oligopolies, often under state protection, in which consumer sovereignty was limited in the way Galbraith describes by such methods as advertising campaigns and the sway of the media. But they were democratic countries in which the planning system was more responsive to public pressure. The military sector is peculiarly immune to outside pressure. The planner is also the consumer; therefore, he (or probably not she) knows best. The national security rationale is also an argument for secrecy to prevent outside prying. Even those nonmilitary sectors most closely related to the military sector, like nuclear power or space, are more publicly accountable. Civil nuclear reactors do have to produce energy at affordable cost; they have, in some degree, to take into consideration public concerns about safety.

In countries like West Germany, Sweden, and Japan, public pressure has led to greater expenditure on such measures as education, local research, and energy conservation, which may well explain some aspects of economic performance. In West Germany, spending on environmental research and development as a share of GNP is four times higher than in the United States or the United Kingdom.[17]

Thus, the relationship of the industrial state to the Cold War is inherently contradictory. The Cold War did and does provide a Keynesian lubricant as well as a way of underpinning a global economic system dominated by the United States. But, at the same time, the Cold War undermines the long-term economic performance of the American economy — the central goal of the industrial state and the basis for American dominance. This contradiction was evident in the Reagan years, when high levels of military spending stimulated high rates of growth and apparent domestic prosperity, accompanied by unparalleled trade deficits.

In the 1950s and 1960s, the system worked rather well. Because the United States still enjoyed technological preeminence, outflows of dollars in the form of overseas military spending returned to the United States in the form of purchases of American goods. Today those same outflows are spent on European, Japanese, and

Taiwanese goods. The system is held together by the willingness of surplus countries to lend to the United States and that, in turn, depends on American dominance — on the Cold War. The United States can get away with a scale of borrowing undreamt of by poor Third World countries because of the role of the dollar and the military alliance system. As Emma Rothschild pointed out recently, there are no central bankers or international economic institutions like the International Monetary Fund or the World Bank applying the financial discipline invented by the United States for other countries to the United States. No one is breathing down the new President's neck, asking "Mr. Bush, can you really afford the Strategic Defense Initiative?"[18]

The Industrial State in the East

In a famous lecture given in Belgrade in 1957, Oskar Lange described the Stalinist-type economy as a *"sui generis* war economy."* By this he meant a system comparable to the organization of capitalist economies during wartime:

> In capitalist countries, similar methods, viz. concentration of all resources towards one basic objective, which is the production of war materials, centralization of disposal of resources in order to avoid leakages of resources to everything that was considered non-essential, i.e., everything not connected with the prosecution of war, were used during wartime.

Lange was of the view that the "methods of the war economy [were] necessary in a revolutionary period of transition." All the same, he was at pains to point out that these methods were not intrinsically socialist. For example, compulsory deliveries of agricultural products "were first introduced by the occupation army of Kaiser Wilhelm the Second, whom I do not think anybody regards as a champion of socialism."[19]

The analogy of the war economy can be taken further. Not only did the Stalinist system devote substantial resources to war prepa-

---

*This was one year after Wladislaw Gomulka's accession to power in the tumultuous events of October 1956. In the revisionist upheaval, Lange was appointed head of the Polish Planning Commission.

rations, but it only really worked efficiently in wartime. During the first five-year plans, starting in 1928, the Soviet Union built gigantic "American-style" factories. Mass production in the Soviet Union was designed not for mass consumption as in the United States but for war. Nevertheless, when war broke out, the Soviet Union was unprepared and humiliated by the German invasion; in many cases, the newly produced armaments proved inferior to German types. The way in which the Stalinist system rallied and went on to win the war was quite an extraordinary achievement. Factories had to be moved eastward; incredible losses were sustained. And yet by the end of the war, war output was comparable to American output and Soviet weapons were comparable in quality to any produced in the West. Although Lend-Lease was significant, it accounted for only a small proportion of the total Soviet war effort. The Stalinist system was tested in war; it was geared up for regulation by battle.

In the late 1940s, the Soviet Union faced in Eastern Europe a situation far worse than the United States faced in Western Europe. The countries of Eastern Europe were much poorer than the countries of Western Europe and had suffered proportionately much greater war damage. Although in several countries the population was socialistically inclined (especially in Czechoslovakia), they were acutely aware of atrocities recently committed by invading Soviet troops (and by departing German troops). The imposition of the Stalinist system and the two-camp doctrine was the most efficient method known to the Soviet leadership for rapidly increasing output.

Of course, there were alternatives. The Soviet Union could have allowed the East European satellites to accept Marshall aid even under the difficult terms on which they were offered — terms which, as Kennan and others have revealed, were fully expected to be refused. They could have tolerated the Yugoslav experiment. That they did not adopt this alternative is not surprising. They had just acquired a buffer zone, they were afraid of the revelations of crimes committed during the war, especially in Poland, and this was the way of doing things they knew best.*

---

*A Polish joke circulating in the spring of 1947, when Marshall aid was proposed, was, "What is it that is red and eats grass?" Answer: "Us, next year."

During the Stalinist years 1947–1953, it has been estimated that the Soviet Union extracted from the East European satellites — in the form of reparations, joint stock companies, and unfair terms of trade — an amount which was equivalent to what the United States provided to the West in the form of Marshall aid.[20]

But, of course, the Cold War was not the same as World War II. Regulation by battle was replaced by regulation by *diktat*. And after Stalin's death, when the conditions of terror, paranoia, and insecurity were somewhat relaxed, regulation by *diktat* became bureaucratic regulation. And the way this worked was very similar to the way the military sector works in the West.

These systems are said to be centralized. But they are not and cannot be truly centralized because, in the absence of any external standard like war or foreign competition, centralized decisions are subjective, introverted, and subject to all kinds of lower-level pressures. Tamas Bauer, the Hungarian economist, speaks of "building up" and "building down" the plan.[21] True, there are vertical directives from top to bottom, but the bottom (the enterprises) contributes to the determination of the directives. This system, argue the Hungarian reform economists, gives rise to shortages just as capitalist economies have a tendency to excess capacity. Actual expenditure always exceeds planned expenditure, even if the planners make allowances for this tendency. This is because enterprises underestimate investment projects either in order to "hook on" to the plan or because they come across unforeseen problems. Since they are state enterprises they do not face real penalties for overstepping their budgets. (This is closely akin to the "cost overrun" problem regularly experienced by Western defense companies.) Shortage is resolved through squeezing those who are outside the planning system and have no power, i.e., households or consumers — hence the investment cycle experienced by socialist countries in which periods of rapid investment are followed by austerity.

Attempts to overcome the problem of shortage through improved efficiency are very difficult. As in the Western military sector the system is prone to inertia. In the absence of external stimuli there is resistance to any form of technical change that might disturb the social structure. Enterprises are unwilling to change suppliers or disrupt established routines which in turn might temporarily impair the fulfillment of planning quotas. Paradoxically, the military sector may be most disposed toward technical change, for this is the only sector where there is some degree of consumer sovereignty and where an external stimulus is transmitted through the arms race. From time to time, other sectors are urged to emulate the scientific-technological efforts that produced Sputnik, land-based missiles, and VTOL aircraft.

The necesssity for reform arises from shortage and inefficiency. Even though consumers are powerless, they revolt from time to time. Hence, reform programs have been undertaken in the mid-1950s under Khruschev, in the mid-1960s, and today under Gorbachev. Reform has gone furthest in Hungary. All the reforms attempt to move toward a market system: to increase autonomy of enterprises, to replace administrative directives by financial incentives, to devolve decision making, to give more emphasis to agriculture and consumption instead of to investment and military spending. But reforms are very difficult to control. Because they are carried out by the planning system, they come up against resistance from within the planning system. Attempts to mobilize support from outside the planning system are risky, as became clear in Czechoslovakia in 1968.

The détente period of the 1970s is interesting because it was an attempt to overcome the problem of shortage *without* reform. A new investment drive was to be supplemented by imports. Brezhnev talked about the "foreign reserve," and Soviet commentators insisted on the link between his "peace program" and the fulfillment of the ninth five-year plan.[22] It was an attempt that failed. In the absence of reform, imports were squandered on ill-conceived projects, on overcoming bottlenecks, or, in the Polish case, on consumption. The consequence was growing indebtedness and the subsequent cutbacks and austerity program of the early 1980s. The Western left argue, rightly, that détente was curtailed because of domestic pressure, especially in the United States, from the neoconservative right-wing groups like the Committee on the Present Danger. But it is worth noting that the Soviet Union's return to economic autarchy and reversion to Cold War ideology did precede, or at least parallel, the political shifts in the West.

Today, different East European countries are pursuing different strategies. The Soviet Union, Poland, and Hungary are press-

ing ahead with détente plus reform: increases in imports and reductions in military spending to release resources, as well as a series
of economic and political reforms. At the time of writing, Hungary
is on the verge of adopting a multiparty system and Poland is on
the verge of legalizing Solidarity. The German Democratic Republic is pursuing a policy of détente without reform — in effect a
continuation of the 1970s. This is made possible by the willingness
of West Germany to offer apparently unlimited credit, even to the
extent of "buying" political prisoners. Czechoslovakia maintains an
autarchic, conservative, Cold Warist stance; critics are still labeled
Western agents. Rumania has adopted a particularly virulent form
of nationalist totalitarianism through which it has been able to pay
off its debts.

The Industrial State or the Market?

The industrial state of the 1950s and 1960s was integrally connected with the Cold War. In both East and West it drew from the
experience of wartime planning. In the West, the Cold War maintained levels of aggregate demand and helped to underpin the
global economic system. In the East, the pseudo–war economy
seemed the only method available for mobilizing resources for
growth.

The Cold War no longer works. It has given rise to differential
rates of growth among capitalist countries, a new pattern of uneven development, and it represents an obstacle to reform of the
international economic system. In the East, high levels of military
spending, stagnating technical performance, and indebtedness have
brought the socialist momentum to a halt.

In both East and West, the culprit is seen to be the planning
system, and the call is for a return to markets. In the East, this is
linked to détente and to the dismantling of the Cold War. In the
West, there is talk of "burden-sharing," spreading the cost of the
Western military effort among the United States, Western Europe,
and Japan.

Many in the West are now saying that the West has "won" the
Cold War because the Soviet Union and several East European
countries are reducing their levels of military spending and ex-

pressing a newfound commitment to democracy and to markets.[23] And there are many in the East, especially in official reform circles, who probably agree with this assessment.

No one can be against the introduction of markets in socialist countries. They do provide autonomy and space in societies where the intrusion of the state into every aspect of social life has been intolerable. All the same, markets operate, in all societies, within boundaries established by political institutions. Up to now, markets in East European societies have been ways of legalizing black activities — the so-called second economy, which emerged to cope with mistakes and lacunae in the planning system. Markets do increase efficiency — small private plots produce a disproportionate share of agricultural output in all East European countries. But they cannot shift the direction of development without a fundamental shift in political priorities.

In the West, the newfound emphasis on privatization and deregulation strengthens the position of large private corporations. Many people have criticized Galbraith for arguing that the trend toward large-scale corporations was inevitable because of the nature of modern technology. It is true that the revolution in information technology and in flexible manufacturing means that mass production is no longer the most efficient form of production in many sectors. The new technology allows for smaller, more decentralized, production units. Nevertheless, control remains centralized — all the more so with modern computers — and the need for large corporations which control flows of information and organize large teams for developing new technologies remains. Privatization and deregulation allow for a shake-up in the composition of the large private corporations. Nevertheless, it is a shake-up within parameters that are politically determined, i.e., the demand for armaments and the emphasis on mass consumption.

A shift of military spending toward Western Europe and Japan could be a solution of sorts. It might slow down the performance of Western Europe and Japan and restore a kind of international equilibrium, but it would leave untouched all the problems raised by Galbraith in *The New Industrial State* which have come to assume much greater significance — the environment, the danger of nuclear war, the submergence of the human personality in a sea of psychologically created wants, not to mention the problems of unemployment, the creation of an excluded underclass, and, above all, the poverty of the Third World.

A solution of this sort in the West, moreover, could foreshorten the process of reform in the East. By sustaining the Cold War in a new guise, it could strengthen those who resist the breakup of the pseudo–war economy. *Perestroika* is by no means inevitable; its layer of intellectual support is thin. The recurrence of shortage, which is inevitable in the short term, and the perpetuation of a Western threat could combine to restore the pre-Gorbachev status quo.

Those who argue that the West has won the Cold War see the choice as state versus market, bureaucratic versus market regulation. They fail to see the choice between the Cold War state and the democratic state, between warfare and welfare, between bureaucratic and democratic regulation. The central problem is how to free the state from the hold of the industrial system, especially the military sector in *both* East and West. And to some extent more markets may facilitate this. But much more important is how to develop a new set of relationships between state and society so that society and not the state is able to set its own goals — how to reinstate the consumer.

In this sense, Galbraith's expectations about the "educational and scientific estate" may not be so far off the mark. The new social movements of the 1980s have largely emerged from the new middle-class strata created by the growth of the state and the needs of the technostructure. Today, in both Eastern and Western Europe, the fashionable term among radicals is "civil society." The term is drawn from Tocqueville and Gramsci rather than Hegel.[24] What people mean by the term is the creation of autonomous social organizations like trade unions, churches, or peace movements through which individuals can establish their own social goals, influence society, and provide a countervailing power to the state. The contemporary concept emerged out of the experience of Solidarity in Poland and the campaign against the Euromissiles in the West.

The central concern now is to create an all-European civil society that can undermine the Cold War through its own efforts. It is recognized that current political institutions are so entrenched in the Cold War system that they cannot reform themselves. A process of what is called détente from below is aimed at protecting reform from below in the East and at shifting political and social priorities in the West. It is not the market or the industrial enterprises that can provide a countervailing power to the New Industrial State. Rather it has to be a new set of public or civic (in the sense of neither state nor private) initiatives — independent groups that are genuinely concerned about public affairs.

The outcome is not determined. We can anticipate a renewed Cold War or a new type of convergence as socialist countries become more market-oriented and less authoritarian, while Western countries, under the sway of economic and military integration (especially after 1992), become less democratic. Or it may be that the current breathing space in the Cold War will allow the evolution of new civic pressures that result in a set of diverse developments according to popular aspirations in individual societies.

NOTES

1. Janos Kornai, "The Hungarian Reform Process," *Journal of Economic Literature* XXIV, no. 4 (December 1986).
2. J. K. Galbraith, *The New Industrial State* (Boston: Houghton Mifflin, 1967), p. 390.
3. Galbraith, p. 399.
4. Clausewitz, *On War* (London: Pelican, 1968), p. 202.
5. John Lewis Gaddis, *Strategies of Containment* (London: Oxford University Press, 1982).
6. Paul Baran and Paul Sweezy, *Monopoly Capital* (London: Penguin, 1967).
7. Michael Kidron, *Western Capitalism Since the War* (London: Penguin 1967).
8. Rosa Luxemburg, *The Accumulation of Capital* (London: Routledge and Kegan Paul 1951).
9. Ron Smith, "Military Spending and Capitalism," *Cambridge Journal of Economics* (March 1977).
10. Seymour Melman, *The Permanent War Economy: American Capitalism in Decline* (New York: Simon and Schuster, 1974); Robert W DeGrasse, Jr., *Military Expansion: Economic Decline* (New York: The Council on Economic Priorities, 1983); Malcolm Chalmers, *Paying for Defence: Military Spending and British Decline* (London: Pluto, 1985).
11. See, for example, Joyce and Gabriel Kolko, *The Limits of Power: The World and United States Foreign Policy 1945–54* (New York: Harper & Row, 1972).
12. Robert Gilpin, *War and Change in World Politics* (Cambridge: Cambridge University Press, 1982); Robert Keohane, *After Hegemony: Cooperation and Discord in the World Political Economy* (Princeton, N.J.: Princeton University Press, 1984).
13. Anne Deighton, "The 'Frozen Front': The Labour Government, the Division of Germany, and the Origins of the Cold War, 1945–7," *International Affairs* 63, no. 3 (Summer 1987).
14. See *Russia and the West*, BBC Reith Lectures 1957 (London: Oxford University Press, 1958).
15. Mary Kaldor, *The Baroque Arsenal* (London: André Deutsch, 1982).

16. M. Kaldor, M. Sharp, and W. Walker, "Military R&D and Industrial Competitive- nesss," *Lloyds Bank Review* (October 1986).
17. Calculated from OECD figures, taken from *The Cabinet Office, R&D 1988. Annual Review of Government — Funded R&D* (London: HMSO, 1988).
18. Emma Rothschild, "Reagan's Economic Legacy," *The New York Review of Books,* (July 21, 1988).
19. Oskar Lange, "Role of Planning in Socialist Countries," in *Problems of the Political Economy of Socialism* (New Delhi: People's Publishing House, 1962), p. 18.
20. Paul Marer, "Intrabloc Relations and Prospects," in David Holloway and Jane Sharpe, eds., *The Warsaw Pact: Alliance in Transition?* (London: Macmillan, 1984).
21. Tamas Bauer, "Investment Cycles in Planned Economies," *Acta Oeconomica* 21, no. 3 (1978).
22. See Peter Volten, *Brezhnev's Peace Program: A Study of Soviet Domestic Political Process and Power* (Boulder, Col.: Westview Press, 1982).
23. See William G. Hyland, "Reagan-Gorbachev III," *Foreign Affairs* (Fall 1987).
24. See John Keane, ed., *Civil Society and the State* (London: Verso, 1987).

Wassily Leontief

Developmental Marshall Plan

CONTINUED EXISTENCE of a shocking disparity between the economic and social conditions under which large masses now live in the poor, less-developed countries and the rich, highly developed countries is an inevitable result of a long, historical process. From time immemorial, humanity advanced like a caravan moving along a winding path across a difficult terrain. Some camels are heading the procession, others follow them, stretched in a long string with stragglers on the other end — if they have not already fallen exhausted by the side — trailing several centuries behind.

Two hundred years ago, triggered by the Industrial Revolution, the pace of economic advance and population growth suddenly increased and became in Western Europe and soon after that in North America almost explosive. At the same time, as a result of unprecedented advances in the technology of transportation and communication, the economic, political, and to a large extent cultural interdependence among all parts of the world, irrespective of the stage of development in which each of them found itself, became so great that we can now truly speak of a complex and greatly diversified but nevertheless single system — the World Economy.

From now on it will be impossible to visualize an effective practical solution of economic, social, and political problems confronting any rich or poor, large or small country located in any part of the world without that mutual interdependence being taken into account.

Interdependence inevitably causes stresses and tensions that, unless effectively relieved, often lead to open conflict. This is particularly true when it comes to a realistic understanding and assesssing of the possibility of enabling the millions of men, women, and children now populating the poorest of the less-developed countries to break out of the vicious circle of undernourishment and ill health.

The public discussion of that problem has for some time been dominated by emphasis on the moral obligation of the relatively prosperous societies to provide the necessary help. Appeal to the natural feeling of compassion proved to be quite effective in inducing thousands of medical and social workers to move to the most distant corners of the world and provide humanitarian assistance to suffering masses in Africa, Asia, and Latin America. Moral suasion also prompted rapid and effective relief action in emergency situations such as earthquakes, floods, and starvation due to disastrous crop failures. The objective of such actions is clear and simple, and practical material obstacles to their realization, while sometimes serious, can usually be overcome.

Emergency relief cannot, however, cure the economic and social ills of the poor, less-developed countries; only accelerated economic growth sustained over a long period of time can do so, and such accelerated growth can hardly be attained without massive economic and technical assistance on the part of rich, developed countries, which can hardly be expected to undertake such a task without a proper combination of moral commitment and enlightened self-interest. However, its practical success will critically depend on a realistic understanding of the technical, economic, and social problems to be solved over a long period of time.

What is called for is a second developmental Marshall Plan designed to accelerate and sustain year after year the economic growth of the desperately poor, less-developed countries. The first Marshall Plan (the fortieth anniversary of which has been recently celebrated) was spectacularly successful in rebuilding Europe after the devastation of the Second World War. This time it will be necessary to move along a yet unexplored path into an entirely new territory — a much more challenging and difficult task.

It is true that a large amount of preparatory work has already been carried out by numerous international and national governmental agencies as well as by private enterprise, particularly by the so-called multinational corporations. These activities — often being carried out without proper overall coordination to serve special interests — focused attention on a great variety of special problems. The interdependence among technical, economic, and institutional aspects of the developmental process, while in principle fully recognized, still has not been realistically and systematically explored and practically taken into account. Past experience has shown that developmental assistance provided without such a systematic approach is bound to be wasteful and in the worst case ineffective.

What is now urgently needed is a pragmatic, realistic assessment of the developmental needs of the poor, economically stagnating countries in Africa, Asia, and Latin America that takes full account of their present and prospective future relation to all others, particularly the developed parts of the world economy.

This will be a difficult and costly task, but fact finding and analytical methods that can be employed in carrying it out are known and have been practically tested. It could be best performed by an independent team of experts under the auspices and supervision of a prestigious international group such, for example, as the United Nations.

Without a proper combination of moral commitment with pragmatic, practical know-how, economic assistance to poor, less-developed countries at best will be very wasteful, and in some particularly difficult cases it will be bound to fail.

Stanislav Menshikov

The Economic Structure of Socialism

JOHN KENNETH GALBRAITH is an author who is valued for, among other qualities, describing real, not abstract or imaginary, economic systems and for recognizing their diversity. In the real world, it has always been normal for two or more economic systems to exist at the same time. While many theoreticians would consider this fact abnormal, indeed objectionable, and would hardly acknowledge in their writings the existence of the less acceptable part of that duality, Galbraith has not only described the modern capitalist system in terms that are not necessarily sympathetic but has also come to recognize the possibility that socialism has a fate different from convergence into God's chosen system.

That is why I feel it is my responsibility to use this occasion for expanding in some detail on what the current system of socialism is and what it ought to be like. I shall do so in my usual Marxist terms. Since some of them may not be familiar to the reader, I shall start with simple definitions.

I shall distinguish economic systems by the dominance within a country of the particular type of property (or ownership) of means of production and labor power.

By dominance I mean that a particular type of property accounts for the majority of GNP (value added) in the country in question and that there are no legal restrictions on that particular type.

By means of production I mean all physical and nontangible

factors, except human labor, employed in production. Labor power is the power of a human being to produce goods and services by applying labor to means of production.

By property or ownership I mean not only the legal title to means of production, but also the control of their economic function, namely, direction of and receipt of income from their use.

Proceeding from these definitions, we describe capitalism as a system in which most means of production are privately owned and where most producers are separated from the ownership of these means and therefore are compelled to participate in production as employed or hired laborers.

Socialism is a system in which most means of production are owned either by the state or collectively by the producers themselves. There is one feature which is common to both capitalism and socialism: in both systems human beings own their labor power.

There are other systems which either are now in existence or have existed in history and which cannot be described as either capitalist or socialist; for example, all systems in which means of production are privately owned by the producers themselves. Such systems are based on small-scale self-employment enterprises and usually exist as parts of larger systems. We shall say more of these forms as we go along.

Historically all systems in which human beings have not been in complete ownership of their labor force — serfdom, slavery, contract, and other forms of forced labor — have disappeared, at least officially, by the middle of this century. The same fate was met by systems in which the principal means of production (land and water) were owned by nonproducers (the state, church, or other elite groups), but other means of production were privately owned by producers who were personally free (the Asiatic system, latifundia).

To avoid details, we shall consider here only modern societies where more than half of the GNP is produced in manufacturing or non-domestic services. It is exactly this area in which the two principal systems of today face each other directly.

A Few Words on Capitalism

One feature of capitalism accounting for its extraordinary vitality is the ability to adjust the notion and institution of private property to the requirements of society and technical progress.

Consider for example the corporate form, which dissociates ownership of means of production from any particular individual or family. It still manages to retain the basic private property principle that applies to both the corporation as a direct collective private owner and to shareholders as individual ultimate owners of its assets. The corporate form is extremely flexible, permitting both the capitalistic separation of means of production from the producers and the private appropriation of net income from the use of means production by non-producers. It also makes possible the separation of legal ownership of means of production from their direction and management; i.e., it makes possible the formal transformation of management into hired labor while at the same time making top management *de facto* corporate owners by giving them the power both to control and self-perpetuate and to enjoy incomes on the level of formal owners of means of production.

The corporate form is in fact so flexible that it can be perfectly well applied to either state or cooperative enterprises under socialism. We shall return to this point later in the article. Perhaps it is this particular feature that in the late nineteenth century forced one of the two distinguished founders of the law firm of Sullivan and Cromwell, that bulwark of capitalism, to castigate the corporation as the one extreme danger to private property. Karl Marx, in more of a dialectical frame of mind than Mr. Sullivan, put the same idea somewhat differently: the corporation is the abolition of private ownership within a system of private ownership.

In general, capitalism has shown itself capable of adopting any seemingly alien form and making that form fully compatible with its basic principles and premises. It does not matter that any such form is collective or even state-controlled, i.e., completely impersonal. The main point has been to keep private property in the means of production universally recognized and unrestricted, both legally (as the right of any individual to acquire and accumulate private property) and economically (in his right to use the income from his property at his will and to increase his personal wealth without limits).

This is very different from the socialist experience. As developed in the Soviet Union, socialism has been mostly, though not always, restricted to certain forms. Since the early Stalin days and until recently, it has lived in a straitjacket of two forms: state-owned enterprises and collective farms. Before Stalin made this restriction a norm, other forms were recognized and permitted: private noncapitalistic enterprises (not using hired labor), private capitalistic enterprises, foreign-owned capitalistic enterprises, cooperatives of various types.

Under Gorbachev, most of these forms have been legally readmitted, with the exception of private capitalistic enterprises. However, both noncapitalistic private enterprises and many cooperatives are still being strictly controlled and taxed so as to make their genuinely free development next to impossible.

My basic proposition is that by restricting itself to any particular form, socialism is making itself an artificial, weak, and largely noncompetitive system. Any viable economic system can gain acceptance and claim superiority only by permitting free competition of various forms within its bounds. Lenin did not consider this principle a danger to socialism, provided that the economy remained predominantly socialistic and that the political power remained in the hands of those favoring socialism. One could believe in the victory of socialism and at the same time see to it that socialism became stronger and more efficient than other forms by actively and openly competing with them and freely choosing the forms of organization which are the most promising in terms of economic efficiency and more consistent with the demands of technology.

There will be many who would consider such an approach a step backward from socialism, a concession to capitalism and private property. To show why it is not such a concession, I would first like to distinguish between facts and fiction about socialism in the Soviet Union as it exists now.

Socialism: Facts and Fiction

One has to recognize that state enterprises in our system are in practice not necessarily as truly socialistic as they appear in our dogma. Collective farms are not truly cooperative and thus also not necessarily socialistic. There are many cases in which both forms have been at least partially transformed into a particular kind of illegal private enterprise which is not necessarily capitalistic either, in any classic sense.

Let us try to prove this point using the example of state enterprises. They are chosen for brevity. Most of the following analysis applies equally or mostly to collective farms as well, since most of these farms are not true cooperatives but rather state-managed enterprises, in which individual members differ from hired laborers only in that their much smaller claims to income and social security are partially compensated by small private plots of land, which are not truly privately owned or managed but are continuously subjected to state expropriation of some kind.

Turning to state-owned enterprises, one has to concede immediately that public ownership is *not* fiction in the legal sense. The enterprises are managed by direct representatives of the state, whether the central government or the republican or local authorities, and most of their income is, in fact, distributed by decisions of the state.

In the economic sense, however, producers employed in the enterprises are not even partial co-owners of the means of production. They receive wages for their labor, some bonuses, and additional income via social benefits from the government budget, but they directly participate neither in the distribution of income of the enterprises where they work nor in management. At least, they will not do so until the new economic reform has been fully implemented. As of now the reform is still in the early stages, and even when it is accomplished it will not make producers co-owners of means of production in any real sense. To make them co-owners indirectly, i.e., through democratic control of state economic and financial management, would need such far-reaching political reforms as have not yet been contemplated.

There is one more significant difference between hired labor in a state enterprise under socialism and hired labor in a corporate or state enterprise under capitalism: employment security. The socialist worker cannot be fired individually or collectively without a specific procedure that defends his right to work and that also includes the right to be reemployed with the assistance of his former employer. This is an important achievement, which it would be extremely dangerous to destroy, as some market socialism reformers have suggested. Another perhaps less important difference is the current use of part of the socialist plant's net income for social purposes (for example, providing housing for the workers, eating and child-care facilities, cultural and sports institutions). However, much more is needed than employment security and social services to make the attitude of the producer in a socialist enterprise significantly superior to that of the worker in a capitalist plant.

Let us turn to management. Under socialism, plant managers were never in complete control of means of production. Plans and quotas were issued from the top, and income was taken away and redistributed by the ministry or other central authority. These bodies possessed the real power; they were the real disposers of the means of production and of their results. Their functions were not unlike the power of top management in capitalist multiplant corporations.

There were important differences, however. Not even the ministries were free to use the income that they appropriated from the enterprises. Even they had to compete among themselves (e.g., with ministries for other industries) for capital investment funds, which were distributed by even higher authorities. Their principal motivation (or objective function) as determined by central directives and tradition was to maximize output measured in physical units or gross value, which meant that they were seeking increased quantity, not quality or higher efficiency.

In a deficit economy, managers were not free to procure the necessary production factors and were therefore at the mercy of those within the central authorities, who allocated their distribution. Therefore they had to maximize quantity, not at minimum but almost at any cost. In other words, though they were disposers and actual directors of means of production, they could not use those means to maximize either output per unit of input, profit per unit of capital, or any other reasonable measure of economic efficiency. The inevitable outcome was that they would direct the production of goods that was not balanced against demand. There would be excess output of some unnecessary products and a glaring deficit of most others.

It follows that *both* workers and plant managers were alienated from means of production — a situation which bred disinterest in good work, inability to attain economic efficiency, and an economic bureaucracy whose main function was collectively and individually to direct and manage means of production in the most inefficient possible way.

The most serious fact was that there was nobody who could step in and act in the name of the real proprietors of the means of production as their agent. The government was supposed to do so, but whatever control it exercised was effected through and by the same bureaucracy whose objective function and motivation were in conflict with this control function. Therefore, the control mechanism that was intended to correct the inefficiencies and imbalances was for all practical purposes paralyzed.

Independent mechanisms of control were attempted at various times, but they were either police methods (under Stalin) with very noneconomic kinds of interference (i.e., terror) or, later, methods without real power to change things (e.g., committees of people's control). Where potentially effective mechanisms of control were initiated as, for instance, the system of state inspection and acceptance of goods produced, those mechanisms worked only in the case of military goods; they met with stiff obstruction and sabotage by plants and ministries in the civilian industries in the earlier days of the Gorbachev reforms.

The other inevitable result was the creation of a shadow economy in the pores of socialist enterprise. Its simplest and most naive business activity is price speculating in scarce goods and gaining from the difference between the official and market clearing price. The easiest way was to make such gains at the expense of consumers who were willing to pay the higher price either to save the time spent in a queue or to be able to obtain the product at all. This form developed faster and more easily than others, because enough consumers were free to spend their money incomes at their will. Neither plant managers nor the bureaucrats could legally do so, a fact which for a while acted as a constraint on the spread of the shadow economy into the non-consumer field.

The Shadow Economy and Its Function

There are a few points to make clear about the shadow economy. First, it was absolutely illegal. The goods sold at nonofficial prices were government property, produced or procured by the state or its organizations, and could not be legally sold to consumers at higher prices. One could consider such sale somewhat legal only if the resale by private persons of goods obtained from a government store were permitted. But it was not. Only farmers producing the products of their plots were permitted to sell their products at free-market prices.

Later on, some basic farm produce and foodstuffs intended for distribution through regular government retail outlets found their way to the free farmers' *(kolkhoz)* market through bribery of officials, inspectors, police, and so on. Selling other consumer goods the same way was not possible, but those goods could be sold at unofficial prices in the government retail units themselves. In all cases this selling had to be done steathily, under cover, and with the support of bribed officials at various levels, including the economic bureaucracy.

Now let us raise an important theoretical point. Most employees of state units (including managers) who are not legal owners either of means of production or of goods may use the fact that they are temporarily in possession of control of such means and goods to use them privately as if they were their property and thus gain individual or collective profits. The general rule is that anybody who controls in practice the use of resources that belong to others (in this case, to the state) is able to use these resources for personal gain (either by himself or jointly with others) if the legal owner does not exercise effective and adequate control. Both managerial and rank and file workers, or at least some of them, are necessarily involved. Police, controllers, and top bureaucrats have to be paid off. The participation of the top bureaucrats is particularly important because of their power to *create* and use shortages by planning and directing the use of resources in a wrong way. This theoretical point is universal, applying to all goods and services, whether consumer, producer, or otherwise. And, indeed, the shadow economy has spread to nearly all industries.

The reader may ask, how is it possible to prosper privately by producing steel or any other producer good at state-owned plants? Here are some of the many ways to do so:

- produce more than you account for and use proceeds for private profit

- resell privately, without accounting, part of your factor inputs
- receive bribes from customers for supplying them with your products
- accept special bribes for timely delivery and quality
- share in payments presumably made to others, for instance, workers, other employees, customers
- profit from selling nonexistent products if customers are willing to certify the receipt of such products and share in profits (this has been done on a large scale in the case of cotton)

In most cases, shortages are a necessary prerequisite for such operations. If there is no real shortage, one may be created with the assistance of the economic bureaucrat in the necessary position and at the appropriate level. Shortages are important not only to compel the consumer or customer to pay a high price but also to involve new managers and bureaucrats in the shadow economy. Most managers in such a system are not able to perform adequately even their official duties without entering into informal and largely illegal deals with their superiors, fellow managers, their own employees, and others. In this way, essential resources are obtained for perfectly legal purposes but in exchange for products and services which are not strictly legal. Even the sale of a scarce good at the official price may be used as a form of bribe. To make such a sale, the manager or bureaucrat would have to withhold part of the supply from general distribution and reserve it for special customers, an action which in itself is an illegal procedure.

It has to be emphasized that the bureaucracy per se, i.e., that part of the managerial class which does not directly participate in the economic process (producing, transporting, selling), is in a position of special power through its control of resources. It can help create shortages by intentionally misallocating resources and working out unbalanced plans, it can allocate resources to those who are willing to pay the additional costs, and it can organize and cover organizers of various profiteering schemes.

Contrary to widely held views, the shadow economy does not in most cases serve any economically useful function. It does not add to the supply of goods and services and therefore does not help achieve market equilibrium. Its profits are not used to increase supply. It benefits by shortages and the underdevelopment of normal market relationships. Were these to develop fully, the whole structure of the commanding economic bureaucracy, which has largely merged with the shadow economy, would become obsolete. It is not surprising that these circles are among the principal and most powerful opponents of the current economic reforms.

The question is asked, would it not be reasonable to legalize the shadow economy and thus make it a positive rather than a negative factor in economic development? The answer is that some parts of this economy can be legalized and others cannot. There are no valid objections to the creation of privately or cooperatively owned units to produce or sell goods and services along with existing government and cooperative units. There is much to be gained by promoting participation of workers and other employees in profit- and revenue-sharing schemes in state-owned units, as well as by the state's leasing plant and equipment to groups of workers under special contracts. It is perfectly proper to expand the payment of bonuses to managers for increasing quality and efficiency rather than quantity. Yet it is utterly irrational to legalize work for private gain in government enterprises, to accept *de facto* false accounting and other kinds of cheating, to permit the use of government-owned resources for private profiteering.

Need for Further Reforms

The system of socialism has a long way to go in order to separate fact from fiction, eliminate the latter, and base itself on reality. Further reforms are needed in pursuit of this goal. It is necessary to permit *all* forms that are consistent with socialist principles and social justice. It is essential to develop democratic control in all socialist forms so that legal owners do effectively control the use of their property.

Why? Because it is the only way.

Historically, new forms of economic organization appear when they are called for by the current or emerging level of productive forces. The appearance of new forms, however, does not necessarily mean that the older ones should disappear. Economic activity can be efficiently organized and performed in different forms depending on, among other factors, the size of the units. In a given period of time, any kind of economic activity will have an optimal range, in terms of size, within which it is bound to survive and show maximum efficiency. This range of size has to be consistent with the available technology, quantity and quality of land, mineral resources, labor power, and other physical factors of production. Size may be measured in different ways. One useful way is by the number of production workers necessary to utilize a given natural resource with a given technology. One to four or five workers are enough to build a small house or operate a relatively small farm. Ten, hundreds, or thousands of workers are needed to operate plants and ships, build railroads and canals.

Historically, economic units have had a tendency to grow, but there have also been movements in reverse. At a certain stage, collective tribal agriculture gave way to individual plots. Large ancient latifundia based on legions of laboring slaves were transformed into feudal landownings, in which many individual farmers operated on a share-crop, share-time, or share-income bases.

Under capitalism there was definite movement from smaller to larger units, a movement largely determined by the level of technology and type of prevailing economic activity. But at any stage of capitalism, including the current one, there has always been a combination of small, medium, large, and super-large units, each with its own rationale for existence.

Many Marxists have traditionally thought that small units are doomed by history, tht the future lies exclusively in the realm of large-scale enterprises. But Lenin recognized that large units cannot exist without small ones. It is not efficient to organize every economic activity in the same way. And there are many additional historical, social, cultural, and other factors which work in favor of small units, helping them to survive and at times to flourish.

This reality also applies to socialism. Obviously, there are many things which individuals, families, and small and medium-sized units in general can do better than large ones. Socialism has suffered in the past, and still is suffering from, gigantomania. Oversized farms, electric power stations, manufacturing plants, service stations, and research institutions are believed in all cases to be economically superior to small ones, but this is not necessarily true. It has turned out that in many cases the large units are the least efficient, the greatest polluters and spoilers of the natural environment, and the least able and willing to innovate, make basic discoveries, or exercise technical leadership.

Socialism cannot hope to survive and win in competition with capitalism unless it recognizes this reality and permits the free development of all sizes of economic units that are consistent with the needs of technology and society at large.

The Case for Private Enterprise

The question arises as to the consistency between the size of economic units and the way they are socially organized, i.e., who owns and directs the means of production in units of different size.

It is clear that private ownership was and still is largely suited to the requirements of a single individual and his or her immediate family. Where families were large, by tradition and culture, collective ownership turned out to be a more appropriate form. Private property historically appeared in a form in which all producers were members of the same family and were thus direct proprietors of the means of production. Within such a form, alienation is possible only when individual members are not adequately provided for within the family itself. Given the physical ability of disgruntled family members to separate themselves and establish their own economic activities, alienation does not become a major social problem.

The limitations of private ownership become apparent when natural resources become scarce: these resources are then in danger of being monopolized by a minority of private owners. Such monopolization becomes a source of social inequality: some people are alienated from the means of production and have to work for those who monopolize them.

Private property also has a tendency to grow. Once it is possible to save part of the product, property is accumulated, wealth starts growing. In economic terms, this condition necessarily leads to a situation where at least some of the private owners accumulate more means of production than they can themselves operate as producers. In order to operate those means efficiently, they need other producers either to share their property with or to work under their control as forced or hired laborers.

The former possibility is not unknown. Family businesses have become partnerships or jointly owned economic activities. But the general rule for many centuries has been to use other people's labor without sharing with them ownership of means of production. Slavery, serfdom, and hired labor are different forms of this private ownership organization. All of them at one point in history or another have been supported by uneconomic (i.e., political or military) force — a factor which was particularly necessary when economic methods of separating the producer from the means of production were not sufficient.

In the more modern age, the corporation became the form which had the advantage of retaining the private features of ownership while making it collective at the same time. Large economic units could not be maintained in any other form, because they had to be almost immortal, not dependent on personal relationships and individual limitations, to assure the access of new proprietors without giving up the possibility of using nonproprietary labor. As indicated at the beginning of this article, the corporation, whether fully private, state, transnational, or in any other form, turned out to be one of the most flexible property forms consistent with capitalism.

In fact, the corporation avoids many of the limitations of private property. It is accessible to anybody who has money savings and is willing to become, at least legally, a co-proprietor of means of production by simply buying shares freely in the market, without any prior permission necessary. It makes concentration of capital much easier and is perfectly applicable to large as well as medium economic units.

What does this say to socialism? First, that the notion of private property (in both the individual and the collective form) is directly applicable to the social organization of small economic units. It is a form in which the producer is directly connected with the means of production and in which, thus, the issue of alienation does not, as a rule, arise. The fact that in the case of small units this form is superior to the state ownership or large cooperative form is accepted to a certain degree in most socialist countries, including now the Soviet Union. This fact applies not only to individual enterprises in retail trade and consumer services, but also, for all practical purposes, to the family-leasing system in agriculture. The minicooperatives that have now been largely recognized, though still frowned upon by many socialist puritans, are really private partnerships using the lease-contract and collective contract as a legal basis for their existence.

But their life is not easy. They are discriminated against and heavily taxed; entry requirements for them are formidable, sometimes prohibitive. Why? Largely because of vested bureaucratic interests and because of the real danger they present as competitors to the old pseudosocialist forms. Ideological conservatives claim them to be nonsocialist, but this claim is simply not valid.

The small private enterprise, as such, is not a basis for a solid and viable socioeconomic system. Historically, it was always part of a larger formation, whether Asiatic, slave, feudal, or capitalist. There is no reason why it cannot be integrated into the socialist economy and both serve it and benefit from it.

Small private enterprises can serve socialism because any activity that is better organized in small units will easily expand without requiring a massive inflow of resources once the barriers to this form are removed. It is an easy and ready answer to the problem, seeming unsolvable under bureaucratic control of achieving market equilibrium. This possibility applies to both consumer and producer goods and services.

Once the barriers to this form are lifted and access to it becomes easy, there will be some outflow of producers now employed in the government plants and collective farms. But there is nothing wrong or dangerous about this. Labor is currently excessive in big plants, and the small private sector will serve as a safety valve to reduce this pressure. Only the more qualified and enterprising employees in the government plants will want to move into the private sector. But this demand will present healthy competition in the markets for both labor and goods and services. In fact, there is no other more powerful stimulus to developing competition within the socialist economy than permitting a sufficient number of successfully operating private enterprises.

Another benefit will be found in the sphere of technical progress. Inventors and innovators should have the option of quickly developing and applying their products in small firms which they themselves own. It is well known that were it not for small entrepreneurs, the video tape recorder and the personal computer would have had to wait quite a while until the large bureaucratic corporations were ready to risk their capital in these areas. Socialism should permit and promote its own Apples and Microsofts if it wants to compete successfully with capitalism.

The question of integrating small private enterprises into socialism raises a number of issues. First, their relations with government and other institutions in terms of producing, selling, and buying should be fully contractual. It is useless to subject them to any kind of administrative commands or planning. The small entrepreneur should work either for the consumer goods and services market, which does not necessarily make him a party to contractual obligations, or for the producer goods market, in which case he will have to enter into contracts with other private and government-owned plants and organizations. But in any case, he should be free to risk his investment in the hope of achieving an expected income. Since most of his customers and suppliers will inevitably be government enterprises, he will find himself integrated into the system and highly interested in its efficient performance.

Second, from a social standpoint the private entrepreneur should be fully integrated into the legal system that provides social security and social benefits to all workers. He should be compelled by law to observe working-hour limits and to pay part of his income to general and social insurance, including provision for his own medical care and old-age pension. When and if he hires labor — we shall come to this point later — all legislative provisions safeguarding the rights of workers will have to be applied on a par with government-owned enterprises.

Third, the private entrepreneur will have to be taxed for part of his net income. The tax need not be excessive. The principal purpose of taxation is not in this case to maximize income to the government budget, but to maintain a decent and adequate system of accounting and control (in addition to bank control, if he uses credit, and to government supervision if he leases productive funds from government enterprises).

The question usually arises as to the social function of taxation in this case. As indicated above, private property has a tendency to expand. What limits, if any, should be set on such expansion by the state? To answer this question we have to consider three additional issues: the permissible limits of income inequality, the inevitability of hired labor in private enterprises, and the size limit of private enterprises.

Private Capitalist?

Under socialism there is a tendency to limit severely income from private entrepreneurship in order to keep it within the bounds of a hired worker's wage. This practice is hardly reasonable and will serve only to restrain the initiative of the entrepreneur in expanding production of necessary goods, providing badly needed services, and pioneering in innovations. Initiative needs incentive, i.e., additional income in cases of success.

The private entrepreneur is also involved in a risky operation, since by definition he has no guaranteed minimum income. Therefore, in principle there should be no fixed maximum limit to his income. But since progressive income taxation may become nearly prohibitive (at rates approaching the point where increments in net income do not cover increments in effort), such taxation can be used as an instrument to control and regulate the expansion rate of the private sector. Tax rates could be low until market equilibrium is reached. Thereafter, the optimal tax rate could be found by experimenting with small marginal rate corrections.

The fact that the individual entrepreneur is paid better than the average hired worker should not be a matter of social concern. The important thing is to maintain a certain balance between his income and that of the skilled workers (including engineers, managers, scientists), who should have the freedom to choose whether to stay in the government's employ or transfer to the private sector. There will always be a healthy differential between incomes of skilled and nonskilled workers, but there should also be an automatic or semiautomatic mechanism equating the highest income of the private entrepreneur with the wage/salary of the highest-paid government employee. In other words, the bureaucrat should not have an incentive to remain a bureaucrat.

Once the income of the private entrepreneur exceeds a certain level, he will inevitably undertake to use hired labor. And even before that happens, there will be many economic activities requiring a unit larger than even a numerous family can manage, and that will not be adequately developed by the state-owned plants and collective farms.

In the Soviet Union, the current answer to this problem is the creation of minicooperatives. In many cases, these private partnerships may be true cooperatives. In other cases, they are fronts for hired labor, when the income is not divided equally or according to the shares and when the acting head receives more than those who work under his direction. This is inevitable, and one has to recognize the existence of *de facto* private enterprises using labor. It is better to legally admit their existence than to proceed on an illegal basis that will necessarily lead to the *de facto* hired workers' not having their rights being defended and guaranteed in any way.

The income of such a proprietor should be taxed with a view to produce a net income equal to that of the highest-paid manager in government service plus payment for risk and technical innovation. In all other respects, such enterprises should be subject to legislation intended for government and cooperative units: social funds, bonuses for employees, participation in management, profit-sharing, and so forth. The one important limitation should be that the owner cannot be voted out of management except under the condition of full compensation for the value of his property.

It would probably not be useful to permit private ownership separate from management, since this practice would tend to create a leisure class. The owner, on retirement, should be entitled to a pension based on his average net income and payable as income from securities that are given to him by the state either in exchange for his property or, if he wishes, in exchange for the cash proceeds from the sale of his property to the new proprietor. He should be able to sell, lend, or bequeath his property to members of his family with the understanding that they take over the management of the enterprise.

It may be useful to give the enterprise council (which exists in any enterprise under the current legislation) the right to decide on the ability of the proprietor to manage the unit efficiently. If they decide that he is not fit, they should have the right either to buy him out or to quit. This procedure should be specified in detail in order to avoid economically unfounded decisions.

Are we admitting the appearance of a capitalist class under socialism? Yes, to a certain extent, but one that is integrated into the overall and prevailing socialist system. The possibility of such a class achieving a commanding position in society should be minimized primarily by political means. But there is also an economic aspect to the issue.

Is it really possible that private plants will significantly increase in size? Suppose that the average age of a person starting a business is between thirty and forty and that the effective time span of ownership by one person is about twenty years. At an average net profit rate of 20 percent, and assuming that half of the profit is reinvested, the capital of the enterprise will increase eightfold. Allowing for an increase in productivity half as rapid as that of capital, the total number of workers would expand fourfold. It is hard to conceive of large privately owned enterprises emerging this way.

The more probable perspective for the further growth of such business would be in the form of partnerships in which a number of managers would jointly own an enterprise while also using hired labor. Such a partnership may further develop into a corporate form. At that point it will be for the state to decide whether to take over and buy out the proprietors.

Before considering the corporate form, however, let us turn to state-owned enterprises, which should remain the preferred type of organizing large and most medium-sized units.

Minimizing Alienation

Currently the chief negative feature of the state-owned enterprise, as mentioned above, is alienation of both workers and management from the means of production. The problem is therefore to find a way to minimize alienation while preserving the form of public ownership.

There are many advantages in making such enterprises operate efficiently while keeping them in the public sector. The largest advantage is that a substantial part of the additional income incurred by risk and through innovation, which in a private plant belongs to the entrepreneur, can go to the state and be used in the interest of the public at large. Some activities that lead to natural monopolies, such as electric power stations and public transportation, yield additional income that should not be part of private profits in any case.

But can government-owned plants work and be efficient in the general case? In any large plant, from the point of view of dealing with the means of production and of the interest of various groups involved, a few principal functions are to be distinguished:

1. the actual use of means of production for producing and selling goods and services,
2. managing (directing and coordinating) the actual use of means of production,
3. controlling management by or in the name of the legal proprietor of the means of production,
4. distributing the net income obtained as a result of the use of means of production.

In the current state-owned enterprises, alienation arises largely because of the improper separation of these functions and the inability of some of them to be performed adequately. Actual producers (function 1) have almost no say in controlling management (function 3) or in deciding how income is distributed. Managers are not free to perform their main function (2) or to participate decisively in distributing most of the income. Controlling management is vested in a bureaucracy which is not interested in maximizing efficiency and is not able to exercise any real meaningful control. It does incompetently interfere in management and in the distribution of income, in such a way as to maximize rather than to minimize alienation.

Apparently quite a lot has to be done to sort out matters and rearrange the performance of functions. Some of this work is taken care of by the current reform legislation, but this legislation is not sufficient.

The most pressing task is to eliminate the interference of the bureaucracy in the function of management and income distribution. The reform, if pursued relentlessly, will eventually succeed in doing this — an important step forward, but only one of many needed. The next most important task is to tie the performance of all four functions to the basic aim of achieving and maintaining maximum economic efficiency. Higher efficiency means higher in-

comes for all groups performing the functions, excluding the useless bureaucracy.

The first step is to make the income of the producers directly
and significantly dependent on their productivity. There is a current dogma, prevalent in the bureaucracy, that labor productivity
has in all cases to rise faster than labor income per worker. Otherwise, it is claimed, investment funds will diminish and inflationary pressure will build up in the economy. This dogma, however,
is totally incorrect. Provided that labor productivity increases as
fast as wages, not more slowly, there should not be unsatisfactory
effects at any level. Assume that both rise at the same rate. Then
the share of labor income in total income remains constant. The
principal source of net investment (profits) will increase at the same
speed as net product. If investment funds are used efficiently (i.e.,
if the marginal productivity of investment does not fall), there is
no reason why there should be inadequate investment funds or an
upward movement of unit labor costs.

Why, then, has this dogma gained currency and been repeated
insistently even in the last few years? Because actual productivity
was rising much more slowly than its official statistical measure,
and the marginal productivity of investment was continuously falling; hence, the pressure to restrict wage increases and to disasso-
ciate them from productivity. But if the worker knows for sure
that his wage will increase in line with his productivity, then he
becomes directly interested in higher efficiency, provided that
productivity is measured correctly and not falsified by various
methods.

There are basically two ways in which the worker's productivity
can be increased: by the worker himself working better and using
more efficiently the means of production at his disposal and by
improving the worker's productivity by innovations in technology.
The first way depends on the worker's personal efforts and the
collective efforts of those who work with him and coordinate their
joint operation. However, the second method depends largely on
the decisions made at the management (and even high bureaucratic) level on how to invest in means of production. It is therefore in the worker's immediate interest, provided that his wage is
directly determined by his productivity, to participate in collective
decisions on the organization of work at the team or shop level, as

well as in decisions on investment reached by the employees' council.

A direct material interest is also promoted by workers' participation in decisions on net income distribution. There is some conflict of interest involved in this process. Wage maximization may eat into the profit and lead to slower wage growth in the long run. However, it is much better to have this decision made consciously and with the worker's participation than to determine labor income without any direct correlation to either productivity or profits. And the conflict referred to may be minimized by setting a rigid connection between the wage and labor productivity, so that it is clear that the worker's personal gain from his own effort and that of his colleagues is guaranteed but that he has still more to gain by maximizing the profit in which he would have a share according to some progressive scale.

The direct interest of the worker in the net income of the state-owned enterprise would also be stimulated by expanding the current experience of selling shares in the enterprise to the worker. This form of personal saving would bring a revenue proportional to the profit of the enterprise and would be additional to all other forms of labor income. This is another way by which the worker can become a *de facto* co-owner of means of production that legally belong to the state.

There are a number of complicated additional issues that would inevitably accompany the introduction of shares. Can they be bought by anybody, including nonworkers of the enterprise in question? How does the shareowner dispose of his shares when he wishes to do so? What is the maximum extent to which individual (and thus *private*) share ownership should be permitted or tolerated? Could there be other forms of securities issued by state-owned enterprises? We shall not go into these details at this time. The important immediate problem is to expand individual share ownership as one of the methods to overcome alienation caused by the very impersonal character of state ownership, which at the same time seems to make everybody a legal co-owner of means of production while actually separating each person from all direct connection with this property and the results of its use.

The notion that the worker is legally co-owner of the enterprise where he works is, in fact, rather misleading. *All* items of public property belong to *all* members of society, whether they work in a particular enterprise or not at all. This is the definition of state property as distinct from the cooperative or collective forms of property. Therefore, one should clearly distinguish among the worker's rights as the ultimate co-owner of public property in general, his *specific* co-ownership in the particular state enterprise through his ownership of its shares, his title to part of the net income of the enterprise as a result of his *de facto* involvement in controlling management and participating in net income distribution, and, finally, his wage as direct payment for his labor contribution.

This distinction may seem a bit complicated, but it is, in fact, what distinguishes a worker in a socialist enterprise from the one working within the capitalist system. The rights associated with ultimate ownership are clearly those associated with guaranteeing the right to work, freedom from compulsory unemployment, and the entitlement to social services of the general type, such as free medical service, free education, and low-cost housing. What we were mainly concerned with in the previous discussion were the worker's rights *directly* associated with his participation in the work of a particular enterprise. The basic principle here is that work gives him wider rights than in a capitalist enterprise. He is entitled to participation in controlling management and distributing profits. Therefore, it is the principle not just of the sale of his labor-power to an employer but also of his entitlement to certain additional rights and privileges as a result of his *active* participation in productive activity. Perhaps the term "capitalization of labor" is a true expression of this specific ownership interest deriving from membership in a socialist enterprise. Labor power is considered a valid co-partner of technology and entails co-ownership rights.

The system described above will lead to wage and other labor income differentiation between workers in different plants, industries, and regions. This differentiation is inevitable and should not be considered a social danger. Envy of higher incomes of other groups of workers should serve as a stimulus to improve one's own performance and not as a basis for demands to level off all worker's incomes. Additional movement of labor into higher-paid and out of lower-paid occupations should serve as a mechanism for correcting the possible social injustices involved in such pay and income differentials.

Disalienating Management

We now turn to means of overcoming the alienation of management in state-owned enterprises. Organizing and coordinating the work of many people within one collective in an efficient way is a highly skilled and professional job that should be adequately paid. The salaries of managers should reflect this basic fact. At present, managers in state-owned plants are receiving not much more than qualified rank and file workers, and some managerial categories are receiving even less. It is only natural that they feel inadequately compensated for their skills and responsibility. In addition, continuous interference from the bureaucracy makes their work increasingly unsatisfying personally. These conditions lead to various illegal ways of self-emolument.

The basic income of top management in state-owned enterprises should be negotiated between the plant and the particular person, specified in a legally binding contract, and decided by a competitive procedure. It should be specifically recognized that managers are in fact selling their special skills and should be paid a fair price for doing so. Within a system where there is a free choice between establishing one's own business and working for a state or cooperative enterprise, there should be a market mechanism of equalizing income from these two different kinds of management activity.

The enterprise council that hires top managers can never agree to pay them salaries in excess of a certain share of the enterprise's income. Part of a manager's income would be a fixed salary within a range determined by the government's control body, but the other part should be flexible and depend directly on the profit. The period of the contract and terms of its termination should be specified in such a way as to guarantee the rights of both sides in case of conflict.

There will be the ticklish problems of relations within the enterprise council. On this council there should be representation of all parties performing the functions denoted above: the hired workers, the management, the state control body, but also the customers, the consumers, and the share owners, if any. No particular party should be strong enough to exercise control. Once this rule is broken, the functions will get mixed up: management will start hiring itself or be ordered around by state bureaucrats or become a simple representation of the workers. And the council itself should not become a source of interference in the day-by-day management of the enterprise.

A very important role is to be played by the representatives of the government's control body. In a socialist system, that body's main function is to ensure that the microeconomic efficiency of the enterprise is maximized but is necessarily subject to that of the macroeconomy and of society at large. Let us note in passing that this is very different from the interest of the stockholders in a capitalist corporation: they will have only the profit of the corporation in mind.

Making these two criteria work together is not an easy task. A high short-range efficiency of the enterprise can be harmful to its long-range stability as a continuously efficient unit. The individual plant may not be able to correctly foresee and assess its future, and it may not be aware of the industry-wide implications and macroeconomic consequences of its own actions. The state, as the agent of the public, has the obligation to foresee and correctly estimate all contingencies and to pursue the highest goal of society at large, which are general well-being, social equality, and social justice.

There are many ways the state can affect the operation of its enterprises without interfering in their affairs in a command fashion. It can provide contracts for the work it needs done, fix taxes on profits, establish rules of accounting and reporting, provide financial assistance, give advice on management and other matters, observe implementation of economic and social legislation, and provide other economic incentives or disincentives. The main responsibility of the state is not to the individual plant but to the economy and society in general. Participating in the enterprise council will provide it with current information and a position of some direct influence on its day-to-day affairs, without the possibility of unduly commanding and taking over.

This is only one of the possible ways large government enterprises can be organized. Life and experience will create others. For example, some state-owned enterprises in the Soviet Union are being leased to their workers and management for ten to fifteen years and are being run on a co-ownership basis. The problem with this form is that eventually workers will be moving in and out and the question will arise as to who is responsible (i.e., who is the effective owner) and who is only selling his labor power without any additional obligations. The state will feel satisfied as long as the leased enterprise achieves the expected or contractually specified financial or other goals. But if it does not? The answer is not exactly clear.

It may be that the lease form will prove viable only in the case of middle-sized plants, where the collective is small enough to discuss and realize jointly the terms and implications of the lease agreement. But could it work in the case of larger enterprises, which do not lend themselves easily to cooperative leasing? Such questions are too practical to be answered theoretically and in advance. But one thing is clear: all such forms are attempts to find efficient ways of overcoming alienation and for that reason should be considered positive experiences.

Competing with Capitalism

Thus, the future socialist economy is seen as a combination of different forms of government, cooperative and private enterprises, all of them functioning within one system where the dominant form is directly socialist, i.e., state-owned or cooperative in its true sense, and where there is a strong central planning but not commanding authority, charged with maximizing macroeconomic efficiency and maintaining the basic socialist principles of social equality and social justice.

The questions are, can such a system be more efficient than the capitalist one and can state-owned enterprises be more efficient than privately owned ones? The answers to both questions depend largely on the answer to the second one. If a socialist (state or cooperative) enterprise cannot be more efficient, then it will not win in the historic competition with capitalism and will not be able to remain the basis of the system, however equal and just are its generally proclaimed principles and objectives.

People measure the relative merits of a social system not only by relative equality of income and wealth or by guarantees of minimal satisfactory conditions of existence, but also by the extent to which their needs in goods and services, both material and spiritual, are satisfied. If the majority enjoys a relatively high level of satisfaction of consumer demand while a minority suffers from relative poverty and deprivation, the society will still remain viable, because it is the majority and not the minority who are satisfied.

A high consumer standard for the majority can be maintained only on the basis of high productivity. Therefore, the socialist system will be viable only if it shows the ability to reach higher levels of productivity than capitalism, and it may do so only if it becomes a leader in technology and its application to the needs of the majority. It is the socialist enterprise which has to prove that it can be more productive and more creative.

It would be interesting to compare directly the work of the socialist state-owned enterprise with that of a capitalist firm in the same industries and producing the same range of products. What are the concrete advantages and disadvantages of each — that is, provided the overcentralized bureaucracy of the command type is eliminated? Which will be more competitive in a free market competition? The answer is not clear.

Comparative productivity and efficiency are not totally determined by the extent of alienation. There are other very important factors: organizational, sociopsychological, cultural, physical, natural, macroeconomic (size of market), and so on. Given minimal alienation, productivity may be either higher or lower depending on these other conditions.

But let us take the effect of the alienation issue per se. It is not as simple as it may seem. For example, the American worker has at no time had any sense of direct closeness to means of productions in terms of owning or co-owning them. Therefore, the sense of alienation, disinterest in hard productive work, should be, and should have been, relatively low. Quite the contrary, however, labor productivity has always been very high, partly as a result of the better organization of the production process, ready access to a wide internal market and thus to economies of scale, and the urge to modernize equipment in order to replace high-cost labor, but also as a result of the very high personal performance of the American worker. Why?

My guess is that alienation in American industry has been minimized not in any formal way but where it was really important, where it counted, i.e., the worker has known he does not own the means of production and that the profit is not his in any part, but he has also known that higher productivity will always bring him higher wages. That is a minimum condition, but it has been satisfied.

The proprietor and the manager also have known that they are free to operate their means of production economically in any way consistent with profit maximization and without any major political or legal constraint. Even strong trade unions did not turn the tide once it was found that it was more efficient to replace high-cost labor by machines and better organization than to rely exclusively on antilabor legislation and the police force. Thus alienation was *de facto* minimized, a fact which together with many natural and historical advantages helped guarantee high productivity.

Under socialism it is a more complex problem. There are always three, not just two parties: labor, management, the state. There is also no desire to let these parties work in opposite directions and fight it out. The desire is to have them all work together and reach decisions which will be both economically efficient and satisfactory to all parties.

If all parties representing the four functions analyzed above were free to pursue what they are supposed to do, there would inevitably be clashes of different, sometimes contrary interests. There has to be a good and workable machinery to reach common consensus. If alienation is to be minimized in the state-owned socialist plant, it should be possibly in the most important, most essential points, rather than in all points. This may be a more realistic and easily achievable objective. If the capitalist can achieve it without giving up his private ownership and profit maximization, the socialist state should be able to do at least as well.

Once socialism has solved its basic microeconomic efficiency problem, it will also have to show its ability to make economic efficiency consistent with social justice. Whether capitalism is able to compete in this matter only the future can show.

The proof of high economic efficiency is direct competition of different social forms of organization. Socialism will be able to develop its full economic and social potential only in market competition with capitalist enterprises — private businesses at home, capitalist corporations abroad. Protectionalism of socialist enterprises by the state vis-à-vis its competitors is undesirable and harmful. Integration with the world economy will be an essential condition for the survival and, it is hoped, superiority of the socialist economic system.

Jan Tinbergen

Development and Armament

GLOBAL INTERNATIONAL RELATIONS are determined to a considerable extent by two large problem complexes, often identified as the East-West problem and the North-South problem. Without better solutions of these two problem complexes, stable international relations will not be possible. The East-West problem is mainly a security problem, while the North-South problem is mainly one of welfare creation and welfare distribution. Each has a public finance component: the East-West problem requires military expenditure, among other expenditures; the North-South problem, development assistance.

The Reagan administration decided not to participate in a 1987 United Nations Conference on the relationship between disarmament and development, because in that administration's opinion such a relationship does not exist. Since both military expenditures and development assistance are burdens on the public budget, the Reagan administration's opinion is somewhat surprising. Such a qualitative reaction to this opinion is not satisfactory, however; it should be completed by a quantitative answer.

The present paper tries to contribute to such an answer. Since the security and welfare of the global community are at stake, a satisfactory quantitative answer can be expected only from a global approach, the world at large and its main groups of nations, or rather their governments, being the actors to be introduced. They will be identified as the First, the Second, and the Third World (W1, W2, and W3). By the usual definition of these "Worlds," W1 comprises the developed market economies, W2 the Communist countries, and W3 the underdeveloped countries. Later we will discuss one dilemma in this subdivision of the global economy.

Our approach will be a macroeconomic approach. We choose such a setup in order to understand the main problems, but we must keep in mind that some of the policy makers introduced do not (yet) exist: we assume a higher degree of integration of national economies than now exists. Apart from that simplification, we also make this choice because we believe more integration to be desirable.

The policy makers in our models are the governments of W1, W2, and W3. Policy makers aim at maximizing their area's generalized welfare, by which we mean welfare-cum-security (cf. Tinbergen and Fischer, 1987) security being considered a component of welfare.

The means used by the policy makers are their world's military expenditures, nonmilitary expenditures for each world's own satisfaction (consumption and investment), and expenditures for development assistance and security assistance. In all these cases, expenditures are both public and private. By security expenditures we mean financial transfers to other worlds to enhance security. Examples are the financial equivalent of the efforts to make available to the other side grain or high-tech products for peaceful purposes.

It should not be overlooked that the concept of security is still far from clear, i.e. it is underdeveloped. A scholar like B. V. A. Röling, in his book *International Law and Peace* (1985), defines security only vaguely but calls it a four-dimensional concept. The Palme report, *Common Security* (Palme et al., 1982), provides us with no clearer definition. Quite a bit of research will be needed to elaborate sharper definitions and methods of measurement. The setup chosen in this paper admittedly is provisional, offered for discussion. To facilitate its presentation we first list the variables used and their notation.

For each "world" i ($i = 1, 2, 3$) we indicate the variables as follows:

n_i = population of World i as a ratio to that of World 1,

x_i = total income, expressed in U.S. dollars with 1975 purchasing power,

y_i = nonmilitary expenditure for World i's own use,
a_i = military expenditure,
v_{ij} = for $i = 1$ and $j = 3$, development assistance; and for $i = 1$ and $j = 2$, security assistance as defined before,
ω_i = welfare-cum-security of World i.

The relations occurring in our models consist of, first, restrictions and, second, other relations. The restricions are, in all cases,

$$x_1 = y_1 + a_1 + v_{12} + v_{13} \qquad (R1)$$
$$x_2 = y_2 + a_2 - v_{12} \qquad (R2)$$
$$x_3 = y_3 + a_3 - v_{13} . \qquad (R3)$$

Welfare-cum-security, or generalized welfare, is assumed to be a function of y_i and some a_j. Two forms of the function have been used, to be called the logarithmic and the parabolic utility function, respectively. (Utility stands for generalized welfare, in order to remind the economic reader of a well-known area of discussion.) We assume that as long as World 1 does not conclude more treaties than were concluded up to June 1988,

$$\omega_1 = \ln (y_1 + 1) + \alpha_{11} \ln (a_1 + 1) - \alpha_{12} \ln (a_2 + 1). \qquad (1)$$

The first term at the right-hand side reflects the impact of nonmilitary expenditures, both for civil and for security purposes, on the generalized welfare of World 1. The second term indicates the effect on World 1's security of its own military expenditures, and the third, negative, term the effect of World 2 military expenditures. For each term a value 0 of the variable yields a value 0 to that component of utility.

The coefficients α_{11} and α_{12} can be estimated from observed armament expenditures if one assumption is added, which is discussed elsewhere (J. Tinbergen, 1989).

After the conclusion of important new treaties, such as the reduction by 50 percent of the number of strategic missiles, the values of the α coefficients will change, and further assumptions will be needed as long as no additional research is done.

The impact of World 3 military expenditure on ω_1 has been neglected. It can be shown that the expression (1) for another "world" with a population n_k times the population of W1 contains n_k in the following way:

$$\omega_k = n_k\left[\ln{(y_k + n_k)} + \alpha_{kk}\ln(a_k + n_k) - \alpha_{kl}\ln{(a_l + n_k)}\right] \quad (2)$$

where l is the index of the "world(s)" of which the armament is relevant to world k (Tinbergen, 1989).

The choice of the logarithmic utility function is based on two arguments. First, that function shows diminishing marginal utility for all values of y_1. Second, work by Van Herwaarden and Kapteyn (1981) on a number of alternative utility functions used by Van Praag and the authors shows that the logarithmic function fits the observations used in similar research slightly — but significantly — better than all other functions considered.

We also used another utility function, called parabolic, where

$$\omega_1 = \frac{1}{y_{10}^2}(y_{10} - y_1)^2 - 1 \quad (3)$$

for one component. This function shows the phenomenon of satiation: utility attains a maximum for $y_1 = y_{10}$, and it falls for $y_1 > y_{10}$. For $y_1 = 2\,y_{10}$ utility becomes equal to its value of $y_1 = 0$, i.e., zero. So from $y_1 = y_{10}$ the phenomenon of satiation occurs. This utility function is more realistic for large values of y_1 and even more so for the component in a_1, military expenditure.

For the maximization of utility, the value of the constant is irrelevant, of course.

Two versions of this parabolic utility function are conceivable. One is that the satiation level y_{10} is an autonomous parameter: a given psychological feature of an individual or of a population. The other version is that the satiation level is the subject of ethical or political propaganda, with a certain ethical or political objective. Idealistic or political groups may recommend a relatively modest level of y_{10} in order to improve their own population's health or — a politically very important consideration — to facilitate larger amounts of development assistance to the Third World. In that case the satiation variables become instruments of international economic policy, and it appears that the objectives of such a policy enter into the set of data needed to solve our problem.

The core of our analysis consists of three calculations. The first aims at finding the optimum values of our variables to maximize $\omega_1 + \omega_2$, in an attempt to arrive at a treaty between W1 and W2 on the most desirable amounts of military expenditure. The second

TABLE 1

Worlds considered and the corresponding notation
of the variables used (y as an example)

Definition of world	Symbol	Notation of y
Non-Communist developed countries	W1	y_1
Communist-ruled countries (incl. China)	W2	y_2
Communist-ruled developed countries*	W2'	y_2'
Underdeveloped non-Communist countries	W3	y_3
All underdeveloped countries (incl. China)	W3'	y_3'
China, when considered separately	W4	y_4

*All East European countries, Yugoslavia not included.

calculation aims at finding the optimum values of the variables by maximizing $\omega_1 + \omega_3$, in an attempt to find the most desirable values of development assistance. The third calculation is to maximize $\omega_1 + \omega_2 + \omega_3$, so as to test whether there is a relation between disarmament and development — the problem of the United Nations Conference mentioned.

A difficulty arose with regard to China: should it be considered as part of W2 or as part of W3? It appeared that only when China was considered as part of World 2 was a positive value found for security assistance of W1 to W2. With China in World 3 we found a negative value, which does not make sense. So an additional setup was chosen wherein China was isolated as a W4, and calculations were also made whereby four worlds were distinguished. As a consequence, two alternative definitions of W2 and W3 had to be made, with the variables corresponding to these definitions. A survey of the definitions and notations is given in Table 1. We will not add another complication (considered elsewhere) with regard to W1, which may be subdivided into NATO and non-NATO-developed market economies.

The main sources of our figures are two publications by Kravis et al. (1978, 1982), in which figures about x_i are calculated in real terms, that is, in dollars with purchasing power in the United States in 1975. Another important source, for military expenditures, is Ruth Leger Sivard's *World Military and Social Expenditures*, of which

TABLE 2

Optimal values, in billions of $ with 1975 purchasing power, of the variables when they are the result of (A) maximizing welfare of W1 and W2, (B) maximizing welfare of W1 and W3, and (C) maximizing welfare of W1, W2, and W3. Based on logarithmic welfare functions.

Variable	A W1, W2	B W1, W3		C W1, W2, W3
		(i)	(ii)	
y_1 Nonmilitary expenditure of W1	2,050	1,458	1,527	1,370
y_2 Nonmilitary expenditure of W2	3,792	—	—	2,535
y_3 Nonmilitary expenditure of W3	—	4,156	4,352	3,905
a_1 Military expenditure of W1	40	167	0	26
a_2 Military expenditure of W2	40	—	—	26
a_3 Military expenditure of W3	—	98	0	59
v_{12} Security assistance	1,790	—	—	519
v_{13} Development assistance	—	2,255	2,353	1,964

(i) Military expenditure of W1 and W3 as in 1975.
(ii) Complete disarmament.
These are the extremes between which the armament expenditures will be situated.

we took the tenth anniversary edition of 1985. These figures are expressed in current dollars, so we took relative figures, i.e., military expenditures as a percentage of national income. Such figures are independent of general price movements over time but not from deviations between types of goods and services. A fourth source of data is the World Bank *World Development Report,* of which we used the 1981 edition; a fifth is Denison's (1967) studies about the growth of production and, in particular, the role played by technological development.

In Tables 2, 3, and 4 we present the results of the three types of calculations.

The "equity" criterion is chosen to be equal incomes per capita; differences in average capability (schooling, experience, and so on) are neglected. The value chosen for v_{12} in alternative (ii) presumably reflects today's order of magnitude. Alternatives (iii) and (iv) are those chosen in Table 2 (i) and (ii).

TABLE 3

Optimal values, in billions of $ with 1975 purchasing power, of the variables when they are the result of (A) maximizing welfare of W1 and W2, (B) maximizing welfare of W1 and W3, and (C) maximizing welfare of W1, W2, and W3. Based on parabolic utility functions where satiation values are chosen so as to maximize world welfare.

Variables	A W1, W2 (i)	A W1, W2 (ii)	B W1, W3 (iii)	B W1, W3 (iv)	C W1, W2, W3
y_1 Nonmilitary expenditure of W1	2,043	3,791	1,458	1,527	1,355
y_2 Nonmilitary expenditure of W2	3,779	2,031	—	—	2,507
y_3 Nonmilitary expenditure of W3	—	—	4,156	4,352	3,862
a_1 Military expenditure of W1	50	50	167	0	50
a_2 Military expenditure of W2	50	50	—	—	50
a_3 Military expenditure of W3	—	—	98	0	98
v_{12} Security assistance	1,787	39	—	—	515
v_{13} Development assistance	—	—	2,255	2,353	1,961

(i) Degrees of freedom choices: $a_1 = a_2 = 50$ and $y_2 = 1.85\, y_1$ ("equity").
(ii) Degrees of freedom choices: $a_1 = a_2 = 50$ and $v_{12} = 1\%$ of x_1 (3,880).
(iii) Military expenditures of W1 and W3 as in 1975.
(iv) Complete disarmament.

The main conclusion to be drawn from Tables 2, 3, and 4 is that, in most cases considered, the optimal values of security assistance and development assistance are lower under C than under A or B, because the assumptions on which A and B are based are incompatible. The exceptions are (1), Table 3, alternative (ii), value of v_{12}, where we presupposed an upper limit to v_{12}, and Table 4, alternatives (i) and (ii), value of v_{13}, where an excessively low value of v_{12} was found. In seven cases, however, our main conclusion is valid. The average difference between the assistance figures under C and those under A or B is 644, which is one third of the average assistance amounts under A or B (1914). In these seven cases, there appears to be a relation between development assistance and security assistance in the sense that if both have to be provided, there is less for one of them than would be available if only it were being offered. This is what we called in our introductory argument the

TABLE 4

Optimal values of the variables, in billions of $ with 1975 purchasing power, when they are the result of (A) maximizing welfare of W1 and W2', (B) maximizing welfare of W1 and W3' and (C) maximizing welfare of W1, W2' and W3'. Based on logarithmic ultility functions.

Variables	A W1, W2'	B W1, W3'		C W1, W2,' W3'
		(i)	(ii)	
y_1 Nonmilitary expenditure of W1	3,238	1,234	1,295	1,231
y_2' Nonmilitary expenditure of W2'	1,814	—	—	1,198
y_3' Nonmilitary expenditure of W3'	—	5,123	5,374	5,108
a_1 Military expenditure of W1	40*	167	0	54
a_2' Military expenditure of W2'	40*	167	0	54
a_3' Military expenditure of W3'	—	145	0	277
v_{12}' Security assistance	602	—	—	0
v_{13}' Development assistance	—	2,479	2,585	2,595

(i) Military expenditures of W1 and W3' as in 1975.

(ii) Complete disarmament.

*Chosen equal to value in Table 2.

qualitative reaction to the absence of the United States from the U.N. Conference. The quantitative answer is that the effect of the necessity to make available both types of assistance (that is, to aim at both security and development cooperation) lowers by one third the amounts ideally required, i.e., the "optimal" amounts.

A second conclusion that may be derived from the tables is that the order of magnitude of the differences found is about the same for the two types of utility functions used. Of the seven cases, three are obtained with the parabolic utility function (the three shown in Table 3). Here the average difference is 30 percent as against 36 percent in Tables 2 and 4, where logarithmic utility functions have been used.

A third conclusion we can draw from the results obtained is that, in the cases where values for military expenditures of the two superpowers were derived from the maximization of welfare-cum-security, not chosen autonomously, a pronounced reduction in military expenditures was found. This applies to the figures under C in Tables 2 and 4: $26 and $54 billion in 1975 dollars.

It seems appropriate to deal with one other aspect of the results obtained, namely, the very high optimal amounts found for both types of assistance. The average amounts of both types of assistance are as much as 49 percent of the real income x_1. The average amounts of development assistance even constitute 59 percent of x_1, the income of W1 (3,880 billion).

These figures seem to undermine completely the credibility of our setup. For this reason the author hopes to publish elsewhere an in-depth analysis of the problem of the optimal amount of development assistance (Tinbergen, 1989). Some of the crucial points of this analysis will be summarized in the remaining part of this paper. First, however, the author wants to state that the avoidance of a nuclear war constitutes an issue of such a high level of welfare that, in the absence of other means, the expenditure of even an amount of half our present income would be rational.

With regard to development cooperation, this degree of urgency does not exist. How, then, must we look at this part of our results? The main point is that our models are static models and their interpretation is that they refer in principle to long-term solutions. What they tell us is that if the present data were to reflect a lasting equilibrium, a better long-term equilibrium would be the one described by our "optimum values." A static model describes a possible goal, but it does not describe how to get there. The road to the new equilibrium can only be a smooth road. We will give a concrete example below.

Yet the high figures in our tables do contain a message. They tell us that there is a tremendous problem that we will not be able to solve if we stick to the present smooth road. Some figures for world income distribution show that in the last three decades hardly any changes in that distribution have occurred. We cannot conclude from this fact that our present policies are adequate. With increasing interdependence, the intolerable inequality will build up tension, and wise politicians — perhaps only the real "statesmen" among them — will understand that something more must be done if we want to avoid an explosion. The fence along the Mexican-American frontier will not help.

What is needed is, for example, a policy such that, in a future when most of the present generation of the Third World is still alive, an observable improvement in their incomes compared to ours will be attained. More concretely, in twenty years something of the order of magnitude of a doubling of their income as a ratio to ours must occur. A simple calculation shows that development assistance must be 2 or 3 percent of our GNP instead of the famous 0.7 percent or the actual 0.35 percent made available at present. The level of 2 or 3 percent is also a consequence of the fact, not always sufficiently realized, that the total population of the Third World without China is about three times the population of the Western industrialized world.

Hence also the "smooth road" to the optimal long-term goals must be different — and significantly different — from today's policies of development cooperation. These different policies require a considerable reduction of armament expenditures, because otherwise the level of our own consumption would have to be lowered in an unacceptable way which would destabilize our internal political equilibrium.

REFERENCES

Denison, E. F. *Why Growth Rates Differ.* Washington D.C.: The Brookings Institution, 1967.

Kravis, I. B., et al. "Real GDP per Capita for More Than One Hundred Countries." *The Economic Journal* 88 (1978): 218–42.

———. *World Product and Income,* published for the World Bank. Baltimore: The Johns Hopkins University Press, 1982.

Leger Sivard, Ruth. *World Military and Social Expenditures,* 10th Anniversary Edition. Washington D.C.: World Priorities, 1985.

Palme, O., et al. *Common Security,* published for the Independent Commission on Disarmament and Security Issues. New York: Simon and Schuster, 1982.

Röling, B. V. A. *Volkenrecht en Vrede (International Law and Peace),* 3rd. ed. Deventer, Netherlands: Kluwer, 1985.

Tinbergen, J., and D. Fischer. *Warfare and Welfare.* Brighton, England: Wheatsheaf Books, 1987.

Tinbergen, J. *World Security and Equity,* forthcoming.

Van Herwaarden, F. G., and A. Kapteyn. "Empirical Comparison of the Shape of Welfare Functions." *European Economic Review* 15 (1981): 261–86.

World Bank. *World Development Report 1981.* Washington D.C., 1981.

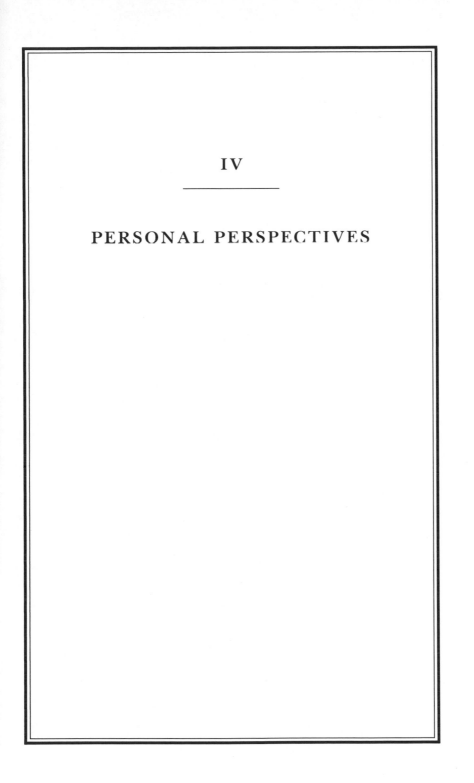

IV
———————

PERSONAL PERSPECTIVES

George W. Ball

Four Decades of
John Kenneth Galbraith

I KNOW THAT a *Festschrift* for a distinguished scholar traditionally consists of erudite monographs by fellow practitioners of his discipline; thus, one who holds no union card as a professional economist lacks qualifications to appear in this volume. Yet, since I have known John Kenneth Galbraith for more than forty years, I cannot forgo the chance to pay him homage on such a notable occasion. Even had he done nothing more, we should celebrate his success in having surpassed the Biblical target age by a full decade — though I understand that, for an academic, that is not such a rare achievement.

If I cannot submit a piece that casts fresh light on some esoteric economic issue, I can at least recount a few incidents in our long, sporadic — but never dull — collaboration. These may help illuminate Galbraith's character and qualities and thus fill out his three-dimensional image — iconic for some, satanic for others — that has become so familiar not merely to academics but to a wide public, which reacts fiercely either to Ken's achievements or his assertive heterodoxy.

Kenneth and I first encountered one another when he was concluding the rough but essential wartime task of controlling prices in the Office of Price Administration during the months after Pearl Harbor. He had already become a center of ferocious controversy — obviously the posture he most enjoys   when, to save the administration from the slings and arrows then being directed at him, the White House arranged for Ken to share his wisdom with the top command of the Lend-Lease Administration, for which I was, at that time, associate general counsel.

In early September 1944, after the Lend-Lease Administration had become the Foreign Economic Administration through one of those transmutations with which Washington was afflicted during wartime, I accepted the invitation of General "Hap" Arnold, commanding general of the air force, to serve as the civilian member of a board of air force officers charged with evaluating the achievements of the United States Air Force, particularly in its attacks on targets in France. It required only two weeks in London for me to conclude that the Air Force Evaluation Board lacked the depth, competence, and independence to make a critical appraisal of the success of the whole air effort. If a study were to do more than lend its *Good Housekeeping* stamp of approval to the Air Force's theories, it would have to be undertaken by a group not responsible to the air force hierarchy but to Secretary of War Henry Stimson.

I therefore wangled permission from General Carl Spaatz to return to the United States, where I found a small group of people in the War Department preoccupied with a similar concern. Together we launched what became the United States Strategic Bombing Survey. At my suggestion, one of the first recruits as a director of the survey was John Kenneth Galbraith; another was Paul Nitze. In November 1945 we embarked together for London to establish the survey under the nominal leadership of General Franklin d'Olier and the practical management of Henry Alexander, a Morgan partner.

Accompanying us was Adlai Stevenson, with whom I had practiced law in Chicago. I had recruited him to serve for an interim term as my deputy to look after my duties on the Evaluation Board, then based in France, while I worked in London with the Bombing Survey. But d'Olier was a cautious man (as befits the retiring head of a major insurance company), and he refused, on security grounds, to permit Stevenson to attend the meetings of the Bombing Survey even though Stevenson had, for some years, been assistant to Secretary of the Navy Frank Knox.

In the spring of 1945 Ken and I decided to move our base of operations from London to Bad Nauheim to provide a more efficient launching pad for our inspection teams that needed access to

German targets. Kenneth had by that time gathered about him a distinguished group of economists and was already tentatively blocking out the report he was to make to the survey directors.

On May 7, 1945, the Flensburg Radio carried Admiral Karl Doenitz's message of defeat and announced the formation of what, Doenitz no doubt hoped, would be recognized by the Allies as an established government. Blackmailers that they were, Doenitz and Alfred Jodl had persuaded themselves that only such a "government" could negotiate a tolerable peace and prevent chaos during the period of surrender.

Of far more interest to Galbraith and me was the news that one of our field teams had found Albert Speer, once in charge of the German war economy, now a member of that rump government. Speer was the man who we had been most eager to encounter ever since the beginning of the survey. So, when I arrived in London on V-E Day, I immediately organized an airplane load of selected survey personnel, including interpreters and secretaries, to fly to Flensburg. Meanwhile, I sent word to Galbraith and Nitze in the field to join me. We flew over the flooded fields of northern Holland, where the dikes had been bombed or sabotaged. It was an unreal scene, since we still instinctively regarded it as enemy territory.

The atmosphere of Flensburg airport has been vividly described by Kenneth in his memoirs and in other writings. It possessed large elements of the bizarre to which Ken and I contributed as, in our paramilitary uniforms, we wandered through units of fully armed Luftwaffe officers and crews, yet could find no Allied military personnel to provide us transport. Finally, we were hailed by one of the majors attached to the survey and taken to a billet on the *Patria*, an old Hamburg-American liner, anchored in the Flensburg Fjord, where the SHAEF Control Party was stationed.

After lunch, Galbraith, Nitze, and I set out for Glücksburg, where Speer was living in a castle belonging to the Duke of Holstein — a picturesque, sixteenth-century château, complete with tower, turrets, a moat, and a complement of S.S. guards. Speer met us in the great hall wearing a dark brown uniform. Friendly and self-consciously affable, he expressed delight that we had come; he had, he said, long hoped to relate the full story of the German war economy to knowledgeable Americans.

For six days after that, the three of us — Galbraith, Nitze, and

I — met with Speer every afternoon, leaving him the morning free to attend cabinet meetings on what he himself referred to as "the opera bouffe Wilhelmstrasse." At one point, during a pause in our interrogation, Speer produced ten or twelve volumes of photo cover consisting of pictures which, he said, included every hydroelectric installation in the western part of the Soviet Union. Speer had had these pictures taken in preparation for an air attack to be made by pick-a-back planes, an operation Göring aborted out of bureaucratic jealousy. Speer gave us the books. "Sooner or later," he said, "you're going to have to fight the Communists, and you may need these."

As the week drew to a close, Robert Murphy, Eisenhower's political adviser, appeared on the *Patria* and told me at dinner that he would like us to try to find out from Speer what had happened to Hitler's political will, but that we would have to act that night, since the Allied authorities would be arresting the entire Nazi group the following morning. So we sent a car to bring Speer to a house we had requisitioned on the outer fringes of Flensburg. Then Galbraith, Nitze, and I sat up till three or four o'clock in the morning (with a whiskey bottle on the table) listening to the exotic tale of the final days in the bunker under the Chancellory in Berlin.

During that long night, Speer spoke with candor about his colleagues, for most of whom he had contempt. Göring, he said, was a morphine addict with unrestrained greed. Goebbels, who posed as an intellectual, was a sycophantic schemer. Himmler dreamed weird fantasies about the future glory of the party while dabbling in astrology and Oriental nonsense. Bormann was a brutal extortionist who used bribery to retain his place at Hitler's side.

Our weeklong interrogation of Speer gave the survey firsthand access to knowledge of what had really happened. Speer not only provided us the addresses of where they had hidden the documents detailing the decline of the German war economy, but also gave us letters of introduction to the members of his staff who had custody of those documents.

The massive Hamburg raids in 1943, when British bombers had produced their first firestorm, had, Speer told us, demoralized Hitler and his colleagues and, had the Allies continued those attacks, German morale would have suffered a critical blow. On the other hand, he suggested, a great deal of our carefully targeted bombing had made only marginal difference. By wiping out many small businesses, we had sometimes freed labor for more productive use. By bombing air-frame factories at a time when aircraft engines were in short supply, we had helped bring Nazi aircraft production back into phase. The statistic that interested us the most was that by June 1944, in spite of months of sustained and intensive bombardment, German war production was roughly three times what it had been at the outset of the war.

In Speer's view, America had dealt the most serious blow to Germany when the Eighth Air Force began to bomb synthetic oil production in June 1944, because, fearing a continued interruption in fuel supplies, the Germans had curtailed flying time to the point where their pilots were pushed into combat with inadequate training.

Later, the saturation bombing of the Ruhr which began in the last quarter of 1944 had critically slowed German industry, not so much because we had smashed up machinery — the Germans always had a large surplus of general-purpose machine tools — but because the bombing destroyed internal transport in plant complexes. The general attack on transportation — which began in September 1944 — produced the ultimate economic collapse. Still — and on this point even our air force friends agreed — our strategic bombing had served the cause well; it had forced an inadequately trained German air force into the air where our fighters could destroy it. As a result, the Allies had gained clear command of the air over the Normandy battlefield.

The perception and analysis reflected in the report made by Ken and his colleagues amounted, in my mind, to an impressive scholarly tour de force, but perhaps Galbraith's most important service to the Bombing Survey was the avidity and vigor with which he manned the barricades in the street fighting that marked the drafting of the survey's final conclusions.

It was an epic of guerrilla warfare reminiscent of the Battle of Algiers. Many top air force officers were, as I suggested, determined that the survey should validate and glorify the achievements of the air force, while the conclusions of Galbraith's Overall Effects Bureau stopped far short of fulfilling that objective.

As a result, the process of persuading the survey top management to accept the conclusions of Ken's operation degenerated into a running controversy that lasted weeks, with Kenneth serving as the champion of rationality against formidable adversaries, particularly General Orville Anderson, who had been in charge of the Eighth Air Force. Ken brought into play his full dialectical armory, complete with satire and ridicule.

The end result was inevitably a compromise. The Bombing Survey would proceed with the publication of its official report, which, to the minds of several of us, was inadequate and misleading, while Ken and his Overall Economic Effects division would publish their own separate report.

But that was not the only successful operation during our life in Bad Nauheim. Out of our discussions evolved two economic predictions that were at least partially confirmed by events.

The first was that the two nations most likely to emerge as the industrial leaders in the postwar world were West Germany and Japan. We arrived at that conclusion because we believed the Allied air forces had done Germany a considerable favor (which our own air forces were then also doing for Japan): they had destroyed both countries' obsolete industry, leaving them not only free of that encumbrance but compelled to assume technological leadership.

Our second tentative prediction was that the postwar world would operate largely without much irksome need for currency. Americans in Germany were then able to procure almost all their necessities by using chits, and sometimes our more imaginative colleagues felt free from the constraints of total probity. For example, one of the captains attached to our survey procured a whole jeepload of liquor by use of a chit signed in the name of P. G. T. Beauregard, General, CSA. The unhappy wine merchant was victimized by his specialized education; his gymnasium had taught him pages of Heine but nothing about the American Civil War. Since then, Galbraith and I have regarded the postwar emergence of credit cards merely as a fulfillment of our prophecy.

But apart from that, we developed no profound academic concepts. Our days were filled with the painstaking work of the survey, interrogating Nazi witnesses whom we brought to our Bad Nauheim quarters (which we turned into a temporary internment camp) and analyzing the data produced by our field teams returning for periodic home visits.

Yet life was not without its intellectual pleasures, for we were frequently visited by such learned colleagues as Arthur Schlesinger, Jr., from the OSS, then based at Wiesbaden, while the survey staff included at least one literary figure, W. H. Auden. Auden, unfortunately, proved disappointing. Although he twice came to dinner with us, far from speaking lyric syllables, he was so drunk on each occasion as to be almost inarticulate.

In the years from 1945 until 1952, my family exchanged periodic visits with the Galbraiths, and we talked together frequently on the telephone, but he and I were not associated in another common enterprise until 1952. Then I helped recruit Kenneth to work with Adlai Stevenson in a glorious campaign that produced a less than glorious result.

Ken was one of the group of prolific academics who based themselves in the Elks Club in Springfield, where they ground out speech materials for the governor. I was a floating member of the campaign staff working directly with Stevenson's manager, Wilson Wyatt.

Thereafter came another time gap in our collaboration until Galbraith and I both joined the Kennedy administration soon after the President's inauguration in January 1961. In part as a result of Kenneth's advocacy, the President had appointed me Under Secretary of State, while making Kenneth our ambassador to Delhi. For the few days before his departure to that post, the Galbraiths stayed at our house in Washington.

I remember only two incidents during Kenneth's tour in India. At one point in 1962, on the President's direction, I flew to Lisbon to hold a conversation in depth with Prime Minister Salazar. He was sorely troubled by our criticism of his Angolan policies, while we wished to obtain a favorable lease of the Azores bases. In the evening of the first day, I sent the following telegram around the circuit to Kenneth in Delhi: "Have just spent long day with Salazar. Now at last I understand what it means to give serious political responsibilities to a professor of economics." Later, after India had effectively swallowed an adjacent small Portuguese colony, Kenneth took mild offense at my reference to Nehru as the "Goa Constrictor."

I must by now have made it clear that this contribution to the *Festschrift* is not serious intellectual food but merely catsup and condiments — for which, I feel sure, Kenneth will forgive me. After all, he is a prime practitioner of adding spice to erudition.

Henry Rosovsky

The Most Famous Professor
at Harvard

IN JANUARY 1966, shortly after joining the Harvard faculty, I
was in a Hoboken, New Jersey, garage waiting for my car to be
serviced following an overseas shipment. In this squalid garage, in
a squalid part of town, the grease-covered mechanic asked about
my place of employment. "I teach at Harvard" was my reply. "Ah,"
said the mechanic, in a muffled voice from underneath the car,
"do you happen to know Professor Galbraith?"

Just a few months ago, I was looking at applications to a freshman seminar. In answer to a query concerning previous studies in
economics, a young woman wrote: "I have read economics texts
and books by such authors as Adam Smith, John Kenneth Galbraith, and Thomas Malthus." What a triad!

Every June, right after commencement, *le tout* Cambridge gath-
ers for "Champagne in the Garden" at the Galbraiths. It is one of
the main social attractions of the season: nearly all recipients of
honorary degrees are regularly in attendance and available for close
inspection; the more glamorous members of the Harvard faculty
are also present; and so are assorted ambassadors, foreign statesmen, journalists, and occasional jet-setters. Even a few students
manage to get an invitation. Over the babble of voices and tongues,
one tall figure floats from group to group extending a hand, bend-

I am very grateful to Jana Van Der Meulen for research assistance and helpful comments.

ing down to pat a back while smiling in a slightly detached way at the hundreds of guests. It is a pleasant enough gathering, but even if one views cocktail parties with loathing, not to be invited would be hellish comment on one's position in Harvard society.

These three vignettes justify the title of this essay. Fame is public estimation, and although our university does not lack individuals of wide reputation, no one comes close to rivaling Galbraith. No Harvard president or Nobel laureate has achieved similar name recognition. Of course, such fame rests on a base of multiple activities. Galbraith's celebrity can be attributed to his achievements as a writer of books and essays (even novels), to his appearances on television, and also to his diplomatic, public service, and political careers. Most of those familiar with Galbraith's work will agree, I believe, that his achievements in these areas do not relate primarily to the university and therefore do not fall within my assigned topic: Galbraith at Harvard. I will have very little to say about the external Galbraith, a category in which I include the professional economist and scholar: others will surely cover these topics in detail. My intention is to focus on the interaction between Galbraith and Harvard, the institution where he has spent most of his life. Even if we narrow our intentions in this manner — by excluding at least 50 percent of Galbraith's labors — it is only possible to touch on a few arbitrarily selected items in a remarkable life of work.

The Second Coming

Galbraith spent two periods at Harvard. From 1934 to 1939 he served in the very junior capacities of instructor and tutor — in between Berkeley and Princeton — specializing in agricultural economics. He returned ten years later as Professor of Economics, a post he occupied for twenty-six years until retirement in 1975 (voluntarily at age sixty-seven). The first period was relatively uneventful: neither Galbraith's arrival nor departure caused a great stir at Harvard. He was just another member of the junior faculty. No doubt it was a period of intellectual growth and excitement: Harvard economics was on the upgrade with faculty stars like Hansen and Schumpeter and graduate students of Samuelson's and Bergson's caliber. But if he had not returned after World War

II, "Galbraith at Harvard" (from Harvard's point of view!) could be confined to a brief paragraph.

One important lesson does emerge from those early Cambridge years. Before the war, Harvard's place in American higher education was unchallenged. Professors received higher salaries than at any other university and lived extremely well, especially during the depression. Hardly anyone refused "a call" to join the faculty. With great benefit to our national system of education, quite a few schools attained high status after the war, creating competition and a decline in the "rent" earned by Harvard professors. I do not mean to suggest that Galbraith opposed competition, but the remembrance of an older Harvard made him determined not to regress to the mean in recent times. In his own words: [1]

> The modern Harvard professor . . . is much less grand, much less affluent, much less secure and I would judge, much less happy. A new academic style, emphasizing a measure of shabbiness in housing, attire and, on occasion, outlook is legitimized by financial necessity. . . . Harvard professors disappear at night into the distant Boston outskirts, there to engage in the suburban middle-class struggle with teenage delinquency and crabgrass. . . . Institutional elitism has declined at Harvard. Authority has weakened. Democracy has advanced. But there has been a price. . . . No one can now afford to seem eccentric.

Galbraith never disappeared into distant suburbs; he lived in a pink mansion on Francis Avenue in Cambridge. I saw no crabgrass on his lawn. I detected no fear of eccentricity. His views were thoroughly modern — on occasion perhaps trendy — but his life-style harkened back to a day when the status of a professor at Harvard was uncontested. And that brings me to the tumultuous second coming.

As the economics department returned to normalcy after World War II, there was much discussion concerning the appointment of an economist with strong policy orientation: someone offering "a type of advanced graduate instruction that deals with problems of the sort that arise in the higher levels of policy-making in government." [2] Galbraith's candidacy for this post was championed by the agricultural economist John D. Black, and in terms of policy experience few could rival his credentials: 1940, Chief Economist, American Farm Bureau Federation; 1940–1941, Economic Advi-

sor, National Defense Advisory Commission; 1941–1943, Deputy
Administrator in charge of price control, Office of Price Administration; 1945, Director, United States Strategic Bombing Survey;
and 1946, Director, Office of Economic Security Policy, Department of State. Black knew, of course, that others were in the running: [3]

> Excluding [Theodore] Schultz, to whom the appointment was of-
> fered, and [Jan] Tinbergen from the Netherlands, he [Galbraith]
> ran neck in neck with [Theodore] Yntema for top place in all of the
> balloting, with [Paul] Samuelson next, and [Arthur] Smithies in sev-
> enth place. Tinbergen owed his strength to the European clique in
> the Department of Economics (by no means all European born),
> who have a European idea of the function of a university, and would
> have been a misfit in this appointment.

By 1947 the leading candidates were Galbraith, Samuelson, and
Smithies — the latter two characterized by Black as simply giving
the Department an opportunity "of getting another high-grade
technical economist." They "would further unbalance the work in
economics at Harvard in the direction of the monetary-fiscal policy
axis," and this would narrow the department more than usual "since
they are Keynesians in addition."[4] Galbraith was different. Instead
of being interested in "refinements of economic and monetary theory . . . a man of his breadth of comprehension is likely to find
himself mainly absorbed in dealing with broad fundamental economic relationships." That is precisely what appealed to Black, as
did the possibility of Galbraith helping with some instruction in
the area of commodity distribution and prices — i.e., agricultural
economics.[5] Eventually, all those on the short list were offered posts.
To our perpetual regret, Samuelson declined. Smithies accepted.
The department voted to invite Galbraith in 1948, but instead of
that being the end of the story it was merely a beginning.

A tenured appointment at Harvard is the culmination of a long
and complex procedure involving internal and external committees, many peer reviewers, and very careful evaluation by the university president. If his conclusions are affirmative, the president
formally recommends the appointment to the two governing boards:
the Corporation and the Board of Overseers. In the matter of academic appointments especially — and in much else — it is expected that the thirty elected overseers will perform their cere-
monial duties swiftly and elegantly by approving the administration's

recommendations. The phrase "rubber stamp" comes to mind; it is usually accurate. Once in a very rare while — I would guess not more frequently than once every fifty years — this smooth procedure fails to work. Objections are raised by the trustees; controversy erupts; the flag of academic freedom is raised. That Galbraith turned out to be a "once in a half century" case will not surprise his friends — or enemies.

All the facts are not available to me. I did not have access to the confidential minutes of the Board of Overseers, and they may well be incomplete. But with the help of Galbraith's own papers and published writings, and some materials from Harvard president James B. Conant's memoirs, it is not too difficult to cover the main points. Three overseers raised questions concerning Galbraith's proposed appointment: Charles Codman Cabot, as the name might lead one to suspect, a prominent Boston lawyer; Sinclair Weeks, a former United States senator (briefly and by appointment) and future secretary of commerce for President Eisenhower; and Clarence B. Randall, president and chairman of Inland Steel. All three were prominent Republicans. Even, so, that these gentlemen should have deigned to take an interest in so prosaic a matter as the appointment of a Harvard professor was most unusual. Of course, the issue was not just any ordinary scholar. They were considering a man who, despite being only forty years old, brought along all sorts of controversial baggage. Galbraith already was a public figure, and there appeared to be two problems: one specific and especially affecting Cabot; the other was much more general and was of greater interest to Weeks and Randall — and eventually Thomas Lamont.

Let us begin with Cabot and the United States Strategic Bombing Survey. The survey was an attempt by the government to assess the accomplishments of our long-range bombers over Germany. Formed as a civilian agency in 1944, "The objective was to improve the efficiency of the attack on Japan and to appraise the return on the considerable investment in lives and resources in strategic bombing. During the period of hostilities the efficiency of the air attacks was, necessarily, speculative."[6] Galbraith joined in 1945 "with the responsibility for assessing the aggregate effects of the attacks on the German economy." Cabot was to serve as secretary for the entire effort and be responsible for the preparation of a final report. Problems quickly emerged, and we need not concern ourselves with details. The initial Cabot draft was rejected as unsatisfactory, and Galbraith was asked to prepare another — and eventually accepted — version. That could not have been helpful to either Charles Cabot's *amour-propre* or *amour* for Galbraith.

There were, however, more important issues. Galbraith's final version minced no words and exposed facts that the air force and some of its backers did not want publicized. The famous Schweinfurt raids did not — as was claimed — greatly impede German ball-bearing production. Attacks on air-frame manufacturers did not prevent production increases throughout the war. And there were other similarly uncomfortable findings. Partisans of air power, and some who believed that the honor of our armed forces had been questioned, were not at all pleased. In the ensuing controversy there were suggestions concerning both the quality of Galbraith's analysis and his patriotism. (He would soon get used to this line of attack.) Galbraith finally prevailed, and nearly all have accepted his version as accurate and truthful: even the air force, though apparently not Mr. Cabot.

In one of his memoranda reconsidering this entire affair, Galbraith made a few observations that have the character of shrewd self-analysis.[7]

> It is of course possible . . . that I am unduly uncompromising in my personal and political views and in my personal relations.
>   I will say that while I set the greatest store by open-mindedness — that habit of mind that learns and unlearns — in scientific and scholarly pursuits, I do believe that there are times when a man must be uncompromising. Facts cannot be compromised; neither can great issues of public welfare. I have no doubt that from my administration of price control considerable evidence of an uncompromising temperament could be adduced. In that context one could not compromise with a few; general compromise would have been fatal. The United States will suffer if it ever finds itself, in a period of danger, with public servants who believe otherwise and so pattern their behavior. The problem of the Bombing Survey was similar. The easy way would have been to accept compromise where the record was troublesome or embarrassing. The result would have been a worthless report. It is also to be recalled that along with the truth, the security of the country was at stake.

Turning now to the more general objections to Galbraith, he was to characterize them this way in later years: "[Sinclair Weeks,

Clarence Randall, and Thomas S. Lamont of J. P. Morgan] . . . thought that I had an excessive commitment to the economics of the late New Deal, and, more alarming, that of John Maynard Keynes. There were already too many Keynesians in the Department."[8] It was an entirely accurate diagnosis. Over a year was needed to get the overseers to approve Galbraith's appointment, and that interval included a special investigatory committee and, it is said, a threat of resignation by President Conant. The appointment was only approved in the winter of 1949. One year later, Clarence B. Randall, as chairman of the Economics Department visiting committee, noting lack of "balance with respect to the viewpoints of its members," made the following additional observations:[9]

> We have in the Department, for example, one or more Socialists, some zealous followers of British economist John Maynard Keynes, and some who advocate the extension of economic controls by Government. Some of these men are nationally known for their views and are both active and zealous in promoting them. But on the other side of the social spectrum, the Department seems to lack men of equal ability and zeal who hold opposing views and are prepared to teach them.

It is obvious that Galbraith's second coming still weighed heavily on Randall's mind. Yet the long-term consequences of this episode are not entirely clear. For Conant, it seemed to confirm a suspicion going back many years concerning the basically unscientific nature of economics. A first-class organic chemist could not reach any other conclusion. Galbraith himself claimed a major long-term effect:[10]

> Often in academic and public life one wonders whether one must speak out on some issue where the emotions or pecuniary interests of the reputable are in opposition to the public good. Perhaps this time one can pass and accept the pleasures of a tranquil life. Always when faced with this decision, I have thought of Sinclair Weeks, Clarence Randall and Thomas Lamont. Surely I must do whatever might be possible to justify their forebodings.

With hindsight, it seems to me that Harvard and the nation owe a debt of gratitude to these three gentlemen. In their absence, Galbraith might have metamorphosed into just another dull empirical — perhaps even agricultural! — economist, and that would have made it pointless to write this essay. Nearly forty years have elapsed since these events occurred. To my knowledge, there has been no overseer restlessness in the matter of academic appointments since the Galbraith affair. If past experience is a guide, we are just about due for another incident.

Degrees for Democrats

Galbraith was only rarely the innocent victim of controversy at Harvard. More usually he joined in instigating controversy, thereby fulfilling his increasingly accepted role as liberal conscience of the university. That would be the friendly interpretation and accords with my own view. Others in Cambridge (and in Belmont where the crabgrass grows) might be tempted to use the less flattering label of gadfly. Support for both interpretations is provided by the dispute surrounding the award of honorary degrees in the late 1950s.

In November of 1959, President Nathan M. Pusey received a letter addressed to the President and Fellows of Harvard College (the Corporation), signed by Arthur M. Schlesinger, Jr., and Galbraith. It is worth quoting the opening paragraph in full: [11]

> We should like, with all respect and good will, to draw your atten-
> tion to present practice in awarding honorary degrees at Harvard
> for public service. We feel that this practice reflects on the fairness,
> liberalism, and, indeed, on the good judgement of the University.
> And we feel that, given the facts, you will wish to agree. We refer to
> the continuing preference for members of the Republican Party and
> the near exclusion from such honors of liberal Democrats. We note
> with equal concern the virtually total exclusion of labor leaders.
> Without attributing undue importance to these awards, we would
> like to urge an end to the present practice as something which can
> only be explained as a vestigial remnant of emotions and attitudes
> now happily far behind us. That the preference for Republicans
> may be in part unconscious makes it neither less genuine *nor* more
> defensible. Political discrimination in such matters is to be regretted
> when it is explicit and also when it is implicit.

This slightly sanctimonious salvo across the bow of Harvard's establishment was then backed by solid and convincing statistics. During the thirteen years following World War II, Harvard had awarded between twenty-two and twenty-seven honorary degrees for public service. Not more than four had been bestowed on active Democrats: thus favoring Republicans by a ratio of between 4 to 1 or 6 to 1.[12] Furthermore, since 1930 only one solitary trade union leader — Clinton Golden — had been honored, and then only after he retired from active duty to the safe (and conservative) haven of the Harvard Business School! And in conclusion, Galbraith and Schlesinger added another sermonette:

> The nation owes much in the last thirty years to those who have been willing to strike out for change. Such men are never fashionable at the moment. They always seem a bit untried and radical as compared with the comfortable and respectable men. But they are the men who earn the applause of history.

We may reasonably assume that, in the view of the authors, there was no shortage of Democrats who would eventually earn the applause of history.

Aside from the fundamental truth of the charges, there are two things that we might note in connection with this episode. First, the original letter was immediately made public by the authors. The purpose was not quietly and discreetly to send a message to Harvard authorities urging them in a friendly fashion to change their practices. An open letter, sent to the *Harvard Crimson* and other papers, is the practice of pressure politics, and that was the intention from the very beginning. Secondly, the G & S Manifesto was no impulsive act — not a few lines drafted in a fit of righteous indignation. We know that one year earlier, Galbraith had attempted to enlist the support of Seymour Harris, at that time chairman of the economics department. Harris declined: "As long as I am Chairman of the Department and have to deal with the Administration in an official way, I think it would not be wise for me to sign this kind of statement." [13]

Galbraith and Schlesinger must have been pleased with the reaction to their effort. The national press gave considerable play in supportive columns and editorials — principally, one suspects, in Democratic newspapers. Philip L. Graham, publisher of the Washington Post approved, as did William Benton, publisher of the *Encyclopaedia Brittanica,* who bemoaned his inability to secure an honorary degree for Hubert H. Humphrey from *any* school. It was also an occasion for a good deal of predictably heavy-handed — largely Republican — humor. A citizen of Allentown, Pennsylvania, suggested this wonderful definition: ". . . the Democratic party is one in which a few aristocrats lead *many* bums, whereas the Republicans have a few bums trying to lead many aristocrats." With impeccable rationality he concludes that G & S favored honorary degrees for bums. H. J. Szold, of Lehman Brothers, declared that a logical extension of the G & S position would be ". . . following the concept of equal time on radio and television and have half of the faculty positions awarded by the Democratic National Committee and the other half by the Republican National Committee." [14] I would award a booby prize to Professors William Yandell Elliot and W. Barton Leach — in those days, big hitters respectively in political science and law — who opined in a letter to President Pusey (December 14, 1959) that "one sure method of avoiding . . . controversy would be to make posthumous awards to persons unconnected with the American political scene." Their preferred candidate: Edward de Vere, seventeenth Earl of Oxford and the real author or the so-called "Shakespeare" works.

Why write about this episode at all? Because it was more than a tempest in a teapot and in some ways showed Galbraith at his institutional best: identifying a real, though perhaps unconscious, prejudice and pushing the university in the direction of desirable change. No one will claim that G & S alone changed either the method of selection or the pool of honorary degree candidates. But change they did. Before the Bok administration, which began in 1971, faculty advice in these matters was restricted to awards given to scholars. The broad public service category — essentially the inevitably political category of all nonscholars — remained entirely in the hands of the governing boards. Since Bok, a committee composed of many different constituencies makes nearly all nominations, with predictable results: many new groups — including Democratic public servants, women, and blacks — are winning deserved recognition. Of course, the world around us — the environment and values within which the university lives — had changed, and new procedures and new sensitivities were an inevitable by-product. However, there are always a few who start the ball rolling, and that has been Galbraith's role more than once. Honorary degrees are only one example.

In June of 1987 one of the more popular honorary degrees at Harvard's commencement was awarded to Galbraith. To use his own words, "Without attributing undue importance to these awards"

I hope that he did not see himself as simply the recipient of an affirmative action prize — category: sometime public servant, Democrat, and, incidentally, scholar of note. Knowing Galbraith, I am certain that these thoughts never crossed his mind — and rightly so. In fact, he had probably forgotten the entire controversy. It was ancient history, and more recent times were eventful enough to occupy his thoughts fully.

Good Forecast; Wrong Conclusion

Relations between Galbraith and Harvard acquired a slightly sour character during the 1960s — so many things turned sour in that cursed decade. Returning from his ambassadorial post to India in 1963, Galbraith gradually identified a number of sources feeding his institutional unhappiness. First, he did not enjoy the drift of economics into a mathematical and technocratic mode and found himself increasingly at odds with the mainstream of his department — middle-aged neoclassical hot shots. These feelings reached a climax in the early 1970s, when the economics department failed to promote a group of highly visible, young followers of the "radical" tradition. But the issue went well beyond individual cases: [15]

> The harmony which one now foresees in the discipline is based on a general commitment to neoclassical economics or its applied refinements. Accomplishment in model-building and refinement is, I think nearly all will agree, an increasingly stern requirement. We would not again hire a labor economist who, like Professor Dunlop or Professor Slichter, made his career out of a practical association with the unions and the problems of labor mediation. Professor Leontief, were he now showing the experimental tendencies that marked his early career, would be in trouble. Even his work, when firmly established, was not strongly supported. We would not have an economist who was too much preoccupied with the practical details of tax reform — unless he protected his flank by suitable theoretical or econometric exercise. My own past tendencies would certainly not be acceptable for promotion . . . What is not in doubt is that we are now very strong in the journals but much less strong in the obscenely practical matters on which many people, including many students, expect economists to be useful.

His suggested — and promptly rejected — solution: two tracks for the Ph.D., one in economics and the other in "social economics," each controlling its own faculty appointments; alternatively, an entirely new and separate department. There was virtually no support for either proposal.

A second issue can perhaps be described as the Vietnam War and its campus consequences. Galbraith's opposition to the war dated to the early 1960s. As university students nearly everywhere began to express their own negative feelings (after 1964) through teach-ins, sit-ins, and demonstrations, he searched for ways to express his sympathy with some of their goals. During the Harvard troubles of 1969 and in the early 1970s, when students occupied buildings and President Pusey called the police — and turmoil prevailed — Galbraith came to be seen as a prominent supporter of undergraduate causes. At the very least he made common cause with the so-called faculty liberal caucus and therefore also with many of the student demands. Years later — in 1986 — he would refer to "these youngsters" as ". . . perhaps the least dangerous rebels in all the long history of revolution."[16] Some colleagues did not share that benign assessment, and Galbraith's relations with a few very old friends remained forever tarnished.

It is not my intention to present either the details of the great happenings at Harvard in the 1960s or to describe Galbraith's role in these events. I would like to discuss a related subject of far more immediate and long-term importance. The student movement was about Vietnam, the draft, civil rights, Afro-American studies, and various other issues. In addition, the movement nearly everywhere attempted to challenge, question, and discredit traditional forms of university governance: students demanded more power for themselves, as did faculties. Sometimes these groups demanded more power for each other, and occasionally a greater voice was urged on behalf of nonacademic employees. Those who were supposed to yield power in the name of democracy, decency, progress, and efficiency — I could go on! — were described as an oligarchy of wealthy trustees and their administrative lackeys: deans, provosts, presidents, and similar parasitic life forms peculiar to the academy. At Harvard, Galbraith was among the first to give a clear voice to this school of thought.

On December 23, 1968, the *Harvard Alumni Bulletin* published a brief article by Galbraith entitled "The Case for Constitutional Reform at Harvard."[17] His argument was simple and provoked, as intended, enormous controversy in our complacent community.

At various campuses — especially Columbia — deep troubles had been created by student militancy. A major causal factor, he alleged, was an archaic system of governance, out of touch with young people, their teachers, and the real world.

> . . . no institution . . . not even Harvard, can assume that its governing arrangements are adequate . . . Better act before rather than after there is trouble . . . There will be little pleasure in saying I told you so after present faults have been fully revealed by some crisis. It will be a pleasure, however, that those who urge modernization can hardly be expected to deny themselves if nothing is done.[18]

These words were a forecast of imminent disturbance and contrasted sharply with the widespread Cambridge view that "it couldn't happen here." Four months later, Galbraith could claim to have been a prophet. As I recall, he did so in dignified fashion, with only very few "I told you so's."

Let us look somewhat more closely into Galbraith's diagnosis. He judged the patients — Harvard's governing boards — to be suffering from obsolescence and anachronism. The Harvard Corporation[19] was unknown to the faculty and everyone else. It was faceless and also profoundly nonacademic, composed almost exclusively of lawyers and businessmen with little understanding of the fundamentals of university life.[20] Galbraith noted as another criticism that all senior academic administrators were appointed, *de jure* by the president and fellows, *de facto* by the president. He urged that faculties (and others?) elect presidents, deans, chairmen and similar office holders.

All of these darts were aimed at internal aspects of university life. One other criticism belonged in a separate category. It did not deal with achieving a greater level of sensitivity or democracy. Rather it invited us to reconsider the very nature of the institution. The passage below refers to Vietnam.

> At Harvard, as elsewhere, many older members of the faculty and academic community have worked hard to reverse public policy on this ghastly mistake and to develop public understanding of the error. *It cannot be said that they have had much help or even encouragement from the university government, either corporately or individually.* On an issue of transcendent importance to the university the governing boards have been largely silent, even by all outward signs indifferent.
>
> *The impression given by the formal Harvard leadership, president and Corporation, is one of neutrality.* This continues to suggest a divorce

from the moral concerns of the university community of which it is
a part.[21]

I find it personally awkward to take issue with these views. Membership in the Harvard Corporation and past service as dean may disqualify me in the eyes of many readers, and in this group I include the object of this tribute. But we already know that it is not Galbraith's style to favor neutrality, so I will not hesitate to suggest some differences with his reading of history.

It is difficult to believe that student disturbances in the United States had very much to do with shortcomings of governance. Indeed, there may be good reasons to change the way universities are ruled — then and now — but the incidents that started at Berkeley in 1965 and eventually swept American campuses were not created by authoritarian and insensitive administrators. (Incidents may have been aggravated by some administrative dinosaurs.) One of the most noteworthy characteristics of the student revolution was its close tie to external factors: the war, especially the draft, and the civil rights movement. The university became a convenient and relatively safe stage on which students and faculty gave vent to their frustrations with and fears of the outside world. Actors occupied the theater not because they chafed under the despotic rule of an uncaring stage manager. The theater was available, the doors were open, and the occupiers wanted an audience.

Galbraith's proposals for constitutional reform, perhaps unknowingly, urged Harvard and by implication other universities to restructure in a distinctly European manner. By any standard, a very odd recommendation. That model suggests electing nearly all academic administrators beginning with the president or rector. These are also institutions in which, traditionally, faculty authority reigns supreme, although more recently the custom of parity has, in some places, introduced students and employees into the process. I am not prepared to argue simple causal relations, but it is true that since World War II there has been a considerable decline in the quality of universities governed in the European fashion. Countries as diverse as Japan, Germany, France, and Israel have been adversely affected. At the same time, the great American research universities have become the standard and envy of the world.

Recent surveys suggest that two thirds of the world's leading universities are presently located in the United States. Where else do we possess a similar share of excellence? I can think only of baseball teams. Of course, America is rich and was not devastated by World War II. And much credit should be given to our philanthropic tradition. But is it not possible that our unusual system of governance in higher education has played a positive role? The system cannot be described in a few words, but essential components are independent trustees, considerable presidential authority, appointed administrators, and the delegation of educational policy to faculties. None of these characteristics are featured in the European model, and my strong belief is that the American model achieves a much higher level of efficiency while safeguarding academic authority and privilege. Above all, the American model is far better at promoting academic change because there exist clearer lines of authority and a more welcoming structure in which to exercise creative leadership.

Galbraith's unhappiness with Harvard's "neutrality" toward the Vietnam War is also slightly puzzling. Is there no valid distinction between being a citizen of a country and a member of a voluntary association? Is it a university's role *corporately* to reverse public policy? It seems to me good practice to have the university limit its corporate voice to matters of education; all the rest should be *delegated* to all of us in our capacity as citizens. Even if Galbraith today saw some validity in this view — and I doubt it — he still expressed regrets that university government did not individually voice more support for his position. I also find that a strange complaint: most likely members of governing bodies adhered to a different political point of view. In my opinion, their views were wrong, but surely that is not a constitutional question.

One last observation: Galbraith fully understood the relation between time horizon and responsibility in running universities. That is why he advocated no role for students outside of responsibility for their own lives. They were transients. But in advocating all power to the faculty he seemed to pay less attention to the equally compelling matter of conflict of interest. A board of trustees — including the Harvard Corporation — is a body that has both the longest time horizon in the institution and the smallest conflict of interest. Trustees will not directly benefit from changes in salary policy, tuition, number of students, or the promotion of individual professors. Higher returns on investment or (say) decapitalizing endowment will not line their pockets. The same is not necessarily true of faculty members who are obviously much more directly affected by these decisions.[22] We have to remember that not *every-thing* is improved by making it more democratic.

Galbraith tells us that President Kennedy once accused him "of being more interested in alarming people with my own designs for reform than in pursuing them."[23] I believe that this episode is a good illustration of President Kennedy's astute judgment. He went on to say that it would have been better for Galbraith "to talk less and do more." When it comes to constitutional reform at Harvard, I am pleased that the president's advice was ignored. At the same time, Harvard was — as usual — in his debt for forcing us to reexamine our structure and our premises.

In Retrospect

In reviewing Galbraith's long relationship with Harvard University, I could have treated many other topics in detail. One of these is Galbraith the Teacher. For most of his career he taught graduate courses, first in agricultural economics and later in various forms of economic policy. As a graduate teacher, he attracted loyal followers especially among those who chafed under the increasingly heavy twin yokes of technocracy and orthodoxy. As an undergraduate teacher, Galbraith primarily appeared in the General Education Section of the curriculum, holding forth on the relations between economic theory and business enterprise (Soc. Sci. 134) and also on the theory and practice of economic development (Soc. Sci. 169). A few passages from the Crimson's infamous *Confidential Guide* give the flavor of undergraduate reaction. The course (Soc. Sci. 134), "is taught in harangues, followed by question periods in which hapless students either serve up items to support JKG's theories or are wittily and thoroughly demolished for failing to do so" (1964). Wittily and unwittingly, the *Confidential Guide* has described the vastly venerated Socratic method. Some years later they added:

> Galbraith has a reputation as an egoist, one which is largely unfounded. A man with a head as large as the one he is said to have would already be on display at the Medical School . . . Galbraith milks his reputation for ego the way Doris Day milks her reputation for virginity — if either were deserved, their owners would have pretty rotten personal lives. (1971)

In undergraduate rhetoric, this is a message of love and admiration. And so it was for many students in the college. Among the "big names," Galbraith was available and friendly. His views were popular; the generation gap was, by comparison with many of his colleagues, very small. Students showed him many signs of public and private affection, which included an invitation to address Class Day in 1975 — the year of his retirement. Very few members of the Harvard faculty have been similarly honored.

Galbraith the Philanthropist should also be mentioned, and here I mean only the donor to Harvard. To supply great detail would, perhaps, be embarrassing and unnecessary, but some outstanding contributions need to be recorded. In 1957, Galbraith sent the following brief note to Dean Erwin N. Griswold of the Harvard Law School:

> It occurred to me after we talked last night that members of the Harvard faculty do expect more of others than of themselves. Anyhow, it is my own slight experience of raising money that it is a most arduous and disagreeable task. So you might consider the enclosed, if not a contribution, at least a small indication of my respect for your efforts on behalf of a very sound establishment.

Enclosed was a check for $50. Griswold's reply is worthy of note:

> You quite take my breath away. As far as I can recall, this is the first time that a member of the Faculty of Arts and Sciences has ever made a gift to the Law School. That is a great event.

A modest beginning, and as Galbraith's fortunes improved — he was collecting an ever larger "rent for some such extraneous skill as a vulgar facility with words."[24] — so did the size and frequency of his gifts to Harvard. I am glad to note that, in general and most appropriately, they remained in the Faculty of Arts and Sciences. Taking away the breath of other deans by giving them money is not my idea of a praiseworthy activity.

Let me just mention a few acts that do deserve our unambiguous approval: the gift of a collection of Indian miniatures to the Fogg Art Museum; stopping all salary increases for himself in the late 1960s — as President Bok points out, the only such request he has ever seen;[25] the presentation to the Economics Department of the *strictly anonymous* Affluent Society Fund, containing the royalties of the second edition of that book, placed at the disposal of the chairman; and also the Galbraith Teaching Prize awarded annually by graduate students to the best graduate teacher in economics. I regret to say that our department did not accept the prize with grace. Before yielding, serious objections were raised because students controlled the award. Somehow this was thought to be an undesirable surrender to populism and consumerism. In nearly a decade, I have not noted any harmful effects.

Not all of Galbraith's philanthropic impulses were equally felicitous. One of his more peculiar initiatives was a suggestion made to Dean Franklin Ford in 1968. It was a time of some financial stringency, and in a memorandum entitled "A Modest Proposal on the Pay Problem at the Higher Ranks,"[26] Galbraith noted that a substantial minority of the faculty were partly or wholly independent of university pay. Reasons included "inherited assets, unacademically skillful speculation, financially circumspect love," an unusual ability to write for a wide audience, and most significantly the opportunities of earning outside income because of a Harvard association. His suggestion was to create a special professorial category "for the man who, as a result of his association with the University or other fortunate circumstance, can afford to forego salary income." While their duties and responsibilities would remain entirely unchanged, their generosity would be recognized by a newly created title: Eliot Professor. Why a new and visible title? "Part of the answer is that vanity and a desire for recognition for good works has not been excised even from the Harvard soul." I cannot imagine that collegial relations would have been improved by making some people walk around with a sandwich board proclaiming: "I am rich." Most of Galbraith's ideas for social reform were more practical.

Galbraith summarized his own Harvard career on Class Day in 1975:[27]

> Harvard has always had two kinds of professors, the inside people and the outside people. The insiders make their lives within the university community; the outsiders are only associated with it. The outside men — most of us, alas, have been men — are the best known; the insiders are the most useful.

This uncharacteristically modest evaluation by an outsider was immediately qualified. Insiders were provincial — suffering from the Belmont syndrome — subsiding too deeply into the comforts of academic routine. It was a dangerous routine because those who lived by its fascinations had no desire to address messy issues of policy. That task was left to the sometimes denigrated outsiders.

Perhaps the distinction proposed by Galbraith applies to average individuals. In his own case, and for other outstanding and colorful members of the faculty, it loses most of its meaning. Galbraith surely was — in his own words — an outsider, but he was a more useful outsider than many insiders, and I mean useful to the university. Many professors served on a larger number of committees, gave more speeches at faculty meetings, and spent more hours with students. Very few — I am tempted to say none — managed effectively to combine so much inside and outside activity.[28] Galbraith's influence and fame as an outsider is a given. But he was also a considerable force within the university, as a scholar, teacher, and liberal social critic who cared deeply about Harvard's present excellence and future well-being.

NOTES

1. John Kenneth Galbraith, *A Life in Our Times* (Boston: Houghton Mifflin, 1981), pp. 59–60.
2. Letter from Professor John D. Black to Provost Paul H. Buck, December 22, 1947.
3. Letter from Black to Buck.
4. All these quotes are from Black's letter. The remark about Keynesians is curious, since that was one of the charges eventually raised against Galbraith by his enemies on the Board of Overseers. See below.
5. In 1947, Black was — with very little assistance — teaching five full courses. In addition, ". . . 12 of the 120 Ph.D.'s reported as conferred in Economics in the United States in 1946–1947 (12 months) were candidates writing theses under my [Black's] direction." These Stakhanovite standards disappeared long ago.
6. Quoted from an unpublished memorandum written by Galbraith in 1948 or 1949. During those years he wrote a number of similar memoranda explaining and defending his role in the survey.
7. Galbraith's unpublished memorandum, 1948 or 1949.
8. Galbraith, *A Life in Our Times*, p. 275.
9. Cited in James B. Conant, *My Several Lives — Memoirs of a Social Inventor* (New York: Harper & Row, 1970), p. 437.
10. Galbraith, *A Life in Our Times*, pp. 275–76.
11. Schlesinger and Galbraith to the President and Fellows of Harvard College, November 23, 1959.
12. Galbraith (and I assume Schlesinger) recognized that party preference was a legitimate issue only because of the public service category for honorary degrees. In a letter to Professor Taylor Starck, dated December 11, 1959, Galbraith wrote: "Were it the policy of the Corporation to give no honorary degrees to political figures, I would be perfectly content. So long as it does, it should see that they are representative of all points of view." This sentence is an excellent expression of Galbraith's basic liberalism.
13. Harris to Galbraith, December 9, 1959.

14. H. J. Szold to Schlesinger and Galbraith, December 10, 1959.

15. Memo from Galbraith to President Derek Bok, Dean designate Henry Rosovsky, Chairman James S. Duesenberry, and members of the department of economics, June 18, 1973.

16. John K. Galbraith, "The Case for Constitutional Reform at Harvard," in *A View from the Stands* (Boston: Houghton Mifflin, 1986), pp. 109–16. This brief piece originally appeared in the *Harvard Alumni Bulletin*, December 23, 1969.

    Lest there be any misunderstanding, it should be noted that Galbraith did not in any sense support all student demands: "I am also far from enthusiastic about student participation in educational policy, academic administration or the selection of faculty. Besides the instability of interest . . . it is nearly inevitable that student concern with educational reform will end up with a proposal for the liberalization of standards, liberalization being a euphemism for the lowering of standards" (*A View from the Stands*, p. 132). Galbraith's aim was not to increase the power of students. He was interested in effecting ". . . a major — and one trusts permanent — shift of power to the faculty" (Letter dated April 18, 1969, addressed to the editor of the *New York Times*).

17. Galbraith, "The Case for Constitutional Reform at Harvard," p. 132.

18. Galbraith, "The Case for Constitutional Reform at Harvard," pp. 111, 113.

19. The principal governing board, composed *ex officio* of the president, treasurer and five other members. The official name of the corporation — sometimes described as a multiple executive — is the President and Fellows of Harvard College. They are the legal owners of the University.

20. When Galbraith wrote, the only academic on the corporation was President Pusey. Shortly thereafter, two professors from other universities were added so that three sevenths of the fellows had respectable academic credentials. But there is no requirement for academic qualifications or professorial status. With the exception of the president and treasurer, all other selections are *ad personam*.

21. Galbraith, "The Case for Constitutional Reform at Harvard," pp. 112, 115. Italics supplied.

22. This scant attention to the conflict of interest problem is especially surprising, because in the early 1970s Galbraith initiated a dispute within the economics department precisely related to this point. He argued that those of his colleagues with outside business interests — i.e., ownership or part ownership of corporations — should be prevented from participating in the appointments process. The issue was raised in the aftermath of failing to promote some of Harvard's "radical" economists. The intended implication was that those with outside corporate interests could not fairly evaluate radical critics of the system. No doubt an argument with some validity, but conflict of interest is not confined to political or economic philosophy.

23. *A View from the Stands*, p. 133.

24. Memorandum from Galbraith to Dean Franklin Ford entitled "A Modest Proposal on the Pay Problem at the Higher Ranks," July 17, 1968.

25. For the sake of historical accuracy, I note that there was one other such request in the Faculty of Arts and Sciences during my term as dean.

26. Does the title suggest that this was a spoof? I do not think so.

27. *A View from the Stands*, pp. 134–35.

28. His only rival may be the redoubtable John T. Dunlop.

Books by John Kenneth Galbraith

Modern Competition and Business Policy. New York: Oxford University Press, 1938. With H. S. Dennison.

American Capitalism: The Concept of Countervailing Power. Boston: Houghton Mifflin, 1952. Revised edition, 1956. Reprinted, with a new preface by the author: White Plains, N.Y.: M. E. Sharpe, 1980.

A Theory of Price Control. Cambridge: Harvard University Press, 1952. Third printing, with a new introduction, 1980.

Economics and the Art of Controversy. New Brunswick, N.J.: Rutgers University Press, 1955.

The Great Crash, 1929. Boston: Houghton Mifflin, 1955. Sentry edition, with a new introduction by the author, 1961. 3rd edition, 1972. 50th anniversary edition, 1979. 4th edition, with a new introduction by the author, 1988.

Marketing Efficiency in Puerto Rico. Cambridge: Harvard University Press, 1955. With Richard H. Holton and others.

Journey to Poland and Yugoslavia. Cambridge: Harvard University Press, 1958.

The Affluent Society. Boston: Houghton Mifflin, 1958. 2nd edition, 1969. 3rd edition, 1976. 4th edition, 1984.

The Liberal Hour. Boston: Houghton Mifflin, 1960.

Economic Development in Perspective. Cambridge: Harvard University Press, 1962. Revised and enlarged as *Economic Development*. Boston: Houghton Mifflin, 1964.

The McLandress Dimension. [Mark Epernay, pseud.] Boston: Houghton Mifflin, 1963.

The Scotch. Boston: Houghton Mifflin, 1964. 2nd edition, with a new introduction and afterword by the author, 1985.

The New Industrial State. Boston: Houghton Mifflin, 1967. 2nd edition, revised, 1971. 3rd edition, revised, 1978. 4th edition, 1985.

How to Get Out of Vietnam: A Workable Solution to the Worst Problem of Our Time. New York: New American Library, 1967.

Indian Painting: The Scene, Themes, and Legends. Boston: Houghton Mifflin, 1968. With Mohinder Singh Randhawa.

The Triumph: A Novel of Modern Diplomacy. Boston: Houghton Mifflin, 1968.

How to Control the Military. Garden City, N.Y.: Doubleday, 1969.

Ambassador's Journal: A Personal Account of the Kennedy Years. Boston: Houghton Mifflin, 1969.

Who Needs the Democrats, and What It Takes to Be Needed. Garden City, N.Y.: Doubleday, 1970.

Economics, Peace, and Laughter. Boston: Houghton Mifflin, 1971.

A China Passage. Boston: Houghton Mifflin, 1973. Reprinted, with a new introduction by the author: New York: Paragon House, 1989.

Economics and the Public Purpose. Boston: Houghton Mifflin, 1973.

Money: Whence It Came, Where It Went. Boston: Houghton Mifflin, 1975.

The Galbraith Reader. Boston: Gambit, 1977.

The Age of Uncertainty. Boston: Houghton Mifflin, 1977.

Almost Everyone's Guide to Economics. Boston: Houghton Mifflin, 1978. With Nicole Salinger.

Annals of an Abiding Liberal. Boston: Houghton Mifflin, 1978.

The Nature of Mass Poverty. Cambridge: Harvard University Press, 1979.

A Life in Our Times: Memoirs. Boston: Houghton Mifflin, 1981.

The Anatomy of Power. Boston: Houghton Mifflin, 1983.

The Voice of the Poor: Essays in Economic and Political Persuasion. Cambridge: Harvard University Press, 1983.

A View from the Stands: Of People, Politics, Military Power, and the Arts. Boston: Houghton Mifflin, 1986.

Economics in Perspective: A Critical History. Boston: Houghton Mifflin, 1987.

Capitalism, Communism, and Coexistence: From the Bitter Past to a Better Prospect. Boston: Houghton Mifflin, 1988. With Stanislav Menshikov.

Contributors

WALTER ADAMS, Distinguished University Professor, Michigan State University

GEORGE W. BALL, lawyer, investment banker, former Undersecretary of State

BARBARA R. BERGMANN, Professor of Economics, American University

KENNETH E. BOULDING, Director of the Program in Research on Political and Economic Change, and Distinguished Professor Emeritus, University of Colorado

SAMUEL BOWLES, Professor of Economics, University of Massachusetts

JAMES W. BROCK, Professor of Economics, Miami University

RICHARD EDWARDS, Professor of Economics, University of Massachusetts

JAMES K. GALBRAITH, Associate Professor of Economics, University of Texas

HERBERT GINTIS, Professor of Economics, University of Massachusetts

ALBERT O. HIRSCHMAN, Professor of Social Science, Emeritus, Institute for Advanced Study, Princeton University

MARY KALDOR, Research Associate, Science Policy Research Institute, University of Sussex

ROBERT LEKACHMAN, (late) Distinguished Professor, City University of New York

WASSILY LEONTIEF, Professor of Economics, Director of the Institute of Economic Analysis, New York University, Nobel Prize in Economics, 1973

STANISLAV MENSHIKOV, Professor of Economics, University of Moscow

MANCUR OLSON, Distinguished Professor of Economics, University of Maryland

HENRY S. REUSS, former Member, U.S. House of Representatives

LLOYD G. REYNOLDS, Sterling Professor of Economics, Emeritus, Yale University

ERIC ROLL, Lord Roll of Ipsden

HENRY ROSOVSKY, Lewis P. and Linda L. Geyser University Professor, Harvard University

PAUL A. SAMUELSON, Institute Professor, Massachusetts Institute of Technology, Nobel Prize in Economics, 1970

WILLIAM G. SHEPHERD, Professor of Economics, University of Massachusetts

LESTER C. THUROW, Gordon Y. Billard Professor of Management and Economics, and Dean, School of Management, Massachusetts Institute of Technology

JAN TINBERGEN, Cleveringa Professor, University of Leiden (retired), Nobel Prize in Economics, 1969

SHIGETO TSURU, formerly Professor of Economics and President, Hitotsubashi University